NATIONAL ECONOMIC PLANNING IN FRANCE

To Carole and Emma

National Economic Planning in France

DAVID LIGGINS
Economist,
County Treasurer's Department,
West Midlands Metropolitan
County Council

SAXON ⬤ HOUSE | LEXINGTON BOOKS

Published by
SAXON HOUSE, D.C. Heath Ltd
Westmead, Farnborough, Hants., England.

Jointly with
LEXINGTON BOOKS, D. C. Heath & Co.
Lexington, Mass. U.S.A.

ISBN 0 347 01028 8
Library of Congress Catalog Card Number 74-26359

Printed in Great Britain
by Unwin Brothers Limited
The Gresham Press, Old Woking, Surrey
A member of the Staples Printing Group

Contents

List of tables

List of figures

Preface

This book brings together a mountain of material I have acquired in the last six years while teaching courses on planning in France to post-graduate students following the National Planning Programme at Birmingham University. I first taught these courses in 1968, and successive generations of my students have suffered under misconceptions and misunderstandings caused by working with inadequate and incomplete source material. This was unfortunate but also inevitable because the preparation of the Sixth Plan did not get properly under way until September 1969, following a 'closed' administrative phase. Very little published material was therefore available, and we had to rely on badly typed, indecipherable French working papers solicited from patient members of the Planning Commission (CGP), the Ministry of the Economy and Finance (MEF), and other branches of the economic administration, during all too infrequent short visits to Paris.

Now for the first time this material has been put into some sort of order, and presented in this book for the benefit of future students (and probably past students who should now recognise what I have been talking about). The book is essentially about *balances*. What is the right balance between bigger and better models (which require longer administrative phases in the plan preparation process) and more time for discussion and 'concertation'? How does one achieve balance on the statistical side between better existing statistics and broadening the statistical base into such areas as social indicators? Can improvement be made in these two areas and at the same time a better balance achieved between the centrally prepared parts of the plan and the regional consultations? How can the role of the plan be adapted to a changing situation in which France is now faced not only with national economic problems but international economic responsibilities (mainly within the European Economic Community) too? These and many other adjustment processes are constantly taking place, and this book attempts to shed some light on how well synchronised the French Plan is to them.

To begin with, my modest aim was to describe the technical methods of plan preparation used in the Sixth Plan, but as time went on I became more intrigued by some of the problems the use of these techniques had created. As more material was released, and the French themselves began to analyse their own experience, it became clear that a straightforward technical description would not be sufficient to do justice to what is now quite clearly a social process and not just simply a sophisticated numerical exercise. Inevitably, the vast amount of tables, data, and diagrams in this book will still support the latter impression (which I must confess I held originally) in many readers' minds, but if they go back and read between the tables and chase up one or two of the non-technical references I think they too will realise that the Plan is something more than men, models, and machines.

I have made very little attempt to get involved in the usual controversy about the Plan and whether it is important or not, although in places I have tried to indicate where this argument is relevant. My main aim is more to clear away a mass of misunderstanding and false argument which I think stems from people not realising what the Plan is, how it is prepared, what role the models play, and where the really critical areas are. I regard it as a paradox to read that 'the Plan is dead' and that 'much of the usefulness of French planning has disappeared now that France is in the Common Market'. In my view, as long as the French economy continues to experience high growth rates, people will willingly participate in the planning process (or most of them will), because as long as there are fruits of growth to share out, people will turn up to argue for their share. It is when the economy starts to slow down and possibly enter a period of zero growth that the danger signals go out for the Plan. Planning for decline is something of which very few economies have experience, but it is well known that in regions that decline the planner who still talks of growth gets very little credence, and the 'social partners' take up entrenched positions to defend what they hold; participation becomes very difficult in such circumstances.

Whatever some political and economic commentators may write, therefore, the Sixth Plan at least was prepared in a climate of opinion which acknowledged that the Plan had an important role to play. But new cracks began to appear in the structure, and the planners were forced to adapt to prevent them widening. The misunderstandings that surrounded the first results produced by the FIFI model, and the later realisation that the model was not politically neutral are causes for concern. The calls for more openness in the technical preparation phases became louder as the Plan went on and was analysed, and it will be interesting to see what effect they will have on the preparation of the Seventh Plan. Reference is made in many parts of the book to demands for deeper structural analyses and more time for the discussion of social and regional problems. Limitations on time and space meant that these issues do not get the airing they deserve here, but limits do have to be drawn somewhere or the book would grow and grow. Chapters 2, 8, and 9 in particular could benefit from much more discussion and analysis; the areas these chapters cover will certainly be the ones on which most of the seminar time is spent in my future French planning courses.

Finally, in addition to the people who have allowed me to make such extensive use of their material and who are acknowledged below, I must express grateful appreciation to the many friends and colleagues whose help has made this book possible: to Tom Kronsjö for introducing me to planning, and then allowing me the freedom to develop my own ideas; to Andrew McKay, for constructive criticism at the right times, and cover on many visits to Paris; to Wolfgang Pfaffenberger and Ross Bull who have collaborated in joint courses on French planning and analysis of other European economic systems; to my many friends in the French economic administration, particularly Alain Bernard and Raymond Courbis for giving their time and ideas so readily, MM Anfré, Aujac, Berthet, Bessière, Boyer, Cazes, David, Delange, Didier, Donzet, Faiveley, Gordon, Guesnerie, Horps and Lenco, Mlle Lori, MM Malgrange, Marczewski, Montbrial, Nataf, Olive, Pagé, Scheer, Seibel, Ternier, Younès, and others too numerous to mention, for information, meetings, and interviews; to my students for continual criticism, encouragement, interest, and assistance with translations, and especially to David Little, who gave up his Ph D programme in despair when my other duties prevented me writing this book three years earlier and thus helping his research; to Birmingham University for granting me leave eventually to finish off the book, and to their Inter-Library Loans office whose valiant efforts to satisfy my unfair requests for difficult sources are evident throughout the book; to the West Midlands Metropolitan County Council for allowing me time to finish the book in spite of being appointed to a post with them some months ago; to the secretaries in the National Economic Planning Unit at Birmingham University, particularly Linda Baker, Ilse Browne, and Maxine Edwards, for help with typing, general organisation, phone calls to Paris, etc.: their endless patience and constant good humour went far beyond the normal requirements of their job; to Andrea Jackson who typed the whole of the final draft: some of her tables and diagrams are works of art, especially considering the illegible handwriting in which I gave them to her. I hope I have not taken her away from her family too much. My own family have forgotten what I look like, and it feels totally inadequate to make the customary thanks to my parents for the original spark of inspiration, and to my wife Carole and daughter Emma for accepting the countless lost summers, weekends and nights. They deserve better!

D. Liggins, University of Birmingham, April 1974

Acknowledgements

Acknowledgement is made to the following for giving permission to use their copyright material:

J. Antoine	J.-P. Page
J. Ardagh	M. Rousselot
M. Astorg	B. Ullmo
J. Billy	G. Weill
L.-P. Blanc	Atreize
R. Bonety	Commissariat Général du Plan
A. Cairncross	DATAR
B. Cazes	Droit Social
Prof. Courbis	Études et Conjoncture
K. B. Griffin	Futures
H. Guitton	Longmans
J. Hayward	Long Range Planning
F. Hetman	Omega
A. Kidel	Revue d'Économie Politique
J. Lesourne	Revue Économique
J. A. McArthur	The Economist Newspaper Ltd
G. Olive	

1 The Preparation of the Sixth Plan

Like the five earlier Plans, the Sixth Plan is, among other things, the culmination of a long process of studies, discussions and concerted action among many thousand people in the Modernisation Commissions, committees, study groups and inter-groups sponsored by the Office of the Commissioner-General for the Plan, as well as in the various regional bodies.

But substantial progess has been made since the Fifth Plan; concerted action has undoubtedly become more efficient in the Commissions of the Plan and in the Regional Councils; planning techniques have improved thanks to the use of integrated economic models and the application of the principles of programme budgeting to collective functions as well as the increased attention paid to long-term trends.

But even more than this it is the whole nature of planning which has been modified to take account of the new operating conditions of the French economy, which has become more sensitive to international fluctuations and the spontaneous behaviour of economic transactors. Thus, the Plan has been streamlined by omitting secondary detail while, on the other hand, stress is laid on certain priority actions whose importance is emphasised by 'declarations of policy'.

> (From the Foreword to the English translation of the *General Report on the VIth Economic and Social Development Plan*, La Documentation Française, Paris 1973).

The purpose of this first chapter is to provide an informational and institutional context against which to set the later chapters on medium-term planning. It is also intended to fill out the points made in the above official French statement on the preparation of the Plan, a statement that like many official statements perhaps, puts forward an all-too-brief and seemingly contented version of the actual situation. Admittedly, there is evidence later in the General Report on the differences of opinion that occured during the Plan preparation stages, but there is little or no account of the role played by 'integrated economic models' in either creating or resolving these differences. It is into this area that we delve more deeply in this and later chapters.

But first we need to set the scene: what were the different stages involved in the Sixth Plan preparation process? What were the roles of the various participants, particularly on the Government side? Where do the economic models come in, and what problems did they create? Where are the weaknesses in the procedure, and what is being done about rectifying them? We hope to give the answers to some of these questions here, and to lay the ground for more extended discussions of some of the others in later chapters.

1.1 The chronological sequence of events

The preparation of the Sixth Plan[1] took over four years, and involved over 5,000 people at the national level, although all of these people were not involved for the whole of the four-year period. Indeed, there was a short period just after the Sixth Plan preparations got under way when very few even of the civil servants and Government participants were involved: they were redirected to work on adapting the Fifth Plan, following the social crisis of May–June 1968. It should be borne in mind, therefore, that the whole preparation process was delayed by approximately one year, a delay that at least allowed more time for the model builders to build and sell their product to the other participants.

Looking only at the national aspects (the regional aspects are considered in Chapter 8), the Plan preparation process can be broken down into three main phases:

(i)   the administrative phase, from early 1966 to mid-1969 but including the one year's delay due to the 1968 events;
(ii)   the options phase, from the autumn of 1969 to June 1970;
(iii)   the Plan specification phase, from the autumn of 1970 to July 1971.

These stages are essentially the same as those in the Fifth Plan preparation process, but they contain a number of innovations with respect to the Fifth Plan, as we point out in the next two sections of this chapter.

The administrative phase started one year after the preparation of the Fifth Plan had ended. Its task was to define the framework of the analyses and discussions that the Plan Commissions and their study groups were supposed to take up in two and a half years' time. This phase was also to include a considerable amount of exploratory technical work aimed at providing the Plan Commissions with the fullest possible information about the problems most likely to be met during the Sixth Plan period (1971–1975) and beyond. One of the main tools used to generate this information was to be the FIFI model, on which work started in earnest in the autumn of 1966, and about which we say a great deal in the next few chapters. The way in which the period beyond the Plan (post-1975) was considered was also reorganised, a considerable programme of long-term studies getting under way in the autumn of 1967 and continuing through to early 1969. We examine this work in more detail in Chapter 2. Consideration was given to the problems encountered during the preparation of the Fifth Plan, and an enquiry was conducted amongst those who had participated.

While most of this work was of a technical nature and took place mainly within the Commissariat Général du Plan (CGP), the National Institute of Statistics and Economic Research (INSEE), and the Ministry of Finance's Forecasting Directorate (DP), the main outward signs of its progress were in November 1967, when the Government was consulted on the general timetable of the work and the broad outlines of the Plan Commissions' programme; July 1969, when the CGP reported to the Government on the problems which the 1975 projections (produced by the FIFI model) and the long-term studies had highlighted, and asked for guidelines to feed into the options phase; and early autumn 1969, when the list of Plan Commission members and their work programme were finalised. We shall be looking at the internal progress of the work in the remaining sections of this chapter.

The starting point of the options phase was the departure account,[2] a picture of 1975 drawn up with the aid of FIFI and attempting to put across to the Plan Commissions what 1975 might look like if past trends persisted and current policies were maintained. Unfortunately, the message did not get across to all the participants, and a great deal of confusion surrounded the Commissions' early discussions. This confusion derived both from the structure of the model that had produced the departure account, and the role the model was supposed to play in the planning process. We shall come back to both these points later: they are central to our presentation of medium-term planning. Leaving aside for the moment the confusion that existed, the departure account revealed the problems that France was likely to face by 1975 if nothing were done to modify undesirable trends and change inappropriate policies. It was the Plan Commissions' job to search for solutions to these problems, mainly by using the FIFI model to produce variants, which are projections of the economy, as is the departure account, with some of the initial assumptions and exogenous variables and parameters deliberately modified in order to try and produce a better picture of 1975. As has been mentioned, the variant procedure was also misunderstood, and several of the participants (mainly the trade unions) refused to approach the problems in this way.

Many variants were however requested, and duly produced by the model (they are shown in Figure 1·2 and listed in Tables 1·2–1·6); we shall be examining some of them in Chapter 4. The Plan Commissions submitted intermediate reports on their discussions in February 1970, and from these documents the CGP and a number of ministries prepared a preliminary report on the options. Three basic options (characterised by annual growth rates of the economy of 5·5, 6·0 and 6·5 per cent) were being considered at this time, and all of them submitted to the Government in March 1970. After modifications, the report then passed to the Economic and Social Council (ESC),[3] who have the facility to recommend, but no executive authority to enforce, further changes, and finally to Parliament, which approved the options account (characterised by a 5·9 per cent p.a. growth rate) in June 1970.

The Plan specification phase then saw the start of the 'filling out' of the Plan proper in the autumn of 1970. The Plan Commissions were reconstituted, and asked to investigate the conditions necessary for the fulfilment of the options account, and to recommend action programmes for realising these conditions. This they did in reports to the CGP early in 1971,[4] after which the same stages as were followed in phase two were repeated: the CGP sent a summary report to the Government, the report then passed to the ESC, and then on to Parliament who approved the Plan in June. The Plan finally became law on 15 July 1971, just over six months after it should have started to be implemented.

1.2   The main institutional innovations

Compared with the preparation of the Fifth Plan, the main innovations on the institutional and administrative side concerned the development of long-term studies, the restructuring of the Plan Commissions, and the formation of administrative work groups and Plan-Finance groups. The long-term work is analysed in detail in Chapter 2, so we move straight on to the Plan Commissions.

There were 25 Plan Commissions involved in the second and third Plan-preparation phases:

(i) seven horizontal commissions:
        general economic and financing (CEGF),
        employment,
        social benefits,
        research,
        economic information (CIE),
        National Commission for Regional Development (CNAT),
        overseas departments;

(ii) nine commissions dealing with productive sectors:
        agriculture,
        agricultural and foodstuffs industries,
        energy,
        industry,
        transport,
        communications,
        commerce,
        handicraft and artisan industries,
        tourism;

(iii) nine commissions dealing with social functions:
        rural affairs,
        towns,
        social action,
        sport and socio-educational activities,
        cultural affairs,
        water,
        education,
        housing,
        health.

This restructuring was part of a conscious attempt to allow the Plan Commissions more time to focus on economic and social policy problems rather than on quantitative work; there was a strong feeling after the Fifth Plan that so much time had been spent seeking mathematical consistency and economic equilibrium, that very little discussion of 'real' issues had taken place. Consistency is important of course, but it was hoped that FIFI would take a lot of work off the Commissions' hands in this respect; this was indeed the case, but, as we shall see, other problems were created.

Previous Plans had seen a gradual increase in the number of vertical commissions [10] dealing with productive sectors, and the change in the Sixth Plan was to reduce their number but still allow for discussions on

5

specific sectors by the creation of Sector Committees: there were, for instance, 22 under the Industry Commission, and four under the Energy Commission.

As a sign of the increasing awareness and growing importance of social problems, more commissions were created in this area, specifically to focus on the main areas of public authority intervention. Several of these social commissions dealt with problems that were the responsibility of more than one ministry, giving more opportunities for increased co-operation, and as a further step in this direction a number of inter-groups were set up to deal with special 'horizontal' problems, including leisure, old people, handicapped people, etc.

To synthesise the work done in the 18 sector and social commissions, there were seven horizontal commissions, the most important of which was the CEGF. This acted as a forum where the more general development aspects were discussed, and had below it three specialist committees on financing problems, foreign trade, and competition (three key areas of the Plan), plus a technical group (CEGFTG) with the very important and difficult job of easing the planning participants' access to the technical tools used to produce projections and variants. The critical comments that we make at the end of this chapter are largely drawn from the CEGFTG's Report [1]. The CIE was created for the Sixth Plan, as a partial response to a strong pressure to fill the gaps in this field, which were, and still are, both at the information generation level and the diffusion to users level. Even with a CIE, it seems that many participants still were not getting sufficient information to be able to participate fully in the public debate on the problems of economic and social development.[5] This might seem surprising, especially when one considers the vast information-gathering network maintained by the INSEE and others (see Chapter 9), but the Sixth Plan has seen a marked change of emphasis in the sorts of problems being discussed, and in any case the data that are currently being collected are of more direct use to the national accountants and short-term policy-makers. Finally on the horizontal commissions, we shall be coming across the CNAT again in Chapter 8.

It is useful at this stage to abstract from section 1.1 those parts of the Plan preparation process that directly involved the Plan Commissions:

Phase two (options phase)[6]
(a) to evaluate the situation of the Fifth Plan in their area of responsibility;
(b) to explore the future on the basis of the 1975 global projections (the departure account derived using FIFI) or other quantitatively expressed

6

information (perhaps derived using other models), and the long-term studies;
(c) to study the problems raised in (b);
(d) to propose policy to deal with (c).

Phase three (Plan specification)[7]
(a) to quantify the projections and specify the objectives for their particular area of responsibility, within the global framework of the options account;
(b) to study the conditions for realising the projections and objectives made in (a), and to propose means for creating these conditions.

The increasing number of policy studies and sector analyses have prevailed upon Government departments to co-operate with and involve themselves in the Plan preparation process far more than in previous Plans. It is probably fair to say that effort was more readily put into administrative 'concertation', because of bigger guarantees over eventual co-operation, than into general 'concertation' at the Plan Commission level. As Pagé says, ' ... it would be an illusion in the present state of socio-political relations to wait for an expression of consensus on the choice [of economic policy measures]...'.[8] Thus, a large number of administrative work groups were formed, to co-ordinate the work being done by the newly created research and forecasting departments in the ministries, and to service the Commission. We have already mentioned the long-term study groups (a full list is given in Chapter 2), and other groups joined in the search for options and the study of economic policy measures.

In spite of this increased involvement by the general administration, the key roles still fell to the Ministry of Finance (MEF) and the CGP, and a special structure of Plan-Finance (CGP–MEF) work groups was set up. These built on the experience gained in the somewhat similar Budget Workshops (*ateliers budgetaires*) in the Fifth Plan. But they were given more status in the Sixth Plan, (they were constituted at a higher level), and their primary aim was to avoid, or at least open channels for the resolution of, the traditional rivalry between MEF and CGP.[9] With the uncertainties surrounding the 'concertation' in the Commissions, it was essential that there should at least be a consensus on the economic administrations' side. The structure of the Plan-Finance groups was extensive and complicated: there were two main groups, with a common secretariat provided by the INSEE and the DP, eight specialist groups, and nine sub-groups, as follows:

(i) main groups:

central group, consisting of MEF department heads and the Deputy Plan Commissioner,

preparatory group, consisting of civil servants representing each of the members in the central group;

(ii) specialist groups:

consisting of civil servants from the MEF, the CGP and the Bank of France, and responsible for

foreign trade,

invisibles,

*public budgets (two groups),

taxation,

*public industrial sector,

*financial operations and structures relating to industrial policy,

prices and competition policy;

(iii) sub-groups:

those specialist groups asterisked above formed themselves into nine sub-groups.

They began their work early in 1968 and their job was to estimate the feasibility and significance of the departure account. To do this, of course, they had to familiarise themselves with FIFI, a step that constituted a highly original feature of the whole exercise: for a group of senior civil servants to sit around a table discussing and examining the intricacies of a complex macro-economic model is indeed an event that is probably unique in the history of western-style economic planning and management. [11] Unfortunately, this activity was short-lived: the May—June 1968 crisis took the senior members away to other duties, [12] and the November 1968 policy measures (to deal with the monetary crisis) [13] and the August 1969 franc devaluation meant that the original departure account was no longer accurate.

But the delay did allow more time for the misunderstandings and disagreements that the first 1975 programme had aroused to be reduced, mainly by operating the model in variant mode. There was, unfortunately for avoiding similar feelings in the Plan Commissions, no corresponding delay in the open 'concertation' phases, and as we shall see later, although the economic administration now understood the tool reasonably well, they were unable to transmit their understanding to all the other participants.

Because the second departure account (based on the new policy measures, the devaluation, and the new national accounting base year) [14] was available only in September 1969, one month before the Commissions started their first discussions, there was insufficient time for the Plan-Finance groups to consider policy questions, or at least to put forward a summarised view for the benefit of the other participants. Nevertheless, the groups did produce a lot of interesting material, [15] and more importantly they encouraged the use of forecasting and simulation models in other work, because of all the attention that was given to FIFI in the early stages of the groups' work, and the time spent during the following year in clearing up the uncertainties. We now move on to look at developments in the use of models during the Plan preparation phases in more detail.

1.3   The main technical innovations

Although macro-models were used in the preparation of the Fifth Plan [16], a number of defects were encountered, in particular:

(i)   the operation of bringing together the detailed projection studies carried out within the 'concertation' framework was very slow and clumsy;

(ii)   it was not possible to examine a very wide range of possible futures because the study of variants had not been made sufficiently fast, for reasons connected with the model and its programming;

(iii)   prices were determined in an unsatisfactory way;

(iv)   economic policy objectives were put forward in normative terms, without the corresponding economic policy means to ensure their realisation.

The FIFI model was designed to overcome these difficulties, and to meet the following objectives assigned to it by the CGP:

(a)   to reveal the macro-economic medium-term development problems in an economy exposed to international competition;

(b)   to study over this same period the influence of economic policies (relating mainly to public finance) or foreseeable uncertainties on macro-economic trends;

(c)   to enable the detailed studies of the Commissions to be synthesised. [17]

It is not the purpose of this particular section of the book to describe FIFI in detail, nor to show how its structure responds to these objectives; this is left to Chapter 3. At this point a brief outline of the whole range of technical tools used in preparing the Sixth Plan, together with some indi-

9

cation of the difficulties that arose over the use of FIFI in the planning process, are required. However, if readers feel the need at this stage to know what FIFI looks like, then they should jump ahead to Chapter 3; they should then pick up the story again here, and make certain they appreciate the points made in Chapters 4 and 5 before forming their own views on FIFI. And even then, there is much more that can be said (and is said in the French sources listed in the notes) both for and against the model and its use. [18]

To begin with, the model has been used in the way anticipated by the above objectives. The departure account was drawn up with the model, and it gave a quantitative expression to the medium-term macro-economic development problems. The economic policy and uncertainty variants, established with the model, have been used to explore various development directions. The way in which the model was used to synthesise the Commissions' work to produce the options account at the end of phase two, and the Plan account at the end of phase three, demonstrates the effective realisation of objective (c).

But FIFI was one tool amongst many. Apart from the other models that are frequently used both separately and as part of a model system involving FIFI as the central model (see Chapter 3), there are several other types of tools that have been used by the Commissions and the work groups. These include:

(a)   retrospective studies, which seek to identify past trends and shed light on the underlying mechanisms operating in a particular sector or the whole economy;

(b)   partial simulation models, similar to FIFI but focused on specific problems: they are frequently based on the mechanisms revealed by a retrospective study;

(c)   simple projections;

(d)   decision studies, designed to test the effects of economic policy instruments on the medium-term equilibrium: they sometimes involve a cost-benefit type analysis, and are supposed to be used most often in the third phase of Plan preparation;

(e)   transition dictionaries, enabling projections which essentially express the same phenomena, but which use different forms of expression at the concept and structure level, to be compared. By use of this tool (which is usually computer programmed), policy-makers who find it difficult to suggest an appropriate policy because the projection is expressed in an unfamiliar language (e.g. the national accounts, whereas they are used to working with enterprise accounts) can translate the projection into their own language.

10

The main studies carried out involving these tools are shown in Table 1.1.

It is useful at this stage to summarise the stages involved in the technical preparation of the model, and the stages involved in its use. Figure 1.1 gives some idea of the intensive effort put into FIFI and which is still going on. It also shows the allowances that continually have to be made for significant external events, such as the May–June 1968 crisis, the November 1968 policy measures, and the August 1969 devaluation. Hence the need for 'uncertainty' variants that in some sense try to show the effects on the economy of external events and changes in behaviour. The various central accounts, policy variants and uncertainty variants that were established in phases two and three with the help of the model are shown in Figure 1.2, and listed in full in Tables 1.2–1.6; we shall be having a closer look at some of these accounts in Chapter 4. These variants, except for the ones listed in Table 1.6, do not for the most part contain any normative elements. Each variant is a re-run of the model, with one or more of the model's parameters changed. There are basically four types of variant:

(i)   sensitivity variants, so called because they show the effects of a change in a parameter which is due to statistical, econometric or technical error;

(ii)   economic uncertainty variants, different in conception from (i) but frequently the same in practice, in which there is uncertainty surrounding particular parameters that reflect the behaviour of domestic agencies or international forces;

(iii)   policy analysis variants, in which a deliberate change is made in one or more (but usually a small number) policy parameters;

(iv)   policy synthesis variants, in which several policies are to be tested simultaneously, and which therefore require changes in several parameters.

There is a central file holding all the parameters relating to the departure account, and a change in one of them will produce a variant when the model is fed with the file and run on the computer. The transition from one central account to another is formally achieved by a variant in which about 500 parameters are changed simultaneously. It is important to note here that a great deal of work can be involved in the definition of a variant. Once a policy has been put forward and a corresponding variant requested, then the measure has to be specified in great detail, the instruments used have to be detailed, the possible effects on the agencies affected estimated, explicit relationships that have not been taken into account in the model allowed for, and finally a numerical value for the changes in parameters (or sometimes only one parameter, after all this work) arrived

11

Table 1.1

Main studies carried out in phase two (without FIFI) for the Plan Commissions

Field of analysis		Tool used	Administration involved		Plan Commission or work group requesting the study
			INSEE, DP or CGP	Division	
1	The economic situation in 1985	PSM	INSEE CGP	Programmes, Quantitative economic analysis	Long-term groups
2	Demographic projections: total population, families	P	INSEE	Demography	Analysis, problems, population, housing, CNAT, towns
3	Demographic projections: regions, towns	P	INSEE	Regional studies	Regions
4	Projections of total working population and agricultural working population	P	INSEE	Employment	Employment, agriculture
5	Manpower projections by qualification	PSM	INSEE	Employment	Training, education
6	Length of working week	DS	INSEE	Employment	Employment
7	Employment in the regions in 1985	PSM	INSEE	Regional studies	CNAT, regions
8	Changes in factors of production (investment, productivity)	RS +PSM	INSEE	Programmes, research	CEGF
9	Projection of domestic consumption	PSM	INSEE	Consumption	All commissions
10	Projection of production and agricultural prices, by product	PSM	INSEE	Agriculture	Agriculture
11	Public enterprise accounts	PSM +TD	INSEE DP	Enterprises, productive economy	Energy, transport
12	Industry file	RS	INSEE	Enterprises	Industry
13	Branch file (engineering, chemicals)	RS	INSEE	Industry	Sector committee
14	Prices and output by branches (1959–67)	RS	INSEE	Goods and services	Productive sector commissions
15	Housing finance	PSM	DP	Productive economy	Housing

Table 1.1 *continued*

| Field of analysis | Tool used | Administration involved | | Plan Commission or work group requesting the study |
		INSEE, DP or CGP	Division	
16 Social security systems projection	PSM	DP	Public administration	Social benefits
17 Social overhead capital index	RS	DP	Public administration	Social commissions
18 Central government account into budget terms	TD	DP	Public administration	Budget group, CEGF, Budget Directorate (MEF)
19 Local authorities account	PSM	DP	Public administration	Local finance
20 Weight of taxation	RS	INSEE	Enterprises	Taxation
21 Structure of taxation (1949–69)	RS	DP	Taxation	Taxation
22 Foreign investment in France	RS +PSM	DP	External	Foreign trade
23 Penetration of French products into foreign markets	RS	DP	External	Foreign trade
24 Foreign trade account into balance of payments	TD	DP	External	Foreign trade
25 Interest, dividends, financial institutions	RS +PSM	DP	Financial programming	Finance
26 Financial operations table	PSM	DP	Financial operations	Finance

Key: RS = retrospective study   PSM = partial simulation model
      P   = projection   TD   = translation dictionary

Source: see note 19

at. Once the variant has been defined in this way, then it takes only a few minutes on the computer to produce its results. But it may take days to define the variant, and it is not surprising that there is now considerable activity engaged in building satellite models to speed up this 'auxiliary' work (see Chapter 3). It is generally true that the results of a variant clearly reflect the quality of the work that has gone into defining it.

But this technical progress has raised new problems, as we now see in the final section of this chapter.

14

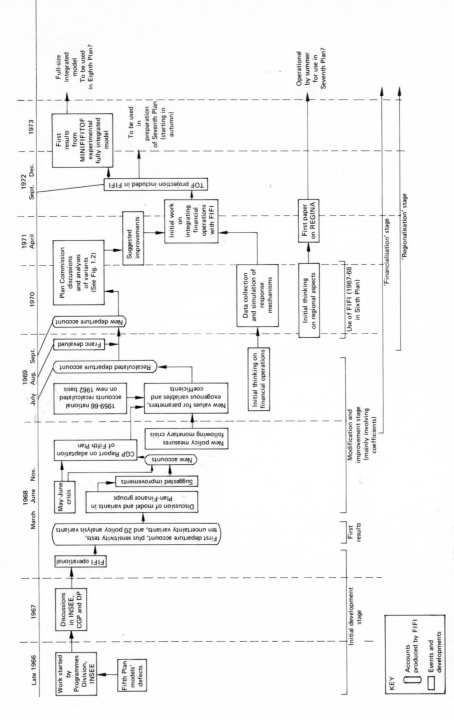

Fig. 1.1   Stages in the development of the FIFI model
Source: see note 20

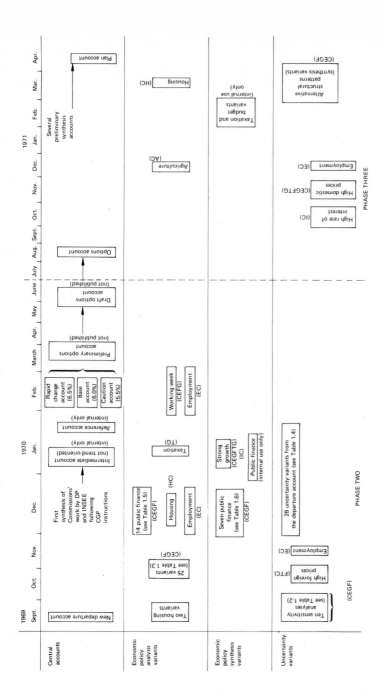

Fig. 1.2 Accounts and variants constructed using the FIFI model in phases two and three

Note: The commissions and other groups for which the accounts were drawn up are shown in brackets; where none are shown, the accounts and variants were used by more than one body.

Abbreviations used: FTC, Foreign Trade Committee; EC, Employment Commissions; IC, Industry Commission; CEGFTG, CEGF Technical Group; HC, Housing Commission; TG, Taxation Group; AC, Agriculture Commission

Source: see note 21

Table 1.2

The ten sensitivity variants
accompanying the September 1969 departure account

Uncertainties connected with the international environment
1 Increased pressure on domestic prices following the devaluation.
2 More aggressive behaviour of foreign exporters following the devaluation.
3 A bigger price handicap than before the devaluation.
4 Higher foreign prices and production.

Uncertainties relating to the structural characteristics of the French economy
5 Effects of higher growth in available manpower.
6 Effects of higher growth in labour productivity.
7 Consequences of less inflationary behaviour.
8 Smaller difference between the growth of wage-earners' incomes and individual entrepreneurs' incomes.[29]
9 Changes in industry's desired rate of self-financing.
10 Change in households' saving rate.

Source: see note 22

1.4 The role of the central model in the planning process

We look more closely at FIFI in Chapter 3, and we examine in some detail the opinions of some of its users in Chapter 5. But it would be wrong not to mention in this chapter some of the things that FIFI *cannot* do, and some of the feelings aroused in various of the participants when they discovered these shortcomings.

At the outset it was acknowledged that as a medium-term planning model, FIFI had certain limitations and weaknesses. These included:

(a) a limited degree of detail: the model distinguishes only seven sectors, including a very large 'industry' sector;
(b) no fully integrated financial operations: although one of its original features is the manner in which it treats enterprises' self-financing behaviour, the operations distinguished by the TOF[27] all had to be projected outside the model, with no consequent feedback on the model's physical equilibrium (Fig. 1.1 shows the work going on to rectify this weakness);

Table 1.3

The 25 specific economic policy variants submitted to the CEGF in November 1969

1, 2, 3	Additional manpower training.
4	Increased competition in the sheltered sector.
5, 6, 7	Reduction of the length of the working week.
8, 9, 10	Changes in income tax.
11	Decrease in VAT.
12, 13	Reduction in the business licence tax ('la patente').
14, 15, 16	Raising national insurance contributions.
17, 18, 19	Faster growth of the minimum wage ('SMIG').
20	Reduction in social security benefits.
21	Encouragement of households' savings.
22, 23	Improving enterprises' external financing possibilities (i.e. leading to a reduction in their desired rate of self-financing).
24	Increased gross fixed capital formation by administrations.
25	Increased housing gross fixed capital formation.

Source: see note 23

(c)   the model is essentially static: FIFI gives a picture only of the Plan's terminal year, assuming smooth trajectories between the base year and this terminal year;

(d)   it gives the national dimensions of medium-term changes and problems: Fig. 1.1 again shows the efforts to put this right;

(e)   social variables are largely excluded: FIFI describes reality in national accounting terms, and thus acknowledges only those actions and problems that are capable of conversion into national accounting flows. There is thus no internal analysis of collective functions, the non-market sphere of the economy, structural phenomena, socio-economic relationships, or the satisfaction of social needs via social indicators.

The hope was that all these things that FIFI could not do would induce other analyses to take place outside the model. But the Plan Commissions had at their disposal only two, roughly six-month, periods in which to do *all* their work, including attempting to understand the model. For many of them, a fair proportion of this time was taken up in arriving at the

Table 1.4

The 28 uncertainty variants associated with the departure account,
derived to show the sensitivity of FIFI to all its main parameters
and to contribute to the analysis of the hazards confronting the Sixth Plan

---

Factors of production

1 Increased manpower availability.
2 Accelerated agricultural exodus.
3 Shorter working week in non-agricultural branches.
4 Shorter working week in industry.
5 Changing the relationship between available population seeking employment and the activity rate.
6 Bigger increase in non-agricultural productivity.
7 Increased industrial productivity.
8 Increased productivity in building and public works, services and commerce.
9 Increased productivity in other sectors.
10 Increased global rate of productive investment.
11 Increased rate of investment in industry.
12 Increased rate of investment in building and public works, services and commerce.
13 Increased rate of investment in other sectors.
14 Less significant change in stocks in industry.

---

correct conclusion that FIFI is one tool among others; it essentially clarifies macro-economic, medium-term regulation problems, rather than problems connected with the structural transformation of the economy and social conditions. Because each participant brings his own ideas and objectives to the 'concertation' process, the model thus corresponds very unequally to the participants' preoccupations, and is therefore of differing uses to them. The main users of the model have in fact been the CGP, the CEGF, various Government departments, those Plan Commissions with economic equilibrium functions (see Fig. 1.2), and the CNPF (Comité National du Patronat Français − National Committee of French Employers − a union-style organisation frequently referred to just as the 'Patronat'), who used it to study several strong growth variants. It has hardly been used at all by the Plan Commissions concerned with social problems, and not at all by the CGT (Confédération Générale du Travail − General Confederation of Labour − a trade union) and the CFDT (Con-

Table 1.4 *continued*

Behaviour and the international environment
15   Stronger constraint on industrial prices.
16   Lower rate of self-financing in industry.
17   Smaller wage coefficient in industry.
18   Smaller wage coefficient in non-industrial sectors.
19   Smaller difference between per capita incomes of non-agricultural individual entrepreneurs and wage earners.
20   Lower rate of self-financing in building and public works, services, and commerce.
21   Higher constant term in the wage–price–unemployment relationship.
22   Bigger unemployment effect in the wage–price–unemployment relationship.
23   Smaller price effect in the wage–price–unemployment relationship.
24   Higher rate of interest.
25   Increase in households' saving rate.
26   Change in domestic consumption away from industrial products to agricultural products.
27   Change in domestic consumption away from industrial products to services.
28   More rapid world growth.

Source: see note 24

fédération Française Démocratique du Travail – French Democratic Labour Confederation – a trade union).

It is true that concerted planning practised on the French scale needs clarity, and that a computerised model is able to provide this regularly and quickly. The public administrations need a lot of detail, and in their own language, and a model such as FIFI (which is much larger than other macro-economic models used in western-style planning processes) speeds the information flow between them. But the planning process involves participants from outside the public administrations, and models tend to be rather esoteric. They are especially difficult and off-putting when they are as large as FIFI. Several participants said they felt dominated by the model, and overwhelmed by the masses of information it produced. Consequently, they said, imagination and innovation were effectively paralysed, and the initiative passed from the hands of the decision-makers to the technicians. This resembles the old criticisms about the power of the

Table 1.5

The 14 public finance policy analysis variants
submitted to the CEGF in December 1969

Effects of a 6 milliard fr. (6 × 10⁹ fr.) 'ex ante' improvement in the public finance balance caused by:

1   increasing employers' national insurance contributions;
2   increasing employees' national insurance contributions;
3   increasing VAT;
4   increasing income tax;
5   decreasing public administrations' expenditure on goods and services;
6   decreasing social security benefits;
7   decreasing subsidies to the productive sector;
8   decreasing the number of central government employees (and hence wages).

Effects of a 6 milliard fr. 'ex ante' deterioration in the public finance balance caused by:

9   decreasing VAT;
10   decreasing income tax;
11   combined decrease in income tax and company tax;
12   combined decrease in income tax and VAT;
13   increase in Government consumption and gross fixed capital formation;
14   increase in Government wage rates.

Source: see note 25

'technocrats', [28] but they bear re-stating, and they take on fresh meaning with the arrival of FIFI in the planning process. Other participants, confusing the model and the results produced by it, tended to look upon FIFI as an oracle and to use it as an authoritative argument only when its results matched their own viewpoints.

While it is certainly true that the use of FIFI in the preparation of the Sixth Plan allowed more time for discussion than in previous Plans (a variant took two months to calculate by hand in the preparation of the Fifth Plan), it cannot be denied that the feeling of dissatisfaction among the participants at the end of the preparation period was higher than at the corresponding stage in the Fifth Plan. A closer analysis of the causes

Table 1.6

The seven public finance policy synthesis variants
submitted to the CEGF in December 1969

1	Central government account: achieving balance by adjusting expenditures to the level of receipts shown in the departure account;
	Social security account: achieving balance by increasing contributions to the level of benefits shown in the departure account.
2 – 6	Achieving balance in the social security and central government accounts when Government taxation stays the same as in 1970.
7	Achieving balance in both accounts when total taxation stays at the 1970 level.

Source: see note 26

of this feeling is made in Chapter 5, where we also see what conclusions were drawn by the CEGF's technical group to avoid a repetition of the situation in the Seventh Plan.

Notes

[1] Nearly all the sources in this chapter (as indeed in the whole book) are French official reports and papers, which one can find in Paris if one knows where to look, but which are not generally available in any great numbers outside France, especially in non-French speaking countries (like England!). I have made many fruitless telephone calls and visits to libraries all over the United Kingdom, and have discovered that not one single issue of even the 'popular' INSEE journals (like *Les Collections de l'INSEE*) can be had. Whenever a source is quoted which might cause some readers difficulties, I have attempted to provide additional information to help locate the source.

The main sources for this chapter are [1] and [2] (see list of references following these notes). [1] is available from la Documentation Française at 29–31 quai Voltaire, 75 Paris 7, and [2] from the Service du Bulletin de l'Economie et des Finances, Ministère de l'Economie et des Finances, 93 rue de Rivoli, 75 Paris 1. Copies of the *Bulletin* will usually be sent without charge. An English translation of [2] is available in [3], but this was prepared for the benefit of students following my course on French planning at Birmingham. It is accordingly very rough and ready, and only available in limited numbers. While stocks last, copies can be obtained from the Secretary, National Economic Planning Courses, Faculty of Commerce and Social Science, University, Birmingham B15 2TT.

[2] The departure account was included in a report submitted to the CEGF (see section 1.2 for definition of these initials) in October 1969. This report is reproduced in full in [4] pp. 7–82; it was prepared by Michel Aglietta, Paul Dubois, Christian Sautter, Claude Seibel and Bernard Ullmo of the INSEE Programmes Division. INSEE publications are available from INSEE, Bureau d'Information du Public, 29 quai Branly, 75 Paris 7.

[3] A very good analysis of the Economic and Social Council, how it works and what its impact has been up to and including the Fifth Plan, is given in [5].

[4] Over 65 reports (from Plan Commissions, committees, inter-groups, technical groups, etc.) were published by La Documentation Française in 1971. A full list and current prices are available from them.

[5] The CIE mentions in its report 16 priority areas where more work on statistical and economic information is needed. In addition to being discussed in CIE's report, these priority areas are also discussed in brief in an INSEE monthly publication: the first five priorities are in [6] and other 11 priorities are in [7].

[6] The Plan Commissions' work programme for the options phase has been published by La Documentation Française in [8]. Note that the title of this report refers to the 'first phase', whereas we describe the options preparation as the second phase. Both are correct: the title in [8] refers to the first phase involving the Commissions.

[7] The work programme for the Plan Commissions in the Plan specification phase is published in [9]. The explanation of the number of the phase is similar to that given in note 6 above.

[8] See [2] p. 17 and [3] p. 11.

[9] 'It is often said that France is governed by the Ministry of Finance, and while the idea is somewhat exaggerated, it still contains a measure of truth', [10], p. 184.

[10] In total, there were eight Plan Commissions in the First Plan, rising to 32 in the Fifth Plan.

[11] I should be delighted to be proved wrong on this!

[12] The CGP published the *Rapport sur les problèmes posés pour l'adaptation du Ve Plan* ('Report on the problems created by the adaptations of the Fifth Plan, La Documentation Française, Paris, 69 pp.) on 5 November 1968. This was the first step in the work that the Government thought

necessary to redirect medium-term economic and social policy following the May—June events. The FIFI model was used in the analyses behind this first step.

¹³ For a very brief summary of the monetary measures taken in November 1968 see [11], pp. 800—1. Available from Aménagement du Territoire et Développement Régional, Institut d'Études Politiques, Université des Sciences Sociales de Grenoble, 17 Grenoble—Gare (38), France.

¹⁴ The data used in FIFI was initially calculated on 1959 as base year, that being the base year of the French national accounts when work first started on FIFI. In 1968 the first results of the national accounts with 1962 as base year were published *(in Études et Conjoncture*, which ceased publication soon afterwards and became *Economie et Statistique)*. See [12]. Later results are in [13], [14], [15], and [16].

¹⁵ Cossé briefly describes the work done by the specialist groups in [2], pp. 22—4 (also in [3], pp. 15—17).

¹⁶ See Appendix IV below.

¹⁷ Quoted in [1] p. 41.

¹⁸ Particularly in Part III of [1], which is a critical report on the model and its use, and includes statements from members of the CEGF technical group describing their opinions on FIFI and its role in the planning process. We analyse these statements in Chapter 5.

¹⁹ The source of Table 1.1 is [2], pp. 34—5; I have slightly modified the presentation. The same is also in [3], pp. 25—7. Note that the DP Divisions are now different (see Appendix I below).

²⁰ This diagram is not based on any known similar source; it is built up from descriptions one can find on the early development of FIFI (in [1] and [2] for example), and on the 'financialisation' and 'regionalisation' sources quoted in Chapter 10.

²¹ Figure 1.2 is very similar to Table 1 on pp. 32—3 of [1]; I have added some additional information on central accounts, and separated the analysis variants from the synthesis variants. The base, caution and rapid change accounts are included in an appendix to *Rapport sur les principales options qui commandent la préparation du VIᵉ Plan*, Imprimerie Nationale, Paris 1970. Available from Imprimerie Nationale, 39 rue de la Convention, 75 Paris 15. The alternative structural patterns are given in [17].

²² More information on these variants is given in [4], pp. 25—31. Nine out of the ten are described numerically in [4], pp. 35—44; we reproduce some of this data in Chapter 4.

²³ See [4], pp. 153—7. Numerical details in [4], pp. 159—89, and Chapter 4.

²⁴ See [4], pp. 86—7. Numerical details in [4], p. 92—149 and Chapter 4.

25 See [4], pp. 193–5, and Chapter 4.

26 See [4], pp. 197–201, and Chapter 4.

27 The financial operations table (TOF) is defined and explained in Appendix II below.

28 See [10], pp. 158–62, and [18].

29 By 'individual entrepreneur' is usually meant a one-man business, a partnership, or an unincorporated firm. The term 'self-employed' is sometimes used instead.

There are additional notes and references to this and other chapters at the end of Chapter 10.

References

[1] Commissariat Général du Plan, *Le modèle physico-financier dans la preparation du VIᵉ Plan* (The physico-financial model in the preparation of the Sixth Plan), Report of the Technical Group of the General Economic and Financing Commission, La Documentation Française; Paris 1971, 95 pp.

[2] J. P. Pagé, P-Y. Cossé, M-O. Mouriau and C. Seibel, 'La préparation du VIᵉ Plan' (The preparation of the Sixth Plan), *Bulletin de Liaison et d'Information de l'Administration Centrale de l'Economie et des Finances* no. 55, April–June 1971, pp. 7-59.

[3] D. Liggins, 'The preparation of the Sixth French Plan' (translation of [2]), *NEP Research Papers* no. 63, University of Birmingham, March 1972, 38 pp.

[4] M. Aglietta, P. Dubois, J-P. Pagé, C.H. Sautter, C. Seibel, and B. Ullmo, 'Études macroeconomiques pour 1975' (Macro-economic analysis for 1975), *Les Collections de l'INSEE*, série C (Comptes et Planification), no. 9, March 1971, 207 pp.

[5] J. E. S. Hayward, *Private Interests and Public Policy. The Experience of the French Economic and Social Council*, Longmans, London 1966, 115 pp.

[6] INSEE, 'Le.développement de l'information statistique pendant le VIᵉ Plan' (The development of statistical information during the Sixth Plan), Part I, *Économie et Statistique* no. 27, October 1971, pp. 60–6.

[7] Part II of [6], *Économie et Statistique* no. 28, November 1971, pp. 60–6.

[8] Commissariat Général du Plan, *Programme de travail des commis-*

sions de modernisation du VIe Plan – preparation du rapport sur les options (1re phase) (The Sixth Plan commissions' work programme – preparation of the options report (first phase)), La Documentation Française, Paris 1969.

[9] Commissariat Général du Plan, *Programme de travail des commissions de modernisation du VIe Plan – préparation du VIe Plan (2e phase)* (The Sixth Plan commissions' work programme – preparation of the Sixth Plan (second phase)), La Documentation Française, Paris 1970.

[10] P. Avril, *Politics in France* (translated from the French by J. Ross), Penguin 1969, 304 pp.

[11] Institut d'Études Politiques, *Aménagement du territoire et développement regional: les faits, les idées, les institutions* (Spatial planning and regional development: the facts, the opinions, the institutions), vol. III, published by the Centre d'Étude et de Recherche sur l'Administration Économique et l'Aménagement du Territoire, Grenoble 1970, 876 pp.

[12] INSEE, 'Retrospective des comptes nationaux dans la nouvelle base' (Past national accounts recalculated on the new base year), *Économie et Statistique* no. 6, November 1969, pp. 54–9.

[13] INSEE, 'Les comptes de la nation base 1962. Résultats d'ensemble des comptes. Séries 1959–1966' (The national accounts to 1962 base year. Results of all accounts from 1959 to 1966), *Les Collections de l'INSEE*, série C, no. 7, May 1970.

[14] INSEE, 'Rapport sur les comptes de la nation 1970' (1970 Report on the national accounts), 3 vols, *Les Collections de l'INSEE*, série C, no. 11, June 1971.

[15] As [14] but 1971 Report, *Les Collections de l'INSEE*, série C, no. 15, June 1972.

[16] As [14] but 1972 Report, *Les Collections de l'INSEE*, série C, no. 23, June 1973.

[17] M. Guillaume and B. Ullmo, 'Six schémas structurels pour 1975' (Six structural analyses for 1975), *Économie et Statistique* no. 32, March 1972, pp. 3–36.

[18] P. Bauchard, *Les technocrates et le pouvoir* (The technocrats and national power), Arthaud, Paris 1966, 319 pp.

2 Long-term Studies and the Preparation of the Plan

> In France, futures research is immersed in a planning context which is essentially macro-economic, and one might ask whether this creates an impediment to a fruitful dialogue between the futures researchers and the planners.
>
> Bernard Cazes, [19].

This quotation from Bernard Cazes symbolises one of the serious problems facing long-term studies (or futures research) in France at the present time: what should its relationship be with the medium-term national planning process that created it and feels it ought to depend on it? Medium-term planning is now well-established and reasonably well-organised in its preparation phases and it is supported by a clearly defined methodology (at least on the macro-economic side). Long-term studies, on the other hand, have developed only comparatively recently; they exist both within the planning framework and outside it, and there is no general agreement on the methodological side. Political scientists are involved in major studies on the future of international relations; urban sociologists are demanding more resources to analyse the 'crisis of urbanisation' and the structure of society at the local level; and, somewhere in between, the national planners feel that they too should be looking to the long-term future, setting the medium-term plan in some longer-term context, and at the same time integrating the results of the international and local studies going on around them.

Attempts have been made ever since the preparation of the Third Plan to analyse long-term developments, and establish links with medium-term planning. A ten-year projection in volume terms, with 1965 as the target year, was prepared for the Third Plan (1958—1961),[1] focusing mainly on total population, working population, and output per capita, and laying the groundwork not only for the later studies which we describe in this chapter, but also the regional population and employment projections which we consider in Chapter 8. The long-term studies prepared during the work on the Fourth Plan (1962—1965) were not published, but it is known that they consisted of a similar projection in volume terms, based on 1956 and extending to 1975.

27

The impression given by the various commentaries[2] on these early efforts in long-term studies is that they were merely extended macro-economic trend extrapolations, and did not really come to grips with France's long-term development problems. It was not until the preparation of the Fifth Plan (1966–1970) that any serious attempt was made to build a logical structure for long-term studies. Pierre Massé, the head of the CGP at that time, had a considerable influence[3] on initiating what Cazes calls this 'second stage of long-term studies', and he created the 1985 Group, a committee of wise men charged with exploring the long-term future. A list of topics, including housing, education, urbanisation, and the regional distribution of activities, was suggested to them by the CGP, and they also had the benefit of another long-term macro-economic projection (the third in the series), covering 1960–1985 and prepared by the INSEE.[4] Although the technical report on the Fifth Plan [77] gives very little space to these long-term studies, and they appear to have had a limited operational character,[5] a structure was established, and the Sixth Plan long-term studies were able to build on it; we give a critical appraisal of them in section 2.2. Before that, we examine the preliminary projections prepared by the INSEE for the Sixth Plan long-term groups, projections that are very much in the same mould as those of previous Plans, but have been updated more recently, as we see in section 2.3. In the section 2.4, we look at French work on social indicators, work that is vital to progress in 'goal-oriented' futures research (a term which is due to Massé). Finally, in section 2.5, we go outside the planning framework and briefly discuss the work going on under the SESAME project ('Système d'Étude du Schéma d'Amenagement', the research programme on the regional development blueprint), an ambitious scheme which has produced some interesting results.

2.1 The preliminary long-term projections

It is important at the outset to be clear on the meaning of the term 'projection' as used here:

> 'The long-term studies cannot ... be classified under the headings of projection, programming or planning.... These studies do not constitute either a programme or a plan.... Nor can they be regarded simply as a projection in the strict sense of the term, since the topics to which they relate do not always lend themselves to a quantitative approach. They provide, rather, an instrument for thought....'[6]

28

This quotation is taken slightly out of context: it refers to long-term studies in the broad sense. But it helps to clarify the nature of the preliminary projections prepared by the INSEE and the CGP in 1967–68: they are very crudely compiled quantitative expressions of a number of development alternatives, constructed with very little historical analysis of growth mechanisms and their consequences, and with no attempt at all to analyse the likely future outcome of known 'social forces'. At best, then, they are an 'instrument for thought', presented to the long-term study groups (listed and described in the next section) at the beginning of their deliberations, and providing a point of departure for them.

Two sets of projections were constructed. The first, designed to give a rough order of magnitude of long-term development possibilities, involved simple index number calculations with numerical assumptions on changes in three factors of production: the size of the working population, the length of the working week, and labour productivity, of the type

$$I_o = I_p I_d I_w \tag{2.1}$$

where I_o = index of output growth;
I_p = index of growth in hourly labour productivity;
I_d = index of growth in the length of the working week;
I_w = index of growth in working population.

The size of the working population is a function of total population, the school leaving age, female activity rates the retirement age. immigration, and the size of the armed forces, about all of which it is possible to make a number of assumptions on change in the 20 years between 1965 and 1985. Combining these assumptions with additional ones on the rate of rundown in the agricultural working population and the likely changes in the administrative working population, three main alternatives were retained for the size of the working population in industry and services in 1985: 21·5 million (low), 23 million (trend), and 25 million (high).

The second factor of production entering into the calculations is the length of the working week. Various studies have been made on likely changes in this factor,[7] including an analysis undertaken for the 1985 Group. This analysis projected the 1985 situation as 40 hours, with five weeks' annual holiday; this was taken as the 'trend' for the Sixth Plan preliminary projection, although not strictly fitting the trend extrapolation of changes in the length of the working week since the end of the Second World War. Two alternatives were artificially constructed on either side of this trend in order to promote discussion.

Finally, assumptions were made on changes in labour productivity,

Table 2.1   The six preliminary 1965–1985 projections of overall growth and changes in production factors (compiled January 1968)

	Level of PIB (with respect to 1965)*	General characteristics	1985 working population in industry and services	Length of the working week in 1985	Annual increase in hourly labour productivity in industries and services (base 1965)
A1	PIB multiplied by 2·5 (i.e. growing at 4·6 per cent p.a.)	Trend pattern: similar growth to that in the post-war period	Extrapolation of past trends: 17 million	40 hours 5 weeks holiday	Trend growth: 4·0 per cent p.a.
A2		Stronger growth of productivity but a bigger reduction in the length of the working week	Extrapolation of past trends: 17 million	Reduction to 36 hours + 4 weeks or 40 hours + 9 weeks	Faster growth: 4·5 per cent p.a.
B1	Doubling of PIB (i.e. 3·5 per cent p.a.)	Growth with low productivity	Extrapolation of past trends: 17 million	40 hours + 4 weeks	Low growth: 3·0 per cent p.a.
B2		Priority to leisure, with average productivity growth	Less activity than in the past: 15 millions	Reduction to 36 hours + 4 weeks or 40 hours + 9 weeks	Trend growth: 4·0 per cent p.a.
C1	Tripling of PIB (i.e. 5·6 per cent p.a.)	Average increase in productivity, with high employment and working hours	More activity than in the past: 19·5 million	Maintenance of longer working hours: 44 hours + 5 weeks or 43 hours + 4 weeks	Trend growth: 4·0 per cent p.a.
C2		Strong productivity growth, shorter working hours, and high employment	More activity than in the past: 19·5 million	40 hours + 5 weeks	Faster growth: 4·5 per cent p.a.

* Agriculture is assumed to grow at 3·0 per cent p.a. between 1965 and 1985, and the table thus refers then to industry and services

Source: Table V, [25], p. 33

mainly by comparing the French situation with that of other industrialised countries, and anticipating how quickly France might catch them up. Again, very little analysis was made of the mechanisms likely to generate such productivity changes, the assumptions being a mixture of expectations on changes in behaviour by industry and households. and reasonable allowances for other uncertainties. With a low, medium, and high assumption on each of the three factors, 27 combinations are possible, but many of these are difficult to reconcile with the low, medium, and high overall growth expectations, taken as 3·5, 4·6 and 5·6 per cent per annum over the 20 year period. Accordingly, six alternatives were put forward (see Table 2.1), constructed in such a way as to satisfy (2.1) when I_0 corresponds to the three growth assumptions. A1 is the 'trend' projection, although the assumption regarding the length of the working week fits the international trend more closely than the trend in France alone.

There are several ways of interpreting the alternatives. Let us consider A2. The argument could be: assume that productivity increases quickly (without looking into why); this allows a reduction in the working week and more holidays, which in turn is likely to encourage different household behaviour and life styles. Thus, the projection is intended to stimulate thought on how to provide for these different life styles in the future. Alternatively suppose there is a demand for shorter working hours and longer holidays; for this to be acceptable without sacrificing growth, there must be faster growth in productivity. To achieve increased productivity requires different investment policies. better organisation, more manpower training, etc., and so another chain of thought is stimulated. Similar interpretations can be placed on the other growth alternatives. thus bringing out the essential purpose of this type of projection.

Following this 'rough order of magnitude' projection, a more detailed projection was produced, using the E_0 model (described in Appendix VIII), and based essentially on the A1 assumptions. Some element of continuity was maintained by using the E_0 model, because the same model was applied to the long-term projection produced for the 1985 Group in the preparation of the Fifth Plan. One or two minor modifications were made to the model: there was a slightly larger sectoral breakdown, and updated parameter estimates were inserted. The same model has also been used more recently to generate a projection of 1980, using the Sixth Plan account (described in Chapter 6) as a reference point; the results are given in [94], pp. 357—67. The model is extremely simple and is really nothing more than a multiple trend extrapolator, but it does introduce important consistency checks and interdependencies (via an input—output table and

Table 2.2
Main assumptions and reference data (past trends or Fifth Plan figures) used in the trend-oriented 1985 projection (compiled January 1968 with the E_0 model)

	Assumptions	Reference data
Factors of production and demography		
Duration of work		
Working week	40 hours in 1985	44½ hours in 1970
		46 hours in 1962
Annual holidays	5 weeks in 1985	4 weeks in 1970
Total population*		
Annual growth rate	0·9 per cent p.a. 1970 to 1985	
Total population in 1985	59 millions	51·2 millions in 1970
		46·6 millions in 1962
Working population	23·12 millions in 1985	
Net immigration of workers	60,000 p.a. 1970 to 1985	
School leaving age	16 in 1985 with diffusion effect beyond 16	
Activity of old people	Extrapolation of 1954–1962 trend	
Female activity	Extrapolation of 1954–1962 trend	
Armed forces	50 per cent in military service by 1985	
Unemployment	350,000 in 1985	
Demand		
Annual growth rate of administrations' gross fixed capital formation	6·5 per cent p.a. 1970 to 1985	8·9 per cent p.a. 1962 to 1970 (Fifth Plan)
		8·5 per cent p.a. 1954 to 1962
Annual growth rate of administrations' consumption	5·0 per cent p.a. 1970 to 1985	7·0 per cent p.a. 1962 to 1970 (Fifth Plan)
		3·5 per cent p.a. 1954 to 1962
Housing		
Number constructed (in dwelling-equivalent units)	550,000 in 1985	480,000 in 1970 (Fifth Plan)
		330,000 in 1962
Increase in quality	2 per cent p.a. 1970 to 1985	
Productive gross fixed capital formation: share of PIB	Maintenance of the Fifth Plan 1970 rate: 14·7 per cent	

* Including external migration, but excluding armed forces stationed abroad

Source: Table IX, [25], p. 39

Cobb–Douglas production functions) which were ignored in the previous index number calculations.

The main assumptions and parameters are shown in Table 2.2. It can be seen from this table that the Fifth Plan's 1970 figures have been inserted as reference points, so that the 1962–1985 projection becomes consistent with the previous Plan. The main results are given in Tables 2.3 and 2.4 (further details and additional results are given in [25]). There is very little need to comment further on these results: they are so clearly trend extrapolations (the last three columns in each of the three parts of Table 2.3 confirm this fact), corresponding to a society in which 60 per cent of value added is industrial (branches 2, 3, and 4), one-third of the working population is employed in services (branch 5), and average living standards are not as high as one imagines the ordinary Frenchman expects. Such then was the basis of the work carried out by the long-term study groups between the autumn of 1967 and the first half of 1969; we now look at the work of these groups in more detail. We shall also discuss some of the criticisms that have been made about comprehensive, synthesising long-term studies of the type just described in this section.

2.2 Sixth Plan long-term study groups

Building on the structure established in the preparation of the Fifth Plan to which we briefly referred above, a much more ambitious analytical approach to long-term studies was attempted during the preparation of the Sixth Plan. Whereas only one main group was formed in the Fifth Plan, there were more than a dozen groups in the Sixth Plan, plus a number of smaller working groups looking into more specific problems. I have been unable to find a comprehensive list of all the groups (Cazes in [26] talks of nine vertical or sectoral policy-oriented groups, six horizontal or problem-oriented groups, and one central co-ordinating group, whereas Pagé in [2] mentions 12 'main' groups (implying that there were others) consisting of five socially-oriented groups, two geographically-oriented groups, and five sectorally-oriented groups, plus a central group, but it is clear from the reports that have been published[8] and various other sources that one or more groups handled one or more of the following sectors and/or problem areas:

Policy-oriented groups	*Problem-oriented groups*
1 Agriculture	1 Population trends
2 Cultural affairs	2 Urban development

Table 2.3

Main results of the 1962–1985 trend-oriented projection (compiled January 1968 with the E_0 model)

Global equilibrium of resources and uses in goods and services	Value (10^9 1959 francs)			Indices			Average annual growth rates		
	1962	1970	1985	1962/70	1970/85	1962/85	1962/70	1970/85	1962/85
Resources									
Gross domestic production	288·3	420·2	818·6	146	195	284	4·8	4·5	4·6
Uses									
Household consumption	199·8	285·2	560·3	143	197	280	4·5	4·6	5·0
Gross fixed capital formation	64·5	104·2	199·1	162	191	309	6·2	4·4	4·8
of which: productive	(40·9)	(62·1)	(120·0)	152	193	293	5·4	4·5	5·0
administrations*	(8·3)	(16·0)	(40·4)	193	253	487	8·6	6·4	7·1
housing	(15·3)	(26·1)	(38·7)	171	148	253	6·9	2·7	4·1
Administrations' consumption*	14·4	24·4	51·0	169	209	354	6·8	5·0	5·6
Other uses†	9·6	6·4	8·2	6·7	128	85	-5·1	1·7	
Total uses	288·3	420·2	818·6	146	195	284	4·8	4·5	4·6

Changes in household consumption by product	Structure (%)			Average annual growth rates		
	1962	1970	1985	1962/70	1970/85	1962/85
1 Agricultural products	11·4	9·9	7·3	2·7	2·5	2·6
2 Energy, metals, chemicals	10·9	13·1	17·2	7·0	6·5	6·7
3 Durable goods	7·3	8·6	11·0	6·7	6·4	6·5
4 Textiles, various food industries	46·3	43·1	37·0	3·6	3·6	3·6
5 Transport and services	24·1	25·3	27·5	5·2	5·2	5·2
Total	100·0	100·0	100·0	4·5	4·6	4·6

Changes in working population	Structure (%)			Average annual growth rates		
	1962	1970	1985	1962/70	1970/85	1962/85
1 Agriculture	19·8	14·1	7·7	−3·4	−3·0	−3·1
2 Intermediate goods industries	8·9	9·0	8·7	1·0	0·6	0·8
3 Capital goods industries	16·5	18·5	18·7	2·2	1·0	1·4
4 Consumer goods industries	13·7	13·0	12·0	0·2	0·4	0·3
5 Transport, services, and commerce	26·3	29·0	33·4	2·1	1·9	1·9
Total employed population working in branches	85·2	83·6	80·5	0·6	0·7	0·6
Outside branches (mainly administrations)	14·8	16·4	19·5	2·2	2·1	
Overall total	100·0	100·0	100·0	0·8	0·9	

* Including financial institutions

† Changes in stocks plus the external balance

Source: Tables X, XI and XIII, [25], pp. 42–3, 45

Table 2.4

The input–output table associated with the 1962–1985 projection
(compiled January 1968 with the E_0 model)

	Branches					Intermediate consumption by product	Household consumption	Productive investment	Other uses†	Total
	1	2	3	4	5					
Products										
1	0	0·2	0	50·5	6·7	57·4	40·7	0	0·8	98·9
2	14·0	0	94·4	28·5	35·5	172·4	96·2	1·3	−20·0	249·9
3	1·1	7·1	0	2·2	15·2	25·6	61·6	117·0	103·2	307·4
4	7·7	11·1	17·2	0	25·3	61·3	207·8	0·4	9·3	278·8
5*	6·0	16·7	18·6	14·5	0	55·8	124·3	1·3	23·6	205·0
Intermediate consumption by branch	28·8	35·1	130·2	95·7	82·7	372·5	530·6	120·0	116·9	1140·0
Value added	45·0	170·5	138·2	109·5	255·1	718·3				
Production at real prices	73·8	205·6	268·4	205·2	337·8	1090·8				
Export price correction	0	17·1	17·8	14·3	0	49·2				
Production at domestic prices	73·8	222·7	286·2	219·5	337·8	1140·0				
Commercial margins	25·1	27·2	21·2	59·3	−132·8	0				
Total	98·9	249·9	307·4	278·8	205·0	1140·0				

Value added   =   718·3
Taxes and duty on imports   =   70·6
Value added of the housing branch   =   29·7

PIB   =   818·6

* Not including housing

† Gross fixed capital formation of administrations and financial institutions + administrations' and financial institutions' consumption + changes in stocks + exports − imports − import duties and taxes + export price correction + gross fixed capital formation in housing

Source: Table XVI C, [25], p. 49

3	Energy	3	Old people
4	Health	4	Leisure
5	Housing	5	Mobility within the labour force
6	Industry	6	Consumption and life styles
7	Posts and telecommunications	7	Change in rural areas
8	Research and development		
9	Transportation		

The choice of these groups reflects the availability of expertise and personnel rather than any preconceived feeling that these are the most important areas requiring long-term analysis. The classification of the groups under the vertical, policy-oriented, and horizontal, problem-oriented headings is also a little artificial, since several of the studies are so broad and multidisciplinary that they do not fit easily into either category. In a field that is so new and underdeveloped, however, it is useful to try and establish some sort of pattern, not only from the viewpoint of outside observers but also from that of members of long-term study groups in future Plans. The framework we describe in this section is essentially due to Cazes, and, whilst not universally accepted by all futures researchers, it can probably reasonably be regarded as the CGP system. Broadly speaking, vertical subjects are characterised by a clearly defined sector of analysis, usually following well-established administrative boundaries (e.g. housing, health, industry and agriculture are each handled by one main ministry and statistics are gathered either by their own services or by INSEE departments that follow the same ministerial demarcations). This means that the area to be analysed is amenable to a quantitative economic approach. Horizontal subjects, on the other hand, spread over several ministerial domains, and encompass global processes (such as urbanisation) or human behaviour (leisure, mobility, etc.). Data on such activities is not readily available; the approach is therefore qualitative and usually depends a great deal on sociological tools of analysis. There is also a third type of analysis within the framework, an example of which we have already discussed in the previous section: synthesising or comprehensive futures research, considered by some to be an extreme example of a horizontal study.

As we have mentioned above, there is disagreement within the field of long-term studies about the nature of the logical structure that should determine the general approach to futures research. Many would argue that vertical long-term studies, emphasising quantifiable variables, is really forecasting, and that the only true futures research is horizontal, while others would criticise some horizontal studies for drifting too close to pseudo-

Table 2.5

Main features of the vertical, horizontal, and comprehensive long-term studies
carried out during the preparation of the Sixth Plan

Feature	Vertical, policy-oriented studies	Horizontal, problem-oriented studies	Synthesising, comprehensive studies
Types of variable used	Prominence to *hard*, easily quantifiable variables, such as demographic, economic and technological variables. Very little attention to such *soft* variables as organisation, utility indicators, etc. Emphasis on supply side.	Mixture of hard and soft variables, with a striking absence of socio-psychological data (i.e. conveying what people actually *feel* about inequalities). Emphasis on demand side.	Wide diversity of concepts covering international issues, social change, and French socio-cultural model; impossible to quantify except on ordinal scale. Little rigour possible.
Interactions between study and outside environment	Tendency to treat the sector as a closed system, ignoring external effects and external developments. Fault lies with the original design of the research.	Name of type of study implies breadth and interaction. Awareness of interaction shown in several studies, but negligible social research to support the predictions. Too little co-operation between compartmentalised social disciplines.	Interdependencies automatically allowed for in quantitative projections (like E_0), but no corresponding methodology on the qualitative side. Have to try and equate demand for social change with capacity of French society to accommodate it.
Development of policy alternatives	Remarkable scarcity of alternatives available to the policy-maker, with partial exception of energy, transport, and agriculture.	Very unclear relationship between the study and policy. Main difficulty is that social problems are horizontal whereas Government departments are vertical.	Better than Fifth Plan. Managed to contrast desirable future and probable future, to show that a *different* policy was necessary. See Chapter 6 of [27] on 'Between the desirable and the probable: a few priority action areas'.
Aspects not covered in the studies	Foreign policy, services, banking, trade, and education, either because of a lack of analytical capacity or low priority to long-term issues in these areas.	Selection of subjects studied is a badly defined function of expertise available and good guesses about the real social issues. Difficult to state omissions because processes and behaviour are unlimited.	No consensus about proper content, but there is a danger of merely predicting without putting forward policy alternatives.

Source: All the material here is taken from [26]

philosophy, an interesting subject but one from which it is extremely difficult to draw policy conclusions. Both views are valid, but they represent rather extreme positions. Ideally, all subjects should be treated in a quantitative and a qualitative fashion, but there are many obstacles between the present stage and this ideal state. This is one of the areas (several others are mentioned later in this book) where the administration and the planners are faced with the delicate task of finding an acceptable balance between two approaches that do not coexist easily. It is a simple matter to use the word socio-economic (and some are even using the term socio-politico-economic), but it is not so straightforward to get economists and sociologists to accept each other's ideas and understand each other's methodology; it is even more difficult to provide quantitative tools for the sociologist (i.e. social indicators, discussed in section 2.4), and to build in social and political factors to macro-economic projection studies (an example of an attempt to do this is examined in the next section). Table 2.5 summarises the work of the Sixth Plan long-term groups, and highlights the major difficulties encountered in trying to reconcile the two approaches. More specifically, the table distinguishes vertical, horizontal, and comprehensive studies, and for each type describes the variables used, the interrelationships established between the study and the 'outside environment', the policy alternatives developed, and finally the subjects or aspects that were not covered for one reason or another.

The picture painted by Table 2.5 is a rather gloomy one, but there are one or two bright spots. The lessons of the Sixth Plan experience have encouraged significant research effort into social indicators, and the added pressure from the medium-term groups (discussed in Chapter 5) for more basic structural analyses into social change mechanisms should substantially improve future horizontal studies. Looked at in a standard policy planning framework ((a) define and establish the current state of the system; (b) determine the underlying development mechanisms; (c) evaluate past experience; (d) explore future contexts; (e) suggest alternative policies), too many of the groups never got beyond stage (a), so it is hardly surprising that some of the results were rather disappointing. Other groups found themselves devoting a great deal of their time to stage (c), which is rather ironic in view of the fact that they were set up to look at the future, but in general (c) was not well covered, possibly because of the fear of exposing poor previous policies. The other main omission amongst these five stages was (e), which reflects the fact that some groups did not have the time to reach this stage (although others deliberately avoided it), and the fact that a lot of the analysis, perhaps because of the example of the medium-term analyses, was carried out at the macro level where it is difficult to be specific unless the data base is good. It is far easier to be more specific at the micro level, working within a smaller, better-defined area: ' ...decisions will undoubtedly have an effect at the macro-equilibrium level, but in the long-term the most important impacts are of another order: productivity and competitiveness at the level of the firm, volume of urban traffic, the working environment, and family life'.[9]

2.3 Further work on the long-term macro-economic projections

We mentioned above that lessons were being drawn from the Sixth Plan experience, and this applies no less to the macro-economic projections prepared at the outset of the Sixth Plan long-term studies exercise, and which we discussed in section 2.1. Since the completion of that early analysis, more work has been carried out, [10] with a view to extending the analysis into stage (e) as defined at the end of the previous section. The same E_0 model was used to generate the growth patterns, but a number of technical improvements and modifications were introduced. In 1970 the base year of the national accounts was changed from 1959 to 1962, the 1968 census results were available, various reports from the long-term study groups had been published, and the options phase of the Plan had produced a number of central accounts up to 1975. In addition to incorporating much of this additional material, the E_0 model was expanded to eight sectors in order to make comparisons with the FIFI model easier (by adding the seventh and eighth sectors in E_0 together, the same seven sectors as FIFI distinguishes are obtained).

Whereas the preliminary projection was a straightforward extrapolation of past trends, the five growth patterns constructed in this exercise were based on assumptions designed to simulate different policies and behaviour. The first two patterns, A and B, were based on assumptions of slower overall growth, due to slower technical progress in A, and unfavourable international conditions in B. The other three patterns maintained technical progress and international conditions at existing levels, but incorporated other distinct changes compared with previous patterns of growth: C is referred to as the controlled tensions growth pattern, D gives preference to collective consumption, and E goes for deliberate industrialisation via faster growth. The three main instruments used for transmitting these intentions to the model are as in the preliminary projection: working population, the duration of work, and labour productivity; Table 2.6 shows the assumptions made about the levels of these

40

Table 2.6

Main assumptions behind the five 1985 growth patterns
(compiled in 1970 with the E_0 model)

Growth pattern	Employed working population in 1985 (millions)	Average working week (hours) and annual holiday (weeks)	Average annual growth rates of hourly labour productivity			
			Industry		Building, services and commerce	
			1965/75	1975/85	1965/75	1975/85
A	24·625	41 + 5	6·85	5·5	3·55	2·70
B	22·75	40 + 5	6·85	6·5	3·55	3·20
C	24·625	41 + 5	7·00	6·5	3·80	3·70
D	26·5	36 + 6	7·00	7·5	3·80	4·70
E	24·625	41 + 5	7·15	7·5	3·80	4·70

Sources: various tables and text in [40]

three instruments. According to the five-stage procedure outlined in section 2.2, the values contained in Table 2.6 should derive from an analysis of the underlying development mechanisms and an evaluation of past experience (i.e. stages (b) and (c)). Only stage (c) was possible, however: 'thought on the mechanisms of social development ... remains necessarily limited in this study'. [11] As a substitute for stage (b), a number of international comparisons were made between France, Japan, Germany, Sweden, Great Britain, the USA and Italy, noting similarities and differences between the economic structure of various sub-groups in this set of seven countries, and making various assumptions about the extent to which the five growth patterns represented these characteristics. According to the way these countries used their resources in 1965, the results obtained by inserting these assumptions, those of Table 2.6, and assumptions on final demand consistent with the 5·5, 6 and 6·5 per cent central accounts (constructed in the first few months of 1970, as shown in Fig. 1.2 and described in more detail in Chapter 6) into E_0 suggested that if patterns A and B were to be realised, France in 1985 would have a similar economic structure to France, Italy, and Great Britain in 1965; that if pattern E were to be realised, France in 1985 would be similar in its use of resources to Germany and Japan in 1965; that if Pattern D were to come about, France in 1985 would be similar to Sweden in economic structure in 1965; and that growth pattern C did not correspond to any of the 1965 structures. Table 2.7 contains a summary of the main results of the five growth

Table 2.7

Main results of the five 1985 growth patterns
(compiled in 1970 with the E_0 model)

*Resources and uses**	1965 value in millions of 1965 francs	A	
		1985 value in millions 1965 francs	1975/85 AAGR*
Gross domestic production (PIB)	438,748	1,246,580	5·0
Household consumption	288,109	805,197	5·1
Gross fixed capital formation in housing	32,297	84,000	4·2
Productive gross fixed capital formation	68,990	218,150	5·7
Expenditures of administrations and financial institutions	36,530	98,369	4·7
Changes in stocks plus the external balance	12,822	40,864	
Structure of the working population (%)	1965	1985	
Agriculture	16·8	6·5	
Extractive and manufacturing industry	30·2	26·0	
Services, building, commerce	31·7	43·1	
Transport and 'non-branch'	21·3	24·4	
Total	100·0	100·0	

Sources: various tables in [40]

patterns. Comparing these results with those of the preliminary projection in Table 2.3, one gets a better feel for the implied policy and behaviour changes. Growth pattern B is the closest to the original projection, and the other four patterns all contain faster growth, although pattern A's growth is slower than the more recent trend (recall that the preliminary projection's trend covers the whole of the post-war period). The deliberate emphasis on collective consumption in pattern D is apparent from the slower growth in household consumption, and the extent to which faster growth means more consumption is illustrated in the results of growth pattern E.

It should be remembered that these growth patterns are supposed to be

B		C		D		E	
1985 value in millions 1965 francs	1975/85 AAGR*	1985 value in millions 1965 francs	1975/85 AAGR†	1985 value in millions 1965 francs	1975/85 AAGR†	1985 value in millions 1965 francs	1975/85 AAGR‡
1,160,294	4·4	1,411,170	6·1	1,400,643	6·1	1,593,585	7·3
734,010	4·3	922,262	6·5	843,461	5·5	979,346	7·0
84,000	4·2	84,000	4·2	110,000	7·0	110,000	6·3
203,051	4·7	258,244	6·7	256,318	6·7	304,375	6·7
98,369	4·7	105,800	4·7	150,000	8·3	105,800	4·4
40,864		40,864		40,864		94,064	
1985		1985		1985		1985	
7·0		5·8		5·4		4·1	
24·8		26·7		26·2		28·3	
42·5		43·2		41·7		43·3	
25·7		24·3		26·7		24·3	
100·0		100·0		100·0		100·0	

* The 1965/1975 average annual growth rate (AAGR) follows the 5·5 per cent central account
† The 1965/1975 average annual growth rate follows the 6 per cent central account
‡ The 1965/1975 average annual growth rate follows the 6·5 per cent central account.

'typical' alternatives (i.e. they are not extreme positions intending to en-compass the most likely 1985 situation somewhere in between): each one corresponds to a particular type of development, a point that is reinforced by the similarity that is drawn with other industrialised countries. Some of the features revealed by the results are clearly desirable, but policies still have to be defined before the growth patterns can really be of practi-cal use to a decision-maker (i.e. stage (e) has to be attempted). This is the purpose of Andréani's later work, reported in [41] and which we now describe. As we pointed out in the previous section, policy recommenda-tions are extremely difficult at the macro level, and consequently An-dréani chose to narrow the analysis to the field of income distribution.

This required a number of additional calculations to bring out the detail of the growth patterns, which deal only with the physical side of equilibrium. They implicitly assume that everything is satisfactory on the financial side (i.e. that savings and investment are in balance), and thus contain implied changes in incomes and taxation.

The initial stage in making these income changes explicit was to expand the resources and uses structure of Table 2.7 into a simplified overall economic table (TEE) (a full symbolic version of the TEE is given in Appendix II). Essentially, the TEE consists of a number of resource—uses balances, with agents' accounts in columns, and operations' accounts in rows. Given the aggregated results of Table 2.7, it is possible to fill out the remaining elements in the table by making additional assumptions; Andreani calls this a 'discretionary projection'. It involves two types of iteration: type one is based on the method of successive approximations in which row and column elements are alternatively fixed and varied until a reasonable set of overall values is obtained; type two iterations are between assumptions and results, the assumptions being the additional assumptions we have just referred to. It is a little unwise to make too many type two iterations because the original assumptions (underlying the growth patterns) cannot be changed (without doing the whole growth pattern exercise again, which is not the intention), and so it is sensible that once the financial assumptions corresponding to them have been established, they should remain fixed. This can lead to some unusual results, but this only serves to highlight the problems and desirable policy directions. There is a similarity here with the construction of medium-term, central accounts using the FIFI model (this process is described in detail in Chapters 4 and 6), but there is one significant difference: the FIFI exercises are exploratory, associating different medium-term futures to varying sets of initial assumptions which are changed as external conditions and internal policies become more clearly defined; these exercises, using a rather crude double iteration procedure, are normative, starting out with a fixed future growth pattern and attempting to determine conditions for its realisation.

It is more meaningful to refer to one of the simplified overall economic tables at this stage. Table 2.8 shows the table associated with growth pattern E; the other results are summarised in Table 2.9. The figures in Table 2.8 are rounded, but the PIB figure of 1,593,585 million 1965 francs shown in Table 2.7 is easily identifiable in Table 2.8 as 1,594 milliard 1965 francs. This is the key datum in the double iteration exercise: it cannot be altered. Other items shown in Table 2.7 in the E columns do have to be switched around, however, because the nomenclatures are not

Table 2.8

The simplified 1985 overall economic table associated with growth pattern E (figures in millions of 1965 francs)

Column key: U = Uses, R = Resources; NFE = Non-financial enterprises, HH = Households, Adm = Administrations, FI = Financial institutions. O+A Acc. = Operating and appropriations accounts; C+F Acc. = Capital and financial account; A Acc. = appropriation account.

	U: NFE O+A Acc.*	U: NFE C+F Acc.†	U: HH O+A Acc.	U: HH C+F Acc.	U: Adm A Acc.	U: Adm C+F Acc.	U: FI A Acc.	U: FI C+F Acc.	U: Exterior	U: Total	R: NFE O+A Acc.	R: NFE C+F Acc.	R: HH O+A Acc.	R: HH C+F Acc.	R: Adm A Acc.	R: Adm C+F Acc.	R: FI A Acc.	R: FI C+F Acc.	R: Exterior	R: Total
Operations on goods and services																				
6a Gross domestic production											1482		112							1594
6b Consumption			1035		26		6			1067										
6c Gross fixed capital formation		314		77		54		3		448										
6d Changes in stocks		19								19										
6e, f, g External balance									60	60										
Total 6		333	1035	77	26	54	6	3	60	1594	1482		112							1594
Distributive operations																				
Gross wages	603		8		141		24			776			776							776
Social security contributions	125		15		11		5			156			-56		212					156
Social security benefits and assistance	7				286					293			293							293
Taxation	258		105				12			375					375					375
Subsidies					69					69	63		6							69
Gross income of the self-employed	244									244			244							244
Self-employed's contribution to the financing of capital formation				34						34		34								34
Others	112									112			24				76		12	112
Total 7	1349		128	34	507		41			2059	63	34	1287		587		76		12	2059
Balances																				
8a Gross savings	196		236		54		29			515		196		236		54		29		515
8c Financing capacity (use) or requirement (resource)				125		0		26		151		103				0			48	151

* Operating and appropriations accounts
† Capital and financial account

Source: [41], p. 20

Table 2.9

Main income characteristics of the expanded 1985 growth patterns

	A (slower technical progress)	B (international stop–go)	C (controlled tension growth)	D (priority to non-marketable goods)	E (deliberate industrialisation)
Incomes					
Wage bill (percentage growth p.a.)	5·7	5·2	6·8	6·5	7·75
Average annual growth rate in the average annual wage (per cent)	3·8	3·8	4·8	4·05	5·6
Social benefits (per cent)	6·3	5·8	6·3	8·5	6·6
Total gross income of the self-employed (per cent)	3·7	3·6	4·3	3·55	4·6
Savings					
Non-financial enterprises rate of self-financing (per cent)	80	82	74	71	69
Households' savings rate (per cent)	11·8	12·1	12·2	13·5	16·3
Administrations' financing capacity (milliard 1965 francs)	0	0	0	18	0
External financing capacity (milliard 1965 francs)	–12	–12	–12	–12	–48
Weight of taxation (percentage of PIB)					
In the narrow sense	24·6	25·3	24·6	34·5	23·5
of which: enterprises	(17·7)	(18·2)	(17·7)	(17·25)	(16·9)
households	(6·9)	(7·1)	(6·9)	(17·25)	(6·6)
Parafiscal weight	16·3	15·8	14·4	19·5	13·3
Global weight	40·9	41·1	39·0	54·0	36·8

Source: [41], p. 22

quite the same in both tables. Assumptions on goods and services operations were made first, followed by assumptions on savings and financing capacities of the different economic agents, and finally by further assumptions on the distributive operations; [41] gives the reasoning behind these assumptions, and Table 2.8 shows the results. The reader can probably get a feel for what is going on between Tables 2.7 and 2.8 without our going into further detail here. Our main purpose is to go beyond the simplified TEE and examine the next stage in Andréani's work.

The objective of this next stage is to discover to what extent more growth means greater income inequality. Leaving aside for the moment the question of how to measure income inequality, the first problem is to project the population of various social categories up to 1985, and then to distribute the resources of households among these various categories. This requires even more assumptions than were made in the previous stages, and since the supporting social and economic arguments and reference points for these assumptions are minimal, the projections necessarily take on less of a 'typical alternative' characteristic and more of a purely mechanical nature. The 1954–1968 population trends largely determine the 1985 projection by social categories, but differences occur between the five growth patterns because each pattern has different in-built assumptions about the activity of women, old people, the speed of the agricultural exodus etc. The results of this projection for growth pattern E are shown in Table 2.10. [12] It should again be emphasised that very little, if any, analysis was done on the way in which the growth patterns' implicit development mechanisms affect the social category distribution of the population. Each of the growth patterns contains, for instance, different rates of technical progress and different sizes of housebuilding programmes, both of which are known to have a significant effect on population and income structure (for example, greater availability of housing is likely to lead to a faster rural exodus and a decrease in 'cohabitation', i.e. young people will leave the family home and form their own household). Research into these structural factors is still in its infancy, however, and studies such as Andréani's can only highlight the need and hopefully encourage others to satisfy it.

Ignorance of the underlying social forces also hampered the breakdown of the household appropriation accounts into socio-professional categories. For growth pattern E, this involves disaggregating the figures shown in the household resources operating and appropriations account column in Table 2.8. The 1965 structure was already available, [13] so that comparison of the 1965 and 1985 resource-type totals enabled average annual growth rates to be derived for net wages, gross income of the self-em-

Table 2.10

The distribution of ordinary households
by the occupation of the head of the household,
corresponding to the 1985 growth pattern E

Socio-professional category of the head of the household	1962* (%)	1968* (%)	E 1985 (%)
Farmers	10·4	8·0	2·4
Agricultural workers	2·8	1·9	0·4
Industrial and commercial employers	9·2	8·1	5·3
Free professions and upper management	4·3	5·1	8·1
Middle management	6·2	7·4	10·9
Employees	7·0	7·5	7·3
Blue-collar workers	29·0	28·0	28·0
Service staff	2·4	2·5	2·2
Other workers	2·1	1·9	1·3
Retired workers	26·6	29·6	34·1
Total	100	100	100
Number of households	14,589	15,778	19,793

* Census years

Source: [41], p. 42

ployed, and so on. These growth rates were then applied within each social category (i.e. farmers' wages and service staff wages were assumed to grow at the same rate), generating the results shown in Table 2.11. This approximate procedure again underlines the paucity of knowledge at this level of analysis. It may seem at first sight that applying the same growth rates to all the categories would tend to reduce the differences between the growth patterns, but this is not so because the number of persons in each social category is different in each pattern, and so is the number of households.

Examination of the data in the lower half of Table 2.11 gives a rough idea of income inequalities over the various social categories, and comparison between patterns of similar figures enables further insight to be gained into the nature of the growth patterns. This measure of income inequality

Table 2.11

The resources of different social categories in 1985 (growth pattern E) (millions of 1965 francs)

Nature of resources	Farmers	Employers and upper managers	Middle managers and other workers	Agricultural workers, employees, blue-collar workers, and service staff	Retired workers, employees,	All ordinary households	Population in institutions	Total
Net wages	4,654	186,819	174,520	309,029	38,025	713,047	6,953	720,000
Gross income of the self-employed	28,205	177,666	7,504	13,535	17,090	244,000		244,000
of which: agricultural	(27,373)	(725)	(137)	(678)	(1,587)	(30,500)		(30,500)
non-agricultural	(832)	(176,941)	(7,367)	(12,857)	(15,503)	(213,500)		(213,500)
Income from capital	3,489	53,856	14,082	25,006	62,467	158,900		158,900
Transfers	2,454	24,657	27,352	77,722	159,933	292,118	6,882	299,000
of which: retirement pensions	(794)	(7,390)	(7,193)	(12,455)	(133,685)	(161,517)	(607)	(162,124)
others	(1,660)	(17,267)	(20,159)	(65,267)	(26,248)	(130,601)	(6,275)	(136,876)
Total gross resources	38,802	442,998	223,458	425,292	277,515	1,408,065	13,835	1,421,900
Direct taxes	1,113	50,109	12,583	14,273	16,322	94,400		94,400
Gross resources after taxes	37,689	392,889	210,875	411,019	261,193	1,313,665	13,835	1,327,500
Number of persons ('000)	1,834	8,661	7,708	26,270	12,827	57,300	1,000	58,300
Number of households ('000)	476	2,657	2,412	2,497	6,751	19,793		
Primary resources per household (fr.)†	76,300	157,448	81,304	46,361	17,420	56,380		
Gross resources per household (fr.)	81,517	166,729	92,644	56,728	41,107	71,140		
Disposable income per household (fr.)	79,179	147,869	87,427	54,824	38,689	66,370		

* This is referred to as 'other primary resources' in the source

† Primary resources = gross resources − transfers

Source: [41], p. 48

is, however, only partial; one really needs to know a great deal more about each category, particularly on the dispersion of income within each category. The extent to which the inequality of incomes in one growth pattern is more acceptable than in another growth pattern is also difficult to measure. The structural factors to which we referred above are important in this type of comparison, each growth pattern containing differing levels and intensities of these factors. Some researchers have attempted to facilitate comparisons of different income inequality situations by eliminating the structural factors as far as possible and working with net income inequality (the corresponding concept when the structural factors are not removed is known as gross income inequality). Others argue that gross income inequality is what is actually suffered by individuals, and so policy should depend on an analysis in 'gross' terms.

The structural factors in growth pattern E operate in conflicting directions. The increased housing programme encourages 'de-cohabitation' (i.e. young people set up their own households, and old people remain in their own homes rather than move in with their families) which creates more lower-income households, and this tends to increase inequalities. On the other hand, the increased rural exodus reduces the number of low-income, agricultural households and this works in favour of greater income equality. Faster growth brings more jobs, and this increases the number of wage earners relative to self-employed workers, another factor that reduces inequalities, because the average income of the self-employed is higher than the average wage. Perhaps the most important structural factor is the change in activity rates generated by faster growth. More old people and more women are attracted into the labour market, and since these workers tend to be from low-income households, income inequalities are reduced. Such a qualitative analysis would need more analytical support before firm policy recommendations could be made, but even in this vague form it helps to point out the appropriate policy directions. By correctly identifying and then harnessing the right structural factors, it need not necessarily follow that a policy of faster growth, as is implicitly followed in growth pattern E, leads to greater income inequalities. Similarly, a policy of greater income equality, which is implicit in growth pattern D, need not necessarily lead to slower growth.

Analyses such as these have their obvious technical and economic shortcomings, but at least they try to give some meaning to socio-economics. There clearly is much to be done before this type of long-term study begins to have a dramatic effect on the preparation of the Plan. An area in which a bigger impact is likely to be felt in the Seventh Plan is that of social indicators, which we discuss in the next section.

50

2.4 Social indicators and the Plan

It is no exaggeration to say that we could easily devote all the remaining chapters in this book to developments in social analysis. There is a great deal of interesting work taking place on social indicators, social accounts, and the preparation of a 'social report'. That we choose not to do this does not mean that we regard the work as unimportant or not worth describing; all the signs point to increasing progress in this field. But our story is concerned mainly with the Sixth Plan, the 'social input' to which was unfortunately not very large. The quantitative support for this social input was even smaller, so that, on balance, we are looking at a relatively minor (in terms of actual contribution to the final shape of the Plan) part of the Plan preparation process. However, criticisms of this process, especially on the technical side, are likely to stimulate appreciable growth in social analysis in future Plans, as we briefly indicate in Chapter 5.

As in other areas (notably regional analysis, see Chapter 8) the need for tools of social analysis has been recognised for a number of years, but the lead-time in building a suitable language (i.e. data and terminology) to support the use of such tools takes longer than the period of one Plan. The move towards social planning encompasses efforts in three separate fields, which eventually will merge into a coherent whole and make a much larger impact than any one of the fields has so far made alone. The first of these fields is social statistics, developments in which were first apparent in the United States. [14] The INSEE now publishes a regular series of social statistics, [15] and these form an important input to the second field: the preparation of a social report. This is intended to provide an indication of the social 'state of the nation', and again closely follows American practice. [16] Neither abundant social statistics nor a social report were available for the preparation of the Sixth Plan (as is confirmed by the very recent appearance of the French sources cited in notes 15 and 16), but there was tangible activity in the third field: social indicators.

This is at first sight rather paradoxical, because social indicators are most needed in areas that can really be adequately defined only by a social report containing sufficient social statistics. On reflection, however, it is clear that the early research into social indicators has done much to encourage activity in the other two fields. There is an iterative process here, which is bound to be somewhat out of phase at the beginning. The essential purpose of a social indicator is to give some quantitative expression to the social well-being of society in different sectors. Collected over a period of years, they should therefore act as warning signals to policy-makers, and, something which is much more difficult to achieve, be capable of reflecting the effects of policy changes so that the effectiveness of social overhead capital decisions can be evaluated. As is shown in Chapter 7, the more usual rate of return on capital is not only difficult to measure in the case of public investment decisions, it is probably not the best choice criterion for an investment that is essentially made in 'the social or national interest'. [17]

The work undertaken between September 1967 and April 1968, at the instigation of the CGP, did not aspire to this degree of sophistication. The work, undertaken by the CGP's Social Affairs department and a group from the National School of Administration (ENA) under the leadership of Jaques Delors, was regarded as preliminary, and designed to answer the following question: 'Is it possible to express by a set of quantified data the state of the nation in different fields of economic and social activity?' [18] Thus, far from an attempt to seek the relationships between public investment policy and social indicators, the study did not even have very ambitious statistical intentions. It was carried out in three stages. In the first stage, six development sectors were chosen, on the basis of discussion with various social groups (it is perhaps significant that after the preparation of the Sixth Plan, demands were made for the participation of social groups in the preparatory analytical stages of the Plan; see Chapter 5). The sectors were: demography, health, and the family, education, employment and social mobility, standards of living and levels of consumption, the social cost of progress, and participation in social life. These six sectors were then broken down into 21 topics:

 (1) life expectancy;
 (2) health protection;
 (3) change in the family;
 (4) participation of women in economic and social life;
 (5) old people's role in society;
 (6) behaviour towards marginal populations;
 (7) employment trends;
 (8) the role of education;
 (9) cultural development;
(10) adaptation to change;
(11) social mobility;
(12) receptivity of society to the outside world;
(13) distribution of national wealth;
(14) utilisation of income;
(15) pattern of assets;
(16) role of welfare;

(17) growth of solidarity;

(18) housing;

(19) organisation of the countryside;

(20) urban development;

(21) use of time.

The second stage involved looking at each topic in depth (at least, as deep as time would allow) and specifying its main components. For the health protection topic (number (2) in the above list), this led to the following list of sub-topics:

1   Measurement of the level of health;
    (a)   general level of health;
    (b)   level of health in relation to a given disease.

2   Characteristics of the health care system:
    (a)   organisation of care;
        (i) hospital care,
        (ii) medical care,
        (iii) pharmacy;
    (b)   financial organisation.

3   Aspects of a health policy:
    (a)   role of the state;
    (b)   pattern of state action;
    (c)   specific action.

In the third and final stage, each of the sub-topics was characterised by one index (or social indicator), efforts being made to satisfy the following criteria: first, is the index ambiguous?; secondly, is the index technically sound as far as reliability is concerned?; thirdly, is the index sufficiently constant to allow comparisons in time and space?; and fourthly, can the index be disaggregated into regions, social categories, etc.? This is a daunting set of conditions to try and meet, but over 400 indices were chosen, not all of which were able to be given a numerical expression. 14 indicators were constructed for the health protection topic:

(1)   life expectancy at birth;

(2)   infant and pre-natal mortality rates;

(3)   main causes of death;

(4)   consolidated indicator of the level of health;

(5)   average length of stay in public hospitals;

(6)   hospital admission rates;

(7)   number of practising doctors;

(8)   annual number of consultations;
(9)   total pharmaceutical consumption;
(10) total cost of the health system;
(11) households' total health consumption;
(12) total amount of sick benefits paid;
(13) extent of the different types of medical practice;
(14) extent of the different kinds of state financial intervention.

Only nine of these 14 indicators, and only about half of the original list of 400, were able to be quantified, for the three years 1936, 1954 and a latest year. A report was drafted on the research, but it was not widely circulated.

To sociologists and 'qualitative thinkers', this approach to social problems may appear rather clinical and mechanical, but it is a necessary first step to the movement away from growth towards social development, and from strictly economic planning to true social planning. As is apparent from the reports of several Plan Commissions and other bodies, the will and demand for such a movement to take place now exists; but can economic and social science come up with the technical tools quickly enough to have a significant impact on the Plan? Will the objectives of future Plans be characterised by social indicators in addition to the more usual economic indicators (such as the rate of growth of gross domestic production)? [19]

2.5   The SESAME project

We mentioned at the beginning of the chapter that there were difficulties in establishing a clear relationship between long-term studies and medium-term planning, and suggested that some of these difficulties derived from the fact that several long-term study programmes were constituted outside the normal Plan preparation stages. Such a programme is the SESAME (Système d'Étude du Schéma d'Aménagement), the research programme on the regional development blueprint. This programme bagan in the latter half of 1968, [20] with the intention of drawing up a 'schéma général d'aménagement de la France' (literally, a general regional development blueprint for France) or SGAF for short. In more detail, its aims were to

(a)   draw up and analyse possible and accessible futures, showing the regional distribution of people, activities, and facilities and taking account of potential technological innovations;

54

(b) examine the consistency of existing long-term schemes in the regional development field;

(c) build appropriate instruments (models and indicators) to measure the effects of possible regional development policies;

(d) construct a computerised tool able eventually to automate the whole SESAME project.

The driving force behind the SESAME is the DATAR (Délégation à l'Aménagement du Territoire et à l'Action Régionale – the Delegation for Town and Country Planning and Regional Action – described in detail in Chapter 8 and Appendix VII), a small, fast, and (to some) irritating body introduced in 1963 to 'get things done' in the regional field. Although the CGP is also involved in the SESAME, it is clearly faced with a delicate problem in establishing a working relationship with an organisation that has a reputation for acting in an 'unplanned' way.

On the face of it, the SESAME, designed essentially to introduce a regional dimension to long-term studies, is a good idea. But many observers, inside and outside the CGP, regard the SGAF as a competitor to the Plan itself, and feel that the SESAME is setting itself up to study the whole future of French society. One has sympathy with this view, but on the other hand it is difficult to see how the future of the regions can be realistically studied without at the same time creating a general long-term picture of the whole of France. Many of the early studies in the programme conformed to the original, more modest expectation of SESAME's contributions to the long-term field: master plans were produced for telecommunications, link routes, aeronautical equipment, water, tourism, rural areas, etc. [21] But the multiplication and diversification of documents and analyses gradually built up an argument for the next controversial stage: 'the realisation dawned that ...a still more global view of the original problems was needed' and that 'the social groups, the French society ... had only been present [in the previous studies] in an implicit manner'. [22]

Thus was launched an ambitious long-term study entitled 'A picture of France in the year 2000. Scenario of the unacceptable'. [23] Its approch and conception are very different to the other studies we have discussed in this chapter, and it bears little resemblance to a long-term projection in the sense an economist would give to the term. We feel it is important to look at the study in some detail here because it is clearly a significant part of a large research effort (over 40 reports have already appeared) [24] and its emphasis on qualitative, sociological methods gives a greater balance to our overall review of long-term work in this chapter; it would be misleading to give the impression that all French long-term analysis is macro-economic based. In the following paragraphs, we shall refer to the analysis as the '2000 study'.

The non-economic nature of the research creates a number of 'language' problems which are distracting to begin with. Indeed, it is rather difficult to summarise the main points on the methodological side because the researchers [24] altered their definitions as they went along. They regarded the main purpose of the study as the creation of a new approach to sociological futures research, as is made clear in the introduction to their final report: 'A tool has been invented.... the content [of the study] matters little'. [25] Consequently, it is necessary to look at the various stages in some depth in order to appreciate their significance. The study is in fact made up of two halves, separated by a period of reflection and criticism in which the whole piece of research was subjected to an appraisal by outside observers and members of the DATAR and the CGP. The first half, which is referred to as the 'stumbling and groping' stage involved a fairly conventional data collection and qualitative projection analysis in which the team sought to construct a trend-oriented scenario. 'Trend-oriented' has a different meaning in this context, and perhaps we ought to explain what a 'scenario' is too. The usual meaning of 'trend-oriented' in economic analysis is associated with an analysis that relies heavily on past data and previously observed behaviour, and then extrapolates them into the future. Existing economic policies are generally maintained, in spite of the fact that they may be inappropriate against the background of the extrapolated future situation (this is, the approach to the medium-term departure account, which we describe in detail in Chapter 4). 'Trend-oriented' in the 2000 study regards mechanical extrapolation as inappropriate, and it therefore initially takes on the meaning of an analysis of the 'natural' evolution of the French regions (i.e. there are no deliberate policy changes designed to block or divert existing mechanisms). In effect, this means that the criteria according to which decisions are taken are fixed over time. On further reflection, it was felt by the 2000 study team that this was still too rigid, and that in reality the decision criteria derive from a comparison of the situation as it exists now and the desire to achieve a given objective (which may be the perpetuating of the system). Accordingly, they used 'trend-oriented' to mean the fixity of the French system in its existing form. But the introduction of sociological ideas and analysis affects this yet again: fixity of the system implies the maintenance of the same institutional framework and the same set of values. There was in the definition no 'man-system' interaction, a relationship that changes (though only slowly) over time, and contradicts the fixity of the system. Finally, therefore, the working definition of 'trend-oriented' in the

2000 study was that the fundamental elements of the system remain, but change takes place in social relationships: 'the 'rule of the game' fixed at the outset (is) the permanence and the preservation of the politico-economic system as it exists now, meaning that the system will react only to defend its fundamental structures from being overthrown'. [26]

The term 'scenario' is a little easier to define. A scenario

> aims at describing some aspect of the future: but, instead of building up a picture of unrestrained fiction or even of constructing a utopian invention that the author considers highly desirable, an operations-analytical scenario starts with the present state of the world and shows how, step by step, a future state might evolve in a plausible fashion out of the present one. Thus, though the purpose of such a scenario is not to predict the future, it nevertheless sets out to demonstrate the possibility of a certain future state of affairs by exhibiting a reasonable chain of events that might lead to it.[27]

> ... they should not be used to 'prove' anything. They are literary and pedagogical tools rather than instruments of rigorous analysis....[28]

The research is thus essentially seeking to determine the dynamics of French society, under a number of simplifying assumptions, the last one of which is that all external (i.e. to France) influences are ignored. It goes without saying that the picture is consequently rather distorted, but the above definitions and initial aims of the research recognise this. The 'stumbling and groping' phase included a historical analysis of capitalist, industrial societies, looking for their natural development, and the potentialities of existing French industries, which were classified as advanced, adaptive, or archaic. The tensions created by industrial development on the urban structure, the rural scene, and the less powerful (industrially speaking) regions enable French regions to be considered in three groups: those experiencing strong tensions because of their low potential for industrial development (and hence little prospect of reducing the tensions); those regions with few tensions; and those experiencing strong tensions but having the potential to overcome them.

This is a rather over simplified description of this stage of the research, which finds little mention in the final report, [53]. This is primarily because the research took on a new aspect after the critical examination given it by Government decision-makers and experts working on other long-term analyses. It was generally agreed that there had been insufficient analysis of social mechanisms in the first half of the study, and that the methodology had proved to be incapable of effective analysis of all natu-

Table 2.12

The characteristics of French rural society, according to the 2000 study

Components that rural society tries to reproduce		Interaction with the other societies		Results	
1	Provision and organisation of services for the agricultural society.	1.1	The urban society gradually takes over the services to the agricultural society, being assisted in doing so by the industrial society.	1.1.1	Rural society is organised as a function of the urban society. It loses its traditional role *vis-à-vis* the agricultural environment.
2	Low density of habitation over a restricted area	2.1	The urban society tends to take over the area occupied by the rural society, either by urbanisation or 'urbaneisation', the former corresponding to a physical integration, and the latter to a sociological integration.	2.1.1	Phagocytosis of the rural area close to expanding towns, increase of principal and secondary residences belonging to townspeople in the rural society, tourist exploitation of bourgs and small rural towns.
3	Place of work close to place of residence.	3.1	The town, exerting its attraction on rural man-power, generates two-way migrations between itself and the bourgs and villages. There are also daily migrations between the towns and the bourgs where the townspeople live.	3.1.1	As above. Duplication of certain social overhead capital.
4	Social structure founded on traditional 'notables' and dispensers of services.	4.1	Townspeople replace, by their presence and their action, the notables (and become new leaders).	4.1.1	Change in the political structure. Diversification of the social structure.

Spatial expression of the rural society: the village, the bourg, the rural town

Source: [53], pp. 106—7

ral phenomena other than economic. The base was thus reconstructed, and the historical analysis repeated, this time distinguishing four sub-systems within the overall system (which was France itself): agricultural society, urban society, rural society, and industrial society. Each of these societies has the capability to reproduce its own characteristics or components, and each of the first three societies forms interrelationships with industrial society, which is the driving force in society as a whole. The relationships between components constitute the operating mechanisms of French society; there are five components in each society:

(i)   the function that it maintains;
(ii)   the modes of production that are peculiar to it;
(iii)   the social structure and system of values of each of the social groups that compose it;
(iv)   the spatial forms that are specific to it;
(v)   the institutions that operate in it.

Tables 2·12, 2·13, 2·14, and 2·15 summarise the special features of the four societies in terms of these five components.

The important element of the 2000 study methodology that we have not yet mentioned is the social regulator: the means by which tensions are reduced, and the fundamental structures of society as a whole preserved. In reality there are many such regulators; in the 2000 study only one was introduced: regionalisation.

> The historical tendency to centralism in France is currently a source of deep conflict....The logical approach to ensure the permanence of the system is to increase the power of the regions. 'Regionalisation', imposed gradually, seems to be the only regulator likely to act against the accumulation of economic, social and political tensions supported by the State. [29]

Again it can be argued that the analysis is distorted by working with this particular regulator and no others. But the choice of regionalisation is significant; it is one of the current obsessions in France (see Chapter 8), and the 2000 study was carried out at a time when intense interest was being shown in the regional reforms (which eventually – after the completion of the 2000 study – *did* give more power to the regions). The story told, step by step, in the 2000 study scenario is, therefore, very plausible. Indeed, to the uninitiated (in reading scenarios), it reads like a novel, written in the present tense throughout, and keeping the reader guessing until the final page! There is no technical jargon, and very little quantification, and the analysis is global, although particular regions are men-

Table 2.13

The characteristics of French agricultural society, according to the 2000 study

Components that traditional agri-cultural society tries to reproduce		Interactions with the other societies		Results	
1	Autarchic production and consumption (polyculture).	1.1	The industrial society introduces the profit and productivity criteria, action on the market related to competition, the concepts of capital, division of labour, and technological know-how.	1.1.1	Organisation of production in order to decrease costs: concentration of agricultural land, mechanisation, use of technical methods (fertilisers, etc.). Organisation of trading networks. Distinction between working time and non-working time (rational organisation of work). Fewer young agricultural workers, farmers, and home helps. Preference for forms of exploitation that are not linked to ownership.
		1.2	The industrial society treats and transforms agri-cultural products.	1.2.1	The agricultural society, and mainly the farmers, are put into a situation of depending on industrial enterprises. Farm workers become poorer and are not able to adapt. Proletarisation.
		1.3	Urban society forms larger and more concen-trated markets. Similarly as far as the Common Market is concerned.	1.3.1	Agricultural society organises its trading net-works or uses those which are external to it. Creation and growth of a capitalist-type industrial sector.
2	Use of arable land exclusively for agricultural purposes.	2.1	Urban society, like industrial society (see 1.2 above), takes over agricultural land for other purposes (weekends, leisure, second homes, principal homes, factories).	2.1.1	Diversification in the use of land. Speculation by farmers and others. Agricultural organisa-tions oppose it. Conflict with the expanding towns.

3 Ownership of the land, conveying privileged status, and its transmission via inheritance: employer status and family operation.	3.1 The phenomena listed above in 1.1 and 2.1 reduce the social standing of land ownership in favour of other forms of wealth.	3.1.1 Development of other forms of wealth not connected to land ownership. The capital that is available to the agriculturalist, and which he increases, becomes an essential factor; contradictory effects: poverty and progress. Devaluation of agricultural land inherited. Replacement of family operations by industrial-type operation.
4 'Personalised-affectionate' relationships with the land and the livestock.	4.1 The phenomena listed above in 1.1, 2.1, and 3.1 cause the land and the livestock to become 'integrated objects in the production and commercialisation cycle'.	4.1.1 See 2.1.1 and 3.1.1.
5 Structure dependent on the land and livestock 'riches' of families.	5.1 Effect of phenomena cited in 1.1, 2.1, and 3.1.	5.1.1 Social structure is linked to economic efficiency and productivity, which tend to be a function of age (the way in which previous generations have developed), living styles, vertical functional relationships, and education.

Spatial expression of the agricultural society: the farm or group of farms in a village

Source: [53], pp. 108–9

Table 2.14

The characteristics of French urban society, according to the 2000 study

Components that urban society tries to reproduce		Interactions with the other societies		Results	
1	Concentration of people and habitation in one area.	1.1	Industrial society strengthens this concentration. Rural society, by perpetuating the 'country mansion myth', makes the organisation of the urban perimeter area difficult (cost of dispersed infrastructure and social overhead capital).	1.1.1	Coexistence of a vertical concentration (densification) and a horizontal dispersion of urbanised human groups.
2	Concentration of very diverse and numerous services and social overhead capital with an extensive area of influence.	2.1	The demand emanating from other societies, mainly the industrial society (economies of scale), encourages this concentration and the introduction of profitability criteria. In the towns where this demand is low (non-industrial towns, towns with reduced services), there is a degradation of component 2; hence, there is little vitality in their development (under-equipped towns, undynamic town centres).	2.1.1	Polarisation of services in the big towns. Stagnation or development of towns with no or a loosely connected urban structure (little interchange between towns in the same region). Decrease in social groups which traditionally provide certain services (small traders).
3	This double concentration enables urban society to intensify its inter-town and inter-society relationships and exchanges, and thus to ensure its production and innovatory diffusion role.	3.1	Relationships, exchanges, creations, and the diffusion of innovations are reinforced by the other societies, and predominantly by the development of the industrial society. But this leads to saturation of town centres and hence imbalances between the different parts of the town (congestion in the centre, lack of facilities on the outskirts, inadequate urban structure for motorised-man). See also 2.1.1.	3.1.1	Appearance of urban, regional development, and national planning machinery. Renovation of urban centres.

| 4 | The three preceding components ensure the development of towns as organisational systems and centres of politico-economic power (the centre function). | 4.1 | The speed of urban growth, pressed for by other societies, mainly the industrial and agricultural ones, on the one hand obstructs the organisational system, and on the other hand dissociates the actions of political and/or economic power 'détente' institutions. | 4.1.1 | Modification of institutions or creation of new ones: search for a new political equilibrium between the social forces concerned with the exercise of authority. |
| 5 | Social stratification according to the share which groups have in urban power, a share that is a function of inherited social prestige. | 5.1 | The industrial society brings with it:
(a) social groups in the town with upper and average incomes and possessing a culture based on technology and the need for efficiency;
(b) a manpower for whom the tasks are socially frustrating.
The conditions of everyday life deteriorate for both groups. | 5.1.1 | Undermining of the influence of the urban notables by new social groups (middle managers, technicians, bureaucrats) looking for political power. |

Spatial expression of the urban society: the town, in the large sense of the word

Source: [53], pp. 110–11

Table 2.15

The characteristics of French industrial society, according to the 2000 study

Components which industrial society tries to reproduce	Interactions with the other societies	Results
All industrial societies		
1 Division of labour: (a) specialisation and collectivisation of tasks; (b) depersonalised relationships with the means of production. Organisation rationality.	1.1 The other societies support the division of labour: (a) availability of manpower; (b) institutions given the job of training it and converting it. But there is still an imbalance between demand and supply (qualifications of wage earners) as well as a refusal of French workers to do some manual jobs (i.e. building).	1.1.1 (a) Increasing specialisation of workers but at a slower rate than that required by industrial growth. (b) Demand for foreign workers to undertake manual jobs. (c) Workers are frustrated in their work.
2 Technological know-how (in a competitive economy or not): (a) production dependent on technical know-how; (b) workers with qualifications. Technical rationality.	2.1 The urban society, centre of creation and diffusion of innovation, encourages the development of technical know-how (a) via formal and informal information circuits; (b) via institutions (universities, laboratories, research centres).	2.1.1 (a) Growing interdependence between industrialised towns (and towns with good educational and scientific research institutions) and industrial society. (b) Numerical and qualitative increase in these institutions. (c) Creation and financing of such institutions by the private industrial sector. (d) Significant numerical increase in qualified workers holding this know-how (higher skilled workers, technicians, middle managers).
	2.2 Agricultural society is transformed into a users' market for the results of this know-how.	2.2.1 (a) Closer relationships between the agricultural society and the industrial and urban societies. (b) Higher agricultural productivity.

3. Capital:
(i) expansion;
(ii) profit;
(iii) profitability;
Economic rationality.
This necessitates:
(a) separation between workers and holders of capital;
(b) search for elasticity of factors of production: labour, capital;
(c) maintenance of the firm as an autonomous decision-making centre;
(d) pressure from the industrial sector on the social body, including the state;
(e) action on the market determined by competition;
(f) the firm adopting the growth imperative.

3.1 (a) Urban (and also agricultural) society, forming bigger and bigger markets, encourage the growth of diversified consumption, thus reinforcing production. But simultaneously, because it is essential to increase collective and social overhead capital, the urban society must find additional financial resources, by decreasing the share of capital available to industrial society.

(b) Urban concentration accelerates the diffusion of ideologies which question 3. In addition, both the unions and the State, discretely and for different reasons, seek to restrict the decision-making autonomy (3b) and the power of the firm (3c). The political and administrative power residing in the urban structure acts in a similar way, seeking to organise the industrial society, not so much as a function of the collectivity in the abstract but more as a function of the industrial society's growth imperatives in the context of a more and more competitive market. But some urban groups (political and professional) and occasionally some agricultural and rural groups, obstruct the industrialisation of the town (and the location of industry in the rural area) for reasons essentially of an ideological order.

3.1.1 (a) Difficulty of avoiding conflict between the requirement to increase the market of goods by consumption and the necessity to stimulate private savings for the investments of industrial society and the state.

(b) Tendency to inflation.

(c) The state fulfils a regulator role, by creating social overhead capital to assist the socio-economic system maintain itself.

(d) Impact of industrial society, which plays a leading and driving role in society overall, both at the national and regional level. Direct lines between economic power and political power.

(e) This impact prevents or obstructs the realisation of all 'rational' regional planning, which is not based at all on criteria of 'economic rationality'.

(f) The search for elasticity in the factors of production (3b) leads to:
(i) the acceptance of frictional unemployment
   – at the enterprise level, where there are strong tensions when the supply of labour increases without there being any demand for it,
   – at the national level, resulting in imbalances which are the sources of social tensions;

Continued on next page

Table 2.15   *continued*

Components which industrial society tries to reproduce	Interactions with the other societies	Results
		(ii) the concentration of capital and the formation of combines (increase of profits) – demanding private savings, – demanding foreign capital (formation of international combines), – leading to an apparent displacement of decision-making centres, but in reality they tend to be concentrated.

French industrial society

4 Family firm:
  (a) family dominance over capital;
  (b) desire for perpetuation of family power;
  (c) distant from changing structures.

4.1 See 3b.
  (a) disappearance of family capital;
  (b) development of power within the firm different from that given by capital;
  (c) introduction of modern organisation and methods.

Spatial expression of the industrial society: the firm

Source: [53], pp. 112–13

tioned. The 1970–1985 period is marked by the granting of more and more power to the advanced industrial regions, until the state begins to abandon its global, social regulating role. France splits even more into two parts as the gap between the advanced and the archaic widens, although there are pockets of progress within the latter. Beyond 1985, the problems of urban society become more prominent, as the regions begin to lose their power to the multinational companies that control the advanced industries.

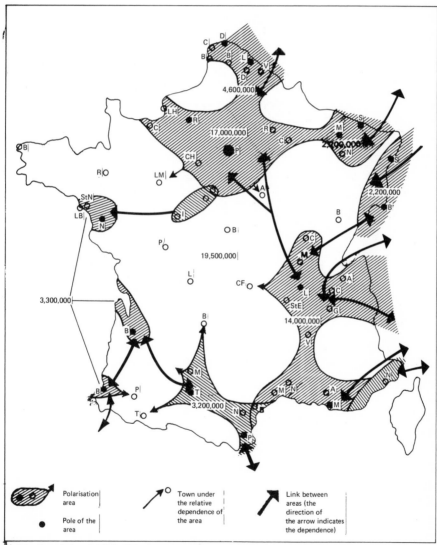

Fig. 2.1   France in the period 1990–2000, according to the 2000 study
Source: [53], p. 161

And so the story goes on; the reader is referred to [53] for all the fascinating details. Clearly, there is no intention on the part of the 2000 study to associate any probability to its picture of France in 30 years' time (see Figure 2.1). Its purpose is to draw up a method for tackling the long-term analysis problem. It is but a short (but difficult) step from trend-oriented social regulators to other regulators which are not constrained to operate in a trend-oriented manner: the more usual name for these is policies. This approach too, then, is capable of conforming to the five-stage policy planning framework we presented at the end of section 2.2 above, and in particular is capable of stage (e): suggesting alternative policies. There is no indication as yet, however, as to when this last and crucial stage might be actually carried out in a real analysis. The 1969 economic budget (compiled towards the end of 1968) states that 'from this work' [i.e. the SGAF and related long-term studies] it will be possible ...rationally to order the major options on which the regional aspects of the Sixth Plan will be based. [30] As we show in Chapter 8, this did not happen, but there were renewed 'expectations' for the Seventh Plan, with particular hopes placed on the computerised tool mentioned in aim (d) at the beginning of this section:

> It will then be possible to carry out automatic simulation, using a very powerful computer, and ranging rapidly and in detail over the whole field of possibilities. This will be possible only by the simultaneous and related development of the computerised tool constructed by the DATAR.... When the Seventh Plan preparation period begins at the end of 1972, one hopes to be in a position to intervene effectively, and to be able to propose both the instrument and the rules of the regional development game. [31]

This still suggests (among other things) that the vital policy stage is to be omitted again, leaving unresolved one of the 'fundamental dilemmas' of futures research. [32]

Notes

[1]   These projections were published (see [20]), and, since they are the only long-term projections for which the target year has been reached, analyses of their accuracy have been published too: Cazes presents such an analysis in the French contribution to the United Nations meeting on long-term planning reported in [21] (part of this same analysis is also given in an appendix to [19]).

68

² Cazes in [19] and [21], and various other unpublished documents that he wrote or edited as CGP's senior co-ordinator of long-term studies.

³ Masse's ideas can be found in [22].

⁴ The report of the 1985 Group was published in [23]. The macro-economic projection was not widely circulated: [24] is no longer available

⁵ According to Pagé in [2], p. 12.

⁶ From [21], p. 64.

⁷ A number of variants were calculated during the preparation of the Fifth Plan, using a linear programming model (see [78], [79], [80] and [81]). The FIFI model, used in the preparation of the Sixth Plan, also requires detailed analyses on this factor in order to establish a number of its parameters (see Tables 4.2 and 6.2 for the numerical results of these analyses, which were input to the model for the elaboration of the departure account and the Plan account).

⁸ All the long-term groups originally submitted their reports to the central group, which then synthesised their work with its own and published its report [27]; Bernard Cazes was one of the rapporteurs of this central group, which was lead by Paul Delouvrier. Not all the reports have actually been published and made available; the Industry Group's rapporteur, for instance, never found the time to draft his report for publication. Eight reports have been published in Armand Colin's 'Plan et Prospectives' series: urban development [28] and [29]; housing [30]; consumption and life styles, mobility within the labour force, leisure, old people (all in [31]); posts and telecommunications [32]; energy [33]; transport [34]; and the central group [27]. Another five have been published by Documentation Française: agriculture [35] (known as the Vedel report); population [36]; health [37]; research and development [38]; and cultural affairs [39].

⁹ [19], p. 16.

¹⁰ This work is reported in [40] and [41], and sometimes incorrectly referred to in other texts as the quantitative projection that was used as background material by the Sixth Plan long-term groups. There is clearly a very close similarity between this work and the preliminary projection of 1968, but this later work came well after the long-term groups had finished their analyses.

¹¹ [40], p. 22.

¹² The results of the projection for the other four growth patterns are given in Table 9 in [41], p. 42.

¹³ In [42].

¹⁴ The French, like other governments, have maintained a close watch on American developments in social analysis, and would probably admit

to modelling their approach on that of the Americans. The INSEE journal, *Économie et Statistique*, carried in 1970 a paper by the Assistant Director of Statistical Policy in the American Management and Budget Office [43], and much of recent French writing on the subject cites American sources, some of which are given below.

[15] 'Early' (really quite recent!) French thinking on compiling a system of social statistics is given in [44] and [45]. This led to the first in a series of annual social statistics handbooks, published in July 1973, [46]. It is significant that in the introduction to [44] is stated, 'It is still premature to think of this as a system of social statistics, but it is possible to define guidelines for research which, when it all links together, will be likely one day to lead to the construction of a consistent system of social statistics'.

[16] Especially work done by Olson and others in 1969 and 1970 [48], and the earlier work of Bauer, Biderman, Gross, Rosenthal and Weiss [49]. The French work took an important step forward with the appearance of [46]. The CGP intends to compile a social report for distribution to all the Seventh Plan Commissions (according to a private communication I have received from Bernard Cazes).

[17] This is another area into which we have deliberately chosen not to venture too far, for reasons of space and also because it leads into more micro-type problems, which are not really the province of this book. Chapter 7 takes up the discussion again, and the interested reader will also find much more interesting material in *Rationalisation des Choix Budgétaires*, a quarterly journal entirely devoted to RCB (the French equivalent of PPBS). The first issue of this journal appeared only in September 1970, again reflecting the recent nature of this type of work, and confirming the fact that not all the Sixth Plan analyses were able to benefit from 'rational' choice techniques. The link between RCB and social analysis is very well sketched out by Bernard Cazes in [47].

[18] This objective for the research is quoted from [21], p. 139. This is part of a section, entitled 'French experience in respect of social indicators', describing the CGP/ENA study that we report in section 2.4.

[19] A recent internal CGP paper [50] outlines the work that will have to be undertaken if the answer to these and other related questions is to be in the affirmative. The timing of this paper indicates, however, that this work will probably not be completed in time to have a major impact on the Seventh Plan. Another source [51] indicates that the Grenoble Economic Research and Planning Institute (IREP) is involved in research on 'the methodology of identifying social variables which are useful or likely to be useful in long-term planning'. (Note: [51] is not the original source. *Problèmes Economiques* reprints French and foreign papers in full and

abbreviated forms. In the case of [51], the reprint is from *Recherche Sociale*, July—August 1972.) [58] provides a useful summary of the state of social planning and also outlines what the next stages should be, on the medium-term and the long-term side.

[20] There is a review of the SGAF in [185], pp. 105—10, and a description of the organisation and intended research of the SESAME in [52]. There is also a brief paragraph on the subject in [186], p. 16.

[21] The SGAF research reports are published by La Documentation Française in the series 'Travaux et Recherches de Prospective' (Futures Research and Analysis). 41 titles are listed in [171], pp. 92—3, plus four in preparation.

[22] [185], p. 106.

[23] This is the title of [53], which is number 20 in the series mentioned in note 21. A complete set of documents on the study is the basis of number 30 in the same series.

[24] The work was carried out by OTAM ('Omnium Technique d'Aménagement'), part of the international METRA group of consultancy companies. There is a report on the work in the METRA journal, [54], and another shorter article by an OTAM member in [56].

[25] [53], p. 13.

[26] [53], p. 20.

[27] Quoted from a very useful dictionary of forecasting terminology, [55], p. 463. The quotation is by Olaf Helmer.

[28] Again from [55] p. 463, this time by Herman Kahn.

[29] [53], p. 44.

[30] [52], p. 315.

[31] [52], p. 320. We should stress here that these are not the words of Weill and his colleagues; they are taken from papers submitted by the DATAR to Weill et al. to edit.

[32] This is Lucien Nizard's term, which he uses in [57]. Much of his paper is on social futures research and policy.

References

[19] B. Cazes, 'Futures research and economic planning: the French case', *Economics of Planning* (forthcoming).

[20] Ministry of Finance, *Perspectives de l'économie française en 1965* (Prospects of the French economy in 1965), Paris, June 1956.

[21] United Nations, *Long Term Planning*, Report of the Seventh Meeting of Economic Advisers to the Governments of ECE (Economic

Commission for Europe (UN)) Countries, Document E/ECE/780, New York 1971.

[22] P. Massé, *Les Étapes de la prospective* (The stages of futures research), Presses Universitaires de France, Paris 1967.

[23] Commissariat Général du Plan, *Reflexions pour 1985* (Thoughts on 1985), La Documentation Française, Paris 1964.

[24] INSEE, *Premières esquisses de croissance pour 1985* (First growth patterns for 1985), Working Paper, December 1962.

[25] INSEE, 'Hypothèses économiques pour 1985' (Economic assumptions about 1985), *Analyse et Prévision* vol. VII, no. 1, January 1969, pp. 27–49.

[26] B. Cazes, 'Applied futures research in France: some critical views' *Futures*, vol. 5, no. 3, June 1973, pp. 272–80.

[27] Commissariat Général du Plan, *1985: la France face au choc du futur* (1985: where France meets the future), Armand Colin, Paris 1972, 220 pp. (vol. 8 in the series 'Plan et Prospectives' (Futures research and the Plan)).

[28] Commissariat Général du Plan, *Les Villes (Towns),* vol. 1: 'Urbanisation' Armand Colin, Paris 1971 (volume 1 in the series 'Plan et Prospectives').

[29] Commissariat Général du Plan, *Les Villes*, vol. 2: 'La Société urbaine' (Urban society), Armand Colin, Paris 1971 volume 2 in the series 'Plan et Prospectives').

[30] Commissariat Général du Plan, *Le Logement* (Housing), Armand Colin, Paris 1970 (volume 3 in the series 'Plan et Prospectives').

[31] Commissariat Général du Plan, *Mode de vie, mobilité, loisirs, troisième age* (Life styles, mobility, leisure, old age). Armand Colin, Paris 1972 (volume 4 in the series 'Plan et Prospectives').

[32] Commissariat Général du Plan, *Postes et télécommunications* (Posts and telecommunications), Armand Colin, Paris 1972 (volume 5 in the series 'Plan et Prospectives').

[33] Commissariat Général du Plan, *L'Énergie* (Energy), Armand Colin, Paris 1972 (volume 6 in the series 'Plan et Prospectives').

[34] Commissariat Général du Plan, *Les Transport* (Transport), Armand Colin, Paris 1971 (volume 7 in the series 'Plan et Prospectives').

[35] Commission de l'Avenir à Long Terme de l'Agriculture Française, *Perspectives à long terme de l'agriculture française 1968–1985* (The long-term future of French agriculture, 1968–1985), The Vedel Report, La Documentation Française, Paris 1969, 64 pp.

[36] Groupe l'Études des Problèms Démographique, *Rapport* (Report of the study group on population problems), La Documentation

Française, Paris 1971.

[37] Groupe Travail sur la Santé, *L'Avenir du système de santé* (The future of the health system), La Documentation Française, Paris 1969.

[38] Comité Consultatif du la Recherche, *Le Progrès scientifique* (Scientific development), La Documentation Française, Paris 1969.

[39] Commissariat Général du Plan, *Rapport du Commission des Affaires Culturelles du VIᵉ Plan* (Report of the Sixth Plan Cultural Affairs Commission), La Documentation Française, Paris 1971.

[40] E. Andréani and A. Gauron, 'Cinq esquises de croissance pour 1985' (Five growth patterns up to 1985), *Économie et Statistique* no. 15, September 1970, pp. 21–44.

[41] E. Andréani, 'Esquisses de répartition des revenus pour 1985' (Income distribution patterns in 1985), *Économie et Statistique* no. 38, October 1972, pp. 3–22 (Part 1), and no. 39, November 1972, pp. 41–52 (Part 2).

[42] H. Roze, 'Les ressources des ménages par catégorie socio-professionelle en 1965' (Household resources by socio-professional category in 1965), *Les Collection de l'INSEE*, série M, no. 10, May 1971, pp. 41–95.

[43] J. Shiskin, 'Le réinforcement des statistiques, fédérales aux États-Unis' (Advances in Federal statistics in the United States), *Économie et Statistique* no. 17, November 1970, pp. 41–7.

[44] INSEE, 'Statistiques sociales: méthodes et sources' (Social statistics: methods and sources), *Les Collections de l'INSEE*, série C, no. 14, April 1972.

[45] C. Girardeau, 'Vers un système de statistiques sociales' (Towards a system of social statistics), *Économie et Statistique* no. 31, February 1972, pp. 3–10.

[46] INSEE, 'Données Sociales. Première édition 1973' (Social data. First edition, 1973), *Les Collections de l'INSEE*, série M, no. 24, July 1973.

[47] B. Cazes, 'What is a rational choice?' *Diogenes*, 1970, pp. 41–56.

[48] M. Olson, 'Rapport social, indicateurs sociaux et comptes sociaux' (Social report, social indicators, and social accounts), *Analyse et Prevision* vol. VII, no. 2, February 1969, pp. 97–114.

[49] R. A. Bauer (ed.), *Social Indicators*, MIT Press, 1966, 357 pp.

[50] Commissariat Général du Plan, *Les Progrès possibles de la planification sociales* (Possible advances in social planning), Social Affairs Dept., August, 30 pp.

[51] P-L. Corteel, 'Le programme français de recherce sur les indicateurs

sociaux' (The French research programme on social indicators), *Problèmes Économiques* no. 1292, 18 October 1972, pp. 11–13.

[52] G. Well et al., 'Vers un schéma général d'aménagement de la France' (Towards a general regional development blueprint for France), *Aménagement du Territoire et Développement Régional* vol. 3, IEP Grenoble January 1970, pp. 311–33.

[53] DATAR, 'Une image de la France en l'an 2000. Scénario de l'inacceptable' (A picture of France in the year 2000. Scenario of the unacceptable), *Travaux et Recherches de Prospective* no. 20, la Documentation Française, Paris 1971, 173 pp.

[54] A. Antunes, C. Durand, P. Hanappe, C. Henry, J. Landrieu-Zemor, 'Une méthode d'analyse prospective. Son elaboration dans le carde d'un scénario tendancial française' (A method for futures research. Its elaboration in the framework of a French, trend-oriented scenario), *Metra* vol. X, no. 4, December 1971, pp. 569–626.

[55] F. Hetman, *The Language of Forecasting* (with a French–English–German vocabulary), SEDEIS, Paris 1969, 540 pp.

[56] A. Antunes, 'Réflexions sur une espérience prospective française' (Reflections on a French futures research study), *Amenagement du Territoire et Développement Régional* vol. 6, IEP Grenoble January 1973, pp. 13–37.

[57] L. Nizard, 'Prospective science et politique: reflexions sur l'impact de la diffusion d'informations sur le futur' (Futures research and policy: reflections on the impact of the diffusion of information about the future), *Aménagement du Territoire et Développement Régional* vol. 6, IEP Grenoble January 1973, pp. 3–12.

[58] C. Girardeau, 'Mieux intégrer les phénomènes sociaux dans la planification à moyen terme' (A better integration of social phenomena in medium-term planning), *Droit Social*, Special issue, no. 4–5, April–May 1972, pp. 51–9.

3 The Theory of the Competitioned Economy and the Development of the FIFI Model

The main methodological innovation in the preparation of the Sixth Plan was the introduction of a large-size mathematical model, solved on the computer, called the medium-term physico-financial projection model, and known to the public by the familiar name FIFI.

> Jacques Mayer, Director of Economic Synthesis, INSEE (translated from the introduction to [82]).

In this chapter we examine in some detail the economic mechanisms that operate in a competitioned economy, a term due to Courbis[1] who developed the theory of a competitioned economy in the late sixties. We shall look at the main assumptions of the theory, the mechanisms that determine sector equilibrium, those operating in the determination of macro-economic equilibrium, and how the theory came to be incorporated in the FIFI model, which was used so extensively in the preparation of the Sixth Plan. As is made clear later in the chapter, the theory and the model were not originally so closely related as might appear at first sight; in fact, initially FIFI was based on the more traditional Keynesian approach to macro-economic regulation problems.

Courbis' first thoughts on the theory of a competitioned economy, so called because it relates to an economy that is subjected to strong foreign competition, were during the preparation phases of the Fifth French Plan in 1963–1965/66. Previous plans had been couched mainly in physical terms, and it was intended to introduce value planning[2] on an extensive scale for the first time. Essentially, this was necessary in order to tackle the problems of a prices and incomes policy. Price forecasts for each branch and group of products were requested, but what was initially conceived of as a technical problem soon took on a deeper meaning. It was realised that the related problem of investment financing had to be tackled at the same time, but in sectors like steel and chemicals which

75

were in direct competition with foreign imports, affecting the price level in the domestic market, the Keynesian-inspired economic mechanisms produced output and investment results that were clearly not compatible with the price constraint.

The competitioned economy theory began in this small way, but it was difficult to get across because it went against the generally accepted principles of the economic policy-makers. It had little effect on the policy followed in the Fifth Plan,[3] but it is clearly reflected in the Sixth Plan 'industrialisation' policy,[4] with the acceptance of which FIFI, based on the theory, had such a lot to do.

3.1 The main assumptions of the theory

It would be impossible in a single chapter to develop the theory to the same level of comprehensive detail that Courbois achieves in his 'magnum opus' and other assorted papers.[5] Instead, we shall give the main assumptions of the competitioned economy theory in this section and then develop it by means of very simplified models in the following sections.[6] The reader is referred to the literature cited in the notes for further illustrations of the theory in terms of larger economic models. Whichever model is used to illustrate the theory, they all rest on the following main assumptions.

To begin with, *exchange rates are assumed to be constant*, or perhaps it would be more accurate to say that occasional, exogenous discrete shifts can only take place within certain fixed limits. This assumption is very much linked with the price constraint imposed on certain domestic firms by foreign procedures, and referred to in the next assumption.

The second assumption is that France, along with certain other countries, is a *competitioned economy*, containing sectors that are *exposed* to international competition, and sectors that are *sheltered* from such competition or at least dominantly competitive with respect to it. The FIFI model also distinguishes *administrated* sectors (in the sense of firms that have their prices set by public authorities), but for most purposes of the analysis (and that includes all purposes while we are still at this simplified level) these sectors can be treated in the same way as sheltered sectors. This sector distinction is not new, either in the context of the French economy[7] or other economies,[8] but it does carry special significance when used alongside the other assumptions of the competitioned economy theory. For those firms in the exposed sector, prices are determined by foreign producers' prices, and, in the absence of an automatically adjusting exchange rate (assumption one), this is a fundamental constraint on the behaviour of these firms. In addition, it is assumed that for the exposed sector there exist perfect substitution possibilities between imports and domestic production. There is no such substitution and no price constraint in the sheltered sector.

Thirdly, it is assumed that firms seek a certain desired level of self-financing of their investments in the medium term. Statistical evidence confirms that there is in the medium term a certain structure between external and internal sources of investment financing, and Courbis also cites a number of theoretical arguments[9] to support this assumption. Expressed in a simplified manner, the desired 'optimal' rate of self-financing is a solution to the following system:

$$r = i + \sigma\,(a) \qquad\qquad (3.1)$$
$$i = f\,(a) \qquad\qquad (3.2)$$
$$a \geqslant a_m \qquad\qquad (3.3)$$
$$A = aI \qquad\qquad (3.4)$$

where r is the marginal productivity or efficiency of investment; i is the rate of interest; $\sigma(a)$, a function of a, is a security or risk margin; a_m is some minimum level of self-financing which must be exceeded or at worst equalled in order for the firm to remain solvent; I is investment and A is self-financing. This is the key assumption in the theory, and is at the heart of sector equilibrium determination, as is shown in the next section.

The fourth assumption is a controversial one,[10] but it is widely used in many western economic models. It states that the growth rate of nominal wages depends on the labour market situation (i.e. that the Phillips mechanism acts on wages, the general level of prices, and unemployment). It is essential to have this assumption in the theory to prevent the possible elimination of the exposed sector by very strong foreign competition. As is shown more clearly in the next section, if foreign competition increases (i.e. domestic prices in the exposed sector rise or foreign prices in the same sector fall), then production in the exposed sector will fall (because imports become more attractive to consumers), thus depressing employment and hence wage increases (following Phillips). This reduces costs in the exposed sector, increases the sector's competitiveness, and thus counteracts the initial effect. The wage—price—unemployment relationship is discussed further in Chapter 5.

The fifth assumption is a technical one, affirming that the analysis is undertaken in the medium term. In the short term, firms fall into two categories. First, there is the non-competitive or oligopolistic category in which the firm can influence the market price. From this follows the simultaneous determination of the level of retained savings, self-financing, and investment. Secondly, there is a competitive category in which firms are price takers. Prices may be determined by domestic market forces or by imports, but the firm does not distinguish these cases. Prices and costs determine self-financing and then investment. In the short term, the exposed sector concept is not operational. However, as the analysis shifts from the short to the medium term, the whole of the non-competitive category is considered as sheltered, as are those firms in the competitive category whose prices are determined solely by domestic market forces. The remaining firms become the exposed sector.

Finally, it is assumed that factor mobility is limited, to the extent that it can be ignored in the analysis. That is to say that capital does not flow or labour migrate quickly enough to act as an important regulating mechanism in medium-term equilibrium determination.

These are the main assumptions behind the competitioned economy theory. They certainly exist in other theories and other models, [11] but not all together.

3.2 Determination of sector equilibrium in a competitioned economy

The special emphasis given to foreign competition in the competitioned economy theory means that it is the relationship between self-financing and investment that is critical in sectoral equilibrium determination. The direction in which this relationship acts depends on the constraints to which the sector is subjected, and, as we have seen, these constraints differ according to the nature of the sector. There are two cases to be considered: exposed sector equilibrium and sheltered sector equilibrium (strictly speaking, there are three if we allow for administered-price sectors, as FIFI does; but there clearly is no iterative price—output mechanism in such sectors). [12]

We shall consider the exposed sectors first. From assumption two, domestic producers in this sector have to follow the price set by their foreign counterparts. For a given rate of taxation and other costs that are not easy to adapt quickly, available profits are determined. Bearing in mind assumption three, it is the firms' self-financing possibilities that then determine their investment possibilities, and hence their capacities and production. Thus self-financing behaviour determines production in this case, and it was briefly indicated in section 3.1 that the firms' desired rate of self-financing depends partly on the structure of external financing and partly on the availability of long-term external finance. Equilibrium of supply

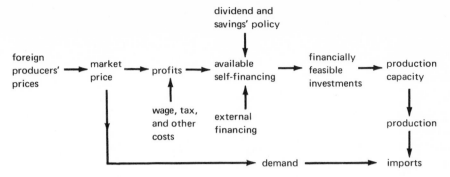

Fig. 3.1   Equilibrium determination mechanisms in an exposed sector

and demand is then assured not through the price mechanism but by imports, as shown in Figure 3.1. This equilibrium corresponds to the solution of the following set of equations, which is again rather simplified (even in comparison with Figure 3.1), but it conveys the essential mechanisms:

$$D = D\,(p) \tag{3.5}$$
$$M + Q = D \tag{3.6}$$
$$p = \bar{p}_M \tag{3.7}$$
$$Q = Q\,(p) \tag{3.8}$$

where $Q\,(p)$ is the domestic producers' supply function and, from the

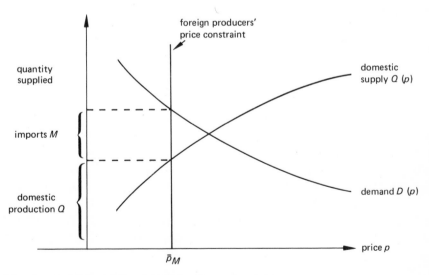

Fig. 3.2   Graphical representation of equilibrium in an exposed sector

79

assumptions made earlier, clearly increases with p; $\overline{p}_M$ is the exogenous [13] foreign producers' price; M is imports and D is demand. This process is represented graphically in Figure 3.2.

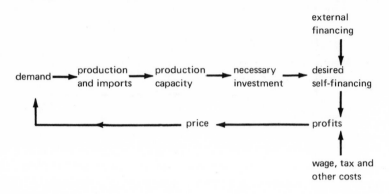

Fig. 3.3   Equilibrium determination mechanisms in a sheltered sector

For sheltered sectors, the mechanisms are quite different. Imports can be determined *a priori* (either there may not be any imports, or if there are they are weakly competitive or complementary) using import functions, and it is demand that determines production. There is no price constraint, and the mechanisms are such (see Fig. 3.3) as to push prices to a level where they enable sufficient self-financing to support the investment that is necessary to keep production at a level to satisfy demand. [14] The simplified system of equations in this case is

$$D = D\,(p,...) \qquad\qquad\qquad (3.9)$$
$$M = M\,(D, p) \qquad\qquad\qquad (3.10)$$
$$p = p\,(Q) \qquad\qquad\qquad (3.11)$$
$$Q = ND\,(p,...) = D\,(p,...) - M \qquad\qquad\qquad (3.12)$$

where $ND(p,...)$ is net demand (i.e. demand after imports have been deducted) and other notation is as in (3.5)–(3.8). This process is represented graphically in Figure 3.4.

It is possible, using the simple models we have here, to demonstrate that the effect of the same general policy is quite different when applied to exposed sectors and sheltered sectors. Consider first a supply policy such that the supply function is moved *ex ante* by $\delta Q > 0$. Then, denoting *ex post* shifts with a capital delta symbol, the reaction in a sheltered sector is

$$\Delta Q = \Delta D \qquad\qquad\qquad (3.13)$$

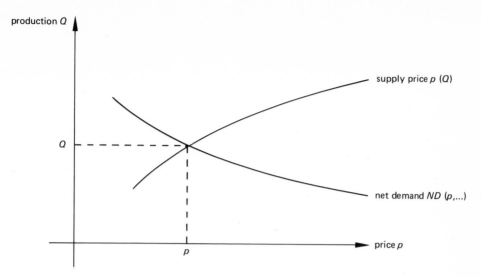

production Q

supply price $p\,(Q)$

Q

net demand $ND\,(p,...)$

price p

p

Fig. 3.4   Graphical representation of equilibrium in a sheltered sector

$$\Delta Q \ = \ \delta\,Q + \beta\,\Delta\,p \qquad\qquad (3.14)$$
$$\Delta D \ = \ -\,\alpha\,\Delta\,p \qquad\qquad (3.15)$$

where $\alpha > 0$, $\beta > 0$ and $\Delta\,p < 0$. Thus, since (3.13) holds, we can solve for Δp from (3.14) and (3.15), to give

$$\Delta p \ = \ -\,\frac{\delta\,Q}{\alpha + \beta} \qquad\qquad (3.16)$$

Therefore, in (3.14):

$$\Delta Q \ = \ \delta Q - \frac{\beta\delta Q}{\alpha+\beta} \ = \ \frac{\alpha}{\alpha+\beta}\ \delta Q \qquad\qquad (3.17)$$

The reaction in an exposed sector is

$$\Delta Q + \Delta M \ = \ \Delta D \qquad\qquad (3.18)$$
$$\Delta Q \ = \ \delta Q + \beta\,\Delta p \qquad\qquad (3.19)$$
$$\Delta D \ = \ -\,\alpha\,\Delta p \qquad\qquad (3.20)$$
$$\Delta p \ = \ \Delta p_M \ = \ \epsilon\,\Delta M \qquad\qquad (3.21)$$

Equation (3.21) is explained by the fact that foreign producers cut their prices to try to retain their share of the market (i.e. p_M is not exogenous in a less simplified model); this interplay between foreign and domestic producers in discussed further in note 13). Solving for Δp again,

$$\Delta p \ = \ -\,\frac{\delta Q}{\alpha+\beta+\frac{1}{\epsilon}} \qquad\qquad (3.22)$$

81

Therefore, in (3.215):

$$\Delta Q = \delta Q - \frac{\beta \delta Q}{\alpha + \beta + \dfrac{1}{\epsilon}} = \left(\frac{\alpha + \dfrac{1}{\epsilon}}{\alpha + \beta + \dfrac{1}{\epsilon}} \right) \delta Q \qquad (3.23)$$

Comparing (3.17) and (3.23), it can be seen that the *ex post* change in output in the exposed sector is greater than that in the sheltered sector, for the same initial change in the supply function.

Looking next at a shift in demand policy $\delta D > 0$, the corresponding analyses are as follows;

Sheltered sector:

$$\Delta Q = \Delta D \qquad (3.24)$$
$$\Delta Q = \beta \, \Delta p \qquad (3.25)$$
$$\Delta D = \delta D - \alpha \, \Delta p \qquad (3.26)$$

where again $\alpha > 0$, $\beta > 0$, but $\Delta p > 0$. Thus,

$$\Delta p = \frac{\delta D}{\alpha + \beta} \qquad (3.27)$$

therefore,

$$\Delta Q = \frac{\beta}{\alpha + \beta} \, \delta D \qquad (3.28)$$

Exposed sector:

$$\Delta Q + \Delta M = \Delta D \qquad (3.29)$$
$$\Delta Q = \beta \, \Delta p \qquad (3.30)$$
$$\Delta D = \delta D - \alpha \, \Delta p \qquad (3.31)$$
$$\Delta p = \Delta p_M = \epsilon \, \Delta M \qquad (3.32)$$

Hence,

$$\Delta p = \frac{\delta D}{\alpha + \beta + \frac{1}{\epsilon}} \qquad (3.33)$$

Therefore,

$$\Delta Q = \frac{\beta}{\alpha + \beta + \frac{1}{\epsilon}} \, \delta D \qquad (3.34)$$

Comparing (3.28) and (3.34), we get the opposite conclusion to the supply policy change: this time, the *ex post* change in output in the exposed sector is smaller than that in the sheltered sector, for the same initial change in the demand function.

Clearly, there are also interactions between the two sectors (which our simple models are not able to handle), and these have to be allowed for in the determination of partial equilibria for both sectors. Courbis analyses these effects in his larger test models. [15] Generally, however, the conclusions are those supported by the above simple analysis: demand policies will be generally ineffective with regard to increases in the output of exposed sectors; investment policies will have relatively greater effects on the level of total output when concentrated upon exposed sectors.

3.3 Determination of macro-economic equilibrium in a competitioned economy

As in the previous section, we do not need a large complex model to demonstrate the essential mechanisms underlying the determination of macro-economic equilibrium in a competitioned economy. Our aim in this section is to show how these mechanisms differ from those which operate in the Keynesian theory, and for this purpose, a single sector model is adequate:

1 Equilibrium between total supply and demand for goods and services (in constant prices):

$$Q + M = C + I + \overline{G} + \overline{E} \tag{3.35}$$

where Q = domestic production
M = imports;
C = household consumption;
I = investment by enterprises;
$\overline{G}$ = (exogenous) domestic demand;
$\overline{E}$ = (exogenous) exports

2 Production function with complementary, non-substitutable factors (note: the same equilibrium properties can also be demonstrated if the factors are substitutable) and constant returns to scale:

$$N = \omega Q \tag{3.36}$$

where N = employment (by enterprises only, in this simple model).

$$I = k Q \tag{3.37}$$

where k = rate of technical investment;
I = technically required investment.

3 Money wage determination:

$$\begin{aligned} w &= \sigma - \lambda u \\ &= \sigma - \lambda \left[i - \frac{N}{\overline{N}_d} \right] \end{aligned} \tag{3.38}$$

83

where u = rate of unemployment;
$\bar{N}_d$ = (exogenous) available labour force;
w = wage rate.

4   Behaviour of households and determination of consumption:

$$R = Nw\,(1 - j) \tag{3.39}$$

where R = household income (from enterprises only in this model) after taxes and social security benefits;
j = net algebraic tax rate;

$$pC = \gamma R \tag{3.40}$$

where p = general price level;
γ = average propensity to consume (i.e. we assume Keynesian behaviour in this simple model).

5   Enterprises' self-financing behaviour:

$$A = pQ - Nw - fpQ \tag{3.41}$$

where A = amount available to enterprises for self-financing;
f = average, constant, net level of tax pressure on firms.

$$pI = \frac{A}{a} \tag{3.42}$$

where pI = investment demand, in value terms;
a = desired rate of self-financing sought by firms.

6   Imports. Equations (3.35)–(3.42) are applicable to both open Keynesian and open competitioned economies. But this relation is different:

(a)   Keynesian: $$M = mQ \tag{3.43a}$$

where m = import propensity.

(b)   Competitioned: $$p = \bar{p}_M \tag{3.43b}$$

where $\bar{p}_M$ = import price (which is exogenous here for simplification)

Since we have introduced a production function (3.36), (3.37), thereby postulating a stable link between output and the level of capital stock, and assumed a stable self-financing behaviour for firms, the equilibrium that this model determines is clearly relevant only in the medium term.
   Solving the Keynesian model first (i.e. (3.35)–(3.43a)), we obtain by

inserting (3.36), (3.37), (3.39), (3.40) and (3.43a) into (3.35):

$$Q + mQ = \frac{\gamma (1-j) Q \omega w}{p} + k\dot{Q} + \bar{G} + \bar{E} \qquad (3.44)$$

At equilibrium there must be compatibility between the financing possibilities and the technically needed investment:

$$pkQ = \tfrac{1}{a} (pQ - fpQ - \omega Qw) \qquad (3.45)$$

using (3,36), (3.41) and (3.42). Therefore

$$p - fp - \omega w - akp = 0 \qquad (3.46)$$

i.e.
$$\frac{\omega w}{p} = 1 - f - a k \qquad (3.47)$$

Combining (3.47) and (3.44),

$$Q = \frac{\bar{G} + \bar{E}}{1 + m - k - \gamma (1-j)(1-f-ak)} = \frac{\bar{D}}{K} \qquad (3.48)$$

showing that output is a function of effective exogenous demand and the Keynesian multiplier. Using (3.48), we can determine employment, wages and prices:

from (3.36),
$$N = wQ = \frac{w\bar{D}}{K} \qquad (3.49)$$

from (3.38),
$$w = \sigma - \lambda \left[1 - \frac{N}{N_d} \right] = \frac{\sigma - \lambda}{1 - \frac{\lambda \bar{D}}{K\bar{N}_d}} \qquad (3.50)$$

from (3.47),
$$p = \frac{\omega w}{1 - f - aR} = \frac{\omega (\sigma - \lambda)}{(1 - f - ak) \left[1 - \frac{\lambda \bar{D}}{K\bar{N}_d} \right]} \qquad (3.51)$$

Looking now at the competitioned economy model (3.35)–(3.43b), excluding (3.43a), and starting with the price constraint (3.43b), we can insert this in (3.46), which is applicable in this model too:

$$w = \left[\frac{1 - f - ak}{\omega} \right] \bar{p}_M \qquad (3.52)$$

Immediately, we have the rather surprising result that wages are independent of the Phillip's parameters, but this is only in the first analysis; in a more realistic situation, the import price p_M is not exogenous,[13] and imports and output interact with p_M and R. From (3.38), the level of employment is

$$N = \left[\frac{w - \sigma + \lambda}{\lambda}\right] \bar{N}_d \qquad (3.53)$$

which, using (3.52), can be reduced to

$$N = \left[\frac{(1 - f - ak)\,\bar{p}_M - \omega\sigma + \omega\lambda}{\omega\lambda}\right] \bar{N}_d \qquad (3.54)$$

From this and (3.36), we have the level of output:

$$Q = \frac{N}{\omega} = \left[\frac{(1 - f - ak)\,\bar{p}_M - \omega\sigma + \omega\lambda}{\omega^2\lambda}\right] \bar{N}_d \qquad (3.55)$$

Using this and

$$Q + M = kQ + \gamma\,(1 - j)\,(1 - ak - f)\,Q + \bar{G} + \bar{E} \qquad (3.56)$$

which is derived in a similar way to (3.44), (3.45) and (3.46) except that M replaces mQ in (3.44), we finally get imports:

$$M = \bar{G} + \bar{E} - Q\,[1 - k - \gamma\,(1 - j)\,(1 - f - ak)]$$
$$= \bar{G} + \bar{E} - \frac{[1 - k - \gamma\,(1 - j)\,(1 - f - ak)\,(1 - f - ak)\,\bar{p}_M - \omega\sigma + \omega\lambda]}{\omega^2\lambda}\bar{N}_d$$
$$\qquad (3.57)$$

There are many more manipulations that could be carried out to bring out policy implications. We shall carry out just one, and leave the reader to consult Courbis[5] for other interesting cases. Consider output in the Keynesian case, as determined by (3.6), (3.38) and (3.46):

$$Q^k = \frac{[p\,(1 - f - ak) - \omega\sigma - \omega\lambda]}{\omega^2\lambda}\,\bar{N}_d \qquad (3.58)$$

Similarly, from (3.55) we have output in the competitioned economy case:

$$Q^c = \frac{[\bar{p}_M\,(1 - f - ak) - \omega\sigma + \omega\lambda]}{\omega^2\lambda}\,\bar{N}_d \qquad (3.59)$$

It is assumed that there is strong foreign competition, and hence $p_M < p$. Looking at (3.55) and (3.58), this means that at equilibrium $Q^c < Q^k$, with obvious implications for growth.

The mechanisms we have attempted to describe in this section can also be shown graphically (see Fig. 3.5). Assuming constant rates of taxation, self-financing and productivity, and the same behaviour by households,

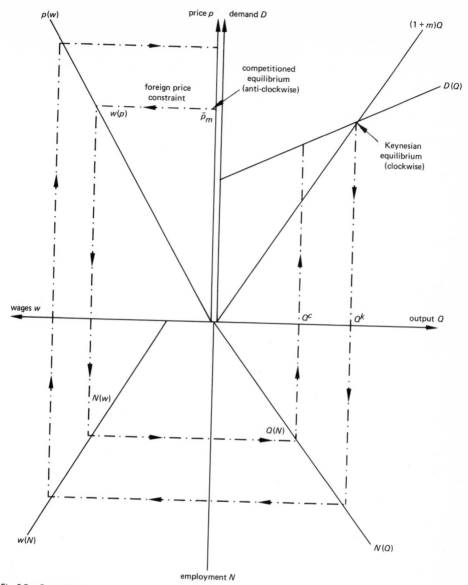

Fig. 3.5 Determination of macro-economic equilibrium in a competitioned and Keynesian economy
Source: see note 16

enterprises and the labour market, it can be seen that equilibrium is determined quite differently in the two cases, both at the sector level and the macro-economic level. The important conclusion is that a rise in effective demand can result in very little difference in overall output, depending on the sector affected by the rise in demand. If it is the exposed

87

sector, then there will merely be a rise in imports (in our simple model, but secondary reactions do take place as we have already noted; they do affect the overall conclusions, however), since it is competitiveness that determines output in this sector. If it is the sheltered sector that experiences the rise in effective demand, then in the short term their output increases, they demand more labour, and this pushes up wage costs. This affects the costs of enterprises in the exposed sector too, and so in the medium term their production falls (because imports get a price advantage), largely offsetting the initial rise in production in the sheltered sector. Action to promote growth must therefore be directed at supply, not at demand.

3.4 From the theory to the FIFI model

As indicated in Chapter 1 (see especially Fig. 1.1), work began on the preparation of a macro-economic model to assist in Plan preparation during the second half of 1966. It is also indicated in Figure 1.1 that this work went on throughout 1967 and into 1968. What is not shown in that diagram, however, is the fact that the competitioned economy theory was not the original basis of the model. We show in this section how the theory and the model did in fact eventually come together, and generally fill out the details of the 1966—1968 period, which is not fully explained in Figure 1.1.

The team set up to construct the model [17] in the Programmes Division of the INSEE began by carrying out an in-depth analysis of several foreign macro-economic models, including the optimisation models being developed at the same time in Hungary under Kornai. [18] The work that Courbis had done in the closing stages of the Fifth Plan preparation on prices [19] was also developed, and although this was not at that time sufficiently advanced to attract the full attention of the team, it was realised that the link between wages, prices and the labour market was likely to be important. The importance attached to prices was such that the optimisation approach was discarded as not sufficiently realistic on the price side. Experience acquired in several other optimisation studies in the Fifth Plan preparation phases [20] supported this decision.

However, there was still no general acceptance of the competitioned economy theory, and indeed the report drawn up early in 1967,[21] putting forward proposals about the structure and the purposes of a model to be used in the preparation of the Sixth Plan, described a neo-Keynesian model. Following this, in February—March 1967, several groups formed within the INSEE and the DP worked on the technical relationships in the model, and the central team started to programme the model in April, deciding against calling in professional programmers, and thereby avoiding delays and making certain that the programming methods were reasonably consistent. [22] The programme converged for the first time in August 1967, and by the end of September the first version of the model was ready.

The model displayed the general characteristics of a Keynesian demand model: foreign trade was complementary to domestic production, prices were determined endogenously to balance supply and demand, and the domestic prices were allowed to differ in exposed sectors. A first departure account was produced,[23] but the results were not satisfactory. Following discussions within the central team, Courbis' competitioned theory was generally accepted, and his exposed–sheltered sector classification and his market-share model (foreign price constraint and imports–production substitutability) written into the model. The solution algorithm was reprogrammed, and convergence was re-established in February 1968. Clearly, a major modification such as this would have been impossible without computer facilities.

3.5   Households, administrations and the exterior

Up to this point, we have concentrated on enterprise behaviour and the industrial sector. This is not unreasonable given the importance of them in the competitioned economy theory and the FIFI model. The other components of the model are more standard, and we deal with them briefly in this section before showing, in the final section, how the whole model operates.

Looking at households first, a number of problems arise from treating them as one single agent, not having full integrated financial operations in the model, and lack of data. As can be seen from the diagrams of the whole model in the next section (see Fig. 3.10), the starting point in the household account is total resources of households available as a result of other blocks in the model. The problem is to break this down into total household consumption, and then consumption by product. The first step is made difficult by the rather crude treatment of savings in the model. The major part of savings is derived by applying a given marginal propensity to save to disposable income, with allowances for the rate of increase of the general price level and households' investment in housing (which is exogenous in the Sixth Plan version of FIFI due to the lack of integrated financial behaviour). No income distribution effects or effects due to differing savings propensities in different socio-professional categories are distinguished.

The second step is to allocate this total consumption in value terms to each of a group of products. This part of FIFI is based on Stone's linear expenditure system, [24] the principle of which is as follows:

$$C_i = \beta_i p_i + \gamma_i \left[D - \sum_{j=1}^{n} \beta_j p_j\right], \quad i = 1, 2, \ldots, n \qquad (3.60)$$

where C_i = consumption of product i, in value terms;

β_i = some minimal consumption level of product i, in volume terms;

p_i = consumer price of product i;

γ_i = coefficients describing the pattern of consumption over and above the minimal levels, with $\sum_{i=1}^{n} \gamma_i = 1$;

D = total consumption expenditure;

n = number of products.

Because of the length of the time-period over which β_i and γ_i have been estimated, it was felt that they would be better represented not as constants but as linear functions of time. Accordingly, the equations used in FIFI for the Sixth Plan were:

$$C_{it} = (\beta_i^0 + \beta_{it}^1) p_{it} + (\gamma_i^0 + \gamma_{it}^1) \left[D - \sum_{j=1}^{n} (\beta_j^0 + \beta_{jt}^1) p_{jt}\right] \quad (3.61)$$

These are more realistic, but it is much more difficult to estimate the coefficients; an iterative scheme due to Stone [25] was used. Although the results were satisfactory, a different version is being prepared for use in the Seventh Plan. This consumption sub-model uses a formulation due to Fourgeaud and Nataf [26] which takes more account of the level of income:

$$\pi_i q_i = \theta_i K(R) \pi_i^\alpha + \gamma_i \left[R - K(R)\right] \qquad (3.62)$$

where

$$R = \frac{D}{p_g}, \quad p_g = \left[\sum_{i=1}^{n} \theta_i p_i^\alpha\right]^{\frac{1}{\alpha}}, \quad \pi_i = \frac{p_i}{p_g}$$

and q_i = consumption of product i in volume terms;

p_g = a general consumer price index calculated not according to the total consumption structure but to the structure of minimal consumption;

$K(R)$ = minimum total volume consumption function of real income R.

90

The linear expenditure system corresponds to the particular case where α = 1 and K is exogenous and independent of R. By using an *a priori* specification of $K(R)$, and also avoiding the problems created by the non-trend increases in income of 1968 for the estimates of β and γ [27] it is hoped to improve this part of the model.

Administrations are treated as six separate agents: civil central government, military central government, semi-public organisations (OSPAEs) which are run very much as firms, [28] local authorities, social security organisations, and other administrations. It has been criticised (see Chapter 5) that all central government decisions are exogenous in FIFI: there are no behavioural assumptions relating to the central government. To include such assumptions would be tantamount to admitting that there was an absolute response on the part of the central government to the actions of other agents included in the model. The model would then be a pure forecasting model, and would lose its policy simulation characteristic, which is so important for its use in Plan preparation. The central government's economic policy is therefore decided outside the model, as are the operations of other administrations if they result directly from central government decisions (e.g. social overhead capital programmes). In other cases, exogenous institutional rules (e.g. on taxation, subsidies, and social security systems) determine operations occuring in administrations' accounts, but there are some behavioural assumptions in the local authority and OSPAE sub-models (although, with financial operations still not fully integrated, these were not so important in the Sixth Plan as they will be in the Seventh, when FIFITOF is expected to be used.[29])

Given the nature of FIFI and the role it was set up to fulfil, it is not surprising that administrations are analysed in great detail. But this detail is not all handled within FIFI: a system of administrations models has gradually developed (see Figure 3.6), not as part of any conscious plan to create such a system but piecemeal, as part of the efforts by separate administrations to improve the quality and speed of information flowing between themselves and the Plan preparation bodies.

Finally, FIFI distinguishes a separate agent known as the 'exterior', which is not really a proper agent but a collection of activities, all involving France and the rest of the world. All assumptions relating to this agent are exogenous, except for the interaction we briefly alluded to earlier between imports and the foreign producers' price. The franc area and the rest of the world are distinguished in the external account, a step which is of course necessary for analyses of balance of payments problems. We have already discussed imports at length and referred to the market share model. Exports are projected exogenously, except for ex-

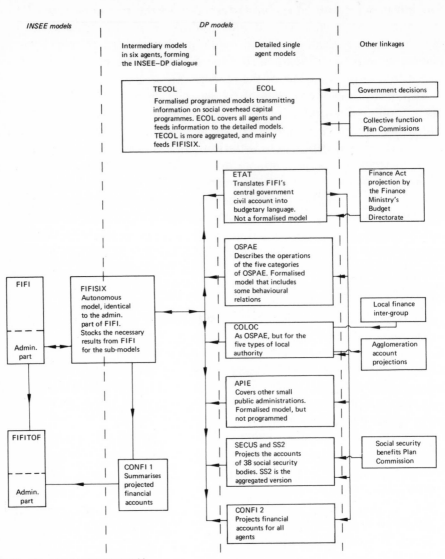

Fig. 3.6 The system of administrations models
Source: see note 28

ports from the exposed sector to the rest of the world. In this case, the following relationship is used:

$$E_{ind} = KD_e^{\alpha} \, Q_{ind}^{\beta} \left[\frac{p_{eind}}{p'_{ind}} \right]^{\gamma} C_{ind}^{-\delta} \qquad (3.63)$$

where

$$\alpha, \beta, \gamma, \delta > 0, \text{ and}$$

92

E_{ind} = industrial (exposed sector) exports, in volume terms;

D_e = gross domestic product of foreign countries (in the rest of the world area), in volume terms;

Q_{ind} = French industrial production, in volume terms;

C_{ind} = consumption of industrial products, in volume terms, by French households;

P_{eind} = the price of industrial exports;

p'_{ind} = the cost of industrial production, assuming industrial production to have the same structure as exports.

The various effects here are readily apparent from (3.63): first, foreign demand affects French exports, and the attraction of French exports is measured by the ratio of foreign prices and French production costs. Reinforcing this, the competitiveness of French producers is reflected via an export thrust effect: exports increase when output grows (which only occurs when French producers achieve a competitive advantage over foreign producers). The negative influence in (3.63) is the growth of domestic demand, indicating that under such conditions French producers concentrate on satisfying domestic needs at the expense of exports.

3.6 The overall structure of the model

In this final section on the FIFI model, the aim is to provide a picture of the overall model. Given the size of the model, the best way of doing this is not to list all the equations; that is done elsewhere,[30] and for completeness we also give an algebraic representation of the model in Appendix V. The version we have chosen to give here is based on the way in which the model is solved on the computer; as is mentioned in section 3.4 above, blocks of the model were programmed 'in parallel', each of the members of the central INSEE team being responsible for parts of one or more blocks. [31] We take advantage of this block structure to give an overall picture of the model in flow-chart form.

The first block is the *physical block*, which assiciates a physical equilibrium (i.e. output, factors of production, employment market) with assumptions on exogenous demand, domestic consumption, exports, and the pressure of foreign competition. Some of these assumptions are later modified in other blocks of the model. There are seven sectors in the model:

(1) agriculture;
(2) agricultural and foodstuffs industries;

(3) energy;
(4) industry;
(5) transport and communications;
(6) housing;
(7) services, building and public works, commerce;

with sectors (1), (3), (5) and (6) being administered, (2) and (7) sheltered, and (4) exposed to strong foreign competition. For some purposes, sector (7) is considered as two sectors, commerce being handled separately (this is the case in the projection of the input–output table used in this block).

We can consider the block in two interrelated parts, the first calculating output, investments in each branch,[32] stock variations, and imports, and the second dealing with equilibrium in the labour market. The output part is shown in Figure 3.7, and the labour market part in Figure 3.8, linkages between them and other blocks in the model being indicated by circled numbers which reappear in following diagrams.

The second block deals with the *enterprise accounts, wages and prices,* and plays a key role in the model. In a preliminary step, the results of the physical block are converted from branch terms to sector terms.[33] There then follows an extremely complex two-stage process involving the matrix decomposition of a large system of equations (several hundred), and itera-

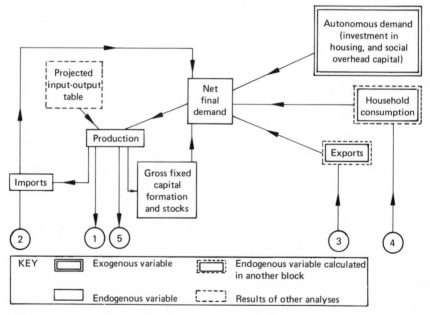

Fig. 3.7   The output part of FIFI's physical block
Source: constructed from Fig. 9, [82], p. 61

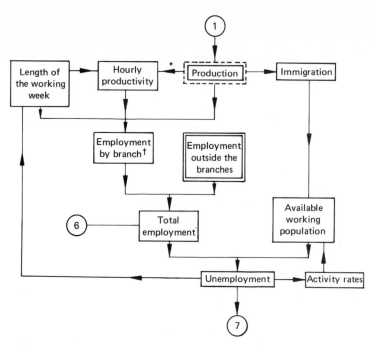

Fig. 3. 8   The labour market part of FIFI's physical block (Key as in Fig. 3.7)

*   For exposed sectors, as a function of foreign competition
     (and hence of output)
†   Except for agriculture where employment is exogenous

Source: Fig. 5, [82] , p. 35

tion between this system and a nonlinear equation involving the general price level and the wage rate. At the end of the first stage, equilibrium of the sector accounts is achieved and a suitable rate of self-financing thus determined. These accounts, however, are usually incompatible with the foreign price constraint, so there follows a second stage in which enterprises manipulate labour productivity, wage costs, and their rate of self-financing. The market share model balances these changes against the reactions of foreign producers, and new import prices and import levels (affecting the physical block too) are determined. A new physical equilibrium is thus established, and so stage one in the sector accounts, wages and prices block is re-entered. There have been problems in achieving convergence in this block, the various stages of which are shown in Figure 3.9.

The third block determines *household, export and administrations' demand*, and carries out the convergence test for the whole model (see Fig. 3.10). On average, the model requires 20 major iterations before converging, with many more minor iterations in the various blocks, all

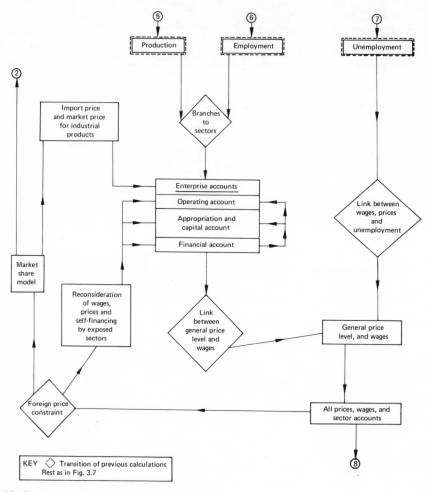

Fig. 3.9   The sector accounts, wages and prices block in the FIFI model
Source: constructed from Fig. 9, [82], p. 61

depending of course on the tolerance limit defining acceptable convergence. The reader is referred to the literature [33] for further technical details.

The results include the input—output table (TEI) in volume and value terms, a price table, production factors, the central government budget, the external account, enterprise accounts by sector, the household account, consumer price elasticities, accounts of administrations and financial institutions, and an analysis of taxation. More detail on the nature of the results can be found in Chapter 4, where the departure account and a number of variants are described.

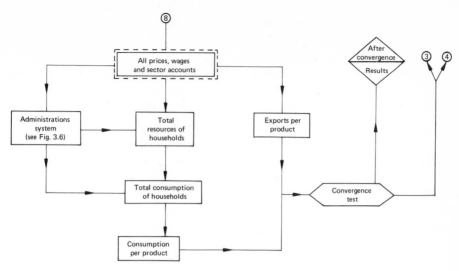

Fig. 3.10   The administrations, households and exports block in the FIFI model
Source: constructed from Fig. 9, [82], p. 61

Notes

[1]   Much of the material in this chapter can be traced to Courbis in one way or another. He is the author of the competitioned economy theory, and consequently one of the main authors of the FIFI model. When his theory was first published, a number of English sources (notably [59], which was not widely circulated) translated its name incorrectly as 'competitive economy', a misleading term because it gives the impression of deliberate action on the part of the economy in question, whereas Courbis' theory relates to an economy which (initially, at any rate) passively suffers very strong foreign competition. Hence the term 'competitioned economy'.

[2]   Value planning attempts to reconcile an equilibrium in physical terms (i.e. at constant prices) with financial flows, and to take more account of short-term economic policy. There is a brief discussion on its use in the Fifth French Plan in [60], pp. 93–9.

[3]   In very simple terms, the Fifth Plan policy was based on Keynesian conceptions: balance of payments problems were tackled by slower growth and increasing unemployment. Imports would fall (it was thought) because they were mainly determined by production.

[4]   The thinking in the Sixth Plan (based on the competitioned economy theory) was that imports could also be reduced by increasing production in the exposed sector (one of the assumptions in the competitioned eco-

nomy theory is that there is perfect substitutability between imports and domestic production in the exposed sector).

⁵ The major source on Courbis' theory is [61], which runs to over 700 pages. Shorter versions can be found in [62], [63] and [64], the latter two sources concentrating more on the treatment of financial flows and monetary variables. References to the theory are also made in many of Courbis' other articles, some of which we cite below.

⁶ The simple models described in this chapter are based on material presented by Courbis in a series of seminars to post-graduate students following the NEP programme and held in Birmingham in February 1973. These seminars were recorded on videotape by the University of Birmingham television service. Persons interested in viewing the tapes or using them for their own teaching should contact the Director of the service.

⁷ Courbis cites a 1935 source [65] in his thesis.

⁸ A number of Scandinavian models distinguish exposed and sheltered sectors, notably the Norwegian MODIS III [66] and PRIM I [67] models and a Swedish model due to Edgren, Faxen and Odhner [68].

⁹ These arguments derive from Kalecki [69], Lerner and Carleton [70], and Courbis himself [61].

¹⁰ See the criticisms made by certain members of the CEGF Technical Group in their report [1]. We discuss these criticisms in Chapter 5.

¹¹ See especially the Japanese medium-term projection model [71], which differs critically from the models described here in that it does not contain an exposed sector (i.e. Japan is considered to be a 'competitive economy', not a 'competitioned economy').

¹² Production in an administered-price sector is determined by demand, (energy, transport), or by the autonomous behaviour of the producers (agriculture), or by investment (housing) (exogenous in FIFI). See section 3.6 for a full list of sectors appearing in FIFI.

¹³ One of the key features of FIFI is the market-share model which describes the way foreign producers change their prices in response to domestic policies, and *vice versa*. See Courbis [72] and [73].

¹⁴ This is not quite the case in sheltered sectors, which are dominantly competitive with respect to foreign competition. See [74], third footnote in section 3.

¹⁵ The test model in [62] contains 79 equations in 86 variables, seven of which are exogenous.

¹⁶ Figure 3.5 is a modified combination of two similar diagrams in [61], p. 277, and a further diagram given in Courbis' TV seminars (see note 6 above).

¹⁷ The members of this team were Michel Aglietta, Raymond Courbis,

98

Patrick Gordon (up to 1967), Alain Saglio, Claude Seibel, and Bernard Ullmo (from October 1967), with leadership from Philippe Berthet and Paul Dubois, and contributions from Jacques Bertherat, Marc Chervel, André Gauron, Christian Sautter and Catherine Girardeau. See [75] for further details of the early work on FIFI.

[18] There are many sources on the early work carried out in Hungary on the application of mathematical programming models to planning. Of particular interest is the special Hungarian issue of *Economics of Planning* (vol. 5, no. 3, 1965) containing papers by Kornai and others. Although there have been further applications since that time, it was at that time that the French were considering using similar models in French planning.

[19] See [76], the publication date of which clearly indicates that, even with two or three years' publication delay, this work came too late to have a profound effect on the Fifth Plan.

[20] Brief reference is made in [77] pp. 114–15 to a linear programming model which CERMAP (later CEPREMAP) built and used to study the effect of changes in the length of the working week. [77] makes no reference to any publications on this model, but there are a number of sources ([75], [79], [80] and the model was picked up by a United Nations survey [81] indicating that the model was used to analyse a number of variants, thus providing an early example of the method of analysis that became so popular in the Sixth Plan preparation phases.

[21] This report was not published originally; it is reprinted in an appendix to [82].

[22] Originally the programming work was allocated as follows: Michel Aglietta was responsible for the enterprise accounts and the overall economic table (TEE); Raymond Courbis undertook the imports–production breakdown, the branch-to-sector conversion, the price sector accounts, wages, and the matrix solution of the whole model; Alain Saglio handled the input–output table (TEI), factors of production, and the variant mode of operating the model; Claude Seibel looked after the accounts of non-productive agents (households, administrations, etc.); Patrick Gordon also worked on the input–output table, and looked after the overall consistency of the programming. The way in which the later version of FIFI was programmed is described in section 3.6.

[23] This was described in a report on 'the first economic perspectives for 1975' which Seibel refers to in [75].

[24] Yoshihara [83] discusses various ways of handling consumption, only two of which are compatible with the theory of choice. Stone's linear expenditure system gave the best results in the FIFI model. It was first used by Stone for the United Kingdom in 1954 [84], and has also recently

been applied in Japan and the United States (see [53] p. 50 for full references).

[25] See the reports published by Chapman and Hall on the Cambridge 'Programme for Growth'.

[26] See [85].

[27] Footnote 2 in [82], p. 53 mentions the problems created in estimating β and γ from time series because there was such an abrupt jump in incomes following the settlement of the May–June 1968 crisis.

[28] There are five categories of OSPAE: autonomous ports, organisations involved in urban development, rural development, motorways, and national markets. Further details on Figure 3.6 are as follows:

(a)   the Finance Act projection model is discussed in [86];

(b)   on the agglomerations account projection, see [87];

(c)   in other administrations (APIE model) are included those organisations involved in adult education and training;

(d)   the social security model is described in [85]; it also acts as a satellite model to the DECA short-term forecasting model (described in Appendix VI).

(e)   the CONFI models were not operational at the time of the Sixth Plan preparation stages; they are expected to play a major role when the FIFITOF model becomes available (see Chapter 10 for further discussion of FIFITOF).

The administrations system is presented in more detail in [89].

[29] It is assumed that local authorities try to achieve a certain level of social overhead capital, and balance between internal and external financing of their activities. These assumptions will take on more relevance when FIFITOF becomes available (see note 28 (c) above).

There are additional notes and references to this and other chapters at the end of Chapter 10.

[30] Courbis describes a simplified algebraic version of FIFI in an appendix to [82]. The full equations are given in [90], to be published later in *Les Collections de l'INSEE*.

[31] See note (22) above for details on the early programming work. The blocks that we describe in section 3.6 are due to the following members of the team: Alain Saglio (physical block), Raymond Courbis (sector accounts, wages and prices block), and Michel Aglietta and Claude Seibel (households, administrations and the exterior block).

100

[32] The French national accounts distinguish between 'branches' and 'sectors': a 'sector' is a group of *enterprises* having the same *principal* activity, and thus preserves the integrity of the decision-making centres constituted by each enterprise; a 'branch' comprises production units, enterprises or parts of enterprises which have the same activity and produce the *same* group of goods and services.

[33] The main sources on the FIFI model are [59], [74] and [82], until [90] is more widely available. The paper in [82] is an updated version of [59], and [74] is a shortened version of [82].

There are additional notes and references to this and other chapters at the end of Chapter 10.

References

[59] R. Courbis, *Le Modèle physico-financier de projection économique à moyen terme FIFI* (The FIFI medium-term, physico-financial, economic projection model), written April 1970. Paper presented at the first Seminar on Mathematical Methods and Computer Techniques, United Nations Economic Commission for Europe, Varna, Bulgaria, 28 September – 10 October 1970, Document UN/ST/ECE/MATHECO/2 (English language version available from UN in Geneva), 84 pp.

[60] G. Denton, M. Forsyth, and M. Maclennan, *Economic Planning and Policies in Britain, France and Germany*, Allen and Unwin, London 1965, 424 pp.

[61] R. Courbis, *Competitivité et croissance en économie concurrencée* (Competitiveness and growth in a competitioned economy), Thesis presented for the Doctorate of Economic Science at the University of Paris, January 1971 (since published by Dunod, Paris 1974), 724 pp.

[62] R. Courbis, 'La détermination de l'équilibre général en économie concurrencée' (Determination of general equilibrium in a competitioned economy) (written January 1970), *Monographies du Séminaire d'Économétrie* no. VII, Paris 1971, 74 pp.

[63] R. Courbis, 'Monnaie, financement et croissance en économie de concurrence' (Money, financing and growth in a competitioned economy) (written August 1969), in Courbis, Fourcade, and Guillaume, *Études de calcul economique* no. 1, PUF, Paris 1971.

[64] R. Courbis, 'Marché international des capitaux et politiques moné-

taires nationales' (The international capital market and national monetary policies) (written October 1970), *Économie Appliqueé* vol. XXIV, no. 3, 1971, pp. 379–411.

[65] J. Dessirier, 'Secteurs "abrité" et "non-abrité" dans le déséquilibre actuel de l'économie française' (Sheltered and non-sheltered sectors in the current French economic disequilibrium), *Revue d'Économie Politique* vol. XLIX, number 4, 1935, pp. 1330–58.

[66] O. Bjerkholt, 'A precise description of the equation system of the economic model MODIS III' *Economics of Planning* vol. 8, no. 1–2, pp. 26–56.

[67] O. Aukrust, 'PRIM I: A model of the price and income distribution mechanism of an open economy' *Review of Income and Wealth*, series 16, no. 1, 1970, pp. 51–78.

[68] G. Edgren, K.O. Faxen, and C.E. Odhner, 'Wages, growth and the distribution of income' *Swedish Journal of Economics* vol. LXXI, no. 3, 1969, pp. 113–60.

[69] M. Kalecki, 'The principle of increasing risk' *Economica* vol. IV, no. 16, 1937, pp. 440–7.

[70] E.M. Derner and W.T. Carleton, *A Theory of Financial Analysis* Harcourt, Brace and World, New York 1966.

[71] Japan Economic Planning Agency, *Econometric Models for the Medium-term Economic Plan 1964–1968*, a report by the Committee on Econometric Methods, Tokyo, August 1965.

[72] R. Courbis, 'Development économique et concurrence étrangère' (Economic development and foreign competition) (written August 1968), *Revue Économique* vol. XX, no. 1, 1969, pp. 37–83.

[73] R. Courbis, 'Echanges extérieurs et partage du marché en économie concurrencée' (Foreign trade and market shares in a competitioned economy), Paper presented at the Franco-Hungarian Colloquium on Foreign Trade, Budapest, 3–6 June 1970.

[74] R. Courbis, 'The FIFI model used in the preparation of the French Plan' (translated into English by D. Liggins), *Economics of Planning*, forthcoming.

[75] C. Seibel, 'L'élaboration du modèle FIFI' (The construction of the FIFI model), *Les Collections de l'INSEE*, série C, no. 22, June 1973, pp. 7–12.

[76] R. Courbis, 'Prevision des prix et étude sectorielle des entreprises pendent la preparation du Vᵉ Plan' (Price forecasting and sector analysis of enterprises during the preparation of the Fifth Plan), *Études et Conjoncture*, November 1968, pp. 1–280.

[77] INSEE (Division des Programmes), 'Méthodes de programmation

dans le Ve Plan' (Programming methods in the Fifth Plan), *Études et Conjoncture*, December 1966.

[78]   CERMAP, 'Un modèle d'étude de variantes d'un plan' (A model to analyse variants of a plan), 1962, mimeograaphed, unpublished.

[79]   A. Moustacchi, 'The interpretation of shadow prices in a parametric linear economic programme', in Hart, Mills, and Whittaker (eds.), *Econometric Analysis for National Planning*, Colston Papers no. 16, Butterworths, London 1964, pp. 205–25.

[80]   A. Moustacchi and Raiman, 'Application d'un modèle d'allocation des ressources à la planification française: ses enseignements' (Application of a resource allocation model to French planning: some lessons), Paper presented to the Econometric Congress, Rome 1965.

[81]   United Nations, *Macroeconomic Models for Planning and Policy-Making*, Geneva, E/ECE/665, p. 185.

[82]   M. Aglietta, R. Courbis, and C. Seibel, 'Le modèle FIFI: tome 1' (The FIFI model: volume 1), *Les Collections de l'INSEE*, série C, no. 22, June 1973, 146 pp.

[83]   K. Yoshihara, 'Demand functions: An application to Japanese expenditure patterns' *Econometrica* vol. 37, no. 2, 1969, pp. 257–74.

[84]   R. Stone, 'Linear expenditure systems and demand analysis: an application to the pattern of British demand' *The Economic Journal* vol. LXIV, no. 255, 1954, pp. 511–27.

[85]   C. Fourgeaud and A. Nataf, 'Consommation en prix et revenus réels et théorie choix' (Consumption in real price and income terms and the theory of choice), *Econometrica* vol. 27, no. 3, 1959, pp. 329–54.

[86]   Direction du Budget, (Ministry of Finance), 'Presentation générale du modèle budgétaire' (General presentation of the budget model), *Statistiques* no. 54, March 1971, mimeographed, 19 pp.

[87]   O. Mouriau, 'Les études financières des agglomérations' (Financial analyses of agglomerations), *Bulletin de Liaison et d'Information de l'Administration Centrale de l'Économie et des Finances* no. 55, April–June 1971, pp. 48–59.

[88]   Pierre Martel, Jean-Pierre Launay and Henri Perdriau, 'Le modèle sécurité sociale' (The social security model), *Statistiques et Études Financières*, Série Orange, no. 6, 1972, pp. 3–27.

[89]   M. Mousel, 'Système de modèle moyen terme "administrations" ' (The 'administrations' medium-term model system), *Statistiques et Études Financières*, Série Orange, no. 10, 1973, pp. 3–15.

[90] M. Aglietta, M. Bussery, R. Courbis, M. Saglio, C. Seibel, et B. Ull-
      mo, 'Les équations du modèle FIFI' (The equations of the FIFI
      model), INSEE Service des Programmes, Note 320/1301 (mimeo-
      graphed), March 1972.

4 Accounts and Variants drawn up during the Preparation of the Sixth Plan

These analyses, especially the variants, enable the mechanisms taken into account in the model to be clearly and concretely appreciated, perhaps in a better way than an abstract description could convey. They enable the feasibility of the model to be tested, and the pertinence of different forms of economic reasoning to be assessed. Finally, they show how to use a large-size model ... to understand the multiple consequences and interdependencies of external events and economic policy instruments.

Translated from the introduction to [4].

This is the first of several chapters in which we examine the central and detailed projections constructed during and immediately after the preparation of the Sixth Plan. The amount of information that is available on these projections, although not widely published in all cases, is enormous,[1] and we are forced to be selective in trying to give an overall but comprehensive picture. It is not difficult to understand the criticisms from some members of the Plan Commissions about the flood of numerical information placed before them, which they were expected to assimilate and, then use as a basis for policy recommendations. We run the same risk of overwhelming the reader, by presenting him with too many vast tables of numbers.

Accordingly, the material used in this chapter relating to the September 1969 departure account and the various types of variant that followed it is only a small sample of that with which the Plan participants were faced. We shall illustrate some of the key features of the FIFI model described in Chapter 3, and provide an example of the difficulties created for many of the participants by an apparent lack of communication between them and the administration about the model's capabilities and limitations. This applies particularly to the departure account, which was completely misunderstood and misinterpreted immediately after it was published in autumn 1969.

We have defined and discussed the various types of variant in Chapter 1, and Figures 1.1 and 1.2 provide an overall picture of the use of variants in the Plan preparation process. Later in this chapter we present several examples of sensitivity, uncertainty, analytical and synthesis variants, bringing out not only the features of each individual variant but additional details of the model and the departure account at the same time. We should emphasise again that the work that goes into the preparation of a variant cannot be appreciated merely by looking at two columns of results comparing the variant and the departure account. Every variant depends on analytical work which in many cases cannot be undertaken with the FIFI model. We describe some of this decentralised work in Chapters 7 and 8.

4.1 The September 1969 departure account

As indicated above, a full description of the assumptions and results of the departure account is impossible within the confines of one section in one chapter of a book like this. We have discarded 90 per cent of the material in the account in an attempt to focus on the key areas as far as the model is concerned, and with respect to the serious economic problems revealed by the account for 1975.

Recall that the two characteristics of the departure account are that it is *trend-oriented* (i.e. economic change is assumed to take place according to observed past trends) and *conventional* (i.e. economic policies in force in September 1969 are assumed to continue up to 1975, and economic behaviour is assumed to follow existing patterns). The projection of 1975 is based on 1965, but trends up to 1968 have been allowed for, and recent events (such as the August 1969 devaluation of the franc) included. It has to be borne in mind that the figures given in the tables for 1968, 1969 and 1970 are only provisional, because the French national accounts, like those of other industrialised countries, are published and updated several times over a five to six-year period.[2] The data quoted for the most recent years comes from the 1970 second economic budget,[3] which includes forecasts for 1970 and figures from the most recently available national accounts for 1969 and earlier years.

Industrial products are expected to constitute 80 per cent of all French imports and 85 per cent of all French exports in 1975, and hence the importance of assumptions about foreign prices and production for the exposed sector. Given the mechanisms described in Chapter 3, these assumptions are critical in determining the external equilibrium and the employment equilibrium. The assumptions made in the departure account

106

Table 4.1

Data on foreign prices and production
(September 1969 departure account: assumptions)

Annual growth rates (per cent)	1970/1965	1975/1970	1975/1965
Foreign gross domestic production (PIB)			
(weighted by French exports)	3·75	4·25	4·00
Foreign PIB price	3·30	2·40	2·85
Foreign industrial prices (including all taxes)	2·20	1·50	1·85

Source: [4], p. 70

are shown in Table 4.1, and one of the sensitivity variants considered in section 4.2 looks at the effect of a change in the import price of foreign industrial products.

The assumptions on working population, labour productivity, and rates of productive investment all follow observed trends, and are shown in Tables 4.2, 4.3 and the top half of Table 4.5. The reader is referred to [4] for the assumptions on the behaviour of enterprises, households, administrations, and financial institutions. Again, we do not have the space to give all those assumptions here, but we pick out as particularly interesting the parameters relating to household consumption by product, which we discussed in Chapter 3 (section 3.5, equation (3.61)):

$$C_{it} = (\beta_i^0 + \beta_i^1 t) p_{it} + (\gamma_i^0 + \gamma_i^1 t) [D_t - \sum_{j=1}^{n} (\beta_i^0 + \beta_i^1 t) p_{jt}]$$

The parameters, shown in Table 4.4, were estimated over the period 1949–1967, so that $t = 0$ in 1949 and $t = 27$ in 1975. In the departure account, all $\gamma_i^1 = 0$.

As can be appreciated from the final sections of Chapter 3 on how the FIFI model is solved, the model produces accounts for all the economic agencies it distinguishes, in addition to results involving the usual macro-economic aggregates. In order to reduce the departure accout to manageable proportions, we have chosen to present the results in terms of the five main macro-economic equilibria, thus omitting many of the sector and agent accounts. The four main features of the physical equilibrium (see Table 4.5) are:

(i) growth is slower (5·4 per cent p.a.) over the ten-year period 1965–1975 than it was in the five years prior to that period (6·2 per cent p.a.); this creates problems in the labour market (see below);

Table 4.2

Assumptions on labour productivity and the working week
(September 1969 departure account: assumptions)

Hourly labour productivity*	Annual growth rates (per cent)				
	1965/1960	1966/1965	1967/1966	1968/1967	1975/1965
2 Agricultural and food industries	4·6	5·6	4·1	4·9	4·4
3 Energy	9·6	7·3	4·6	10·5	9·3
4 Industry	5·5	6·9	5·4	9·7	6·3
5 Transport and tele-communications	4·0	3·5	2·8	8·3	4·8
7 Building and public works, services, and commerce	3·8	3·6	2·7	4·8	3·75
All non-agricultural branches (excluding housing)	4·75	5·0	3·7	6·9	5·0

Length of working week	Hours							AGR (per cent)
	1959	1962	1965	1966	1967	1968	1975	1975/1965
2 Agricultural and food industries	46·0	46·8	46·8	46·7	46·6	46·5	44·9	−0·4
3 Energy	47·4	45·9	44·0	44·3	44·1	43·3	43·0	−0·2
4 Industry	44·9	46·0	45·4	45·6	45·2	45·2	43·7	−0·4
5 Transport and tele-communications	47·2	47·1	46·3	46·3	46·3	45·6	44·2	−0·5
7 Building and public works, services, and commerce	45·0	45·7	45·7	45·4	45·3	45·2	43·0	−0·6
All non-agricultural branches (excluding housing)	45·3	46·6	45·6	45·6	45·4	45·2	43·5	−0·5

* Value added at domestic prices per hour worked

AGR = annual growth rate

Source: Table 4, [4], pp. 47−8

(ii) growth of consumption, compared over the same two periods, also slows down appreciably (from 6·2 per cent p.a. in 1960−1965 to 5·0 per cent p.a. in 1965−1975), as one might expect given the close relationship between PIB growth and consumption;

(iii) investment continues to grow faster than consumption;

(iv) the effects of the August 1969 devaluation rapidly disappear, lead-

Table 4.3

Assumptions on productive investment rates (in volume terms)
(September 1969 departure account: assumptions)

Branches (figures in percentages)	1960	1962	1965	1966	1975
2 Agricultural and foodstuffs industries	11·1	11·9	12·1	11·8	12·2
3 Energy	33·3	29·8	27·7	28·7	26·9
4 Industry (excluding AEC)*	14·6	17·3	15·2	15·1	17·2
5 Transport and telecommunications	36·6	35·1	33·2	36·1	34·9
7 Building and public works, services, and commerce	8·2	10·0	11·5	12·0	14·5
All branches: global rate of productive investment (including AEC)	13·9	15·3	15·7	16·3	17·8

Rate of productive investment = (productive investment) / (value added at domestic prices)

* AEC = Atomic Energy Commission (sometimes included in the chemical industry for national accounting purposes)

Source: Table 5a, [4], p. 48

ing to a slowdown in the growth of exports and problems in the balance of payments (see below).

The labour equilibrium is affected by two main factors; first, there is a marked increase in the growth of working population towards the second half of the ten-year period 1965–1975 (the growth rate is 0·4 per cent p.a. between 1965 and 1970, and 0·9 per cent p.a. between 1970 and 1975), due to the decreasing effect of the raising of the school leaving age; and secondly, there is the already referred to slowdown in growth, which means that full employment cannot be achieved. The unemployment figure for 1975 is 395,000 (1·8 per cent of the total working population), which is not high compared with 1968 but is very much higher than in the 1960–1965 period (see Table 4.6). This increase in unemployment is also in spite of a reduction in the length of the working week (see Table 2.2), thus emphasising the insufficient growth of PIB.

The second major problem brought out by the departure account is the balance of payments deficit. Looking at Table 4.7, the balance of trade is in surplus, but distributive operations are very much in the red, leading to an overall balance of payments deficit in 1975 of 4,817 million francs at 1965 prices (7,000 million in 1975 francs). The impact of this deficit is reduced somewhat by the fact that a sizeable proportion of this deficit is

Table 4.4

Parameters relating to household consumption by product
(September 1969 departure account: assumptions)

		Millions of 1965 francs			%
		β_i^0	β_i^1	$\beta_i^0 + \beta_i^1 t$ (1975)	γ_i^0
1	Agricultural products	13,905	304	22,153	3·13
2	Agricultural and food industry products	33,984	0	33,984	20·07
3	Energy	4,005	55	5,520	6·66
4	Other industrial products	14,363	−35	13,013	39·22
5	Transport and telecommunications	3,794	0	3,794	1·82
7	Services, building and public works (there is no commerce 'product')	19,254	−134	14,586	29·10
					100·00

Source: [4], p. 68

with the franc area, but even allowing for this, the deficit with abroad is still significant. The picture is in fact worse than it seems from looking at Table 4.7: the FIFI model assumes a smooth trajectory between the base year (1965) and the Plan horizon year (1975), so that a deficit in 1965 and a deficit in 1975 means deficits in all the intervening years too. The cumulative balance of payment deficit is, therefore, extremely serious.

The public finance balance also shows a deficit (see Table 4.8) and the growth of total expenditure is slower (6·5 per cent p.a. between 1965 and 1975, compared with 8·6 per cent p.a. between 1960 and 1965). This is a consequence of maintaining conventional policies (a major assumption of the departure account) which are adapted to 1969 and not to the problems of 1975. There is a complete lack of symmetry in the social security account, and, although the local authorities' deficit is much the same in 1975 as in previous years, this is only achieved by cutting back on social overhead capital programmes.

The fifth equilibrium, between savings and investment (see Table 4.9), is characterised by a marked increase in the domestic savings rate, particularly households, and dependence on considerable external financing. The analysis of these problems is not as firmly based as other parts of the account because FIFI does not project financial operations,[5] and so it is not possible to trace the situation of financial markets.

To summarise, the key problems brought out by the departure account are:

Table 4.5

Equilibrium (in volume terms) between production and its uses
(September 1969 departure account: results)

	Totals in millions of 1965 francs		Annual growth rates (per cent)					
	1965	1975	1965/1960	1968/1965	1970/1968	1970/1965	1975/1970	1975/1965
Resources								
Gross domestic production	438,748	739,249	6·2	4·9	6·3	5·4	5·4	5·4
Imports	51,654	136,942	9·8	9·9	12·0	10·6	9·8	10·2
Total resources and total uses	490,402	876,191	6·5	5·5	6·9	6·1	5·9	6·0
Uses								
Total consumption	307,854	503,362	6·2	4·6	5·1	4·8	5·2	5·0
of which:								
households	288,109	474,019	6·1	4·6	5·3	4·9	5·3	5·1
public administrations	17,863	25,943	7·1	3·9	3·2	3·6	4·0	3·8
financial institutions	1,882	3,400	11·8	5·1	6·0	5·4	6·8	6·1
Investment (GFCF)	118,072	218,674	9·9	7·2	7·5	7·3	5·5	6·4
of which:								
productive	68,990	131,416	8·8	7·6	8·6	8·0	5·4	6·7
housing*	32,297	54,633	10·4	5·4	6·8	6·0	4·8	5·4
public administrations	15,823	31,070	13·5	8·9	4·2	7·0	7·0	7·0
financial institutions	962	1,555	8·0	6·1	6·3	6·2	3·6	4·9
Changes in stocks	7,552	18,337	−12·3					
Exports and the balance of services' uses	56,924	135,818	6·9	7·2	14·0	10·0	8·2	9·1

* Investment in housing by enterprises and households. See also note 4, which refers to all tables of results

Source: Table 1, [4], p. 46

111

Table 4.6 Equilibrium of employment (September 1969 departure account: results)

	Levels in thousands of persons					Annual growth rate (per cent)		
	1960	1962‡	1965	1968‡	1975	1965/1960	1968/1962	1975/1965
Population resources								
Total population living in metropolitan France	45,185	46,585	48,795	50,190	52,990	1·5	1·2	0·8
Total domestic working population	19,650	19,830	20,355	20,650	21,540	0·7	0·7	0·6
less military	550	510	300	295	245			
less unemployed*	240	230	270	430	395			
Total employed domestic working population	18,860	18,990	19,785	19,970	20,900	1·0	0·9	0·55
Use of population								
1 Agriculture (01)†	4,008	3,724	3,316	2,952	2,321	-3·7	-3·8	-3·5
2 Agricultural and foodstuffs industries (02)	690	660	689	698	703	-0·1	0·95	0·2
3 Energy (03 to 05)	385	374	374	361	292	-0·5	-0·6	-2·4
4 Industry (06 to 12)	4,615	4,748	4,907	4,802	5,145	1·2	0·2	0·5
5 Transport and telecommunications (14)	925	957	1,027	1,054	1,085	2·1	1·6	0·5
6 Housing (15)	34	35	38	42	47	2·3	3·1	2·15
7 Building and public works, services and commerce (13, 16 to 19)	5,499	5,623	6,277	6,716	7,537	2·7	3·0	1·8
Employment in all branches	16,156	16,121	16,628	16,625	17,130	0·6	0·5	0·3
Employment outside the branches	2,704	2,869	3,157	3,345	3,770	3·1	2·6	1·8
Total employed domestic working population	18,860	18,990	19,785	19,970	20,900	1·0	0·8	0·55
Wage earners	13,535	13,620	14,765	15,255	16,960	1·8	1·9	1·4
Non wage earners	5,325	5,370	5,020	4,715	3,940	-1·2	-2·2	-2·4
Total employed domestic working population	18,860	18,990	19,785	19,970	20,900	1·0	0·9	0·55

* Strictly 'workers looking for a job'
† Population census year
‡ National accounts branch numbers

Source: Table 3, [4], p. 47

(a)   an unacceptable balance of payments deficit;

(b)   a rate of growth in the general level of prices of 3·9 per cent p.a. (see Table 4.10), and faster growth than this of prices in those sectors sheltered from international competition (the latter puts pressure on costs in the exposed sector too, thus reducing their competitiveness);

(c)   insufficient growth to absorb all the available working population, leading to high unemployment;

(d)   slower growth in wages (not shown in the tables presented here: the annual growth of wages paid by the enterprises is 5·4 per cent between 1965 and 1975, compared with 7·4 per cent between 1960 and 1965).

It is worth pointing out again that these problems are due mainly to extrapolating the past into the future, and depend very much on the initial assumption and an economic policy that is not adapted to the situation in 1975.

Based on the figures in the departure account, and the key problems just listed, the Plan Commissions were advised to focus on the analysis of particular structural problems, all directly or indirectly linked to a lack of competitiveness in French industry: production costs too high, inflationary behaviour of certain agencies, lack of symmetry in central government transfers and chargers, and the 'invisibles' problem in the external account. It was suggested that policies to combat these problems be given special attention, and many of the sensitivity variants that accompanied the departure account were designed to demonstrate the effects of the changes in factors bearing on production costs in the exposed sector. The competition policy is central to the Sixth Plan, and one can see in the departure account the beginnings of the attention given to it and the work done on it during the preparation of the Plan.

4.2   Sensitivity variants

Variants[6] were used throughout the Plan preparation period to focus on particular areas of uncertainty and to show the overall effects of policies and changes in assumptions. The variants accompanying the departure account (see Table 1.2 for full list) were considered as examples of the types of analyses that the Plan Commissions might like to use in their initial discussions. In a sense, they were what the planners themselves regarded as the logical first round of variants supporting the departure account, given that attention should be focused on problems involving international competition.

Table 4.7

External account (September 1969 departure account: results)

Imports and exports	Millions of 1965 francs			Annual growth rates (per cent)		
	1965	1975 (1965 prices)	1975 (real value) (1975 relative prices)	1965/1962 (volume)	1968/1965 (volume)	1975/1965 (volume)
I Imports	51,654	136,942	103,966	10·6	9·8	10·2
1 Agricultural products (01)	4,470	4,470	4,117	–0·2	–3·9	0
2 Agricultural and food industries (02)	6,128	8,957	7,565	10·8	5·8	3·9
3 Energy (03 to 05)	8,245	14,209	8,948	11·4	7·6	5·6
4 Industry (06 to 12)	32,781	109,246	83,290	12·2	12·4	12·8
Others	30	60	46	–9·0	0·8	7·2
II Exports	51,458	127,761	100,816	9·4	7·9	9·5
1 Agricultural products (01)	4,194	8,155	6,198	20·0	13·2	6·9
2 Agricultural and food industries (02)	4,451	6,040	5,192	6·7	7·9	3·1
3 Energy (03 to 05)	1,901	1,000	744	11·6	2·8	–6·2
4 Industry (06 to 12)	40,615	112,316	88,428	9·0	7·7	10·7
Others	297	250	254	–	–4·8	–1·7
III Balance of services' uses	5,466	8,057	6,927	7·8	2·5	4·0
IV Balance of trade in goods and services[a]						
Total	5,270	–1,124	3,777			
Trade with abroad	3,421					
Trade with franc area	1,849					

114

Distributive operations and financial balances (in real value terms)

	Millions of 1965 francs		Annual growth rates (per cent)		
	1965	1975	1965/1962	1968/1965	1975/1965
V French operations abroad	16,953	26,058	0·3	2·7	4·4
Social security benefits	775	780	0·3	0·8	0·1
Interest and dividends	1,539	2,628	12·0	6·6	5·5
Transfers	2,444	2,750	8·8	−1·3	1·2
Insurance	152	154	5·6	−10·5	0·1
Various external receipts [b]	8,951	14,237	−7·0	1·6	4·8
Other	3,092	5,509	13·5	7·5	5·9
VI Foreign operations in France	10,962	17,463	0·8	−0·6	4·8
Interest and dividends	2,468	3,482	14·0	5·1	3·5
Transfers	417	1,439	30·0	6·6	13·2
Insurance	65	31	−7·0	−8·0	−7·2
Various external expenditures [b]	6,209	10,047	−5·0	−2·7	4·9
Other	1,803	2,464	3·7	−0·5	3·2
VII Distributive operations balance [d]	5,991	8,595	−3·5	8·2	3·7
With abroad	1,346	3,558			
With franc area	4,645	5,035			
VIII Financing capacity (+) [c] or requirement (−)	721	4,817			
Abroad	−2,074	1,553			
Franc area	2,795	3,264			

[a] II + III − I

[b] External receipts and expenditures come from households (tourism and residents' wage transfers), from public administrations and from financial institutions

[c] The financing capacity (VII − IV) is approximately equal to the balance of payments deficit

[d] V − VI

Source: Table 6, [4], pp. 49−50

Table 4.8

Administrations' expenditures and receipts (in real value) (September 1969 departure account: results)

	Millions of 1965 francs		Annual growth rates (per cent)					
Expenditures	1965	1975	1965/1960	1968/1965	1970/1968	1970/1965	1975/1970	1975/1965
Consumption	17,863	24,653	6·0	3·1	2·4	2·8	3·8	3·3
Gross wages paid	31,982	53,638	9·6	6·5	4·8	5·8	4·8	5·3
Social transfers	80,678	161,921	10·5	6·3	7·3	6·7	7·7	7·2
of which: social security benefits	(69,320)	(146,355)	11·2	6·7	7·8	7·2	8·4	7·8
assistance	(11,358)	(15,566)	6·9	2·9	3·7	3·2	3·2	3·2
Subsidies to enterprises	15,918	29,697	15·7	11·6	−3·1	5·2	7·6	6·4
Subsidies to households	1,207	2,925	13·4	−0·6	12·0	4·3	14·1	9·2
Subsidies between administrations	13,601	36,813	13·2	7·2	7·4	7·3	13·7	10·5
Gross fixed capital formation	15,823	31,017	14·0	8·4	3·9	6·6	7·4	7·0
Other operations on goods and services	744	612	12·9	6·9	5·9	6·5	−10·3	−1·9
Other*	17,607	25,872	−4·5	8·8	0·2	4·3	3·5	3·9
Total	195,423	367,149	8·6	6·7	4·8	6·0	7·0	6·5
Receipts								
Social security contributions	59,641	116,195	11·1	7·2	7·0	7·1	6·7	6·9
Receipts from taxation	112,668	192,959	7·2	4·1	6·4	5·0	6·0	5·5
of which: Direct taxes	(30,568)	(59,231)	6·8	6·5	9·8	7·8	5·8	6·8
on company profits	(9,029)	(12,765)	2·3	1·0	13·4	6·2	0·8	3·5
on personal income	(16,080)	(37,465)	10·1	7·3	9·0	8·0	9·6	8·8
other	(5,459)	(9,000)	6·4	11·4	7·0	9·6	0·6	5·1
Indirect taxes	(82,100)	(133,728)	7·3	3·3	5·0	3·9	6·1	5·0
Subsidies between administrations	13,601	36,813	13·2	7·2	7·4	7·3	13·7	10·5
Various resources†	11,401	14,418	5·8	2·0	4·8	3·1	1·7	2·4
Financing requirement (+) or capacity (−)	−1,888	6,764						
Total	195,423	367,149	8·6	6·7	4·8	6·0	7·0	6·5

Financing requirement (−) or capacity (+) of administrations	Real values in millions of 1965 francs				
	1960	1965	1968	1970	1975
Central government	2,612	5,244	-4,597	5,107	8,262
Local authorities	-1,884	-3,166	-3,761	-3,358	-3,531
Semi-public enterprises (OSPAEs)	-349	-1,114	-1,236	-1,103	-3,096
Social security	1,521	858	1,896	-92	-8,398
Other administrations	10	66	-15	-40	0
Total: all administrations	1,910	1,888	-7,713	594	-6,764

Weight of taxation	1960	1965	1968	1970	1975
Administrations' receipts (central government in brackets) as percentage of PIB	35·2 (24·0)	39·3 (21·9)	39·6 (21·0)	39·9 (22·5)	41·8 (23·5)
Direct taxes	6·8 (6·3)	7·0 (6·4)	7·3 (6·6)	7·8 (7·1)	8·0 (7·4)
Indirect taxes	17·6 (14·5)	18·7 (15·1)	17·8 (14·0)	17·4 (15·0)	18·1 (15·7)
Social security contributions	10·8 (0·3)	13·6 (0·4)	14·5 (0·4)	14·7 (0·4)	15·7 (0·4)
Direct taxes paid by households as a percentage of their consumption	4·6	5·6	6·6	9·0	9·6

* Interest and rents, taxes, war compensations, international co-operation, insurance, external expenditures, various others plus social security contributions

† Interest and rents, international co-operation, insurance, external receipts, various others

Source: Table 13, [4], pp. 54—5

Table 4.9

Equilibrium of savings and investment (in real value terms)
(September 1969 departure account: results)

	Millions of 1965 francs		Annual growth rates (per cent)					
	1965	1975	1965/1960	1968/1965	1970/1968	1970/1965	1975/1970	1975/1965
Gross savings of domestic agencies								
Companies	45,430	83,293	5·1	10·0	9·2	8·2	4·4	6·3
Households	52,848	96,268	8·3	6·6	5·5	6·1	6·3	6·2
of which: CFCFIE[a]	(14,050)	(22,401)	(8·3)	(5·4)	(7·7)	(6·3)	(3·3)	(4·8)
Administrations	18,455	24,865	11·9	−10·1	32·2	4·8	1·3	3·0
Financial institutions	5,989	15,432	6·4	7·3	9·9	8·4	11·5	9·9
Insurance indemnities on capital goods (IICG)	2,181	4,827	17·0	7·8	9·0	8·3	8·3	8·3
Total domestic savings	124,796	224,685	7·5	4·8	10·9	7·2	5·7	6·0
Gross capital formation [b]								
Non-financial enterprises	84,714	151,949	8·3	5·8	9·0	7·0	5·0	6·0
Households	23,381	44,390	14·4	5·3	7·4	6·2	7·0	6·6
Administrations	16,567	31,629	14·0	8·4	3·9	6·6	6·8	6·7
Financial institutions	962	1,537	9·4	6·2	6·1	6·2	3·4	4·8
Total	125,624	229,505	10·1	6·0	7·8	6·7	5·6	6·2
External financing capacity	721	4,817						

	1960	1965	1968	1970	1975
Financing capacity (+) or requirement (−) (millions of 1965 francs)					
Non-financial enterprises	−19,431	−23,160	−24,881	−29,155	−41,633
Households	13,515	14,252	18,806	19,010	26,564
Administrations	1,910	1,888	−7,714	594	−6,764
Financial institutions	4,491	6,299	7,721	9,303	16,712
Exterior	−485	721	6,068	248	4,817
of which: abroad	(−4,371)	(−2,074)	(3,695)	(−1,423)	(1,553)
franc area	(3,886)	(2,795)	(2,373)	(1,671)	(3,264)
Rate of self-financing (per cent)[c]					
All enterprises	67·3	70·2			69·6
1 Agriculture	81·0	73·8			56·7
2 Agricultural and food industries	62·9	72·7			75·1
3 Energy	65·2	63·0			60·0
4 Industry	74·6	79·5			75·9
5 Transport and telecommunications	76·5	86·0			77·5
6 Housing	14·2	15·6			50·1
7 Building and public works, services, and commerce	74·1	72·8			72·8
Savings rate (per cent)					
Domestic savings rate[d]	26·4	28·0	27·9	29·8	29·7
Household savings rate[e]	14·5	15·6	16·1	16·1	16·8

[a] Contribution to the financing of capital formation by individual entrepreneurs

[b] Gross fixed capital formation + changes in stocks + purchases and sales of land

[c] (Savings + CFCFIE) / (GFCF + changes in stocks)

[d] Domestic savings (excluding IICG) / PIB

[e] Household savings (including IICG) / (consumption + savings)

Source: Tables 15 and 16, [4], p. 57

Table 4.10

Change in nominal prices

(September 1969 departure account: results)

	Annual growth rates (per cent)					
	1965/1960	1968/1965	1970/1968	1970/1965	1975/1970	1975/1965
Nominal prices of the aggregates						
Consumption	3·5	3·5	5·9	4·5	3·5	4·0
of which: households	3·5	3·6	5·9	4·5	3·5	4·0
administrations	2·7	2·5	4·9	3·5	3·3	3·4
Investment (GFCF)	3·9	2·5	5·9	3·9	3·5	3·7
of which: productive	3·2	1·9	5·9	3·5	2·1	2·8
housing	5·5	3·5	6·3	4·6	6·0	5·3
administrations	4·0	2·8	5·5	3·9	4·1	4·0
Exports + services' uses balance	1·1	0·5	4·6	2·1	0·9	1·5
Imports	0·7	0·5	4·9	2·2	0	1·1
Gross domestic production (PIB)	3·6	3·3	5·8	4·3	3·5	3·9
Nominal production prices						
1 Agriculture	3·2					2·8
2 Agricultural and food industries	3·9					4·7
3 Energy	−0·2					1·6
4 Industry	2·6					2·4
5 Transport and telecommunications	2·6					4·7
6 Housing	10·2					9·2
7 Building and public works, services, and commerce	4·2					4·5

Source: Table 7, [4], p. 51

We give two of the variants in this section to illustrate the sensitivity of the central account to changes in assumptions and uncertain statistical estimates. The first variant involves a lower rate of growth in import prices, simulating more intense foreign competition. The rate is reduced from 1·1 per cent p.a. to 0·8 per cent p.a. and leads to the new situation shown in column 1 of Table 4.11. From the theory of a competitioned economy, on which the model is based, industrial prices follow import prices and their growth also decreases by three points (from 2·4 to 2·1 per cent p.a.). This leads to slower growth in the overall price level, but it also induces industrial enterprises to lower their rate of self-financing in an attempt to cut their costs. They are not able fully to compensate for the tighter financial situation, however, and the result is a cutback in the rate of growth of production in the industrial sector. As a result, overall growth is cut, but consumption benefits from the reduced import prices of industrial goods and the lower general price level. Consequently imports increase, exports are squeezed by slower industrial growth (although there is some response by French exporters), and the trade balance deteriorates.

In the second variant shown in Table 4.11, an improving financial situation and a reduction in the pressure of international competition are reflected in a reduction of enterprises' *desired* rate of self-financing. The desired rate of self-financing is the rate that enterprises would achieve if there were no pressure from international competition. A reduction in the desired rate means that enterprises are more confident of finding external financing, and thus achieve more investment with a given amount of self-finance. This leads to faster industrial growth (6·5 per cent p.a. compared with 6·4 per cent in the departure account), and all the benefits for the rest of the economy that such a situation brings: more output, more employment, higher wages, more consumption, and a lower financial requirement on the part of the administrations.

4.3   Uncertainty variants

We have already attempted (in Chapter 1) to draw a distinction between sensitivity variants and uncertainty variants (a full list of uncertainty variants is given in Table 1.3), and variants have also been discussed elsewhere in Chapters 3 and 4. But the presentation of numerical examples of actual variants provides the opportunity to make the distinction really clear. A sensitivity variant is nothing more than a straightforward, mechanical sensitivity analysis, the term being used as it is in mathe-

Table 4.11

Results of sensitivity variants on self-financing and foreign producers' prices
(variants accompanying the September 1969 departure account)

	Variant 1 Lower import prices		Departure account (summarised)		Variant 2 Lower desired industrial rate of self-financing	
	1975/1965	1975/1970	1975/1965	1975/1970	1975/1965	1975/1970
Growth						
Rate of growth of **PIB** (per cent p.a.)	5·37	5·34	5·4	5·4	5·45	5·5
Rate of growth of household consumption	5·18	5·56	5·1	5·3	5·2	5·55
Number of people looking for a job (in 1975)	415,000		395,000		360,000	
Wages and prices						
Increase in the general price level (per cent p.a.)	3·7	3·1	3·9	3·5	3·9	3·5
Increase in the average hourly wage:						
nominal (per cent p.a.)	7·34	6·28	7·5	6·6	7·65	6·9
real (per cent p.a.)	3·54	3·18	3·5	3·1	3·65	3·4
Exterior (in 1975)						
Trade balance (10^9 1965 francs)	−5·8		−1·1		−1·4	
Trade balance (10^9 1975 francs)	3·7		5·5		5·4	
Financing capacity (BoP deficit) (10^9 1975 francs)	8·3		7·1		7·5	

Administrations (in 1975)						
Financing requirement (10^9 1975 francs)		12·8		9·9		8·9
Industrial sector (exposed)						
Rate of growth of production (per cent p.a.)	6·28	–	6·4	–	6·5	–
Imports (10^9 1965 francs) in 1975		116·0		109·2		–
Exports (10^9 1965 francs) in 1975		114·4		112·3		–
Trade balance (10^9 1965 francs)		–		3·1		2·8
Employment in industry		–		5,145,000		5,190,000
Rate of growth of industrial production price (per cent p.a.)	2·1	–	2·4	–	2·4	–
Rate of growth of import price (per cent p.a.)	*0·8*	–	1·1	–		–
Rate of growth of export price (per cent p.a.)	1·4	–	1·4	–		–
Actual rate of self-financing (per cent) in 1975		75·4		75·9		*73·0*

The figures in italics in the two variant columns show the key variables defining the variant: the import price is fixed *a priori* in Variant 1; the desired rate of self-financing is reduced to 78 per cent (from 81 per cent in the departure account) in Variant 2

Source: [4], pp. 37, 43

matical programming, for example.[7] Its purpose is to demonstrate the effect of a small change in one parameter on the overall solution of the model. It would be possible to carry out over 3,500 such analyses in the case of FIFI, but a great many of these would not be very meaningful in the sense of shedding light on possible ways of solving the problems revealed by the departure account. An uncertainty variant, on the other hand, is something that attempts to go a little further and deeper than just a mechanical sensitivity analysis. Carried out properly, an uncertainty variant would require not only changes in the relevant parameters but also additional relationships adding to the model to take account of the linkages between the particular uncertainty involved and the mechanisms of the economy. It is not very easy to do this in a planning process that puts a premium on time and the use of a tool that is supposed to supply variants quickly. To add several equations to a model that has already been programmed and set up on the computer requires even greater sophistication on the programming side than the French achieved.

The only way out of this difficulty, given the constraint of not wishing to have to reprogramme the model to solve every variant, is to try to approximate the effects that the added equations would have had by making changes in parameters in other constraints that already exist in the model. This is what was done in each of the uncertainty variants: besides making allowances for the primary effects of a change in a particular exogenous variable or behavioural characteristic, an attempt was also made to estimate the indirect, induced effects and to make those changes in other parameters which best represented these induced effects. This can be illustrated by referring to the first variant, the results for which are listed in abbreviated form[8] in Table 4.12: the variant involves the movement of agricultural working population to other sectors. There is an assumption in the departure account about the annual rate of decrease of the agricultural working population: it is assumed to be 3·8 per cent p.a., which is the observed rate of decrease between 1962 and 1968. The variant described in Table 4.12 includes an increase in this rate, so that there are 200,000 more agricultural workers 'on the labour market' in 1975 than the figure allowed for in the departure account.

The primary effect is thus a reduction in the tightness of the labour market, and the induced effects are: (a) increased competitiveness in the industrial sector (because of lower wage costs); (b) accelerated expansion; and (c) slower price increases. These mechanisms are readily apparent from the description of the exposed sector in a competitioned economy in Chapter 3. In this case, therefore, since FIFI is based on the competitioned economy, all the effects (primary and induced) are *in-*

124

cluded, and the induced ones do *not* have to be approximated by any changes in parameters additional to the initial one involving the non-agricultural working population. But if any of the induced effects had been external to the model, further parameter changes would have been required. This particular variant thus reduces to a sensitivity variant, and indeed, many uncertainty variants have this property. But the important point is that their conception is different, and their practical implementation can involve simultaneous changes in several parameters. They constitute the second stage in the transformation of a mechanical sensitivity analysis into a multi-policy synthesising variant.

The results of variant 1 are interesting because they highlight the criticisms that the agricultural participants made of the FIFI model and which we discuss in the next chapter. All the five main equilibria, except employment, are benefited by the variant, and it is therefore an attractive possibility. But there is another side to the story which the variant is not able to tell; we look at this again in Chapter 5.

The other three variants considered here all involve the controversial wage–price–unemployment relation included in the model. This too is discussed in more detail later because it has come under a lot of criticism. Many participants (and others) feel that it is too simple in that only prices and unemployment have an explicit effect on wages, all the other effects being 'concealed' in the econometric relation's constant term which, as a consequence, is larger:

$$TXH = 7 \cdot 2 + 0 \cdot 39 \, PG - 0 \cdot 664 \, TCHO_{75} \qquad (4.1)$$

where[9] TXH = average annual rate of growth in the nominal hourly wage rate (in per cent);

PG = average annual rate of growth of the PIB price (i.e. of the general price level) in per cent;

$TCHO_{75}$ = rate of unemployment in 1975 (in per cent).

The simple answer to the criticism is that most other large macro-economic models applied to western-type countries have used this sort of relationship, and French data fits reasonably well. However, the departure account is very sensitive to the three coefficients in (4.1): variant 2 replaces (4.1) by

$$TXH = 7 \cdot 8 + 0 \cdot 39 \, PG - 0 \cdot 664 \, TCHO_{75} \qquad (4.2)$$

while variants 3 and 4 consider, respectively

$$TXH = 7 \cdot 28 + 0 \cdot 39 \, PG - 0 \cdot 954 \, TCHO_{75} \qquad (4.3)$$

and
$$TXH = 7 \cdot 47 + 0 \cdot 27 \, PG - 0 \cdot 664 \, TCHO_{75} \qquad (4.4)$$

Table 4.12

Results of uncertainty variants on the agricultural exodus and the wage–price–unemployment relationship (variants submitted to the CEGF in November 1969)

	Departure account	Differential effects of Variant 1*	Variant 2	Variant 3	Variant 4
Growth					
Rate of growth of PIB (per cent p.a.)	5·4	+0·1	5·2	5·5	5·4
Rate of growth of household consumption (per cent p.a.)	5·1	–	5·1	5·1	5·1
Number of people seeking work (1975)	395,000	+32,000	527,000	316,000	348,000
Wages and prices					
Increase in the general price level (per cent p.a.)	3·9	–0·1	4·0	3·8	3·9
Increase in the average hourly wage:					
nominal (per cent p.a.)	7·5	–0·1	7·7	7·4	7·4
real (per cent p.a.)	3·5	–	3·6	3·5	3·5
Increase in the average per capita agricultural GIIE:†					
nominal (per cent p.a.)		+1·45			
real (per cent p.a.)		+1·35			
Exterior (in 1975)					
Trade balance (10^9 1965 francs)	–1·1	+3·0	–6·5	2·0	0·7
Trade balance (10^9 1975 francs)	5·5	+3·8	–1·5	9·7	8·0
Financing capacity (BoP deficit) (10^9 1975 francs)	7·1	–4·0	14·5	2·7	4·5

Administrations

Financing requirement (10⁹ 1975 francs) in 1975	9·9	−2·6	15·0	6·9	8·2

Industrial sector

Production:					
rate of growth (per cent p.a.)	6·4	+0·2	6·0	6·6	6·5
level (10⁹ 1965 francs) in 1975	325·5	+5·9	314·6	331·8	329·2
Imports (10⁹ 1965 francs) in 1975	109·2	−1·0	111·1	108·1	108·6
Exports (10⁹ 1965 francs) in 1975	112·3	+2·1	108·6	114·5	113·6
Household consumption (10⁹ 1965 francs) in 1975	172·9	+0·2	172·6	173·1	173·0
Trade balance (10⁹ 1965 francs) in 1975	3·1	+3·1	−2·5	6·4	5·0
Employment (1975)	5,145,000	+98,000	4,970,000	525,000	5,210,000
Industrial production price‡	127·3	−0·3	128·3	126·7	127·0
Export price‡	115·4	–	115·4	115·4	115·4
Import price‡	111·7	−0·3	112·6	111·3	111·5
Actual rate of self-financing (per cent) in 1975	75·9	–	75	77	76

All per cent p.a. rates cover the 1965–1975 period

* The agricultural variant is with respect to an account similar to the departure account, but not the actual one represented in column 1. The differential effects are valid, but to avoid confusion neither the variant figures nor the similar departure account figures are given. The other columns refer to absolute values, not differential ones

† GIIE = gross income of individual entrepreneurs

‡ 1975 index (1965 = 100)

Source: [4], pp. 94–5, 134–9

127

These are derived by changing each of the three coefficients, one in each case, by one standard deviation (the constant term changes in (4.3) and (4.4) as well as the other coefficients because it depends on the base year values of *PG* and *TCHO*, so that if their coefficient changes it changes too). The results are, in each case, significantly different, particularly with respect to the labour market equilibrium, the external account, and the public finance balance. Although, as an uncertainty variant, the changes in coefficients may be justified (i.e. they can be interpreted meaningfully in terms of enterprise behaviour), as a sensitivity analysis the only conclusion one can draw from the results is that more work needs to be done on this relationship.

4.4   Policy analysis variants

Having shown the sensitivity of the departure account to mechanical changes in parameters, and then tried to analyse the direct and induced effects of changes in parameters about which there is uncertainty, the third stage in variant analysis is to relax the assumption about conventional policy continuing up to 1975, and, for the first time, attempt to adapt economic policy to the by now readily apparent 1975 problems. To begin with, only single economic policy changes are considered, multiple policy changes being evaluated in the fourth and last stage (see next section).

We consider three single policy variants in this section (a larger list is given in Table 1.3). The first one concerns the gross fixed capital formation of public administrations (i.e. expenditure on new social overhead capital), which is assumed to grow at an average rate of 7·0 per cent p.a. in the departure account. This rate is rather low if it is compared with the average rate over a longer period, and the revised assumption in variant 1 in Table 4.13 is a continuation of the rate observed between 1962 and 1970: 9·0 per cent p.a. This effectively means an increase in public administrations' demand of 4 milliard (i.e. 4×10^9) francs at 1975 prices, a quarter of this going to consumption and the remainder to gross fixed capital formation. With these exogenous parameter changes, the results are:

(a)   to increase global production (and especially that of the sector containing building and public works);
(b)   and hence to increase employment and wages;
(c)   the increased domestic demand in sector 7 leads to higher prices there, this effect also being transmitted to the general price level;

128

(d) thus, costs are increased in the exposed sector too and this gives a comparative advantage to foreign producers, so that imports rise and the balance of payments situation deteriorates.

The second variant generates similar reactions, but this time by encouraging households to invest more in housing. The departure account assumes rates of growth in household's gross fixed capital formation of 5·7 per cent p.a. between 1965 and 1970, and 3·1 per cent p.a. between 1970 and 1975. Variant 2 in Table 4.13 assumes that the rate in the first five-year period should be maintained throughout the Sixth Plan, a policy that requires increased subsidies and transfers to housholds. A particular problem that arises in this sort of variant is that an analysis of financial markets is required to judge the possibility of housholds acquiring the necessary loans to invest in housing: as we point out in several places (and discuss mainly in Chapter 10), the Sixth Plan version of the FIFI model did not have this facility.

The third variant shows the effects of a policy designed to increase competition in the sheltered sector, which in this case is taken to be sector 7 (building and public works, services and commerce). This sector is so heterogenous, however, that it was not possible to define the *means* of the policy, and so no estimate of its costs could be made. Because of this, the variant is rather crude, the numerical changes made in various parameters and exogenous variables not being based on detailed analyses. This policy was tranmitted to the rest of the economy by means of five changes in the departure account assumptions: productivity in sector 7 was assumed to grow 0·1 per cent p.a. faster; commercial price mark-ups were decreased slightly; the number of individual entrepreneurs (self-employed) in the sector was assumed to fall by 40,000 with a consequent increase of 20,000 in the number of wage earners; the desired rate of self-financing was reduced by two points; and the sliding wage coefficient [11] reduced by 0·2 per cent p.a. The results are generally beneficial, and give a further illustration of how the equilibrium mechanisms in the model work.

4.5   Policy synthesising variants

Towards the end of 1969, the first attempts were made to pull together the various analyses and decentralised studies that were going on in the Plan Commissions and administrative work groups. This eventually led to improved central accounts (such as the intermediate account and others

Table 4.13

Results of policy analysis variants on social overhead capital, housing and the sheltered sector
(submitted to the CEGF in November 1969)

| | Departure account | | Differential effects of | | | | | |
| | | | Variant 1 | | Variant 2 | | Variant 3 | |
	1965/ 1975	1970/ 1975	1965/ 1975	1970/ 1975	1965/ 1975	1970/ 1975	1965/ 1975	1970/ 1975
Growth								
Rate of growth of PIB (per cent p.a.)	5·4	5·4	+0·01	+0·02	+0·03	+0·06	+0·05	+0·1
Rate of growth of household consumption (per cent p.a.)	5·1	5·4	−0·01	−0·02	+0·04	+0·08	+0·02	+0·04
Number of people seeking work (1975)	395,000		−8,000		−21,000		−16,000	
Wages and prices								
Increase in the general level of prices	3·9	3·5	+0·04	+0·08	+0·05	+0·10	−0·13	−0·26
Increase in the average hourly wage:								
nominal (per cent p.a.)	7·5	6·6	+0·03	+0·06	+0·09	+0·18	0	0
real (per cent p.a.)	3·5	3·1	−0·01	−0·02	+0·04	+0·08	+0·13	+0·26
Exterior (in 1975)								
Trade balance (10^9 1965 francs)	−1·1		−2·4		−3·7		+1·6	
Trade balance (10^9 1975 francs)	5·5		−3·0		−4·5		+2·2	
Financing capacity (BoP deficit) (10^9 1975 francs)	7·1		+3·15		+4·8		−2·5	

Administrations (in 1975)				
Financing requirement (10⁹ 1975 francs)	−9·9	+2·6	−1·6	+1·2
Central government financing requirement	0·2	+1·2	—	—
Local authorities financing requirement	5·2	0·4	—	—
Weight of taxation (percentage of PIB)	41·82	+0·24	+0·09	—
Industrial sector				
Rate of growth of output	6·4	−0·07	−0·09	+0·1
Imports (10⁹ 1965 francs) in 1975	109·2	+1·6	+2·2	−0·7
Exports (10⁹ 1965 francs) in 1975	112·3	−0·8	−1·4	+1·1
Production price index (1965 = 100)	127·3	+0·03	—	−0·01
Export price index (1965 = 100)	115·4	0	—	—
Import price index (1965 = 100)	111·7	+0·03	—	—
Actual rate of self-financing in 1975	75·9	−0·5	—	+0·2
Building and public works, services, commerce				
Production price index (1965 = 100)	154·5	—	—	−3·2
Actual rate of self-financing (per cent) in 1975	72·8	—	—	−1·8

Note: a dash (−) means 'data not given in source' (see also note 10)

Source: [4], pp. 163, 187, 189

Table 4.14

Results of a public finance policy synthesising variant (submitted to the CEGF in December 1969)

	Partial effects of				Total effect
	lower VAT and income tax receipts	increased employers' social security contributions	increased employees' social security contributions	lower social security benefits	
External financing capacity (BoP deficit)	+7·2	−0·8	−1·1	−3·5	+1·8
Numbers seeking jobs (thousands)	−45	+15	+3	+7	−20
PIB growth	+0·18	−0·05	−0·03	−0·05	+0·05
Growth of prices	−0·20	0	0	−0·05	−0·25
Growth of real wages	+0·43	−0·1	−0·03	−0·05	+0·25
Weight of taxation (*ex post*)	−1·05	+0·15	+0·22	−0·15	−0·83
Administrations' financing requirement	+13·0	−1·65	−2·2	−4·05	+5·10

Source: Table 5, [4], p. 199

described in Figure 1.2 and section 1.3), but the initial synthesis was carried out with reference to the original departure account and involved the use of the fourth type of variant, known as policy synthesising variants.

Many of these variants focused on the disequilibrium in public finances (see Table 1.6). This lack of balance was created in the departure account by extrapolating expenditures according to past trends and keeping receipts low by maintaining the 1969 taxation legislation through to 1975. Thus, company tax, value added tax, and social security contributions all remained at 1969 rates, and a further reduction in total receipts was brought about by linking income tax to prices so that the burden on households remained roughly the same in 1975 as in 1970 (see Table 4.8). The variant considered here attempts to trace the effects of a policy that is designed to correct the imbalances shown in the third block of Table 4.8: to match central government receipts to expenditures, and to put right the structural imbalance in the social security account. Other variants consider alternative ways of doing this, but the method in this variant is to keep the weight of central government taxation at 1969 levels (the fourth block of Table 4.8 shows that this weight does increase during the period of the Plan, according to the departure account), and to balance the social security system by increasing contributions and reducing benefits. Accordingly, receipts from value added tax are reduced by 8 milliard 1975 francs, receipts from income tax by 4 milliard, employers' and employees' social security contributions raised by 3 milliard each, and benefits reduced by 6 milliard. The individual and overall effects are shown in Table 4.14. Rather surprisingly perhaps, the financing requirement of administrations is made even larger, mainly due to induced effects, and this clearly illustrates the advantages of using a large macro-economic model in variant form.

An assessment of just how valuable variants like this one and the others we have considered in this chapter really are depends, however, on an assessment of the realism of the model that produced them. The views of several planning participants on this and related matters are discussed in the next chapter.

Notes

[1] The main source on the departure account and the variants drawn up between October and December 1969 is [4]. The three central accounts elaborated in February–March 1970 are in [91]. The central account constructed after the options had been voted by Parliament in the summer of 1970 is available in [92]: it is known as the '4 August' account, and formed the basis for the Plan Commissions' work in the autumn of 1970. The variants constructed from this central account and listed in Figure 1.2 were not published to my knowledge, but the synthesising process which occurred at the end of 1970 was assisted by the structural analyses (or patterns) published in [17]. After the Plan itself had been approved midway through 1971, projections associated with the Plan were established by the CGP and published in [93] and [94]. Literature on disaggregated analyses is referred to in note 1 at the end of Chapter 6.

[2] The various types of economic budget and national account are described in [101].

[3] Presented in the Economic and Financial Report in [95].

[4] Some of the results are presented in volume terms (i.e. at 1965 prices), thus incorporating changes in quantity and quality. Others are in nominal value terms (i.e. at 1975 prices), and yet a third category are given in real value terms, which means nominal values corrected for increases in the PIB price.

[5] The first time that a projection of the financial operations table (TOF) was drawn up was early in 1970, using the reference account (see

Fig. 1.1). It was only after this 'reference TOF' became available that the financial implications of the analysis could be evaluated. Just as central accounts were successively updated and made more relevant and appropriate to the expected 1975 situation, so the TOF was successively reprojected and improved.

6 Notes 22–26 at the end of Chapter 1 give the details on where to find more information about the variants considered in the rest of this chapter, and others which are not considered. Variants have also been published and discussed elsewhere: see [96], [97], [98], and there is a general presentation of the variant concept in [99].

7 There are many different types of sensitivity analysis that can be carried out in mathematical programming, and even more references on the subject. A good, uncomplicated approach can be found in [100], Chapter 5.

8 The complete results of a variant involve several thousand numbers ([4], p. 89). The Programmes Division of the INSEE hold full details of all variants, and interested readers should consult them at the address given in note 2 at the end of Chapter 1.

9 The wage–price–unemployment relationship is derived in detail in Chapter 5.

10 The figures quoted in the tables in this chapter are accurate to a certain degree. I have not consulted the original variants, nor cross-checked any of the results with sources other than [4]. The reason for this is that the variants are presented here for their pedagogic value, not as primary data sources supporting arguments about particular policy choices. As a consequence, there are rather more gaps in some of the tables than might otherwise be the case, simply because there are a number of obvious misprints in [4] which I have not spent a great deal of time correcting. I have left a gap rather than perpetuate the error of the misprint or seek an alternative value.

11 Average wage rates in each of the sectors distinguished by FIFI are calculated from the overall economy average (calculated in the wage–price–unemployment relationship) by applying sliding wage coefficients which reflect the situations in different sectors with respect to overtime working, special bonuses, structural differences, etc.

References

[91]   Commissariat Général du Plan, 'Rapport de la Commission de l'Économie Générale et du Financement au cours de la 1ʳᵉ phase'

(Report of the CEGF during the first phase), Appendix to the Report on the Sixth Plan options, 1970, pp. 47–64.

[92] INSEE (Programmes Division), 'Compte du 4 août 1970 associé aux options du VIe Plan' (The 4 August 1970 account associated with the Sixth Plan options), mimeographed paper, September 1970.

[93] Commissariat Général du Plan, *Projections économiques pour 1975 associées au VIe Plan* (Economic projections of 1975 associated with the Sixth Plan), La Documentation Française, Paris, July 1971.

[94] INSEE and DP, 'Rapport technique sur les projections associées au VIe Plan (Technical report on the projections associated with the Sixth Plan), *Les Collections de l'INSEE*, série C, nos 24–25, June 1973, 379 pp.

[95] DP, 'Comptes prévisionnels de l'année 1969 et principales hypothèses économiques pour 1970' (Forecast accounts for 1969 and principal economic assumptions for 1970), *Statistiques et Études Financières*, Série Rouge, October 1969.

[96] INSEE, 'Variantes de politique économique établies avec le modèle FIFI' (Economic policy variants constructed with the FIFI model), *Économie et Statistique* no. 20, February 1971, pp. 37–43.

[97] R. Courbis, 'Comportements financiers et developpement économique' (Financial behaviour and economic development), *Économie et Statistique* no. 12, May 1970, pp. 27–44.

[98] R. Courbis, 'Tarifs publics et équilibre économique' (Public tariffs and economic equilibrium), *Économie et Statistique* no. 30, January 1972, pp. 19–27.

[99] M. Aglietta and R. Courbis, 'Un outil pour le Plan: le modèle FIFI' (The FIFI model: a tool for the Plan), *Économie et Statistique* no. 1, May 1969, pp. 45–65.

[100] H. Wagner, *Principles of Operations Research*, Prentice-Hall, Englewood Cliffs, 1969.

[101] D. Liggins, 'The models used in French short term macroeconomic forecasting' in *Economics of Planning* (forthcoming).

135

5 Criticisms of FIFI and its Role in the Planning Process

> Exaggerated use of FIFI at the time of the preparation of the Sixth Plan may have created certain problems that the Planning Authority has tried to solve for the Seventh Plan.
>
> Bernard Ullmo, [124], p. 12.

> The FIFI model has made us more demanding and given us an appetite for more rigour in the knowledge of the factual domain that encompasses it.
>
> Alain Bienaymé, [1], p. 81.

> OR is not politically neutral. It can ... contribute solely to the development of rationality in executive and administrative decision-making, augmenting still further the supremacy of these branches within the political system.
>
> Jacques Lesourne, [123], p. 14.

One consequence of using the FIFI model so much in the open preparation phases of the Sixth Plan is that there is no shortage of views and opinions on it. Almost everyone, from administrator, planner and technician, to trade unionist, academic economist and ordinary man in the street, seems to have either put forward or been asked for his opinion. We try to give a representative sample of these views in this chapter, distinguishing technical and theoretical criticisms of the model itself from more philosophical and ideological views on the role of models and technical instruments in the planning process. The technical and theoretical criticisms considered in the first section focus on the emphasis given to international competition in the model, the key role played by the Phillips wage—price—unemployment relationship, and the way in which capital accumulation and productivity are handled. We choose these three particular aspects because most of the criticisms seem to have been directed at

137

them; we briefly refer to other problems towards the end of the chapter. In the second section we examine the effect of the model on some of the main policy choices of the Plan, discovering that there is a limit beyond which no model, however well formulated, can go. Then, progress is reported on work designed to answer some of the criticisms about the model, again looking mainly at the three aspects referred to earlier. Finally, we look beyond the immediate problems of the model, and assess the possible future of such techniques in the French planning process, highlighting the areas in which new developments, some of which have already started, are needed.

5.1 Criticisms on the theoretical foundation and structure of the model

As a way of approaching the three main problems of international competition, wages, and capital accumulation, it is interesting to consider first the criticisms made by Phan and others[1] on the overall structure of the model. Phan presents his argument in the context of the following two-sector equilibrium model;

$$(1 - i_{11}) \, \overline{p}_1 - i_{12} p_2 - \omega_1 w - a_1 \, (\overline{p}_1 k_{11} + p_2 k_{12}) = 0 \qquad (5.1)$$

$$(1 - i_{22}) \, \overline{p}_2 - i_{21} \overline{p}_1 - \omega_2 w - a_2 \, (\overline{p}_1 k_{21} + p_2 k_{22}) = 0 \qquad (5.2)$$

$$w = \mu_0 + \mu_1 \overline{p}_1 + \mu_2 p_2 - \mu_3 u \qquad (5.3)$$

$$u = \frac{1}{1 + x} \left(1 - \frac{N}{\overline{N}_d} \right) \qquad (5.4)$$

$$Q_1 + M_1 = (i_{11} + k_{11}) \, Q_1 + (i_{21} + k_{21}) \, Q_2 + \frac{\gamma_1 R}{\overline{p}_1} \qquad (5.5)$$

$$Q_2 = (i_{12} + k_{12}) \, Q_1 + (i_{22} + k_{22}) \, Q_2 + \frac{\gamma_2 R}{p_2} + \overline{E}_2 \qquad (5.6)$$

$$R = Nw \qquad (5.7)$$

$$N_1 = \omega_1 Q_1 \qquad (5.8)$$

$$N_2 = \omega_2 Q_2 \qquad (5.9)$$

$$N = N_1 + N_2 \qquad (5.10)$$

where sector 1 is the exposed sector; sector 2 is sheltered; there are no taxes (unlike the model we used in section 3.3, where f and j represented the tax system); there is intermediate consumption, which is handled by the i_{11}, i_{12}, i_{21}, i_{22} coefficients (there was no intermediate consumption in the section 3.3 model); and there is now a price effect in the wage equation (5.3) (compare equation 3.38) and an activity rate parameter in (5.4). Apart from these small changes, which do not affect the overall properties of the system, Phan's model is merely the two-sector version (with some equation reduction already carried out) of Courbis' one-sector model[2] which we used in Chapter 3. By seeking a solution that satisfies non-negativity conditions on w, p_2, u, and Q_2, Phan shows that the following inequalities must be satisfied for a solution to exist (asterisks on variables indicate the equilibrium values of the variables):

$$i_{11} + a_1 k_{11} < 1 \tag{5.11}$$

$$i_{22} + a_2 k_{22} < 1 \tag{5.12}$$

$$\frac{1 - (i_{11} + a_1 k_{11})}{i_{21} + a_2 k_{21}} > \frac{i_{12} + a_1 k_{12}}{1 - (i_{22} + a_2 k_{22})} \tag{5.13}$$

$$w^* \leqslant \mu_0 + \mu_1 \bar{p}_1 + \mu_2 p_2{}^* \tag{5.14}$$

$$\frac{N^*}{\omega_2} > \frac{\dfrac{\gamma_2 R^*}{p_2{}^*} + \bar{E}_2}{1 - (i_{22} + k_{22})} \tag{5.15}$$

This shows the *interdependency* of the parameters and coefficients, but, as we have seen in Chapter 4, many of the equations in FIFI are estimated *independently*. Even so, it is still possible to find a set of parameters that satisfy (5.11) – (5.15), but the real point of Phan's criticism is then made: what structural forces caused the parameters to take on such values? Phan goes on to show that not only must the parameters satisfy certain numerical conditions, they must also be known to a high degree of accuracy, and in some cases (particularly the wage–price–unemployment relationship, which we discuss further below) this is not so; the results of some of the variants considered in Chapter 4 confirm that significant changes in the departure account were obtained by varying coefficients and parameters, in some cases within their 95 per cent confidence interval.

It is possible then to criticise the model on structural grounds, but it is the model's basic assumptions that have attracted more attention.[3] We begin with the second assumption discussed in section 3.1, concerning international competition: firms in the exposed sector have their prices determined by more competitive foreign producers. This is one of the key assumptions of the competitioned economy theory, and it dominates industrial policy and employment policy in the Sixth Plan. As we have seen, it supports policies that are far from traditional, and as Courbis himself states in several of his papers, many people refused to accept the 'new' policy recommendations because they did not understand the underlying theory. But even those who did know of the theory and perhaps accepted it in the late sixties, now begin to doubt whether foreign competition acts in this way. The seeds of doubt were sown by the August 1969 franc devaluation: what happens immediately after a devaluation? How quickly do foreign prices and exposed sector prices get back together again? Do the competitioned economy mechanisms cease to function during the recovery period?

And on top of these doubts about the devaluation effect, the persistence of inflation in the industrialised economies has weakened the idea that competition is best transmitted to the economy through prices in the exposed sector. This criticism, it should be pointed out, has gathered adherents since the event (i.e. the Plan) and so it is not really a valid criticism of the competitioned economy theory; the people making the criticism feel that perhaps the problem is now a different one, and so a different theory is required (i.e. the FIFI model was probably well founded, at least with respect to this particular part of the theory, and able to handle the problems of France in the late sixties, but if the model is to be used to prepare the Seventh Plan, then account must be taken of the new conditions facing France, some of which weaken the imposed foreign price assumption in the exposed sector). There is now talk of an 'autonomous economy', reflecting the idea that there is an autonomous inflation factor which tends to produce the inverse action: local increases in costs in exposed sectors get transmitted to neighbouring regions and countries.

The feeling that competition was not best handled through prices was present before the autonomous economy idea, however. The CEGF Technical Group's report [1] feels that the whole structure of the model can be questioned on the basis of this one assumption (and the one on wages, which we deal with below). The point was made in the group that price competition acts only through common products, and not through new ones. Competition via the nature of the product opens up a whole new set of problems, leading into the difficult field of multinational enterprises: clearly, it is argued, flows of products between different branches of the same enterprise in different countries are mainly complementary, not competitive. One can understand why FIFI chose not to try to deal with multinational enterprises, but the point is nevertheless a valid one that sector 4 (industry) in the model is very large and heterogeneous, and perhaps an alternative sector breakdown might have been more beneficial:[4] The heterogeneity of the sector in fact makes it prohibitively difficult to carry out empirical analysis to test the validity of the foreign price assumption for France. But Phan quotes the work of Aukrust on the Norwegian economy, which is far more exposed than France: '... the assumption of an adaptation of Norwegian prices to import prices in the exposed sector has not been confirmed by a comparison made annually over the period 1961−68'.[5]

Two final further criticisms on this aspect of the model make it apparent that whatever the original merits of the foreign price assumption, modifications will have to be made, either inside the model or outside it, by linking it to other analyses, if it is to be effectively used in the preparation of the Seventh Plan. First, the competitioned economy is a national concept, considering France as subjected to foreign competition on a world scale. But recent events have made it clear that two levels (which existed before, but not with such relevance) now have to be distinguished: France within the European Community, and the European Community within the industrial super-league, competing against the Americans and the Japanese. Uncertainty at both levels needs to be reflected in whatever tool is to be used to handle international competition.

The second major target for the model's critics has been the wage−price−unemployment relationship. There is a vast literature on the subject,[6] falling into three particular categories: that deriving from econometricians, trade unions, and economic theorists, with the last category firing the most shots. We shall look at the views of each category in turn. It should be clear to the reader by now what the argument is about: we considered in Chapter 4 several variants that involved this relationship, and the one- and two-sector models described in Chapter 3 and the beginning of this section both include versions of the relationship, which is usually referred to as 'the Phillips relationship' because it follows the link between nominal wages and labour market tensions first statistically observed by Phillips in 1958.

Beginning with the econometricians, reasonable results were obtained when French data were first fitted to the relationship; for example, Courbis gives the following equation, based on 1957−1969 annual data:[7]

$$TXH_t = 8{\cdot}03 + 0{\cdot}55\ TPG_t - 0{\cdot}21\ TPG_{t-1} - 3{\cdot}25\ \frac{D}{N_t} + 1{\cdot}9\ RAP_t$$
$$\underset{(0{\cdot}08)}{}\quad \underset{(0{\cdot}08)}{}\quad \underset{(1{\cdot}41)}{}\quad \underset{(0{\cdot}76)}{}\quad r = 0{\cdot}971$$

$$(5.16)$$

where TXH_t = rate of growth of average hourly wage rate with respect to the previous year;

TPG_t = rate of growth of general price level with respect to the previous year;

$(\frac{D}{N})_t$ = ratio in year t of unsatisfied demands for jobs to the available domestic working population;

RAP_t = effect of Algerian repatriates (applicable only to 1962–63)

and the figures in brackets are the standard errors of the estimates. Because unemployment is measured only in census years in France, the $\frac{D}{N}$ ratio is used instead. By assuming that unemployment $U = 1 \cdot 5D$, and that $TPG_t = TPG_{t-1}$ (because FIFI assumes regular growth-paths), it is possible to convert (5.16) into the approximate relationship:

$$TXH_m = (8 \cdot 03 - 1 \cdot 08 \, u_0) + 0 \cdot 34 \, \overline{TPG} - 1 \cdot 08 \, u_T \qquad (5.17)$$

where TXH_m = average rate of growth of the average hourly wage rate during the period;

$\overline{TPG}$ = average rate of growth of the general price level during the period;

u_0, u_T = unemployment rates for the base year and terminal year of the period.

Courbis does state, however, that the same equation fitted to 1953–1967 annual data gives a coefficient of only $1 \cdot 3$ for $(\frac{D}{N})_t$, thus indicating the instability of the relationship. It is possible to find reasonably convincing changes in behaviour on the part of French firms to explain this shift,[8] and so the structure of (5.16) was retained in the model, with slight changes in the parameters due to including a self-financing term which was not significant.[9]

But similar equations fitted to more recent data do not come out so well: Ullmo[10] states that the predicted increase in nominal wage rates is approximately three percentage points out in comparison with actual increases.

The trade unions' criticism is more political than technical. Although not denying· the technical achievement in building the model, they do refer to the econometric tour-de-force in getting the whole wage behaviour system into one equation.[11] They regard the relationship as passive, since it is nominal wages which are considered, and there is no explicit statement about maintaining purchasing power. Other criticisms relate to the lack of a full employment constraint in the model, and go on to argue its whole theoretical basis, a point that we take up again in the final section of this chapter.

The criticisms of the economic theorists are long and involved.[12] They fall into two groups: first, there is a school of thought that basically accepts the Phillips–Lipsey relationship, but seeks to add other factors to it in order to improve its explanatory power. Some of this work in fact has little theoretical foundation, and is merely looking for a better econometric fit. The extra factors that have been included in the relationship include prices, profits, the bargaining power of the unions, and productivity. There is an argument that states that all these factors are already in the relationship anyway, lumped together in the constant term (which provides a plausible reason for the high value of the constant term in the French case). But the results obtained are in many cases contradictory, and their uncertainty makes it difficult for any firm policy guidelines to be derived from them.

The second school of thought is much more recent, and is usually known as the 'expectation school'. In periods of regular growth no Phillips–Lipsey mechanism operates; there is a natural level of unemployment towards which the economy moves, and once there the Phillips curve is essentially a vertical line, wage growth being determined by the anticipations of participants in the labour market about what the economy can bear. In short periods of sharp changes in the growth pattern, disequilibrium occurs, and the theory then admits that movement in the labour market does follow a Phillips curve, but only for a short period, after which the economy re-establishes the pattern of movement towards the natural unemployment level, but at a different wage level. The important points from this theory which are used by some in criticising the relationship retained in FIFI are that the Phillips–Lipsey mechanism is unstable and essentially applicable only in the short term, whereas FIFI of course seeks to identify medium-term mechanisms. Phan goes further and argues that *all* the competitioned economy assumptions are more applicable to the short term, and that this is implicitly admitted in the way the FIFI model is used: he points out that the importance which is attached to the variant use of the model testifies to the fact that the coefficients of the model *have* to be changed in order to produce a medium-term projection, and hence *without* such changes the wrong mechanisms are being used. He then goes to the point he makes about the coefficients having to satisfy certain inequalities (see above), and that a great deal of external analysis is required to generate satisfactory coefficients which incorporate expected medium-term structural changes.

The third major criticism has been directed at the way in which the model treats productivity and the capital accumulation process. The choice of technology is exogenous in the model, a situation that was largely determined by the lack of suitable data on capital (as is shown in

Table 5.1

The development of planning techniques
to analyse the problems revealed by the first six French Plans

Plan	Problems to be solved	Techniques	Characteristics
I (1947–50, extended to 1953)	Reconstruction. Basic infrastructure.	Basic sector analyses (project choices).	Emphasis on investment and production.
II (1954–57) (1958–61)	Getting the country out of a situation of shortages. Gradual movement towards an exposed market economy.	Construction of a national accounting system, and of an input–output table (TEI) for 1951. Projection of the TEI (plus an experimental overall economic table (TEE) for the Third Plan).	Overall view of global objectives (rate of growth) and search for consistency — emphasis on problems of production.
IV (1962–65)	Entry into the Common Market.	TEI and triangular TEE, plus a first attempt at a forecast financial operations table (TOF), and regional facility analyses.	Projection of incomes at constant prices. No proper financial analysis. Very detailed physical projections.
V (1966–70)		TEI + TEE (at relative prices) + TOF. Manual projections. Regional demographic projections. Sector account projections.	Importance of problems of competitiveness. Emphasis on price equilibria (relative prices). Very clumsy and detailed physical projections.
VI (1971–75)	Competitiveness. Emphasis on equality and living conditions.	FIFI (current prices) + TOF. System of decentralised models. Long-term studies in different fields. First attempts at 'growth paths'.	National–international dichotomy; emphasis on industrialisation. Proper financial analysis of enterprises; very strong cutback in number of detailed projections.

144

| VII (1976–80) | (First indications): Quality of life, and the environment; influence of the international situation. Spatial–national interactions, and local problems; search for common policies. Short-term, medium-term linkages. | FIFITOF. REGINA. MOISE (for international hypotheses). Analysis of the influence of money. Techniques for analysing short-term, medium-term linkages. | Development of integrated linkages between different fields:
a international and national;
b physical and financial (monetary problems);
c national and regional. |

Source: [110], p. 953

section 5.3, recent research has improved this situation). This criticism is very much linked with the other two: in FIFI, it is foreign competition and the lack of domestic resistance to it that is responsible for unemployment; the critics suggest that adjustments in the labour market can be realistically analysed only if capital—labour substitution is endogenised.

To summarise this section, the critics argue that too much importance is attached to the Phillips—Lipsey relationship and the foreign price constraint, which together largely determine employment, with capital—labour substitution allowed only a secondary, exogenous role. The power of decision of exposed sector enterprises is thus underestimated. The work being done to improve the model in these three main areas is examined in section 5.3. For the moment, we consider just how big a role the model, or the analyses it produced, played in the Sixth Plan's key policy choices; if this role was substantial, and the above criticisms are correct and relevant to the Sixth Plan period, then perhaps the wrong choices were made?

5.2   The effect of the model on the Sixth Plan policy choices

In seeking to assess the role of the model and other techniques in the policy formulation stages, it is necessary to appreciate the historical perspective from which the model has emerged, and to understand the problems that have been uppermost in the minds of the decision-makers. Table 5.1 has given an overall picture of the main characteristic problems associated with each Plan, and one obtains from a picture such as this a clear indication of the time-lag that occurs between the appearance of a problem and the later appearance of a technique designed to analyse this problem. Thus, the problem of competitiveness in industry appears during the Fifth Plan period [13] and is largely responsible for the later appearance of the FIFI model, which is specifically designed to analyse this problem. [14] It is to be expected, therefore, that FIFI's main contribution will be to the industrial sector, but even there it can contribute only partial analyses because of its acknowledged limitations in the financial, regional and social aspects of the problem.

Techniques are a function of the state of economic knowledge at the time they are built, and of the arguments and devices that are available and prevalent. But there are always other ways of presenting arguments, based on different representations of reality, and it is interesting to consider the way in which the model's recommendations and the decision-maker's preferences interact. As we shall see, by looking at the Sixth

146

Plan's policy recommendation on taxation, growth, prices and foreign trade, differences can occur because of another time-lag between the availability of the technique and the assimilation of the technique by the decision-makers, or because there is a difference between the various Plan participants' proclaimed and real objectives, or because of interests, preferences and constraints that do not appear until the planning process is under way and which have therefore not been allowed for by the model.

An important objective which appears in the final version of the Plan is 'to stabilise the overall weight of taxation, that is the part raised by obligatory levies within the GDP, as closely as possible at the existing level of nearly 40 per cent'.[15] But FIFI demonstrated that it was not necessarily harmful to industrial competitiveness to increase the weight of taxation by one or two percentage points,[16] and indeed that such a move would be beneficial from the social overhead capital point of view. A necessary condition of increasing taxation was that the structure should be changed at the same time, so as not to overburden the exposed industrial sector with direct taxation[17] and affect its competitiveness. It is clear, then, that the Plan objective came from other considerations: first, a social constraint that the model missed, involving the general belief in a psychological level of taxation that the French would probably bear, and beyond which there would be strong reactions from taxpayers. Although the Plan uses the fight-against-inflation argument for holding taxation at its previous level,[18] there clearly is a lot of weight in the psychological arguments too: 'If there is a choice to be made between lower taxation or higher social investment, the instinct of the government is to choose lower taxation'.[19] The second consideration overriding the model's recommendation was the anxiety (chiefly that of the Patronat (CNPF)) not to overdevelop the public sector at the expense of the private sector. Thirdly, the model's arguments about changing the structure of taxation in order to benefit industry were overruled by an anxiety not to unbalance the central government budget, and further feelings about the sensitive nature of taxation: indirect taxation and parafiscal measures have always been preferred to direct taxation in France.[20] Finally, on taxation policy, FIFI demonstrated that an increase in VAT would not be harmful to industrial competitiveness and would benefit the administration finance balance,[21] but the Plan chose otherwise, putting forward measures to ease certain VAT rates[22] in line with the EEC's taxation structure harmonisation policy (an institutional constraint for which the model did not allow).

Thus, FIFI had little effect on the Sixth Plan's taxation policy, but, as we have indicated above, one would look for a bigger influence on growth, prices and foreign trade. FIFI showed that it was possible to go for rapid growth and external balance, provided that a supply policy aimed at improving competitiveness were pursued in the exposed industrial sector. The policies outlined in the Plan are very much in accordance with this, but it is not altogether certain that they derive from wholehearted acceptance of the model. To begin with, there was resistance to the model's philosophy from those Plan participants who still held to Keynesian beliefs, and the fact that the tax policy was not in line with FIFI's recommendations also imposed further difficulties. The really important point here is that FIFI was generally more of an influence during the pre-options phase, but it declined in importance during the later part of the pre-options phase and the final options phase when the key policy decisions were taken. Even on the industrial policy front, the argument was more that exports should be encouraged in order to improve the external balance, and that industrial prices should not therefore grow faster than those of foreign competitors. This way of thinking overlooked the necessity to allow exposed enterprises sufficient margins to finance their investment, and perhaps resulted from the fact that the whole of industry was considered as one sector in FIFI. It may have been possible to reconcile the two arguments (i.e. allow prices to rise a little in exposed sectors in order to help finance investment (FIFI argument), and stimulate exports by a demand policy in exposed sectors which are dominantly competitive (traditional argument)) if FIFI had been more disaggregated. We have raised this point before, [23] and several of the Plan participants also criticised the industrial structure in FIFI. [24]

Thus, overall, the model made a bigger impression in the pre-options phase than in the post-options phase. It focused attention on some of the key problems, and, although there were criticisms and objections in this early phase, they were mainly against the conception of the system itself rather than against the model. Towards the end of the pre-options phase and during the post-options phase, it is possible to discern the gradual re-introduction of norms and preferences external to the model. Although frustrating for the model-builder, this is reassuring in the sense that if this had not been the case the accusations of over-formalisation and planning by techniques would have been justified. In passing, it also helps to explain why it is so unrealistic to try and use an optimisation model in a planning process like the French one: the objective function is not known until *after* the decisions have been taken; there is a network of constraints and preferences that no model-builder realises is there until it gradually appears during the Plan preparation stages.

These observations strongly support the case for continuing with the open concertation phases in French planning: no model can ever anticipate fully the extent of the preferences that are revealed slowly. It is possible, however, to improve the contributions that the model can make, and the way in which this is being done is analysed in the next section. Following that, we take a broader look at what can be done to avoid some of the mistakes that were made in the use of formal techniques in the Sixth Plan.

5.3 Immediate improvements to the model

Concentrating again on the three main areas considered in section 5.1 (capital accumulation, wages, and international competition), certain improvements will have been made by the time the model comes to be used in the preparation of the Seventh Plan. It will be possible to handle capital–labour substitution endogenously, replacing the complementary factor production function by a Cobb–Douglas formulation. This derives from work by Mairesse[25] on capital series which built on work done by Carré for the Fifth Plan:

$$(c_t - n_t) = 0{\cdot}36\, (k_t - n_t) + 4{\cdot}1 \qquad R^2\ =\ 0{\cdot}30 \\ (0{\cdot}13) \phantom{0{\cdot}36 (k_t - n_t) + }(0{\cdot}7) \qquad D\ =\ 2{\cdot}1 \tag{5.18}$$

where k_t = growth rate of gross capital used;
n_t = growth rate of labour employed;
c_t = growth rate of production capacity;

and these estimates are based on a 1950–1971 time series. This function covers industry as defined in FIFI's fourth sector, and was used in the Sixth Plan to project labour productivity, with the industry Plan Commission providing exogenous estimates of $(k_t - n_t)$. Adding to this the work of Malinvaud[26] on the cost of using capital, Ullmo[27] has suggested that the following relations be included in the model:

$$q - n = a_1\, (k - n) + b_1 \tag{5.19}$$

$$\frac{I}{Q} = a_2\, CU + b_2 \tag{5.20}$$

$$K = K_{-1} + I - \overline{K} \tag{5.21}$$

$$CU = \frac{a_3\, (mp_f + n)}{p_g} \tag{5.22}$$

where Q = industrial value added (and q is its growth rate);
CU = cost of using capital in industry;

149

$$I = \quad \text{industry's gross fixed capital formation;}$$

$P_f =$ price index of non-financial enterprises gross fixed capital formation in producer goods;

$K =$ capital used in industry.

There are still doubts about this formulation, however; the Cobb–Douglas production function is weakly estimated, and alternative investment functions have also been suggested (particularly by the group working on the STAR model, which we discuss in Chapter 10). The reader is referred to Ullmo [28] for a summary of the ongoing research and further references.

There are also several directions of research continuing on the wage–price–unemployment relationship. Work carried out by the INSEE using recent data indicates that the Phillips–Lipsey mechanism may have less of a key role to play in the future. Using DENS as the unemployment indicator, the price coefficient is much closer to unity (0·8) than in previous estimates (such as (5.17), for instance), and the unemployment coefficient is not significant. This could either spell the end for the Phillips relationship (leading virtually to an exogenous real wage, which is incompatible with the competitioned economy theory), or it may mean that a better unemployment indicator needs to be found. Courbis suggested several alternatives in his original work, [29] but estimates calculated at that time still gave very low price coefficients. More recent work by Salais [30] may lead to better results. As indicated in note 6, there has also been a lot of activity on wage differences in different sectors, but this will be difficult to integrate with FIFI because of the model's global industry classification.

The several suggestions put forward to modify the way in which international competition is handled introduce very little that is new; they essentially reduce to an intermediate position between the rigid price constraint of the competitioned economy and the import functions of the Keynesian economy. It is likely that some such compromise arrangement will be incorporated for the early Seventh Plan projections, but it is interesting to note that attempts are also being made to construct an operational definition of the autonomous economy concept, which we mentioned in section 5.1. Ullmo distinguishes the autonomous economy from the competitioned economy and other types as follows: [31]

(a) protected economy:

international context	$\rightarrow$	industrial import price	$\rightarrow$ ($\neq$)	domestic industrial price	$\rightleftarrows$	domestic factors

(b) totally competitioned economy:

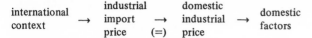

international context → industrial import price → (=) domestic industrial price → domestic factors

(c) partially competitioned economy:

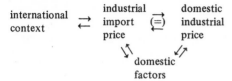

international context ⇄ industrial import price (=) domestic industrial price

domestic factors

(d) competitive economy:

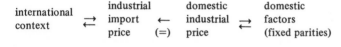

international context ⇄ industrial import price (=) ← domestic industrial price ⇄ domestic factors (fixed parities)

(e) autonomous economy:

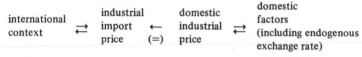

international context ⇄ industrial import price (=) ← domestic industrial price ⇄ domestic factors (including endogenous exchange rate)

Tests are being carried out using the MINIFIFITOF model (a reduced version of FIFITOF, which is discussed in Chapter 10), but it is unlikely that the research will be sufficiently advanced to play a major role in the Seventh Plan projections. This demonstrates once again the way in which techniques are developed to analyse special problems, the theme with which we opened section 5.2. We return to it now in the final section of this chapter.

5.4. Techniques in the Seventh and later Plans

As with forecasting in general, the simple, straightforward approach to the problem of estimating how macro-economic, medium-term planning techniques will develop in the future is to establish the trend, by looking at the development of similar techniques in previous Plans, and then to project into the future on the basis of this trend and other known developments. Whilst this approach will undoubtedly produce a forecast, the accuracy of the forecast depends on the weights given to 'the trend' and 'other known developments', and the content of 'other known developments'. In this section, we look at a model-builder's forecast of the next

20 years in French planning models, and then add some observations on the difficult task facing the planner in deciding how to achieve the right balance between more models and more discretionary methods, a balance that, in spite of the model-builder's predictions, could swing away from models in the immediate future.

The model-builder is Courbis, one of the main authors of the FIFI model, and it is his views, presented at a recent international conference, [32] that we first describe and then query somewhat by assessing the strength of the doubts raised by others on the use of models in planning. Courbis bases his views on a continuation of the trends that are readily apparent from Table 5.1, which is taken from another of his recent papers, [33] and which also includes the first five years of his 'forecast'. Much of the work on the Seventh Plan techniques is already underway (we discuss it in detail in Chapter 10) and so this part of the forecast is reasonably accurate, although even there it is possible that some of the feelings that we identify below might have a restraining effect. Courbis calls the FIFI–FIFITOF–REGINA models the first generation of models to be used in French planning. Their common characteristic is that they are static, and they emphasise economic characteristics. He expects first versions of FIFITOF and REGINA to be used in the preparation of the Seventh Plan, and more complete versions of both models to be used in the Eighth Plan, by which time current research on structural analyses [34] should also have been incorporated.

Courbis' second generation of models is to meet the requirement, already apparent and shown at the bottom of Table 5.1, for dynamic analyses, linking the short term and the medium term, and possibly joining the medium term to the long term. [35] We have already briefly referred in earlier chapters to the STAR model; this is a dynamic model, but it is intended primarily for use in economic budgeting, and does not contain sufficient detail for planning purposes. The report [36] of the Applied Macro-economic Research Group (GAMA, of which Courbis is Director) at the University of Paris mentions a project that was started in 1972 on the CML (the initials of the French words for short, medium, and long) model, but it is not expected that this model will be ready before the preparation of the Seventh Plan is complete, and so the earliest Plan it could be used for is the Eighth. It will probably be built on a modified version of the REGINA model, and its regional–sectoral–dynamic framework will require new developments on the data side.

Looking further ahead, Courbis envisages a third generation of models to analyse socio-economic linkages. and hazards a guess that a static model on these lines may be available for the Eighth Plan.

Even allowing for the considerable uncertainty associated with these future developments in model-building, it is clear that French planning will hold a great deal of interest for students of quantitative national economic planning over the next ten years and probably beyond. But there are clouds on the horizon, and it is by no means certain that things will turn out quite the way Courbis anticipates. As we mentioned in Chapter 1, there was a considerable feeling of unease amongst the participants at the end of the Sixth Plan preparation period, and many observers attribute this to the FIFI model. If future Plans involve increasingly sophisticated models, and the unease of the participants grows as a result, then there is a real possibility of a serious breakdown in the planning process as it is at present known. Louis-Pierre Blanc describes the movement away from the growth objective, a movement that is currently prevalent in many industrialised countries, but which turned from 'passive resistance' to growth into 'open opposition' to growth during the pre-options phase of the Sixth Plan:

> The preparation of the Sixth Plan has been dominated by (this) problem. The first phase..., in a rather confused debate on the rate of growth, saw the partisans of rapid industrial development confronted by those giving priority to the social aspects of development. The preoccupations of the environment and living standards were reaffirmed in the second phase. [37]

It is no coincidence that FIFI was much more involved in this first. controversial phase, and less so in the second phase. Speaking of the increasing use of operational research (OR) in government and planning, Lesourne states that

> at the level of individuals and groups, to a certain extent, everywhere in the world a tendency towards the rejection of rationality is occurring, on the one hand because of the consequences engendered by the local recourse to 'rationality' for questionable objectives, and on the other, as a result of the individual nervous structure. OR has tended to be encompassed within the overall technocratic phenomenon and rejected all the more violently because of the fact that OR studies directly affect the situations of individuals. Under these conditions, the extreme left-wing milieux reject OR and systems analysis because, in their eyes, the problems dealt with by it and the objectives imposed are conditioned by the political system and by the resource allocation system reigning in the collectivity. Information produced by OR is thus not neutral. It is implicitly at the service of

those in power. In the leftist view, systems analysis is an arm of conservatism. OR risks to contribute moreover to the development of over-administration, which we know is one of the characteristics of post-industrial societies. The present institutional system of government was created at a time when statistical data were rare, and studies on the consequences of decisions less complicated. Representatives, who had a profound knowledge of local situations, were at the same time the reflection of their electors and their interlocutors, and were not overly disadvantaged in relation to the executive and the administration. This is no longer true. [38]

The views attributed to the 'extreme-left-wing milieux' in this statement are confirmed by the following remarks due to Dasseto and Rosanvallon, trade-union members of the CEGF technical group:

This structure of the model, reproducing the operations of the capitalist economy, makes its use in the medium-term very doubtful. It boils down in effect to a justification of the capitalist system, and considers capitalism as the only possible form of economic organisation. In this sense, FIFI is not a neutral tool.... [39]

If the advantages that we have attributed to FIFI earlier in this book are to be retained in future Plans, and the difficulties arising from the use of models are to be avoided or at least reduced, then the administration's attitude to further developments in model-building has to be a balanced, open and realistic. This attitude is discernible in the report of the CEGF technical group, a group with the special job of acting as an intermediary between the model and the planning participants. They rate as highest priority for the Seventh Plan preparation period much more work on structural development studies that are not restricted by a national accounting framework (as FIFI is), that extend towards the long-term, and that explicitly allow for the social determinants of development. This attention to structural analyses is to be preferred to more new macro-modelling work in the immediate future. [40] A more recent paper from the administration side confirms this intention, perhaps implicitly questioning whether FIFI should have been used so extensively before deeper structural analyses had been carried out:

'... the question is whether it is suitable to start the planning process with structural studies or with models. Rationality leads us to think that basic problems (structural studies) ought to be solved before formal problems (formal model). In practice, the French experience shows that formalization may be made before basic study... . Presently, for the Seventh Plan, the Director of the Planning Authority does not want the semi-global model to play such a central role. He is tempted to give a certain priority to other instruments such as structural studies or social indicators. [41]

It seems that the CGP have recognised the problem, [42] and that Courbis' forecast timetable may be re-ordered slightly. Structural analyses and social models will have to be brought forward [43] possibly at the expense of some of the anticipated macro-modelling work. Certainly, the acceptance of FIFI by the Plan Commission was misjudged by the administration, but if the views of the CEGF technical group have any standing at all, then the same error of judgement will not be made again. It is now recognised that models can be considered by some participants as a 'privileged instrument for development norms which the government or the dominant class try to impose on social groups. [44] It will be interesting to see how far the administration go in involving the various social groups in actually elaborating the new techniques to be used in the preparation of the Seventh Plan, rather than repeating the Sixth Plan practice of keeping most of the discussion on the central techniques within the administration. This would require constituting the Plan Commissions at an earlier stage, but there are clear advantages in doing so, for reasons that Lesourne again spells out:

> ... a 'commission' .... is a difficult type of interlocutor, because the objectives of its members are often antagonistic. Thus the ground must be carefully studied beforehand, an attempt made to understand the relationship between the members and the interests which they are defending respectively, the goals they are pursuing, their attitudes with respect to operational research. One must avoid being forced into accepting impossible studies, but devote a considerable amount of time *during the course of the study* to making the intellectual orientations of the [OR] team understandable, before submitting any results, and without adopting any premature positions with respect to the most burning questions. [45]

Notes

[1] Phan's criticisms are reported in [102]. They derive from discussions and research carried out in CEPREMAP, a research organisation that does a lot of work on models. Similar arguments were presented in a lecture at CEPREMAP to a group of Birmingham University post-graduate students

whom I led on a visit to Paris in September 1971.

² Since writing Chapter 3, I have discovered that both Courbis' one--and two-sector models are in [103]. The reader can thus compare all four versions of the model (Courbis' two versions, Phan's two-sector version given in this chapter, and the implied one-sector version of which it is an extension) and carry out his own analyses. For instance, equations (5.1) and (5.2) correspond to equation (3.46), illustrating that Phan's two-sector model starts out in reduced form. Similar comparisons can be made between the other equations.

³ As stated earlier in the chapter, there are several sources; the ones mainly referred to here are [1] and [106], the latter forming the basis of sections 5.1 and 5.3. Other sources include [105] and [104]; the author of the latter was a member of the CEGF Technical Group, and a summary of his criticisms and constructive suggestions are included in the Group's report, [1], pp. 73–81. A more general source is [126].

⁴ Desrosières applies factor analysis to FIFI'S industry sector in [107], and concludes that a three-sector breakdown would be more beneficial from several points of view. He also suggests that FIFI's sector 7 should be separated into building and public works, services, and commerce sectors, giving an overall 11-sector breakdown in the model.

⁵ This quote comes from [102], p. 941 and the Norwegian source is [67].

⁶ For example *Revue Économique* in 1971 devoted two complete issues (over 300 pages) to 'wage disparities', and several other papers also appeared in the same journal in the same year, notably the paper by Aglietta [108] on a non-econometric approach to wage determination.

⁷ See [61], pp. 176 and 178.

⁸ Such as the ones described in [61] pp. 179–80, for instance.

⁹ The version retained in the model is given in [82], pp. 38–9. See also note 46 below.

¹⁰ In [106], p. 1037.

¹¹ Florenzano and Pontagnier, representatives of CGT in the CEGF Technical Group, use this term in their contribution to [1], p. 88, and [127]. Courbis answers the unions' criticisms in [110] pp. 979–82.

¹² Rather than give a long list of references, many of which were not inspired by the French case, we refer the reader to Phan [109], who summarises many of the theoretical arguments and gives their original source.

¹³ Maurice Parodi opens his chapter on 'French industry in the search for competitiveness' in [111] with the sentence, 'Since 1968, the under-industrialisation of France has become one of the favourite themes of

official speeches and the press'. Parodi goes on to examine where competitiveness is most lacking in French industry, providing much factual information on all the major branches.

[14] 'It is not just chance that the physico-financial model is centred on the problems of French industry's competitiveness'. [1][110], p. 962.

[15] This quote is taken from the official English translation of the Sixth Plan, [112], p. 28.

[16] See variant 4 in [4], p. 169.

[17] Variants 10 ([4], p. 141), 7 ([4], p. 176), and 11 ([4], p. 194) show this generally to be the case (the variants are not dealt with in numerical sequence in [4] but according to type.

[18] Parodi shows that the overall weight of taxation had been held just below the psychological 40 per cent level for many years, well before the Sixth Plan period. The following figures are taken from Table 30 in [111]: Overall weight of taxation (taxes and social security contributions) as a percentage of gross national product (Parodi's source is the OECD, and so the more usual French concept of gross domestic production (PIB) has been standardised to gross national product (PNB) between 1958 and 1966):

1958	1959	1960	1961	1962	1963	1964	1965	1966
34	34·7	33·8	35·1	35·4	36·6	37·8	38·3	38·6

Further useful sources here are [125] and [129].

[19] This quote is taken from [113], p. 6.

[20] The same source, [113], gives the following diagram on p. 46, showing France's relatively high indirect taxation in the pre-Plan year, compared with other industrialised countries:

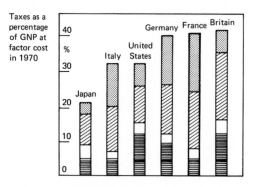
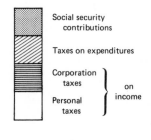

Source: *Economic Trends,* October 1972.

[21] See variant 13 in [4], p. 194: there is no change in industrial growth following an increase in VAT.

[22] See [112], p. 30.

[23] See note 4 above.

[24] 'As several participants have remarked, certain industrial activities are sheltered, whereas certain non-industrial activities, such as transport for example (shipping and air transport) are exposed'. [1] p. 45.

[25] See [114], [115] and [116] for the essential aspects of this work and details of the production function for French industry. Ullmo gives additional references in [106].

[26] See [117].

[27] See [118] and [119]. [106] also contains brief comments.

[28] [106] again.

[29] Courbis devotes a chapter to these alternative versions in his thesis [61].

[30] This work is being done in the INSEE. It is attempting to construct a typology of unemployment, distinguishing frictional, structural, and temporary unemployment.

[31] This information is taken from a diagram that appears in [106], pp. 1064—5.

[32] The annual assembly of the Swiss Society of Statistics and Political Economy, held in Sion, 10—11 May 1973, and devoted to medium and long-term socio-economic programming. Courbis' paper is in [120].

[33] See [110], p. 953.

[34] Work on structural problems is going on in the INSEE and the CE-PREMAP, involving Seibel and Sautter among others.

[35] Bienaymé emphasises the constraints that working towards a medium-term horizon imposes, in [1], pp. 78—80: 'The interactions between decisions that are inspired by long-term objectives (new technologies, education, new towns, etc.), and decisions that are taken within the medium-term plan, are very little explored'. He suggests that more effort be put into exploring linkages in both directions, as illustrated in one of his diagrams:

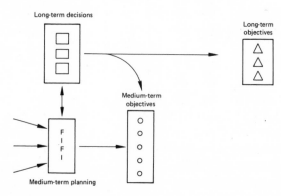

[36] 'The work that will be carried out for this project (on behalf of the CGP (contract No. 72–45)) consists of a preliminary analysis of the structure of a sectoralised, dynamic model adapted to the needs of planning'. [121], p. 12. The address of the GAMA is Université de Paris-X à Nanterre, 2 rue de Rouen, 92000 Nanterre.

[37] This quote is taken from [122], p. 58. The whole of the same issue of *Revue d'Économie Politique* is devoted to the subject 'The costs of growth'.

[38] Taken from [123], pp. 13–14.

[39] This quote is in the short article written by Dasseto and Rosanvallon, representatives of the CFDT on the CEGF Technical Group, in [1], p. 84.

[40] 'Priority must be given to "structural development analyses" rather than to the immediate development of new macro-economic modelling work'. [1], p. 63.

[41] In [124], pp. 7 and 12.

[42] See quote by Ullmo at the very beginning of this chapter.

[43] Several planners have spoken to me of the lack of progress in producing operational social research in France. Their feelings are adequately summarised in the following quote from Courbis and Pagé: 'It is not an accident that the study of so-called "social" problems (concerning the distribution of incomes and the national wealth, and more generally all the inequalities of the present situation, living standards, and the satisfaction of "needs") has lagged a long way behind the study of economic *regulation* problems in French planning. Certainly, the fact that it was essential to get the economy going before looking at other things partly explains this order of priority. But on the other hand, the undeniable backwardness of research in the social field and above all the incapacity of the human sciences to put forward workable systems at the level of aggregation at which planning operates, have constituted (and still constitute) a significant handicap to the analysis of social problems'. [110], p. 963. Suggestions are beginning to come forward however: see Aujac's proposals in [125] for a national social balance, and a long-term socio-economic simulation model.

[44] Taken from [124], p. 12.

[45] [123], p. 12.

[46] The keen-eyed reader will have noticed an apparent contradiction between (5.16), (5.17), and (4.1); the situation is further confused by the same relationship being given in [108], p. 75 with different coefficients. To clarify the situation, I asked Courbis to explain the various sources in more detail; the following is his reply, suitably modified in parts to tie in with the references in this book:

The value of the coefficient of D/N in the wage determination relationship in FIFI is not inconsistently given in my texts ([61] and [82], and [4], p. 73). It is equal to 3·67 if TXH and D/N are expressed in percentage terms (i.e. the units which I use). If TXH is expressed in percentage terms (%) but D/N is given in %₀ terms (which is the case in [4], p. 73), then clearly the coefficient is equal to 0·37. You will see that [4] indicates that D/N is given in %₀.

To understand the value of the coefficient given in [4], p. 135 (i.e. equation (4.1)), three elements have to be taken into account:

(a) first of all (see [82]), the econometric relationship takes D/N as explanatory variable, whereas FIFI includes the rate of unemployment U/N, where U is unemployment (in the sense of the French census); D on the other hand is the number of unsatisfied demands for work (i.e. registered unemployed). Thus, U is greater than D, and in fact U is approximately $1·7D$ (a lower coefficient of U/D is taken now because of the impact of the National Employment Agency). The coefficient of U/N is clearly smaller, and equal to $3·7/1·7$;

(b) it is assumed (see [82]) that all change is *regular* during the period of the projection. Therefore, $TPG_t = TPG_{t-1}$' and U_t varies regularly between year 0 and year T. The average rate of growth of wages is therefore calculated by taking

$$U = \tfrac{1}{2}[U_0 + U_T]$$

As U_o is given, only U_T remains, but with a weight of $\tfrac{1}{2}$ (see the details in [82]).

(c) the variants in [4], p. 135 (described in section 4.3 of this book) refer to 1970–1975, but the supporting argument is fictitiously given in terms of the original ten-year period on which FIFI is based; the known 1970 values of PG and PW have been introduced. If PG_{70} and PW_{70} are the indices (base 1965) of the general price level and the wage rate, and if the wage–price–unemployment relationship is

$$TW = \alpha_1 + \beta_1\ TPG + \gamma_1\ u_{75}$$

where u_{75} is the rate of unemployment in 1975, then the wage rate in 1975 is equal to

$$PW_{75} = PW_{70}\ (1 + \alpha_1 + \beta_1\ TPG + \gamma_1\ u_{75})^5$$

with $$TPG_{75/70} = (PG_{75}/PG_{70})^{\frac{1}{5}} - 1$$

160

But for a number of reasons connected with the way the model is written, the argument has been maintained as if one were dealing with a ten-year period, and therefore:

$$PW = (1 + \alpha_2 + \beta_2 \ TPG + \gamma_2 \ u_{75})^{10}$$

with appropriate coefficients α_2, β_2, γ_2, and

$$TPG = (PG_{75} / PG_{65})^{\frac{1}{10}} - 1$$

The coefficients α_2, β_2, and γ_2 should satisfy identically

$$PW_{70} (1t \ \alpha_1 + \beta_1 \ TPG_{75/70} + \gamma_1 \ u_{75})^5 = (1 + \alpha_2 + \beta_2 \ TPG + \gamma_2 \ u_{75})^{10}$$

with $\qquad TPG = (PG_{75} / PG_{65})^{\frac{1}{10}} - 1$

and $\qquad TPG_{75/70} = (PG_{75} / PG_{70})^{\frac{1}{5}} - 1$

Thus, α_2, β_2, and γ_2 can be determined, and the coefficient γ_2 is clearly smaller than γ_1. This explains the value given in [4], p. 135, but it has no economic meaning. It is merely a device that I have used to make FIFI (which was written to operate over a ten-year period) work with certain known 1970 values introduced into the 1965–75 projection (but then the 1975 displacements should be interpreted not as 1965–1975 changes but 1970–1975 changes). The values α_2, β_2, and γ_2 should not have been given in [4], only the true values α_1, β_1, and γ_1, (as on p. 73), with an explanation that the variants had been carried out over 1970–75 by introducing a fixed 1970 point.

There is therefore no contradiction, but poor editing in [4] (which is due to the fact that this text is a reproduction of administrative papers).

(28 February 1974)

There are additional notes and refences to this and other chapters at the end of Chapter 10.

References

[102] D. L. Phan, 'Le modèle FIFI et la politique à moyen terme' (The FIFI model and medium-term policy), *Revue Économique* vol. XXIV, no. 6, November 1973, pp. 923–50.

[103] R. Courbis, 'La théorie des "économies concurrencées", fondement du modele FIFI' (The competitioned economy theory, basis of the FIFI model), *Revue Économique* vol. XXIV, no. 6, November 1973, pp. 905–22.

[104] J. Bernard, *Comptabilité nationale et modèles de politique économique* (National Accounting and Economic Policy Models), Thémis French University Press (PUF), 1972.

[105] A. Bienaymé, 'Le passage critique de l'économie concurrencée à l'économie compétitive' (The critical transition from the competitioned economy to the competitive economy), *Revue Économique* vol. XXI, no. 3, May 1970.

[106] B. Ullmo, 'Trois problèmes posés par le modèle physico-financier' (Three problems posed by the physico-financial model), *Revue Économique* vol. XXIV, no. 6, November 1973, pp. 1026–71.

[107] A. Desrosières, 'Un découpage de l'industrie en trois sectors' (A three-sector breakdown of industry), *Économie et Statistique* no. 40, December 1972, pp. 25–39.

[108] M. Aglietta, 'L'évolution des salaires en France au cours des vingt dernières années' (Changes in wages in France during the last 20 years), *Revue Économique* vol. XXII, no. 1, January 1971, pp. 69-117.

[109] D. L. Phan, 'Aperçu de la littérature théorique sur la courbe de Phillips' (Survey of the theoretical literature on the Phillips' curve), *Revue Économique* vol. XXII, no. 5, September 1971, pp. 751–91.

[110] R. Courbis and J-P. Pagé, 'Techniques de projection macro-économique et choix du Plan français' (Macro-economic projection techniques and the choices of the French Plan), *Revue Économique* vol. XXIV, no. 6, November 1973, pp. 951–87.

[111] M. Parodi, *L'Économie et la Société Française de 1945 à 1970* (The French economy and society from 1945 to 1970), Armand Colin, Paris 1971 (2nd edition), 374 pp.

[112] Commissariat Général du Plan, *Sixth Economic and Social Development Plan. General Report. The General Objectives and Priority Actions of the Sixth Plan,* La Documentation Française, Paris 1973, 307 pp.

[113] J. Radice, 'Pompidou's France: an economic survey' *The Economist,* 2–8 December 1972, 46 pp.

[114] J. Mairesse, L'évaluation du capital fixe productif' (The evaluation of productive fixed capital), *Les Collections de l'INSEE,* série C, no. 17, October 1972.

[115] J. Mairesse, 'L'estimation du capital fixe productif' (The estimation

of productive fixed capital), *Économie et Statistique* no. 25, July–August 1971, pp. 33–55.

[116] J. Mairesse and A. Saglio, 'Estimation d'une fonction de production pour l'industrie française' (Estimation of a production function for French industry), *Annales de l'INSEE* no. 6, January–April 1971, pp. 77–117.

[117] E. Malinvaud, 'Peut-on mesurer l'évolution du coût d'usage du capital productif?' (Is it possible to measure changes in the cost of using productive capital?), *Économie et Statistique* no. 22, April 1971, pp. 5–20.

[118] B. Ullmo, 'La substitution capital-travail dans l'industrie, proposi tion de modelisation' (Capital–labour substitution in industry: proposals on a model), INSEE (Programmes Division) internal paper, August 1972.

[119] B. Ullmo, 'Test à l'aide du MINIFIFITOF, du modèle proposé dans la note INSEE, août 1973' (Use of MINIFIFITOF to test the model proposed in the INSEE paper of August 1972) INSEE (Programmes Division) internal paper, January 1973.

[120] R. Courbis, 'Les méthodes de planification française: évolution et perspectives' (French planning methods: past trends and future prospects), *Revue Suisse d'Économie Politique et de Statistique* vol. 109, no. 3, 1973, pp. 3,7–340.

[121] GAMA, 'Rapport d'activité pour 1972' (Report on work done in 1972), *Paper no. 22*, February 1973, 17 p.

[122] L-P. Blanc, 'La prise en compte des coûts de la croissance dans les plans de developpement' (Allowing for the costs of growth in development plans), *Revue d'Économie Politique* vol. 83, no. 1, January–February 1973, pp. 56–75.

[123] J. Lesourne, 'Operational research in government and planning', to appear in *Omega*.

[124] B. Ullmo, 'Usefulness of planning models', Paper presented at the Rehovot Conference on Economic Growth in Development Countries, Israel, 5–11 September, 1973, 13 pp.

[125] H. Aujac, 'Deux instruments de programmation sociale: le bilan sociale de la Nation – le modèle à long terme de simulation économique et sociale' (Two instruments for social programming: the national social balance, and the long-term, social and economic simulation model), *Revue d'Économie Politique* vol. 83, no. 1, January–February 1973, pp. 171–94.

[126] J-P. Page, 'L'étude des comportements socio-économiques dans le modèle d'ensemble du VIe Plan' (The analysis of socio-economic

163

behaviour in the Sixth Plan global model), *Droit Social*, special issue, no. 4–5, April–May 1972, pp. 31–9.

[127] M. Geistdoerfer-Florenzano, 'Le modèle physico-financier, essai de critique syndicale' (A trade-union criticism of the physico-financial model), *Droit Social*, no. 4–5, April–May 1972, pp. 40–50.

[128] J-J. Branchu, 'Signification et mesure de la pression fiscale' (The meaning and measurement of the weight of taxation), Report of the Taxation Group to the CEGF, reproduced in *Économie et Statistique* no. 11, April 1970, pp. 3–19.

[129] J. Fournier, 'Pression fiscale et politique sociale dans le VIᵉ Plan' (The weight of taxation and social policy in the Sixth Plan), *Droit Social*, special issue, no. 4–5, April–May 1972, pp. 113–22.

6 Projections of 1975 based on the Contents of the Sixth Plan

> But — and this is certainly one of the most astonishing paradoxes —
> the definitive version of the Sixth Plan, submitted to the Economic
> and Social Council and to Parliament, finally contained very few
> numbers compared with earlier Plans!!!
>
> René Bonety, in [130], p. 218.

The paradox to which Bonety is referring in this quotation is the fact that
in no previous Plan had such extensive use been made of a formalised
model (FIFI), and yet at the same time no previous Plan contained as
little numerical detail as the Sixth Plan. The reasons for reducing the
numerical content are well known and adequately reported elsewhere;[1] it
is the aim of this chapter to show that the availability of FIFI has in fact
made it possible to produce *more* detail than in previous Plans, but very
little of this detail appears in the official documents. It is made clear in
the introduction to the General Report on the Plan that the economic
projections for 1975 are constructed under the responsibility of the CGP,[2]
but they do not form part of the Plan itself. The projections, published
nearly two years after the approval of the Plan,[3] are clearly *forecasts* and
not targets: the simplest way of putting it is that they constitute just
another central account, constructed in exactly the same way as the departure account, but obviously based on better information and much
firmer economic policy indications.

Having presented the initial departure account in Chapter 4, we give the
same tables in this chapter, this time drawing the figures from the 'Plan
account', as the projections produced after the Plan had been approved
have come to be called. We look at the different assumptions in the first
section, and the consequent different results in the following section. In
section 6.3, we go through some of the central accounts that were constructed in the intermediate stages of the preparation of the Plan, seeking
to indentify where the difference occurred on the path between the departure account and the Plan account. Finally in this chapter, we see how
the aggregated Plan account (based on FIFI, and hence only seven sectors)
can be broken down into more detail for the purposes of disaggregated
analysis, and we give an overall view of the detailed projections produced

165

for particular aspects of the Plan, normally with techniques other than the FIFI model.

6.1 The main assumptions of the Plan account

The Plan account is designed to illustrate what the objectives retained in the Plan involve, in the way of behaviours and actions on the part of various economic agencies. The figures that we give in the next section (and the assumptions given in numerical form in this section) are not to be confused with the Plan, and they in no way commit the Government or the authorities, although in an ideal situation they reflect the decisions that will have to be taken if the Plan is to be fulfilled. But even at the outset, many features of the preparation of the account are far from ideal. To begin with, the FIFI model was used to produce the account, and that means that all FIFI's in-built assumptions are also built into the account. Following the criticisms made on the model (reported in Chapter 5), and the relatively small influence that the model had on policy formulation in various parts of the Plan (see section 5.2), this is a significant point. The way in which the final version of the Plan was arrived at was according to an *implicit* model constituted by the Plan Commissions, the Government, Parliament and all the other decision-making centres involved. It is quite clear that this implicit model is different from FIFI. The best way to produce a projection associated with the Plan would be explicitly to quantify, formalise, and then use this implicit model; to use another model in which there are acknowledged shortcomings and differences is to adopt a second-best approach.

This is recognised by the authors of the projection, who point out that in many cases it would indeed be more meaningful to give a range of values for some of the aggregates, rather than a single figure.

The Plan account, then, is really a separate forecasting excercise, providing a picture of 1975 based on information contained in the Plan. Many of its assumptions are similar to those behind the departure account, because FIFI was used in both cases. But the Plan account should be more meaningful and more realistic because it was prepared two years after the departure account, and consequently contains more information. It also has a significant advantage over the departure account in that it is based on expressions of Government intentions (the policies outlined in the Plan) rather than on policies not specifically designed for 1975, as was the case in the departure account. It should be pointed out, however, that it is not a straightforward matter to 'feed-in' the Plan policy to FIFI.

Certainly in some cases, like central government expenditures for instance, it is just a question of making an appropriate change to a few exogenous variables. But in other cases, sizeable auxiliary analyses have to be undertaken, in order to estimate the effects of vocational training policies on productivity, for example, or the influence of certain parts of the Plan's competition policy and finance policy on rates of self-financing.

To summarise the general assumptions behind the Plan account before moving on to the details, we can say that there are three types: first because FIFI is used as the main forecasting instrument, all the assumptions behind the model (see section 3.1) are carried over to the projection; secondly, various assumptions are made about the international situation, general development factors, and the behaviour of domestic agencies, in much the same way as in the departure account, but using more recent and more accurate data; and thirdly, interpretations and translations of the policies contained in the Plan are incorporated in the projection, but in some cases this process is either rather arbitrary (because the Plan does not specify a policy) or impossible (the Plan specifies full employment as an objective, but as we know from previous chapters, there is no full employment constraint in the model, and no way it can be enforced).

We have discussed the assumptions of the model at length in Chapter 3, and so we look first at the second set of assumptions behind the Plan account: those relating to the international environment, general development factors, and the behaviour of domestic agencies. We shall follow the pattern established in Chapter 4, highlighting the same features and assumptions, and thus comparing the two accounts. There are four fundamental assumptions in this category:

(i)   the possibility of a major crisis is discounted, international growth will be maintained, and inflation contained by 1975;
(ii)   wages will return to pre-1968, non-inflationary growth rates;
(iii)   there will be increased competition within the sheltered sectors, leading to greater efficiency and slower price rises;
(iv)   in this sort of favourable situation, the exposed sector will experience rapid growth under the influence of the greater financial flexibility allowed by higher foreign prices.

The translation of (i) is shown in Table 6.1 which is directly comparable with Table 4.1. One gets the impression here that the departure account was a little pessimistic about the 1965–1970 period, and that this lead to lower expectations for the 1970–1975 period; this impression is supported in some of the later tables, and one wonders whether the problems revealed by the departure account were not exaggerated by an

Table 6.1

Data on foreign prices and production (August 1971 Plan account: assumptions)

Average annual growth rates (per cent)		Departure account		Plan account	
	1960/1965	1965/1970	1970/1975	1965/1970	1970/1975
Foreign PIB (weighted by French exports)	5·1	3·75	4·25	4·6	4·9
Foreign PIB price	3·2	3·30	2·40	4·4	3·2
Foreign industrial prices	1·9	2·20	1·50	3·2	1·9

Source: columns 2 and 3, see Table 4.1; other columns from Table 1, [94], p. 19

over-cautious estimate of economic performance in 1970. There is certainly more flexibility for industry in foreign prices rising at 1·9 per cent p.a. compared with 1·5 per cent p.a. in the departure account.

Looking at Table 6.2, and comparing the figures with those in Table 4.2, there are some marked differences between the two accounts, but these are in part due to the Sixth Plan policy choices, which are summarised in Table 6.3, choices that had clearly not been made at the time of the departure account; as is mentioned above, several of the policy decisions in the Plan are transmitted to the projection by changes in productivity parameters. There is also a direct link between the two sets of figures in Table 6.2: it is assumed that a reduction of 1 per cent in the length of the working week is accompanied by a 0·5 per cent increase in productivity. There is a definite policy statement in the Plan, limiting the overall reduction in hours worked to no more than $1\frac{1}{2}$ hours per week if the high growth target is to be maintained; Table 6.2 thus shows that the departure account was generous in allowing industry's week to fall to 43·7 hours; the additional growth decided upon in the Plan requires the Plan account to raise this to 43·75 hours, a move that is not reflected in other sectors, especially energy (an important factor in this sector is the run-down in the coal industry; note how the productivity figure is very high, as a direct consequence). The productivity gains are relatively low in sector 7, in spite of a significant reduction in the length of the working week; this highlights a particular effort to be made in the Plan to modernise construction (a move very much tied up with efforts in housing), and introduce more efficient methods in commerce.

The energy sector is again prominent in Table 6.3: the departure ac-

168

Table 6.2

Assumptions on labour productivity and the working week (August 1971 Plan account)

Hourly labour productivity	Average annual growth rates (per cent)			
		Departure account	Plan account	
	1960/1965	1965/1975	1965/1970	1970/1975
2 Agricultural and foodstuffs industries	4·8	4·4	5·8	5·7
3 Energy	9·7	9·3	10·3	9·2
4 Industry	5·1	6·3	6·6	7·0
5 Transport and telecommunications	4·3	4·8	5·5	6·1
7 Building and public works, services and commerce	3·9	3·75	3·1	3·9
All non-agricultural branches (excluding housing)	4·7	5·0	5·1	5·4

Length of working week	Hours			
		Departure account	Plan account	
	1965	1975	1970	1975
2 Agricultural and foodstuffs industries	46·8	44·9	45·95	43·9
3 Energy	44·0	43·0	42·3	40·1
4 Industry	45·5	43·7	44·6	43·75
5 Transport and telecommunications	46·3	44·2	44·6	43·5
7 Building and public works, services and commerce	45·7	43·0	44·45	42·9
All non-agricultural branches (excluding housing)	45·6	43·5	44·5	43·2

Source: definition and column 2, see Table 4.2; other columns from Tables 12 and 13, [94], p. 42

count failed to make proper allowance for the end of the hydroelectric programme, and the consequent fall-back from the very high investment rates of the sixties (the rate for 1960, not shown in Table 6.3, was 33·5, which puts the Plan account figure very much in line with the decreasing trend). Similarly, the high priority accorded to transport infrastructure and telecommunications in the Plan is reflected in another significant

Table 6.3

Assumptions on productive investment rates (in volume terms) (August 1971 Plan account)

Branches (figures in percentages)	1965	1970	Departure account 1975	Plan account 1975
2 Agricultural and foodstuffs industries	12·1	15·7	12·2	15·0
3 Energy	27·7	21·3	26·9	17·2
4 Industry (excluding AEC)	15·2	18·3	17·2	16·7
5 Transport and telecommunications	33·2	36·1	34·9	39·5
7 Building and public works, services and commerce	11·5	15·5	14·5	19·2
Global rate of productive investment (including AEC)	15·7	18·2	17·8	18·9

Source: column 3 and definitions from Table 4.3; other columns from Table 9, [94], p. 39

difference between the two accounts. The construction modernisation policy referred to in the previous paragraph explains the third major disparity.

To explain the policy assumptions built into the Plan account requires a summary of the Plan itself, a task that could well take several chapters. In order to present the essential aspects of the Plan without diverting attention too much from the main purpose of the chapter, we have chosen to include the major objectives and policies in one large table, to save the reader from having to dig around for the facts in the main text. 19 major objectives are listed in Table 6.4, together with corresponding numerical translations of the objectives, where possible and appropriate. The Plan itself is far more explicit and detailed on the policy side than we have room to be in this table, especially with respect to financial and budget policy intentions. A further difficulty in trying to compress all the essentials into one table is that the 'living conditions' and 'solidarity' goals tend to be overshadowed by the third key objective of the Plan: competitiveness. To redress this imbalance, Tables 6.5, 6.6, and 6.7 are also presented, illustrating the intentions and expectations with respect to social overhead capital expenditures.

We have already mentioned the problems involved in transcribing Tables 6.4, 6.5, 6.6, and 6.7 and the rest of the Plan into a suitable form for input to the model, and so there is little to add here except to point to

Table 6.4
Summary of the Sixth Plan's major objectives and policies

General targets and objectives	Quantitative expression of objective included in official Plan	Main related policy recommendations
Competition and growth		
1 Strong and balanced growth to ensure full employment.	1 The average annual rate of growth of PIB to be between 5·8 and 6·0 per cent.	This corresponds to an increase of PIB of one-third over the five-year period. This will be achieved mainly via the industrial, price and trade policies below, but there is also a three-point *competition policy:* (i) changes in certain laws; (ii) more powers to a renamed Technical Commission on Competition; (iii) special consumer regulations.
2 Particular emphasis on industrial growth.	2 The average annual rate of growth of industrial production to be around 7·5 per cent. 3 At least 250,000 new jobs to be created in the industrial sector.	This corresponds to a doubling of industrial output in ten years. *Industrial policy* consists of incentives to restructuring (too many small firms), priority investment programmes for mechanical engineering, chemicals, and electronics, and specific recommendations on glass, iron and steel, ores and non-ferrous metals, motors, shipbuilding, aircraft, and others. Strong internal competition policy in construction industry and commerce.
3 Foreign trade to be in surplus in 1975.	4 Currency reserves of at least $5,000 million to be maintained. 5 Sufficient margin to be created to be able to devote 1 per cent of GNP to foreign aid. 6 Trade surplus to be 1,000 million fr. in 1975. 7 Surplus on trade in industrial products to be 15,000 million fr. in 1975.	*Trade policy* mainly consists of export promotion via a reformed credit system, and improved overseas sales networks. Incentives to firms to establish branches abroad. The price policy is also critical in achieving these targets.

Table 6.4, continued

General targets and objectives	Quantitative expression of objective included in official Plan	Main related policy recommendations
4 Reduction of the structural imbalances in the labour market.	8 Doubling of adult education and manpower retraining facilities between 1970 and 1976.	The employment policy involves considerably strengthening the National Employment Agency, and setting up an extensive vocational training programme, regarded as the main priority for Government investment. School leaving age to be raised to 16 in all schools, and no child to leave school without the beginnings of a vocational training (see also Table 6.7).
5 Considerable expansion of industrial capacity and productivity.	9 Average annual rate of growth of productive investment to be 7 per cent. 10 Investment rate in industry to be 16·7 per cent in 1975.	In broad outline, the Government's *financial policy* is to introduce measures to increase the supply of long-term capital, and to reorient the financial circuits towards industry.
6 Continued efforts in favour of shorter working hours.	11 Absolute maximum working week to be reduced from 60 hours to 57 hours. 12 Average maximum to come down from 54 to 50. 13 Average reduction not to exceed 1½ hours.	Appropriate regulations to be drafted. But to go further than this would compromise the growth targets, as would a general reduction in the retirement age. The latter would also lead to financing difficulties.
7 Prices should grow at most only as fast as prices in the countries that are France's main trading partners.	14 At present (1971) this means that the average annual rate of growth of the general price level should be less than or equal to 3·2 per cent.	The *prices policy* to be aimed mainly at the sheltered and administered sectors because international competition should be sufficient to keep prices down in the exposed sector. The policy involves: (a) a return in stages to uncontrolled prices for products subject to foreign competition; (b) the conclusion of agreements between the administration and services, whereby the latter will undertake to keep their prices stable;

172

Table 6.4, continued

General targets and objectives	Quantitative expression of objective included in official Plan	Main related policy recommendations
		(c) the formulation of agreements to which tradesmen in certain sensitive commercial sectors will subscribe individually;
		(d) the possibility for public enterprises in energy and transport to apply more flexible tariffs that will be better adjusted to market conditions.
8 Further major requirements of competitiveness are (a) increased technical progress in the industrial sector; (b) more secure energy supplies; (c) a properly adapted infrastructure.	15 Proportion of research and development expenditure devoted to competitive industrial sector to be increased from 35 per cent in 1970 to 43 per cent in 1975. 16 Telephone density comparable to that of other EEC countries by 1977, and improved telecommunications. 17 Opening of 875 miles of motorways (see Table 6.9). 18 Completion of port schemes at Dunkirk, Fos, and Lower Seine. (see Table 6.6).	Redirection of Government investment programmes (see Table 6.6). Priority will be given in the *energy policy* to (a) more crude oil storage facilities; (b) incentives to French oil groups to prospect outside main oil regions; (c) 8,000 MW nuclear building programme; (d) faster growth of electricity consumption.
9 'Strategy for change' in industrial redeployment, trades and agriculture.		Coal rundown to be compensated by more jobs in some areas (see objective 17), and agricultural exodus to be 'co-ordinated'. Special role for vocational training programmes (see objective 4), and housing policy (see objective 13). Efficiency drive in commercial and business activities (linked with objectives 2, 3, and 7).

General targets and objectives	Quantitative expression of objective included in official Plan	Main related policy recommendations
10 Public finances must remain in balance over 'average' period, and taxation remain stable.	19 Financing requirement of administrations less than or equal to zero. 20 Weight of taxation to stay at 40 per cent of PIB approximately. 21 Savings rate should exceed 30 per cent of PIB.	Key 'management of public finances' policy, including (a) better utilisation of civil servants; (b) increased contributions from firms to pay for the vocational training programme; (c) tighter control on state contributions to various social security schemes; (d) savings on education, housing, and aircraft expenditures.

Distribution of benefits of growth

11 To permit productive capacities to expand, net disposable resources will grow slightly slower than output.	22 Aggregate consumption to grow at 5·5 per cent p.a., including an average per capita increase of 4·5 per cent.	This corresponds to a doubling of living standards in 15 years.
12 Reduction of share of military expenditures and redeployment of civil expenditures so as substantially to increase expenditure on social overhead capital.	23 Macro-target is an average annual rate of growth of 9 per cent (with a 'low hypothesis' of 8 per cent) in social overhead capital expenditures.	See Table 6.5 for overall figures and Table 6.6 for priority expenditures. A substantial increase in 'living conditions' is one of the three key targets of the Plan ('competition' and 'solidarity' are the others).
13 Increased housing effort.	24 An average of 510,000 new dwellings per year to be completed (with 565,000 in 1975, 315,000 being low cost and social units). 25 Average of 250,000 old dwellings per annum to be improved to a minimum level of amenities	Special investment programme, guided by expected interregional movement of population, and areas of 'badly housed'.
14 Improvement in 'social equity' (the solidarity objective).	26 Conversion of wages to monthly basis by 1975 ('mensualisation'). 27 Regular increases in the minimum wage (SMIC). 28 Increases in overall social benefits of at least 45 per cent during the Plan.	Part of overall management of public finances (see objective 10).

Table 6.4, continued

General targets and objectives	Quantitative expression of objective included in official Plan	Main related policy recommendations
Regional development		
15 Development of economically underdeveloped rural areas.	29 Share of jobs in manufacturing and service industries to be raised to 80 per cent by the end of the Plan in those regions where the percentage is currently (1971) below 75 per cent.	Incentives to firms to locate new jobs in Lower Normandy, Brittany, Midi-Pyrenees, Loire country Poitou-Charentes, Auvergne, Limousin, and Aquitaine.
16 Restructuring of declining industrial areas.	30 At least 30 per cent of net new jobs in motors, machine tools, and chemicals to be located in these areas.	This policy applies to the North, Lorraine, Alsace, and Franche-Comté.
17 Significant progress to be made in the special 'blueprints' for Paris, Lower Seine, Marseille-Fos, and Lyons.		Priority ratings for special projects. (see Table 6.6)
18 Development of middle-towns.		Regarded as important balancing factors in terms of environment and industrial development.
19 Protection of rural amenity areas.		Priority expenditure programmes.

Source: all the material in this table appears in various parts of [112]

another problem, which is more readily apparent now that these tables have been reached: some of the targets in the Plan are five-year targets (such as those in Table 6.6, for example), and so a further element of uncertainty is introduced into the Plan account by having to make additional assumptions about the proportion of the overall amount that refers to 1975 (FIFI, one recalls, is a static model, generating a projection for the final year only of the Plan).

Thus forewarned about the status of the projection, we now consider the results of the Plan account.

Table 6.5

Sixth Plan social overhead capital five-year expenditures by function (millions of 1970 francs)

Functions	Block votes based on a 9 per cent p.a. growth in social overhead capital GFCF		Lower assumption 8 per cent programme appropriations
	Programme appropriations†	GFCF*	
1 Functions for which a GFCF block vote has been provided			
Education and training	19,150	28,350	18,800
Social action	1,800	4,400	1,600
Health	3,600	12,400	3,100
Sporting and socio-educative activities	2,500	8,800	2,250
Cultural affairs	2,000	2,850	1,700
Urban development	19,050	77,400	17,850
Rural development	9,800	30,700	9,300
Transport	15,250	27,600	14,300
Telecommunications	28,400	35,500	27,300
Sub-totals	101,550	228,000	96,200
2 Other functions			
Research	21,400	–	19,500
Overseas departments	2,900	–	2,700
Overseas territories	920	–	850
Posts	2,800	–	2,500
Total	129,570‡	–	121,750

All these figures are estimates only, although the word 'target' is used in respect of the lower figures

* Administrations' share of GFCF
† Central government's contribution
‡ Total financing of public utility services creation by the central government

Source: [112], p. 141

Table 6.6

Sixth Plan social overhead capital priority declarations
(millions of 1970 francs)

Facilities with priority declarations	Five-year programme appropriations*
1 *Goal oriented programmes* (see Table 6.7)	2,850‡
2 *Social facilities*	
Technical education	4,500
Child welfare	95
Training of social workers	70
Crèches	75
Training of health personnel	220
Improving hospital care	320
Cultural action	200
Acquiring land for outdoor, sporting and socio-educational activities in old and, where appropriate, new urban areas	315
Training senior staff in sporting and socio-educational sphere	175
3 *Living conditions*	
Research and experiments with new urban transport methods, and studies of urban traffic movement	650
Urban and provincial motorways	4,300
Public transport in Paris region	1,100
Refuse collection	115
Land tenure activities	1,650
Green spaces	100
Tracked public transport (Lyons and Marseilles)	_†
Research into plan construction	240
Research into nuisance abatement	230
Water treatment stations	700
4 *Transport and communications*	
Link-motorways programme	1,950
Dunkirk port programme	440
Le Havre port programme	430
Marseilles-Fos programme	420
Operations in river ports and inland waterways:	
(a) northern	330
(b) Seine (priority)	190
(c) Saône–Rhône	245
Mechanisation of mail handling and sorting	730

Table 6.6, continued

Facilities with priority declarations	Five-year programme appropriations*
5 *Research*	
Life sciences	490
Human sciences	120
Atmospheric, space, land and sea	540
Electronic components	815
Research and development in other industrial sectors	1,350
Mathematics	20.
Multi-purpose computer centre installations	240
Science information and documentation	40
Total (without 2)	26,255

* These are only central government contributions. Other public administrations (mainly local authorities and OSPAEs) also contribute, in some cases substantially more so than central government. They have to be respected in the annual national budget unless there is a revision of the Plan at mid-term

† Not determined at time of approval of Plan

‡ Not confirmed at time of approval of Plan. In addition to this figure, another 830 million of the figures listed under 2, 3, 4 and 5 are in goal-oriented programmes. See Table 6.7. Of this figure of 2,850, 2,680 are included in Table 6.5.

Source: [112], pp. 142–3

6.2   The main results of the Plan account

As with the departure account, the results of the Plan account are extensive, and it is not possible to relate them in full without making the chapter unusually long in comparison with the others. Accordingly, we have again been selective, picking out the results that correspond to those reported in Chapter 4. We begin with the reduced overall economic table (TEE) shown in Table 6.8, which also contains some of the departure account details given in Table 4.5. The first striking feature in comparing the two accounts is again the marked conservatism of the departure account estimates for 1965–1970: production, imports, consumption, investment, and exports are all under-estimated in the departure account. One wonders what effect the Plan account's 1965–1970 figures would have had on

178

the actual Plan figures if they had been included in the departure account. The other main features of the Plan account are, first, that PIB growth is much higher, reflecting objective 1 in Table 6.4, and secondly, that imports grow more slowly than in the departure account, reflecting faith in the competition policy (but one should bear in mind that all previous Plans have optimistically under-estimated imports). Thirdly, total consumption is growing slightly faster, as a result of the increase in output, but there is a clear indication of the public finance policy (objective 10) in the relative cut-back in administration consumption.

Looking at the employment figures in Table 6.9, the high Plan growth rate has a clear effect on immigration and activity rates, increasing the domestic working population by over 600,000. Lower unemployment contributes to an increase in total employment of 710,000, compared with the departure account. There is confirmation here of the fact that FIFI cannot accept a full employment constraint, and it is not difficult to understand why the Plan account was not published in the Plan itself, being in clear contradiction with the 'full employment' objective (al-

Table 6.7

Sixth Plan goal-oriented programmes

---

1 *New towns:* to create autonomous urban units so that the population can find work ɔn the spot.

2 *Road safety:* to prevent increases in the number of fatal accidents.

3 *Mother and child care:* to reduce the number of children affected by lasting handicaps as a result of sickness or accident during pregnancy or childbirth.

4 *Labour market:* to ensure a third of placements through better organisation of the public guidance and placement facilities.

5 *Old people:* to stabilise the number of persons cared for in institutions, and to improve the home care service.

6 *Mediterranean forests:* to safeguard and exploit the forests in the Mediterranean area.

See parts 1 and 3 in Table 6.6.

Appropriations for goal-oriented programmes are given in an appendix to the Finance Act.

Source: [112], p. 140

Table 6.8

Equilibrium between production and its uses (in volume terms)
(August 1971 account: results)

	Average annual growth rates (per cent)			
	Departure account		Plan account	
	1965/1970	1970/1975	1965/1970	1970/1975
Resources				
Gross domestic production (PIB)	5·4	5·4	5·8	5·9
Imports	10·6	9·8	12·4	9·3
Total resources and uses	6·1	5·9	6·5	6·4
Uses				
Total consumption, of which:	4·8	5·2	5·1	5·3
households	4·9	5·3	5·2	5·4
public administrations	3·6	4·0	3·4	3·3
financial institutions	5·4	6·8	4·9	6·0
Investment (GFCF), of which:	7·3	5·5	7·8	6·4
productive	8·0	5·4	9·0	6·8
housing	6·0	4·8	5·5	4·6
public administrations	7·0	7·0	7·3	7·6
financial institutions	6·2	3·6	6·4	6·5
Exports and balance of services' uses	10·0	8·2	11·3	10·0

Source: columns 1 and 2, see Table 4.5; columns 3 and 4, Table 5, [94], p. 36

though an unemployment rate of 1·5 per cent would be regarded by some as full employment). Allowing for the fact that the agricultural exodus is more rapid than anticipated in the departure account, 1,050,000 new jobs have to be created in the Sixth Plan period, 250,000 being in industry (in conformity with objective 2) and almost all the remainder being in sector 7 (the other four sectors balance out, reductions due to run-downs in coal and the railways being compensated by increases in telecommunications). 800,000 extra jobs in sector 7 may seem high but it actually corresponds to a slower growth rate in the sector, compared with previous years (1,150,000 were created between 1962 and 1968). Employment

180

outside the branches (mainly in public administrations) is higher, in spite of the aim to use civil servants more efficiently (see objective 10), but colums 4 and 5 do indicate a slowing down in the growth rate (this is further emphasised by the 1960–1965 figure which is 2·8).

The overall foreign trade picture (see Table 6.10) is much improved compared with the departure account. Although imports in all sectors are higher, exports are even better, demonstrating the expected effects of the trade policy described in Table 6.4. The trade balance of 13·4 billion francs (1975) is completely due to the very high balance of trade in industrial products, which exceeds the target contained in the Plan. The balance of payments is slightly in deficit, but this situation is mitigated by the positive balance with the non-franc area part of the world.

Three particular policy guidelines are apparent in the top part of Table 6.11: first, social transfers are kept at their high departure account rate, in line with objective 14; secondly gross fixed capital formation is slightly higher, corresponding to objective 12 (the Plan target rate of 9·0 per cent includes telecommunications, but the rate shown in Table 6.11 does not); and thirdly, there is a big cut-back in subsidies to enterprises, which is part of the 'management of public finances' policy.[4] On the receipts side, company profits are taxed much more highly in the Plan account than in the departure account, but personal incomes slightly less, thus showing further evidence of the psychological barrier that we referred to in Chapter 5. This barrier is very obvious in the bottom part of the table, where the policy of holding taxation around the 40 per cent mark (objective 10) has a marked effect in comparison with the departure account. In this same part of the table, the increased social security contributions' share is largely responsible for eliminating the huge social security administrations' deficit in the departure account.

Looking at savings and investment in Table 6.12, there is a clear move not to overburden households, relying on increased efforts from all other agencies. The overall total is growing slightly more slowly than in the departure account, again following a better-than-expected performance in the 1965–1970 period. All the self-financing rates are higher, except for sector 7, reflecting once again the competition policy in that sector. The other high increases, in energy and transport in particular, are due to the policy of reducing subsidies to public enterprises (objective 10, see note 4), and the policy of directing the financial circuits towards industry (see objective 5).

Finally, on prices (see Table 6.13, there is a significant difference between the two accounts in the growth of the general price level (the PIB price). This reflects the price policy listed in Table 6.4, and is well within

Table 6.9

Equilibrium of employment (August 1971 Plan account: results)

	Departure account		Plan account		
	Level in 1975 (thousands)	1965/1975 average annual growth rate	Level in 1975 (thousands)	1965/1970 average growth	1970/1975 annual rates
Total population present in metropolitan France	52,990	0·8	53,233	0·8	1·0
Working population resources					
Total domestic working population	21,540	0·6	22,133	0·9	0·9
less military in metropolitan France	−245*		−180		
less available working population looking for a job	−395		−343		
Total employed domestic working population	20,900	0·55	21,610	0·9	0·9

182

Use of working population

	1	2	3	4	5
1 Agriculture (01)	2,321	−3·5	2,223	−3·8	−4·0
2 Agricultural and food industries (02)	703	0·2	645	−0·2	−0·4
3 Energy (03 to 05)	292	−2·4	335	−1·7	−0·7
4 Industry (06 to 12)	5,145	0·5	5,311	0·6	1·0
5 Transport and telecommunications (14)	1,085	0·5	1,127	1·2	0·6
6 Housing (15)	47	2·15	80	3·1	0·5
7 Building and public works, services and commerce (13, 16 to 19)	7,537	1·8	8,009	2·6	2·2
Employment in the branches	17,130	0·3	17,730	0·6	0·7
Employment outside the branches	3,770	1·8	3,880	2·4	2·1
Total employed domestic working population	20,900	0·55	21,610	0·9	0·9
Wage earners	16,960	1·4	17,528	1·8	1·6
Non wage earners	3,940	−2·4	4,082	−2·2	−1·8
Employed total domestic working population	20,900	0·55	21,610	0·9	0·9

* This figure is all military (see Table 4.6, and [94], Second Part, Chapter 1, for explanation of the distinction)

Source: columns 1 and 2, see Table 4.6; columns 3, 4 and 5, [94], p. 41

Table 6.10

External account (August 1971 Plan account: results)

Imports and exports	Departure account		Plan account			
	1975 (at 1965 prices) million francs	1965/1975 average annual growth rate (volume)	1975 (at 1965 prices) million francs	Average annual growth rates (volume)		
				1965/1970	1970/1975	1965/1975
I Imports	136,942	10·2	144,553	12·4	9·3	10·8
1 Agricultural products (01)	4,470	0	5,117	2·3	0·5	1·4
2 Agricultural and food industries (02)	8,957	3·9	11,000	7·5	4·6	6·0
3 Energy (03 to 05)	14,209	5·6	17,935	9·1	7·1	8·1
4 Industry (06 to 12)	109,246	12·8	110,441	15·1	10·8	12·9
Others	60	7·2	60	–	–	–
II Exports	127,761	9·5	147,087	12·0	10·2	11·1
1 Agricultural products (01)	8,155	6·9	9,300	10·9	5·7	8·3
2 Agricultural and food industries (02)	6,040	3·1	10,770	12·2	6·4	9·2
3 Energy (03 to 05)	1,000	−6·2	2,960	6·2	2·9	4·5
4 Industry (06 to 12)	112,316	10·7	123,807	12·4	11·2	11·8
Others	250	−1·7	250	–	–	–
III Balance of services' uses	8,057	4·0	9,267	3·3	7·6	5·4
IV Balance of trade in goods and services (II+III−I)	−1,124		11,801			

Source: columns 1 and 2, see Table 4.7; others, [94], p. 56

Summary balances

	Plan account (10⁹ current francs)		
	1965	1970	1975
1 Merchandise trade balance	−0·2	−4·8	0·5
with abroad	(−0·5)	(6·4)	(−0·5)
with franc area	(0·3)	(1·6)	(1·0)
2 Services' uses balances	5·5	7·8	12·9
with abroad	(3·9)	(5·6)	(9·2)
with franc area	(1·6)	(2·2)	(3·7)
3 Distributive operations balance	−6·0	−7·0	−14·3
with abroad	(−1·3)	(−1·5)	(−5·7)
with franc area	(−4·7)	(−5·5)	(−8·6)
4 Exterior's financing requirement (1+2+3)	−0·7	−4·0	−0·9
abroad	(2·1)	(−2·3)	(3·0)
franc area	(−2·8)	(−1·7)	(−3·9)

Source: Table 31, [94], p. 59

Table 6.11

Public administrations' expenditures and receipts
(August 1971 Plan account: results)

Expenditures	Average annual growth rates (real values)			
	Departure account		Plan account	
	1965/1970	1970/1975	1965/1970	1970/1975
Operations (wages, etc.)	5·8	4·8	5·9	6·1
Gross fixed capital formation	6·6	7·4	6·8	7·6
Social transfers	6·7	7·7	6·5	7·7
Subsidies to enterprises	5·2	7·6	3·0	4·0
Other expenditures (including military)	*	*	2·7	3·8
Total (excluding subs between administrations)	6·0	7·0	5·5	6·5
Receipts				
Social security contributions	7·1	6·7	7·2	6·8
Receipts from taxation	5·0	6·0	4·5	6·1
of which: Direct taxes	7·8	5·8	7·9	6·3
on company profits	6·2	0·8	10·0	3·2
on personal incomes	8·0	9·6	6·2	9·2
other	9·6	0·6	9·4	3·4
Indirect taxes	3·9	6·1	3·2	6·0
Subsidies between administrations	7·3	13·7	7·8	11·6
Various resources	3·1	1·7	6·9	2·3
Financing capacity in 1975	−6764 m. 1965 francs		1549 m. 1975 francs	
Total	6·0	7·0	5·7	6·9

the corresponding objective (the foreign PIB price grows at 3·2 per cent, see Table 6.1). Consumer prices grow more quickly, however, mainly because of the increased services content in household consumption relative to PIB. Another clear policy effect is the remarkable cut-back in the housing GFCF price, due to the assumption of significant productivity gains in the building industry.[5]

186

Table 6.11, continued

Financing requirement (−) or capacity (+)	Real values (million fr. 1965) Departure account		Nominal values (million fr.) Plan account	
	1970	1975	1970	1975
Central government	5107	8262	7835	6432
Local authorities	−3358	−3531	−5080	−5520
Semi-public enterprises (OSPAEs)	−1103	−3096	−1449	−4261
Social security	−92	−8398	3114	1800
Other administrations	−40	0	−77	0
Total: all administrations	594	−6764	4343	−1549

Weight of taxation (percentage of PIB)	Departure account		Plan account	
	1970	1975	1970	1975
All administrations (central government in brackets)	39·9 (22·5)	41·8 (23·5)	38·8 (20·4)	39·7 (20·7)
Direct taxes	7·8 (7·1)	8·0 (7·4)	7·7	7·9
Indirect taxes	17·4 (15·0)	18·1 (15·7)	16·5	16·6
Social security contributions	14·7 (0·4)	15·7 (0·4)	14·6	15·2

* This table is not exactly comparable with the corresponding part of Table 4.8; the figures in these two columns are therefore approximate, and it is not really possible to give a figure for 'other expenditures'.

Source: columns 1 and 2, see Table 4.8; others, Tables 18, 20, 21, [94], pp. 49—51

6.3   From the departure account to the Plan account

It is interesting to examine the changes that took place in the values of the main aggregates during the period between the appearance of the departure account in September 1969 and the Plan account in August 1971. Table 6.14 summarises these changes, presenting the values contained in

Table 6.12

Equilibrium of savings and investment
(August 1971 Plan account: results)

	Average annual growth rates (real values)			
	Departure account		Plan account	
	1965/1970	1970/1975	1965/1970	1970/1975
Gross savings of domestic agencies				
Companies	8·2	4·4	9·1	5·5
Households	6·1	6·3	7·5	4·7
of which: CFCFIE	(6·3)	(3·3)	(7·9)	(4·6)
Administrations	4·8	1·3	7·5	3·7
Financial institutions	8·4	11·5	7·7	12·7
Insurance indemnities on capital goods				
(IICG)	8·3	8·3	5·4	12·4
Total domestic savings	7·2	5·7	8·1	5·3
Gross capital formation				
Non-financial enterprises	7·0	5·0	9·2	4·8
Households	6·2	7·0	6·2	4·6
Administrations	6·6	6·8	6·9	7·3
Financial institutions	6·2	3·4	6·2	6·6
Total GCF	6·7	5·6	na	na

Source: definitions and columns 1 and 2, see Table 4.9; other columns,
see Tables 32, 33 and 37, [94], pp. 60, 61 and 64

15 different central accounts. The departure account is, as we have seen,
trend-oriented and conventional, but this is not the case with any of the
other accounts shown in the table. Indeed, as shown in Figure 1.2 , policy
changes were evaluated very early on in phase two, the first stage in the
gradual movement towards a synthesising account being the intermediate
account. This was the forerunner to the reference account, prepared in
January 1970 to act as a basis for the Forecasting Directorate (DP) to
draw up a preliminary financial operations table (a reference TOF). This
TOF was consistent with stronger growth and a better balance of payments situation than in the departure account, and enabled a more detailed
investment analysis to be carried out.

Table 6.12, continued

	1970	1975	1970	1975
Financing capacity (+) or requirement (−)	(millions 1965 francs)		(million francs nominal values)	
Non-financial enterprises	−29,155	−41,633	−47,586	−63,083
Households	19,010	26,564	27,744	39,311
Administrations	594	−6,764	4,343	−1,548
Financial institutions	9,303	16,712	11,484	24,389
Exterior	248	4,817	4,015	931
of which: abroad	(−1,423)	(1,553)	(2,292)	(−3,038)
franc area	(1,671)	(3,264)	(1,723)	(3,969)
Rate of self-financing	(per cent)		(per cent)	
All enterprises	na	69·6	69·1	70·8
1 Agriculture	na	56·7	na	60·8
2 Agricultural and food industries	na	75·1	na	79·9
3 Energy	na	60·0	na	88·4
4 Industry	na	75·9	na	76·2
5 Transport and telecommunications	na	77·5	na	83·4
7 Building and public works, services and commerce	na	72·8	na	67·8
Savings rates				
Domestic savings rate	29·8	29·7	31·2	30·3
Household savings rate	16·1	16·8	17·0	16·0

na = not available

Following the reference account, three more central accounts were simultaneously constructed in February 1970: the base account and two variants of it, the main results of which are shown in Table 6.14. The caution (5·5 per cent) account made a deliberately prudent assessment of the growth potential of the economy, and of the international environment. On the economic policy side, priority was given to balance of payments equilibrium and a more balanced public financial position, as the results in column two of Table 6.14 confirm. The base account (6·0 per cent) and rapid change account (6·5 per cent) both went for more rapid growth, the first by means of a supply stimulation policy, and the second by following an accelerated structural transformation policy. Both

189

Table 6.13

Changes in nominal prices (August 1971 Plan account: results)

	Average annual growth rates (per cent)			
	Departure account		Plan account	
	1965/1970	1970/1975	1965/1970	1970/1975
Nominal prices of the aggregates				
Consumption	4·5	3·5	4·5	3·5
of which: households	4·5	3·5	4·5	3·6
administrations	3·5	3·3	3·1	2·3
Investment (GFCF)	3·9	3·5	4·1	2·7
of which: productive	3·5	2·1	3·7	2·6
housing	4·6	6·0	5·0	2·7
administrations	3·9	4·1	4·1	2·9
Exports and services' use balance	2·1	0·9	2·6	0·9
Imports	2·2	0	2·9	0·7
Gross domestic production (PIB)	4·3	3·5	4·65	2·9

Source: columns 1 and 2, Table 4.10; columns 3 and 4, Table 15, [94], p. 46

accounts show marked improvements compared with the departure account (but the reader should bear in mind that a central account consists of several thousand results, only ten of which are shown in Table 6.14), although the public finance deficit is still a problem.

In the period leading up to the choice of the options account, the economic policy means were specified in more detail, and several further sets of results were produced. Column five in Table 6.14 shows how the main aggregates of the options account eventually appeared, in August 1970, after the vote on the options. This account is very similar to the base account, on which it is 'based', but shows improved unemployment, price, and public finance figures. In fact, at first sight, one might well ask why the options account was not left alone: it is marginally better than the eventual Plan account on growth, unemployment, prices, wages, public finance and taxation. The answer is, of course, that the policy input to the options account was not based on any proper analysis of possible means or measures, but only on hypothetical policies that would achieve the 'norms and objectives' written into the account. It was for the Plan Commissions to examine realistic policy measures, and as we know from previous chapters, they made their choices as a result of many separate sector analyses and studies, a lot of which did not involve the FIFI model. In addition, the reservations that we made at the beginning of this chapter about the status and accuracy of the Plan account also apply when comparing it with other central accounts. It is clear, however, that special attention was focused on the external deficit in the options account; the deficit is reduced by almost 50 per cent in the Plan account.

The six structural patterns shown in Table 6.14 examine the effects of changes in the parameters relating to the behaviour of domestic agencies, for a given international situation. In effect, they are sensitivity analyses constructed around these parameters, and they can also be used in connection with the analysis of policies designed to counter the effects of unforeseen behavioural changes; some of the results are shown with and without such corrective policies. Ideally, this type of analysis should be undertaken in a dynamic context, since it is important to understand when to apply corrective policies and for how long; FIFI, of course, is a static model, but a number of alternative approaches to this problem have been tried, some of which are discussed in Chapter 10.

6.4 Disaggregation of the Plan account

All the central accounts and associated variants that we have described at length in this and previous chapters contain a seven-sector breakdown. For many of the Plan Commissions and their sector committees this is not detailed enough, so that additional tools have to be employed to get down to the problems that they regard as important. Later in this section we give an overview of the detailed projections that were carried out during the preparation of the Sixth Plan, but first we describe the way in which the Plan account was disaggregated into 36 branches, to show, purely for illustrative purposes, what the Plan meant in terms of specific industries. This level of disaggregation was chosen in order to correspond as closely as possible with the number of sector committees. It is interesting to note that although there was a deliberate move in the Sixth Plan to reduce the amount of technical consistency work done by the Plan Commissions, many of them found that the FIFI model by itself was not an adequate substitute: this is yet another aspect of the conflict between those who feel the need for more detail generated by bigger models, and those who feel that there is already too much to understand and assimilate with the present model.

In this particular instance, the case for using the 36-branch breakdown in all Plan preparation phases is not a strong one. To attempt to formulate

Table 6.14

Changes in the main aggregates, from the departure account to the Plan account

Main aggregates	Departure account (Sept. 1969)	Three central accounts (Feb. 1970)			Options account (Aug. 1970)	(1)
		Caution account	Base account	Rapid change account		
1 Average annual growth of PIB (in 1970/1975)	5·4	5·5	6·0	6·5	5·95	6·4
2 Average annual growth of industrial production (1970/1975)	6·4	7·0	7·4	7·7	7·5	8·
3 Average annual growth of household consumption	5·3	ng	ng	ng	5·2	5·
4 Number of people looking for a job (in 1975) (thousands)	395	375	345	275	295	295
5 Average annual growth of the general price level (1970/1975)	3·5	2·7	3·0	3·3	2·7	2·
6 Average annual growth of real wages (1970/1975)	3·1	3·65	3·8	4·4	4·65	4·
7 Public finances deficit (in 1975, in 10^9 1975 francs)	10	1·7	7·2	8·4	1·4	−1
8 Exterior's financing capacity (in 1975 10^9 1975 francs)	7	4·5	0·5	−0·9	1·7	−3
9 Weight of taxation (per cent of PIB in 1975)	41·8	ng	ng	ng	39·3	39
10 Industrial products trade balance (in 1975, in 10^9 1975 francs)	ng	15·1	13·3	11·7	ng	ng

ng = not given in source

Source: see note 6

the mechanisms operating between 36 branches rather than seven and include them in all the central accounts and variants would clearly be a monumental task requiring resources to be taken away from more important priorities (as we described in Chapter 5), and the approach to the disaggregated Plan account is consequently simple and straightforward,

6.14, continued

uctural patterns f 1970 – March 1971)									Plan account (Aug. 1971)
t tive	(2) with corrective policy	(3) without corrective policy	(3) with corrective policy	(4)	(5)	(6) without corrective policy	(6) with corrective policy	
	5·3	5·2	5·1	5·6	4·75	5·1	5·0	5·9
	6·4	6·2	6·5	6·8	4·3	5·9	6·0	7·5
	3·4	4·7	4·3	5·2	4·2	3·6	3·2	5·3
	350	400	420	305	340	290	305	340
	3·3	3·6	3·6	3·8	4·6	4·0	4·0	2·9
	3·55	4·4	4·3	4·9	3·4	3·0	2·9	3·9
	1·0	9·0	1·5	3·0	14·5	8·3	−0·6	1·5
	−1·1	7·8	−0·9	9·0	31·3	6·8	−0·3	0·9
	43·1	39·7	40·1	39·8	41·9	41·3	41·8	39·7
	ng	ng	ng	ng	ng	ng	ng	16·6

acknowledging its many shortcomings but nevertheless providing a further useful insight to the Plan. It involves the use of an input–output table, which is constructed in a rudimentary manner, bringing in assumptions about developments in particular industries made in sector committee analyses and the FIFI model. Household consumption and foreign trade

Table 6.15

Disaggregated sector breakdown of exports and imports associated with the August 1971 Plan account

Products	Exports				Imports			
	Average annual growth rates (volume) (per cent)		Share of exports in total uses (per cent)*		Average annual growth rates (volume) (per cent)		Share of imports in total resources (per cent)	
	1965/1970	1970/1975	1965	1975	1960/1965	1970/1975	1965	1975
1 Agriculture	10·5	6·1	5·8	10·3	1·4	0·8	6·1	5·6
2 Agricultural and foodstuffs industries	12·0	6·5	4·8	8·2	7·4	4·4	6·6	8·4
3 Solid combustible minerals	26·1	−20·3	1·2	1·7	1·0	1·0	23·1	33·7
4 Factory gas	–	–	–	–	–	–	–	–
5 Electricity, water and others	17·4	−18·2	6·0	4·3	21·6	5·3	22·0	24·4
6 Oil, natural gas, and motor fuels	4·0	5·9	6·0	4·3	11·6	8·0	22·0	24·4
7 Construction materials	9·2	8·4	4·2	5·5	16·4	8·3	4·9	7·0
8 Glass	8·7	9·3	16·6	18·0	25·1	10·1	5·3	16·3
9 Iron ore and iron and steel products	3·7	3·2	24·5	21·4	6·0	0·9	14·2	17·2
10 Non-ferrous ores, metals, and semi-finished products	12·5	8·8	19·5	26·1	5·9	7·6	35·2	40·4
11 Primary steel products	10·9	10·4	7·3	9·8	18·0	16·5	4·6	10·3
12 Precision machinery	16·9	11·8	12·5	19·2	17·2	10·3	13·1	17·9
13 Other mechanical equipment	–	–	–	–	–	–	–	–
14 Electrical equipment	17·7	12·4	9·1	14·8	24·9	10·1	8·0	13·4
15 Electronic equipment	16·3	18·0	11·3	19·9	28·0	13·4	8·3	14·7
16 Automobiles and cycles	19·3	8·5	17·4	23·5	30·6	17·9	8·4	15·9

	1	2	3	4	5	6	7	8
17 Shipbuilding	8·1	15·2	37·5	37·7	5·4	8·7	13·2	9·3
18 Aircraft	10·4	13·9	29·3	43·3	-7·5	0·0	11·4	15·4
19 Armaments and munitions	-0·3	11·3	35·4	47·5	30·9	15·4	4·6	7·0
20 Various minerals	3·0	4·2	17·3	13·7	7·2	8·1	23·1	28·5
21 Basic chemicals	16·2	17·0	18·3	25·5	20·3	10·8	17·6	23·4
22 Other chemical industry products	14·5	12·2	10·8	14·6	7·5	8·1	6·8	7·8
23 Textiles	7·0	8·5	19·2	22·7	3·3	11·2	15·0	23·7
24 Clothing	13·1	12·1	3·3	6·9	30·6	19·6	1·1	5·3
25 Leather	4·9	7·2	13·6	15·3	11·7	15·9	6·6	15·5
26 Wood products	5·9	11·4	5·1	6·3	15·2	12·3	9·4	14·4
27 Paper and cardboard	10·7	16·8	7·5	12·0	11·4	11·0	14·6	22·2
28 Newspaper and printing	6·0	10·6	4·2	5·4	22·9	10·5	3·6	6·3
29 Plastics	20·5	24·7	4·0	8·9	60·7	16·0	3·1	7·0
30 Miscellaneous industrial	12·2	10·1	12·2	11·8	20·4	8·2	6·8	6·3
31 Building and public works	7·5	5·5	–	–	–	–	–	–
32 Transport	5·4	7·3	14·2	14·9	–	–	–	–
33 Telecommunications	0·6	-0·6	1·5	0·7	–	–	–	–
34 Housing services†	–	–	–	–	–	–	–	–
35 Other services	-11·3	12·6	–	–	-1·5	10·2	–	–
Total	11·3	10·0	7·2	10·5	9·8	9·1	6·6	9·7

* Total uses as defined in the TEE. The ratio is calculated using exports and total uses valued in 1965 francs. Similar remarks apply to the imports side.
† This is the sector that we have called just 'housing' in other tables

Source: columns 1 to 4, Table 194, [94], pp. 324—5; others, Table 196, [94], pp. 328—9

Table 6.16

Disaggregated sector breakdown of employment and gross fixed capital formation associated with the August 1971 Plan account

Branches		Employment Thousands		Average annual growth rates (per cent)			GFCF Annual average growth rates (per cent)	
		1965	1975	1960/1965	1965/1970	1970/1975	1959/1969	1965/1975
1	Agriculture	3,316	2,223	-3.7	-3.8	-4.0	7.4	5.9
2	Agricultural and foodstuffs industries	664	645	0	-0.2	-0.4	9.8	6.8
3	Solid combustible minerals	165	68	-3.6	-7.5	-9.5	-6.7	-12.1
3B	Factory gas	25	30	1.0	0.8	2.7	1.8	5.9
4	Electricity, water and others	100	125	1.4	2.0	2.6	3.3	1.6
5	Oil, natural gas, and motor fuels	86	112	3.9	2.8	2.6	7.7	6.3
6A	Contruction materials	224	215	1.7	0.7	-1.5	11.4	6.7
6B	Glass	70	82	3.1	1.1	1.9	7.3	1.7
7	Iron ore and iron and steel products	203	168	0.1	-2.7	-1.1	3.8	9.9
8	Non-ferrous ores and metals	31	32	2.0	-0.8	1.5	-2.5	2.0
9A	Primary metal transforming	484	540	1.7	0.8	1.4	4.2	4.7
9B	Mechanical machines and apparatus	781	907	2.1	1.9	0.9	8.6	8.4
9C	Electrical machines and apparatus	352	470	3.8	2.7	3.2	8.7	8.2
9D	Automobiles and cycles	291	414	1.8	4.0	3.2	11.3	12.1
9E	Shipbuilding, aircraft, and armaments	148	170	1.2	0.6	2.1	5.6	9.8
10	Chemical industry products	377	499	2.3	2.3	3.4	7.6*	8.3*

11A	Textiles	520	398	−1·2	−2·7	−2·5	7·8	3·1
11B	Clothing	375	309	−1·3	−2·1	−1·8	13·8	11·3
11C	Leather	185	142	−1·2	−3·1	−2·1	6·0	4·0
12A	Wood products	300	272	0·5	−1·2	−0·8	9·6	8·7
12B	Paper and board	137	149	1·8	0·8	0·9	12·5	10·2
12C	Newspapers and printing	219	275	4·1	2·6	2·0	17·9	13·6
12D	Miscellaneous industries	206	269	3·1	2·0	3·5	13·2	10·6
13	Building and public works	1,940	2,165	4·1	1·5	1·0	12·4	7·5
14A	Transport	721	687	1·9	0·3	−1·2	4·3	5·1
14B	Telecommunications	307	440	2·9	3·4	3·8	15·0	13·7
15	Housing services	68	80	1·5	2·7	0·6	6·7	4·9
16	Other services	2,239	3,209	2·3	4·1	3·2	15·2	11·8
19	Commerce	2,146	2,635	1·9	2·0	1·9	15·2	11·6
Total		16,680	17,730	0·6	0·6	0·6	8·7	7·9

* Excluding the GFCF of the Atomic Energy Commission

Source: columns 1 to 5, Table 197, [94], pp. 330–1; others, Table 198, [94], p. 332

figures from detailed analyses carried out by the INSEE and DP specialist divisions are combined to produce detailed final demand estimates, and their combination with the projected input—output table generates a first simplified overall economic table (TEE) for each branch. These figures have to be consistent with the Plan account, other detailed analyses (see Table 6.17 for full details), and the CGP's guidelines contained in the Plan. It is not possible to ensure complete overall consistency, but various adjustments and modifications are made to the input—output table, and new branch projections are constructed.

This process may be repeated several times before an acceptable resources—uses equilibrium is obtained. The production figures are then taken from this final version, and gross fixed capital formation and employment figures calculated for each branch, following much the same consistency check, modification procedure. All this is done in 1965 price terms because too little is known about individual branch price mechanisms to be able to produce a current price projection. The results of this disaggregated projection are given in [94], and we present a sample in Tables 6.15 and 6.16.

There are 35 products described in Table 6.15 (commerce is the thirty-sixth branch and has no product), export growth rates being given for each one. The relationship with the seven FIFI sectors is as follows (with the disaggregated branch numbers in brackets): 1 (1), 2(2), 3(3 to 6), 4(7 to 30), 5(32,33), 6(34), and 7(31,35,36). Looking at columns two, four, six, and eight in Table 6.15, it is possible to obtain a better appreciation of some of the Plan objectives described in Table 6.4. For instance, import growth rates are lower in 1970—1975 than in 1960—1965 in 16 out of the 23 industrial products, confirming the intention to increase the competitiveness of French industry; but there is still some way to go: for 21 out of the 23 industrial products, the share of imports in total resources is higher in 1975 than in 1965.

The employment and investment figures in Table 6.16 are given in terms of the French 29-branch national accounts classification.[7] More Plan objectives are discernible here: employment in agriculture, coal, and transport (mainly the railways) is seen to be declining, and investment is also at rates below the Plan average. The telecommunications branch behaves according to the priority to be given to this area in the Plan, and confirms objective 8 in Table 6.4. Steel, textiles, clothing and footwear are clearly declining in terms of employment opportunities, and emphasise the urgency of creating new jobs in areas where these industries are located (mainly the north and east, thus highlighting objective 16 in Table 6.4).

198

Table 6.17

Detailed projections and disaggregated analysis carried out during the preparation of the Sixth Plan

Type of analysis	Title of analysis and Main division involved	References
Demography and employment		
1 Demographic projections: total population, households, working population, and school population.	'Demographic projections for France' (Calot, Bodin, Salais and Hémery). INSEE: Demography, Employment.	[133], [134].
2 Demographic projections: regions, towns, ZEAT* etc.	'Regional pattern no. 2: first results' (Cazin, Perras, and Muet). INSEE: Regional studies.	[135] and Chapter 8.
3 Manpower projection by qualification.	'Trend projections of French needs for manpower by profession, 1968–1975–1980' (Bégué). INSEE: Employment.	[136].
4 Regional outline on employment in 1985.	'Regional outline on employment in 1985'. INSEE: Regional studies.	Internal papers, and Chapter 8.
Enterprises and production		
5 Agricultural production and prices (by product): simulation models.	'Agriculture in the Sixth Plan'. INSEE: Agriculture.	[94], pp. 93–110.
6 Energy: the FINER model.	'The financing model in the energy sector'. 'The EdF accounts projection models'. DP: Productive economy. INSEE: Enterprise analysis.	[137]. [138]. [94], pp. 111–39.
7 Transport: the public enterprises model.	'Transport in the Sixth Plan'. INSEE: Enterprise analysis.	[94], pp. 141–6.
8 Projection of goods and services in 36 branches: input–output table.	'Disaggregation of the Sixth Plan into 36 branches'. INSEE: Goods and services synthesis.	[94], pp. 319–44.
Consumption		
9 Semi-global integrated model.	'Analysis of substitution effects in a complete system of demand functions' (Nasse). INSEE: Research.	[139].

Type of analysis	Title of analysis and Main division involved	References
10 Consumption broken down by products	'Projection of food consumption in 1975' (Fouquet).	[140].
	'Projection of the demand for automobiles in 1975' (Thomas).	[141].
	'Consumption models and projections' (Vangrevelinghe).	[142].
	'The household budget in 1975 according to the Sixth Plan' (Fouquet). INSEE: Consumption enquiries, and Household accounts.	[143].
11 Medical consumption.	'The consumption of medical services will continue to grow rapidly'. CREDOC[†]	[144].
Housing		
12 Construction programme.	'Housing in the Sixth Plan'. INSEE: Programmes.	[94] pp. 147–63.
13 Financing: completion of the FILO model.	'The housing finance model'. DP: Financial operations.	[145].
14 Policy: completion of the POLO model.	'The housing policy model'. DP: Financial operations.	[146].
Public finance and administrations		
15 Social security systems: the SECUS model.	'Model for projecting social security operations' (Martel, Lannay, Perdriau). DP: Administrations.	[88] and [94], pp. 243–54.
16 Local authorities account: the COLOC model.	'Public finances in the Sixth Plan'. DP: Administrations.	[94], pp. 211–34 and pp. 255–70.
17 OSPAE accounts: the OSPAE model.	Ditto.	Ditto.
18 The financial accounts of administrations by sub-agents: the CONFI model.	Used to construct the financial operations table. DP: Administrations.	See Figure 3.6 in Chapter 3 on these five models.
19 Financing of social overhead capital: the ECOL model.	Ditto.	Ditto.
Taxation		
20 Taxation projection models.	'Taxation in the Sixth Plan'. DP: Taxation analyses.	[94], pp. 271–88.

Type of analysis	Title of analysis and Main division involved	References
The external account		
21 Translation of the external account into balance of payments terms: transfer dictionary.	'Foreign trade in the Sixth Plan'. DP: External.	[94], pp. 183–209.
22 Wage transfers abroad.	Simulation model. DP: External.	Internal papers.
Financial problems		
23 Financial operations table: simulation model.	'Financial networks in the Sixth Plan'. DP: Financial operations.	[94], pp. 259–303.
24 Long-term financing table.	As above.	
Regional aspects		
25 Regional local authority and household accounts.	INSEE: Regional studies.	Internal papers.

* ZEAT = zone d'étude et d'aménagement du territoire (regional development and analysis area). There are eight ZEATs covering the whole of France (see Chapter 8)

† CREDOC = Centre de Recherches et de Documentation sur la Consommation (Research and documentation centre on consumption).

Source: [82], pp. 109–10

The priority to be accorded to chemicals and electronics (objective 2 in Table 6.4) is also apparent.

Thus, although the Plan contains fewer figures compared with earlier Plans, and certainly does not include targets for individual industries, it is possible to give a detailed quantitative expression to many of the objectives and priorities stated in the Plan. Such indications, although approximate and unofficial, are invaluable in drawing attention to the problem areas and the key sectors. They are the end product of many detailed projections made during the preparation of the Plan (referred to as 'sector committee analyses' and 'work of specialist divisions' in Figure 6.1), some aimed specifically at the Plan but many supporting other work (which goes on outside the formal Plan preparation phases) as well. These pro-

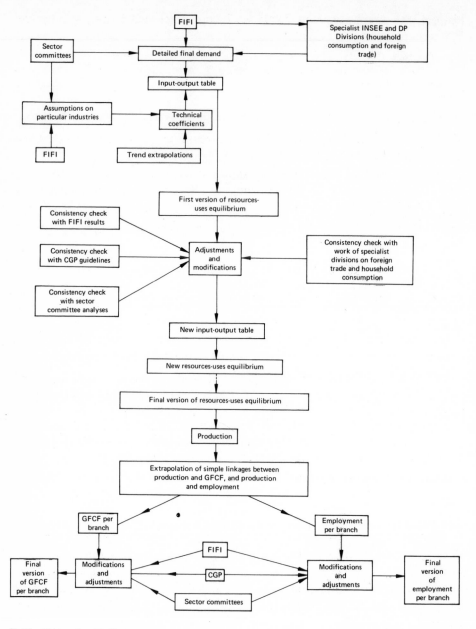

Fig. 6.1   Disaggregation of the Plan account
Source: based on a diagram in [94], p. 320

jections are summarised in Table 6.17, and discussed in detail in several other chapters of this book.

Notes

[1] See, for instance, 'the role of the "projection" redimensioned' in [147], pp. 158–161, and the rest of Lutz's discussion on Pierre Massé's 'new Look' planning (see her Chapter XV).

[2] The full text of the statement appearing in the introduction to [112] is 'Valuable light will be thrown on this Report, which the Government now submits for the approval of Parliament, by the many studies made during the two years of its preparation, which are the necessary complement of this Report. They are as follows:

— the reports of the commissions and committees, *published on their own responsibility*, which provided the groundwork for the Government decisions, and which afford an invaluable source of information for the authorities as well as for the other economic and social transactors;
— the 'long-term' studies which made it possible to identify long-term trends well beyond the terminal date of the sixth Plan and to draw on them for the initial guidelines for action;
— the economic projections for 1975, *constructed under the responsibility of the Office of the Commissioner-General for the Plan*, with the participation of the National Institute of Statistics and Economic Studies (INSEE) and the Directorate of Forecasting of the Ministry for Economic Affairs and Finance, which plot the expected consequences on the economic situation of France in 1975 of the choices proposed by the sixth Plan.'

[112], p. 6 (my italics).

[3] The projections are given in full in [94], the source from which much of the material in this chapter is derived. A summarised version was in fact published much earlier in [131], but without any information on the detailed projections. The main co-ordinators of [94] were Bernard Ullmo and Michel Jura of the Programmes Division, and [131] was prepared by the CGP's Quantitative Analysis and Synthesis Division (DESQ).

[4] 'Efforts will be directed to ... a reform in the relations between the state and enterprises in the public sector, and an improved economic return on these enterprises will make it possible in the next few years to reduce the amount, in real terms, of subsidies paid under this head.' [112], pp. 29–30.

⁵ See objective 2 in Table 6.4. The following quotation from the Plan also supports this assumption: 'The building industry, where traditions still have a strong influence on the behaviour of the many and various building trades, is experiencing even worse difficulties. Despite the progress made, especially in new constructions, the industry is still far too marked by scattered and compartmentalised structures in parallel with a multiplicity of contractors and the fragmentation of work by building firms which are rarely responsible for planning and marketing their output; the industry is also characterised by bad management and the poor use of technical advances, and finally by low wages paid to its workers and the lack of financial means which would enable enterprises to break out of the vicious circle.

'The repetitive character of an increasing number of building operations as well as promising but isolated developments which are taking place today tend to encourage rapid considerable progress in productivity, prices and quality...', [112], p. 193.

⁶ All the data in Table 6.14 were taken from [132]. The original sources are listed in note 1 at the end of Chapter 4.

⁷ There are two commonly used branch classifications in the French national accounts: the 29- and 78-branch classifications. Table 6.15 contains a number of products that correspond to categories or combinations of categories from the 78-branch classification.

There are additional notes to and references to this and other chapters at the end of chapter 10.

References

[130]   R. Bonety, 'Les points de vue des partenaires sociaux: la CFDT' (The social participants' viewpoints: the CFDT), *Droit Social, Numero Special sur les aspects sociaux du VIe Plan*, no. 4–5, April–May 1972, pp. 218–222.

[131]   Commissariat General Du Plan, 'Projections economiques pour 1975 associées au VIe Plan' (Economic projections of 1975 associated with the Sixth Plan), La Documentation Française, Paris 1971, 91 pp.

[132]   J–J. Bonnaud and J–P. Pagé, 'L'utilisation d'un modèle de simulation économique dans la procédure de préparation du VIe Plan (1970–75)' (The use of an economic simulation model in the

Sixth Plan (1970–75) preparation procedure), *Revue Économique* vol. XXIV, no. 6, November 1973, pp. 988–1025.

[133] G. Calot, J–L. Bodin and R. Salais, 'Projections démographique pour la France' (Demographic projections for France), *Économie et Statistique* no. 8, January 1970, pp. 3–19.

[134] G. Calot, J–L. Bodin, R. Salais, and S. Hémery, *'Projections démographiques pour la France' (Demographic projections for France), Les Collections de L'I'INSEE*, serie D, no. 6, March 1970.

[135] P–A. Muet, 'Fresque régionale no. 2: premières synthéses' (Regional Pattern no. 2: first results), *Économie et Statistique* no. 10, March 1970, pp. 62–4.

[136] J. Bégué, 'Projections tendancielles des besoins français en main d'oeuvre par professions (1968–1975–1980)' (Trend projections of French needs for manpower by professions (1968–1975–1980), *Les Collections de l'INSEE*, serie D, no. 8, June 1970.

[137] D. Blain and P. Magnant, 'Le modèle de financement dans le secteur de l'energie' (The financing model in the energy sector), *Statistiques et Études Financières*, série Orange, no. 5, 1972, pp. 15–29.

[138] P. Nasse, 'Analyse des effets de substitution dans un système complet de fonctions de demande' (Analysis of substitution effects in a complete system of demand functions), *Annales de l'IN-SEE* no. 5, September–December 1970.

[139] D. Blain and P. Magnant, 'Le modèle de projection des comptes d'EdF' (The EdF accounts projection model), *Statistiques et Études Financières*, serie Orange, no. 6, 1972, pp. 25–41.

[140] A. Fouquet, 'Projection de la consommation alimentaire pour 1975' (Projection of food consumption in 1975), *Les Collections de l'INSEE*, série M, no. 5, October 1970.

[141] C. Thomas, 'Projection de la demande d'automobiles en 1975' (Projection of the demand for automobiles in 1975), *Les Collections de l'INSEE*, série M, no. 12, September 1971.

[142] G. Vangrevelinghe, 'Modèles et projections de la consommation' (Consumption models and projections), *Économie et Statistique*, pp. 17–31.

[143] A. Fouquet, 'Le budget des ménages en 1975 d'après le VIᵉ Plan' (The household budget in 1975 according to the Sixth Plan), *Économie et Statistique* no. 30, January 1972, pp. 3-17.

[144] B. Couder, G. Rösch and S. Sandier, 'La consommation de services médicaux continuera à croître rapidement' (the consumption of

medical services will continue to grow rapidly), *Économie et Statistique* no. 37, September 1972, pp. 3–19.

[145] Y. Carsalade and F. Nicolas, 'FILO: modèle de financement du logement' (FILO: housing finance model), *Statistiques et Études Financières*, sèrie Orange, no. 9, 1973, pp. 3–23.

[146] Y. Carsalade and R. Pincon, 'POLO: modèle de politique du logement' (POLO: housing policy model), *Statistiques et Études Financières*, serie Orange, no. 10, 1973, pp. 17–51.

[147] V. Lutz, *Central Planning for the Market Economy: an Analysis of the French Theory and Experience*, Longmans, 1969, 194 pp.

206

7   Industry and the Plan: the Rate of Actualisation

An important aspect of our planning these last few years has been to encourage, within a market economy, investment behaviour. A more and more rational generalisation of decentralised behaviour should correspond to the search for conditions favourable to the establishment of a central rate of actualisation.

R. Montjoie, translation of statement in [148], p. 3.

One searches in vain among Plans for a statement that '...the temporal preferences of our country are such that we should apply such and such a time rate of discount ...'; yet the notion of time preference is inherent in all plans. ...

Keith Griffin and John Enos, [149], p. 41.

We have already devoted a great deal of attention to the industrial sector of the French economy: the exposed sector and international competition have played key roles in the last three chapters. In spite of this, we have not yet examined in detail the fascinating relationship between private industry and the Plan. To do so in great detail is not the purpose of this book, but it would be wrong to leave the subject entirely untouched, especially as there is some most interesting quantitative work going on involving the related concept mentioned in the title to this chapter and the quotation of the Plan Commissioner below it: the rate of actualisation. This rather awkward-sounding expression has taken on an important meaning in recent years, and we hope to show in this chapter how it is intended it should be used in investment appraisal.

By discussing the rate of actualisation and ways of calculating its numerical value, we shall attempt to shed some light on such questions as: what effect does the Plan have on the private sector? What sort of guidance can small and medium-sized private firms obtain from the Plan? How can the planners advise such firms in their investment decisions so that the 'national interest' is safeguarded? Other texts[1] look at other aspects of these questions: we focus on the research that has been undertaken into evaluating a rate of actualisation associated with the Plan, and which has used formalised models. The result of this research is regarded as a key instrument in 'decentralising the Plan'. We have seen in Chapter 6 how the Plan account can be disaggregated into 36 branches; but this is not detailed enough, even for the largest firms. There is also the famous 'network'[2] through which many large firms are able to maintain contact with the planners and administrators, and thus derive first-hand information on what the Plan really means for them. But again, this network is small and close-knit, and excludes the majority of private firms. It is clear that some sort of link has to be established between the planners and this very important section of the economy, in addition to the indirect links that the representatives of these firms maintain in the Planning Commissions, the Economic and Social Council and various other remote (from the firms' viewpoint) bodies. The significant investment effort that is required of these firms in the Sixth Plan is apparent from the description of the Plan targets and policies given in Chapter 6, and the rate of actualisation is to be used primarily to co-ordinate this effort, and synchronise it with other private and public investments.

In the first section of this chapter we bring out the real meaning of the rate of actualisation by discussing the factors that affect firms' investment intentions, households' savings behaviour, and the rigidities of the French capital market. This is followed in section 7.2 by more formal definitions of the concept, relating it to the discount rate and various other parameters, and examining the conditions and assumptions that it is necessary to make in order to be able to measure it. The third section reports on the work undertaken in the sixties to calculate a value for the rate of actualisation associated with a given programme of growth; several formalised growth models were used, but the estimates of the rate of actualisation were not very accurate. Finally, we describe a more recent attempt to calculate the rate, and show that the value originally retained for the Sixth Plan was remarkably accurate.

7.1 Investment, savings, and the capital market

A firm contemplating a set of investment projects takes a number of factors into account. In the most straightforward situation, the firm considers the cost of capital (i.e. the rate of interest) and the expected profits from the projects, and then accepts those projects that are profitable at this rate of interest. But there are several other factors which complicate this simple behaviour; to begin with, many investment projects are not susceptible to economic appraisal: it is frequently impossible to evaluate all the benefits of such projects as building a new head office, or laying out a new internal transport network. Then there are investments that are undertaken for reasons other than immediate profitability, such as prestige projects (although there is implicit acknowledgement of benefit derived from the expected prestige in the decision to accept the project). The prevailing rate of interest plays only a minor role in the appraisal of such projects. Other more important factors are — depending on the type of project — the degree of risk involved, forecasts of future markets for the firm's products, the general economic situation, and so on, all of which can be evaluated by recourse to economic and financial indicators, and then weighted in some way in the final decision. Perhaps the most important factor of all is the firm's solvency constraint. In many cases, the decision to invest does not primarily depend upon the degree of profitability of the projects but upon the structure of the firm's existing indebtedness. That is to say that, assuming a certain minimum level of profitability has been set by the firm as a basis for accepting projects, the financing constraint usually acts before this profitability condition: projects are therefore discarded not because they are unprofitable but because accepting them would compromise the financial independence of the firm.

The conclusion then is that changes in the rate of interest (of the magnitude experienced in the late sixties: no more than two or three per cent either way) do not have a very great influence on a firm's decision to invest. Research has also shown, perhaps rather surprisingly, that the rate of interest has very little influence on the other side of the capital market: the inflow of funds in the form of savings. The decision to save is conditioned by other socio-economic reasons, supporting the argument that saving is a requirement rather than an act conditioned by the prospect of earning interest. Although there is a certain elasticity with respect to the rate of interest, policies that merely adjust the rate will not have a drastic effect on individuals' savings behaviour. The rate *is* effective, however, in determining *where* the individual puts his savings, and *for how long*: i.e. the rate is unimportant in the original decision to save, but it plays a key role in directing savings towards particular locations. This implies that long-term savings (a perennial problem in France)[3] could be stimulated by the right sort of encouragement in the form of a high enough rate of interest, but additional long-term funds attracted in this way would probably be the same savings redirected from other sources.

It can be fairly stated, therefore, that the price of the capital that the banks and other lending sources offer to firms is largely independent of the supply of available capital (i.e. savings). The rate of interest reflects the *cost* of the capital, but it does not reflect its *scarcity*. At this stage, we can introduce the 'national interest', and assume that in some sense this is what the Plan is seeking to maintain. We shall also refer to the planners as the representatives of society as a whole, but this is in no way meant to be a political statement: it is merely a device for achieving brevity and simplicity in the remaining paragraphs. Planners in this sense are the implementers of the Plan, which society as a whole has participated in producing (it should be clear to the reader that this sort of plan is very idealistic, and that when we transfer the argument to the actual French Plan we are implicitly making rather strong assumptions about the nature of the Plan and the way it has been prepared). The planners intervene in the capital market in two ways: first, they require capital for social investments such as schools, hospitals, roads, etc; and secondly, they seek to promote economic development at the national level, and this means that they assume responsibility for the stability of the capital market equilibrium. How is this responsibility translated into effective action?

There are two ways: the first is by means of 'compulsory savings', deducted from people's incomes in the form of taxation. This is saving in name only, because there is very little prospect of the individual being able to recoup his 'contributions' other than in the form of better facilities and amenities financed by the capital created in this way. In periods of low spontaneous savings (i.e. savings in the more usual sense of the word), the central government could increase taxation as a compensatory measure, but, as we have already seen in Chapter 5, the authorities are loath to increase taxation beyond a certain psychologically-acceptable level. The second way is to ration the capital that is available, but there is also a limit to the extent to which physical controls could actually be imposed. The French have probably already come close to reaching this limit: many would argue that the rigidities of the capital market are caused by the innumerable separate sources of funds that have been created to favour particular types of investment (agriculture, housing, etc.), but which are frequently left holding spare capital that cannot be used by potential investors because they do not meet the narrowly-defined qualifying conditions of the funds.[4] If it is acknowledged that further action in this direction is limited, then the planners must resort to more subtle approaches that essentially amount to the same thing; and this is where the rate of actualisation comes in.

Defining the rate of actualisation as 'the profitability threshold that it is necessary to require of investments in order that demands for capital do not exceed savings resources',[5] there are a number of consequences to be drawn on the social policy side and the capital distribution side in order to ensure the most efficient use of very scarce capital. For productive investments in the private sector, a high rate of actualisation (the recommended value for the Fifth Plan was 7 per cent in real terms) is only an acknowledgement of an existing situation: firms seeking to fund large projects were already working with rates between 10 and 15 per cent. For other private firms 'the norm of profitability given by the Plan should provide a useful indication for assessing their investment programme, and an incentive not to undertake less profitable programmes even when they have the capital'.[6] A special booklet[7] was prepared by the CGP prior to the Sixth Plan (for which the recommended rate was 10 per cent) in order to get this message across to private industry; the quotation at the head of this chapter is taken from it. It is admitted in the conclusion to this document that the firm's own interests (subsumed under the single objective of profit maximisation) are by no means always compatible with the national interest, and that for private industry to attempt to satisfy both would seriously compromise efficiency. The firm is thus recommended to follow a single-minded objective (profit maximisation) and to choose its investments as far as possible with the national interest in mind (by using the national rate of actualisation as its discounting rate).[8] But there will be a significant divergence between the two aims as long as the firm is not charged the real cost of its involvement in 'society': thus, the firm has to be financially responsible for all the infrastructure amenities it uses, as well as the more usual marketable goods and services; for the inconvenience and benefits it creates with respect to the environment; and for the expenditures that are necessary to ensure population mobility. Only when the firm is so charged (or recompensed) will the two objectives agree. The present system of financial incentives to firms (mainly regional, see Chapter 8) coupled with the system of company taxation would be rather stretched to fit this interpretation of economic and social rationality; hence the need for the additional psychological incentive that is conveyed by the rate of actualisation.

For productive investments in the public sector, the rate of actualisation is something more than a recommendation, although it is likely to affect only the type of technique chosen (i.e. labour intensive approaches will be favoured), once the decision to go ahead with a project has been taken on other criteria. This also applies to social overhead capital investment projects, where there is the additional problem of dealing in non-marketable goods. For this type of investment, the rate of actualisation has no impact on the choice of the overall volume of investment nor on its allocation to different projects, but it can affect the choice of technique.

This section tends to suggest, therefore, that in defining an investment policy that is consistent with the social optimum that the Plan is supposed to represent, two homogenous instruments should be used: the rate of interest, which reflects the cost of capital, and the rate of actualisation, which reflects the scarcity of capital. To proceed to such a definition, we need a measure of the rate of actualisation, and for that we need a more accurate definition of the rate itself than that used in a descriptive way in this section; we deal with the latter point in the next section, and look at the measurement problem in the sections after that.

7.2 Relations between the rate of actualisation and other concepts

It is not difficult to incur the wrath (and, after that, the total disregard) of an economist; a particularly simple way is to misuse a piece of his jargon. It instantly exposes one's weaknesses, and devalues one's arguments in his eyes. Mindful of this, we spend some time in this section trying to relate the rate of actualisation (as we, and others who translate French literally call it) to other concepts that occur in the literature,[9] and which, economists might already have suspected, are the same thing.

To begin with, we consider the instantaneous rate of actualisation, and relate it to the social time preference discount rate, which reflects society's choice between doing something today or doing it in the future.[10] Suppose it is possible to increase consumption in period $t + 1$ by decreasing consumption in period t, and to do so without changing the pattern of later consumption; then the instantaneous rate of actualisation at time t is defined by $i(t)$:

$$1 + i(t) = \frac{\Delta C_{t+1}}{\lceil \Delta C_t \rceil} \tag{7.1}$$

where Δ denotes 'change in', and C_t is consumption at time t. Another way of putting this is:

$$\Delta C_t + \frac{\Delta C_{t+1}}{1 + i(t)} = 0 \tag{7.2}$$

i.e. the overall benefit of this operation is zero when future consumption is discounted at the rate $i(t)$. But $i(t)$ is not necessarily society's time preference discount rate: to see this, consider a welfare function

$$U = \sum_{t=0}^{T} e^{-dt} u(C_t) \tag{7.3}$$

where U = a measure of society's welfare, and is to be maximised;

212

$u(C_t)$ = an index of utility associated by society to consumption at time t;

d = society's time preference discount rate.

Then the necessary conditions for the consumption pattern to be optimal are:

$$1 + i(t) = \frac{U'(C_t)}{U'(C_{t+1})} \tag{7.4}$$

If $u(C_t)$ is consumption itself, then (7.4) becomes

$$1 + i(t) = \frac{e^{-dt}}{e^{-d(t+1)}} = e^d \tag{7.5}$$

i.e. $$i(t) \simeq d \tag{7.6}$$

Thus, the rate of actualisation is approximately the same as the social time preference discount rate when the value of consumption itself is taken as the utility of consumption.

Starting again from the definition (7.1), it is also possible to relate the instantaneous rate of actualisation to the net marginal productivity of capital in the same period. Consider a growth model that allows the definition of this concept:

$$Y(t) = f[K(t), L(t)] \tag{7.7}$$

where $Y(t)$ = output at time t;

$K(t)$ = available capital stock at time t;

$L(t)$ = available labour supply at time t.

The same decrease of consumption at time t is balanced by an increase of net investment

$$\Delta I_t = |\Delta C_t| \tag{7.8}$$

which generates an increase in output at time $t + 1$:

$$\Delta Y_{t+1} = \left(\frac{\partial Y}{\partial K}\right)_t \Delta I_t \tag{7.9}$$

$$= \left(\frac{\partial Y}{\partial K}\right)_t |\Delta C_t| \tag{7.10}$$

where $\left(\frac{\partial Y}{\partial K}\right)_t$ = the gross marginal productivity of capital at time t. Consumption at time $t+1$ is increased in two ways: firstly via ΔY_{t+1}, and secondly via $(1-g)\,\Delta I_t$, which is the reduction in savings needed in period $t+1$ due to the residual effects of the additional investment undertaken in period t (g is the capital depreciation rate). This means that

$$\Delta C_{t+1} = \Delta Y_{t+1} + (1-g) \Delta I_t$$

$$= \frac{\partial Y}{\partial K}_t \mid \Delta C_t \mid + (1-g) \mid \Delta C_t \mid \qquad (7.11)$$

Combining (7.1) and (7.11),

$$i(t) = \frac{\partial Y}{\partial K}_t - g \qquad (7.12)$$

showing that the instantaneous rate of actualisation is equal to the net marginal productivity of capital.

Finally, definition (7.1) can be generalised to define the constant rate of actualisation associated with a given development programme (i.e. the Plan):

$$\sum_{t=1}^{T} \frac{\Delta C_t}{(1+i)^t} = 0 \qquad (7.13)$$

The thinking behind this is that the Plan, which includes a household consumption programme, has been chosen in preference to all other alternatives, including the one in which initially less consumption would be accepted in the expectation of later gains. This means that society does not consider worthwhile an additional savings effort aimed at increasing future consumption. There exists, therefore, a rate of actualisation implicitly associated with this programme such that the future gains in consumption, discounted at this rate, are not sufficient to compensate for immediate losses, and at best (i.e. a *marginal* savings effort compared with the Plan) these future discounted gains just compensate for immediate losses. Valuing consumption in this way, it is clear that we have the situation represented by (7.6): in this definition, which is used widely in the remaining two sections of this chapter, the rate of actualisation associated with a given development programme is approximately the same thing as the social time preference discount rate.

7.3 The rate of actualisation associated with the Sixth Plan period

It is clearly a more straightforward proposition to calculate i according to (7.13), than $i(t)$ according to (7.1), if only because one is dealing with a static case rather than a dynamic one. It can be shown, however, that the value of i associated with a given development programme is always contained

214

within the range of variation of $i(t)$ over the period covering the same development programme, so this means that we could use (7.1) or (7.12) if the model associated with the particular development programme makes it more convenient to do so. This is what the planners in fact did in the early stages of their work on finding a rate of actualisation associated with the Sixth Plan period; there were several production functions and growth models available, and it was thought advisable to obtain as many estimates of the rate as possible, in order to see how big the range of variation was, so that the later research could be focused on values within this range.

The projection model used in the preparation of the Fifth Plan [11] contained a Cobb–Douglas production function, and Malinvaud pointed out that the implicit rate of actualisation could be derived from

$$i = e\frac{Y}{K} - d = e\frac{Y}{K} - \frac{A}{K} \qquad (7.14)$$

which is of the same form as (7.12), and in which

Y = gross value added of industry and transport;
K = net capital stock of industry and transport;
e = the elasticity of output with respect to capital (i.e. $1-\alpha$ in the usual Cobb-Douglas notation);
$\frac{A}{K} = g$ = the economic depreciation rate.

We have seen in Chapter 5 that estimates of capital were not very accurate, even in the models used in the preparation of the Sixth Plan. Consequently, the estimates five years earlier were even more uncertain, and so the results of applying (7.1) are very approximate. Two variants were calculated: for $e = 0.30$, the average value of i was 13.0 per cent, with extreme values of 10.0 per cent and 18.0 per cent; for $e = 0.50$, the average value was $i = 27$ per cent within a range of $21-35$ per cent. The most plausible value was regarded as $i = 13$ per cent, with support also for the lowest value $i = 10$ per cent.

The simulation models used by CGP to calculate the rate of actualisation (described in more detail below) also contain production functions that, used separately, enable the net marginal productivity to be calculated. Both are Cobb–Douglas production functions, the first with autonomous technical progress and the second with incorporated technical progress. According to the first production function, the instantaneous rate starts at 15.5 per cent in 1962 and gradually decreases to 10.9 per cent in 1990. The second production function leads to a modified form of (7.12):

$$i(t) = e^{ht}\left(\frac{\partial Y}{\partial K}\right)_t - (g+h) \qquad (7.15)$$

where h is the re-evaluation rate of investments (the rate of obsolescence), and the K in (7.15) is not the same K as in (7.12). The results from this function are: $i = 19\cdot9$ per cent in 1962 and falls gradually to $14\cdot6$ per cent in 1990.

Optimisation models can be used to generate estimates of the rate, even if they were not originally designed specifically to do so. Most of the models of this type that were current in the mid-sixties had an objective function based on (7.3), so that (7.4) is then the appropriate way of calculating i. The CGP team obtained estimates from three global models: the Massé, CERMAP, and SEDES models. The Massé model[12] contains the following objective function:

$$U = \int_0^\infty e^{-dt} \log\left(\frac{C}{M}\right) dt \qquad (7.16)$$

where $M = Le^{\frac{\beta}{\alpha}t}$ is an index of labour, re-evaluated to allow for technical progress, and α and β are the usual Cobb–Douglas production parameters, i.e. they are defined by

$$Y_t = Ae^{\beta t} L_t^\alpha K_t^{1-\alpha} \qquad (7.17)$$

Applying (7.4) to (7.16), the rate of actualisation is given by

$$i(t) = d + a_c^t \qquad (7.18)$$

where a_c^t is the rate of growth of consumption at time t. In a situation of balanced growth, this can be written as

$$i = d + a$$

where a is the constant rate of growth of the economy. Using the same data as in the two CGP models described below, and applying the same procedure of synchronising the results of the model with given 1970 and 1985 projections of the economy (this procedure is described in more detail below), it was found that d had to be set at $10\cdot0$ per cent, so that initially $i = 16$ per cent and asymptotically $i = 15$ per cent. Very little confidence was expressed in these estimates, however, because some of the other results produced during the same solution of the model were not very credible.

The CERMAP model[13] is a linear programming model, constructed to analyse the effects of reductions in the length of the working week during the Fifth Plan. It is a two-period model, and has the following objective function:

$$U = C_1 + \frac{C_2}{1+i} + \Sigma_j M_j (i) K_j \qquad (7.19)$$

where i is the rate of actualisation (and also the time preference discount rate in this case), C_1 and C_2 are consumption in each of the two periods, $M_j(i)$ is the residual value of a unit of capital installed in branch j, and K_j is the terminal capital stock in branch j; the third term in (7.19) is necessary to counter the 'edge-effect', found in all global linear programming models that work with a finite time horizon and an objective function based on the choice between consumption and investment. [14] Fixing the rate of actualisation, and then attempting to adjust the results of the model to a given development programme, the best fit was given for $i = 14$ per cent, but this was found to be very sensitive to the productivities of the model's modern production technique; and those productivities were not accurately estimated.

Finally, the SEDES linear programming model [15] was used to generate a very approximate value for i of 20 per cent. The conclusion to be drawn from these six preliminary studies is, therefore, that the appropriate value for the rate seems to be somewhere in the range 10–20 per cent, with more confidence in a value towards the lower end of this range. More detailed work then proceeded along the following lines.

Two versions of a five-sector simulation model were constructed, model 1 assuming autonomous technical progress, and model 2 assuming incorporated technical progress. Both models were also run as global models (i.e. one sector), and very similar results obtained; to simplify the presentation, we shall describe the global models. In addition to the usual data problems involved in such exercises, there are three important problems that have to be resolved: first, the question of what to take as society's agreed development programme; secondly, how productive investment should be defined; and thirdly, how the model should be adjusted so as to coincide with the given development programme. We shall deal with each of these in turn, before examining the results of the analysis.

Choosing a development programme was relatively straightforward. The base year was taken as 1962, for which the national accounts data were quite accurate (it takes five to six years in France to produce 'firm' national accounts, figures produced earlier than this being regarded as 'forecasts' or 'provisional'); the Fifth Plan projection of 1970 was taken as the first intermediate benchmark; and the 1985 projections produced by the Fifth Plan's long-term group (see Chapter 2) were taken as the second intermediate benchmark. All the simulations were adjusted to agree as closely as possible with these 1962, 1970 and 1985 figures.

The second problem is a little more difficult. The rate of actualisation calculated according to (7.13) will vary with the definition of consumption and investment. Should all private, public, and collective investment be classified as 'investment', or is some fraction of collective investment more realistically considered as 'consumption'? There is no completely satisfactory answer to this question; detailed analysis of all collective investment is required, almost on a project-by-project basis. The assumptions made by the CGP team are given in an appendix to [154], and the outcome of the calculations summarised in Table 7.1.

Table 7.1

Definition of total productive investment
used in the given development programme
associated with the rate of actualisation study

	1962	1970	1985
Productive investment in the strict sense (I)			
(10^9 1959 francs)		39·3	58·3	109·5
Collective investment (10^9 1959 francs)	9·9	19·8	52·3
of which: productive part (per cent)	47	49·3	51
Additional productive investment (ΔI)			
(10^9 1959 francs)		4·6	9·8	27·2
Total productive investment ($I + \Delta I$) (10^9 1959 francs)	43·9	68·1	136·7

Source: [154], p. 25

An additional difficulty on the investment side is technical progress. There are two conventional ways of handling this, and CGP have allowed for both by working with two models, one of which assumes autonomous technical progress and the other incorporated technical progress. It was felt that the first model tended to underestimate and the second overestimate the efficiency of investment, so that the real value is probably somewhere in between; the results are, therefore, to be interpreted with this point in mind.

The adjustment of the model's results to the given development programme is achieved only at a very global level, by means of changes in the production funtion parameters. Although statistical estimates of elasticities and stocks are used as far as possible, a trial and error procedure is resorted to to improve the fit, a compromise eventually being arrived at between the best statistical estimate of a certain parameter and the value that gives the best fit. This will become clearer below.

Model 1 is as follows:

$$\frac{Y_t}{Y_0} = e^{\beta t} \left(\frac{L_t}{L_0}\right)^{\alpha} \left(\frac{K_t}{K_0}\right)^{1-\alpha} \tag{7.20}$$

218

$$K_{t+1} = (1 - g) K_t + s_t Y_t \qquad (7.21)$$

$$C_t = (1 - s_t) Y_t - G_t \qquad (7.22)$$

where Y_t = global value added;

I_t = labour employed in production;

K_t = capital stock in service;

C_t = household consumption;

G_t = exogenous demand, consisting of the external balance, investment in housing, and the non-productive fraction of collective investment;

S_t = savings rate;

g = capital depreciation rate.

Table 7.2

Data relating to the given development programme
in the CGP rate of actualisation study

Year	Labour L_t (millions)	Savings rate s_t (per cent)	Exogenous demand G_t (10^9 1959 francs)
1962	16·02	15·5	47·3
1964	16·20	15·7	51·2
1966	16·32	15·9	57·2
1968	16·19	16·1	59·8
1970	16·01	16·3	63·8
1972	15·94	16·5	68·1
1974	15·96	16·7	72·6
1976	15·89	16·9	77·6
1978	15·88	17·1	82·4
1980	15·87	17·2	86·5
1982	15·89	17·3	93·2
1984	15·89	17·4	99·3
1986	15·88	17·5	106·0
1988	15·87	17·5	116·0
1990	15·87	17·5	125·6
>1990	15·87	17·5	growth rate of 7·0 per cent

Source: [154], p. 28

The data is given in Table 7.2, and reflects available statistical information and the 1970 and 1985 projections as far as possible. The best statistical estimate of α was found to be 0·70, but $\alpha = 0·74$ gave the best fit; the compromise value of $\alpha = 0·72$ was finally decided upon. The other production function parameters used were: $\beta = 2·95$ per cent p.a., $g = 5·5$ per cent p.a., $K_0 = 375,000$ million 1959 francs, and $Y_0 = 282,000$ million 1959 francs.

Applying (7.13) to the results given in Table 7.3 leads to $i = 8·4$ per cent for a 30-year time-horizon, and $i = 10·9$ over a 60-year period. As stated above, the five-sector model gives similar results.

Table 7.3

Results of CGP model 1 (autonomous technical progress)

Year	Consumption C_t		ΔC_t
	Central account (adjusted to the development programme) (s_t given)	Variant ($s_t + 1\%$)	
1962	190·9	188·1	−2·8
1964	211·0	208·9	−2·1
1966	230·7	229·2	−1·5
1968	252·7	251·9	−0·8
1970	274·4	274·2	−0·2
1972	299·3	299·8	+0·5
1974	328·1	329·1	+1·0
1976	357·4	359·1	+1·7
1978	391·1	393·3	+2·2
1980	429·4	432·1	+2·7
1982	469·3	472·7	+3·4
1984	513·1	517·1	+4·0
1985	536·2	540·5	+4·3
1986	560·4	565·0	+4·6
1988	610·1	615·4	+5·3
1990	665·2	671·2	+6·0
2000	1028·4	1038·7	+10·3

Source: [154], p. 28

Model 2 with incorporated technical progress is as follows:

$$\frac{Y_t}{Y_0} = \left(\frac{L_t}{L_0}\right)^{\alpha'} \left(\frac{J_t}{J_0}\right)^{1-\alpha'} \tag{7.23}$$

$$J_{t+1} = (1 - g) J_t + e^{ht} s_t Y_t \tag{7.24}$$

$$C_t = (1 - s_t) Y_t - G_t \tag{7.25}$$

where J_t = efficient stock of capital = $\sum_v a_v K_v(t)$ = weighted sum of residual stocks of capital at time t, the weights a_v reflecting the technical efficiency of the capital, which decreases with age.

Assuming that investment grows at the rate a, it can be shown that

$$J_0 = \left[\frac{a+g}{a+g+h}\right] K_0 \tag{7.26}$$

Taking $a = 6\cdot0$ per cent p.a., $g = 5\cdot5$ per cent p.a., $h = 10\cdot0$ per cent p.a., and the K_0 value from model 1, this means that J_0 is approximately 200,000 million 1959 francs; the actual value used in model 2 was 223,000 million 1959 francs, taking into account the acceleration in the rate of growth of investment and the goodness of fit with the given development programme. The results obtained using this data, $\alpha' = \alpha = 0\cdot72$, and L_t, G_t, and s_t as in model 1, are shown in Table 7.4. The associated rate of actualisation is $i = 15\cdot4$ per cent over a 30-year time horizon, and $i = 16\cdot0$ per cent over 60 years.

An estimate of the sensitivity of these values for i can be obtained by considering the instantaneous rate as being approximately equal to the rate associated with a given development programme, and differentiating (7.12) and (7.15) The most uncertain production function parameter is α, and the derivative with respect to α yields, for autonomous technical progress

$$\Delta i \simeq -\frac{Y_0}{K_0} \Delta\alpha = -0\cdot80 \Delta\alpha \tag{7.27}$$

and a similar result is obtained in the incorporated technical progress case. This places quite a high degree of uncertainty around the rate associated with the Sixth Plan: the CGP eventually recommended a central rate of 10 per cent, with the further recommendation that all projects should also be evaluated at 8 and 12 per cent to allow for the imprecise nature of the central rate. It also expressed the hope that these estimates would be revised if and when improvements in the production functions had been

221

Table 7.4

Results of CGP model 2 (incorporated technical progress)

Year	Consumption C_t		ΔC_t
	Central account (adjusted to the development programme) (s_t given)	Variant ($s_t + 1\%$)	
1962	190·9	188·1	−2·8
1964	219·8	218·9	−0·9
1966	231·8	231·3	−0·5
1968	253·7	255·1	1·4
1970	274·8	276·4	1·8
1972	298·6	300·9	2·3
1974	325·8	328·7	2·9
1976	353·2	356·7	3·5
1978	384·5	388·6	• 4·1
1980	420·0	424·4	4·4
1982	456·5	461·6	5·1
1984	496·3	501·6	5·3
1985	517·6	523·1	5·5
1986	538·9	544·8	5·9
1988	583·3	589·7	6·4
1990	632·1	639·3	7·2
2000	948·1	959·0	10·9

Source: [154], p. 31

made. As we have reported in Chapter 5, such improvements have since appeared, and the rate of actualisation has been revised as a result. We discuss this more recent research in the next section.

7.4 A new rate of actualisation for the French economy

The work we have described in the previous section was undertaken well before any projection associated with the Sixth Plan was available. In the light of the new long-term growth patterns for 1985 (see Chapter 2) and the Plan account, which we discussed at length in Chapter 6, it is interesting to see whether a better estimate of the rate of actualisation associated with the Sixth Plan can be obtained. This was the purpose of Alain Bernard's work in the CGP, [16] which we look at in this section.

In addition to the new 1975 and 1985 projections, advantage can also be taken of the work done by Mairesse and others on improving the capital series (see Chapter 5). This extra confidence in the data encouraged Bernard to extend the previous CGP work in at least two directions: first, he divided the capital elasticity e into two components, e_1 and e_2, the first referring to non-financial enterprises capital stock and the second to that of administrations. With certain assumptions about the allocation of capital between the two sets of agencies and between productive and non-productive uses, this allows a more detailed analysis, as we see below, and means that, formally at least, a distinction can be made between marketable and non-marketable goods. The second extension of the previous CGP exercise involves the way in which the model is adjusted to the given development programme. Bernard uses three adjustment instruments (four, if the initial rate of actualisation is included): (i) the change in the rate of actualisation over the period covered by the model; (ii) the variation in the rate of autonomous technical progress; and (iii) the variation in the elasticity of capital in the production function. Other parameters in the model are not altered. Two goodness of fit indicators are used: (a) the average rate of growth of output over the whole period; and (b), the rate of productive investment in the last period. Essentially then, only two of the three adjustment indicators need be used at any one time, and it is possible to use only one. In a first series of partial adjustments, Bernard in fact did use only one instrument and one indicator: (ii) and (a); this enabled some idea to be obtained of the changes in the rate of productive investment for a constant (i) and (iii), thus facilitating a comparison with the earlier CGP exercise described in the previous section. A second series of complete adjustments was then carried out, involving (ii), (iii), (a) and (b) to begin with, and then (i), (ii), (a) and (b). We should point out here that the indicators of the goodness of fit between the model and the given development programme are very global and static: they are not dynamic in any sense. Once the adjustment has been satisfactorily achieved, according to whichever indicator(s) is (are) being used, the time-paths of the indicator parameters have to be examined. It is possible for wide divergence between the individual values of the model and the individual values of the development programme to exist. If this is the case, then a slightly less good fit at the global level will probably have to be accepted in order to bring the individual values more closely into line.

The model used in this new exercise is an optimisation model that 'solves itself', without requiring an explicit application of an optimisation algorithm. It is interesting to follow through the stages that lead to this situation, because it reveals some of the key assumptions behind the whole analysis. The classical formulation of the model is as follows:

maximise
$$\int_0^T L \left[u\left(\frac{C}{L}, \frac{Y_c}{L}\right)\right] e^{-dt} \, dt \tag{7.28}$$

subject to
$$Y_p = f(K_p^1, K_p^2, L, t) \tag{7.29}$$

$$Y_c = g(K_c) \tag{7.30}$$

$$Y_p = I_p^1 + I_p^2 + I_c + C + G \tag{7.31}$$

$$\dot{K}_p^1 = I_p^1 - \mu_p K_p^1 \tag{7.32}$$

$$\dot{K}_p^2 = I_p^2 - \mu_p K_p^2 \tag{7.33}$$

$$\dot{K}_c = I_c - \mu_c K_c \tag{7.34}$$

where the notation here is similar to that in the CGP models of the previous section, with the important exception that productive capital, investment and output (subscript p) are now distinguished from non-productive capital, investment and output (subscript c), and non-financial enterprises (subscript 1) are distinguished from administrations (subscript 2).

One of the key assumptions mentioned above is that there is an efficient allocation of capital between the public sector (sector 2) and the private sector (sector 1). This means that the separate capital stock factors in the production function can be combined:

i.e.
$$F(K_p, L, t) = \max \quad f(K_p^1, K_p^2, L, t) \tag{7.35}$$

and
$$K_p^1 + K_p^2 = K_p \tag{7.36}$$

so that in the case of a Cobb–Douglas production function the capital elasticities are added together. The constraints are also simplified, and further reduction is possible if it is assumed that the allocation of capital between productive uses and collective uses in the given development programme is efficient. The variables I_c, K_c and Y_c can then be determined exogenously (the development programme values are used), and the important deduction made that the net marginal productivity of productive capital equals the net marginal productivity of total capital (productive plus collective) and hence the rate of actualisation. It is easy to miss the strength of these assumptions when considering them in the context of a

224

formalised growth model: one is apt to consider them as devices for the sake of mathematical convenience. They are more than this. They are critical for the whole exercise, and the fact that they are so strong highlights the precariousness of the results.

Taking the value of consumption as its utility (a move that enables the social time preference discount rate to be approximated by the rate of actualisation), the classical model defined by (7.28) to (7.34) can be written as

maximise
$$\sum_{t=1}^{n} (1 + i)^{n - t} C_t \tag{7.37}$$

subject to
$$C_t + I_t + G_t - A_t K_t^{1 - \alpha_t} L_t^{\alpha_t} \leqslant 0 \tag{7.38}$$

$$K_t - m_{t-1} I_1 - m_{t-2} I_2 - \ldots - m_1 I_{t-1} \leqslant K_t^r \tag{7.39}$$

where K_t^r is the proportion of the initial capital stock still remaining at time t, and the other notation is as before. Because the development programme has C_t, K_t and I_t positive in all time periods, this means that the dual of (7.37) to (7.39) is a system of equations to which the usual optimality conditions can be applied and the optimal solution derived. Given the optimal dual solution, the optimal primal solution follows automatically, and hence the statement above that the model 'solves itself' without any explicit need for a formal optimisation algorithm. The full solution is

$$K_t = L_t \left[\frac{(1 - \alpha_t) A_t}{r} \right]^{(\frac{1}{\alpha_t})} \tag{7.40}$$

$$Y_t = \frac{r K_t}{1 - \alpha_t} \tag{7.41}$$

$$I_t = \frac{1}{m_1} \left[K_{t+1} - K_{t+1}^r - \sum_{\theta = 1}^{t - 1} m_{t+1-\theta} I_\theta \right] \tag{7.42}$$

$$C_t = Y_t - I_t - G_t \tag{7.43}$$

where
$$r = \frac{1}{\sum_{t=1}^{\infty} \frac{m_t}{(1+i)^t}} \tag{7.44}$$

Thus, i (which determines r), α_t and A_t are the key parameters, and justify Bernard's choice of adjustment instruments.

The results of the partial and complete adjustments of the model to the development programme defined by the base account (one of the three, pre-options central accounts constructed during the first half of 1970, and

225

Table 7.5

Results of different adjustments of Bernard's model
to a given development programme

	Development programme	Partial adjustment via technical progress	Complete adjustment via technical progress and the capital elasticity	Complete adjustment via technical progress and the rate of actualisation
Numerical results				
Average annual growth rates of output:				
1965–1970	5·7[a]	5·75	5·9	5·8
1970–1975	6·0[b]	6·1	6·2	6·1
1975–1985	6·1	6·1	6·0	6·05
Rates of productive investment:				
1965	16·3	16·3	16·3	16·3
1970	–[c]	16·8	17·6	17·2
1975	18·0[d]	18·0	18·7	18·5
1985	18·9	18·2	18·7	18·9
Adjustment parameters				
Variation over the whole period of:				
rate of technical progress		–0·7	–1·2	–0·8
elasticity of capital		–	+0·009	–
rate of actualisation		–	–	–0·5

[a] The observed rate for 1965–1970 was slightly higher (5·85 per cent)
[b] The Plan account rate was slightly lower (5·9 per cent)
[c] The observed rate in 1970 was 18·8 per cent
[d] The Plan account rate is 19·6 per cent

Source: [158], p. 525

mentioned in several places in previous, chapters; see, for instance, Fig. 1.2, and Table 6.14) and growth pattern C (one of the five growth patterns constructed by Andreani and Gauron, and discussed in Chapter 2; C is in fact based on the base account, so there is some element of consistency between them) are given in Table 7.5. The initial values of the adjustment parameters were taken as 10 per cent, 4·0 per cent p.a. and 0·22, for the rate of actualisation, rate of autonomous technical progress, and non-financial enterprises' capital elasticity, respectively. The partial adjustment, as is to be expected, is not as good with respect to the rate of productive investment as it is on the overall growth rate. The two complete adjustments are both reasonably good fits, but it is a little misleading to fit the results of the model to the development programme shown in column 1 of Table 7.5 because, as the notes below the table indicate, events have rather overtaken the programme as originally defined. Fitting the model instead to the observed 1970 figures and the Sixth Plan account 1975 figures (i.e. replacing the given development programme by another, which Bernard calls the Fifth—Sixth Plans' programme, and shortening the model's time horizon to ten years, 1965—1975), satisfactory adjustment is achieved with a fall of 0·5 per cent in the rate of autonomous technical progress and a reduction of 0·75 per cent in the rate of actualisation (i.e. it takes the value 9·25 per cent in 1975).

The overall conclusion from Bernard's study is that a rate of actualisation of 10 per cent is probably about right for the capital situation in 1965, and that in the medium to long term the variations are unlikely to be so great as seriously to question the use of the same constant rate in the economic appraisal of investment projects.

Notes

[1]   See, for instance, the work of McArthur and Scott [150], which looks at the way the national planning process has influenced the strategies of major French companies. Their work looks outwards from the planning process towards industry, whereas our purpose is to examine, within the planning process, the efficiency and usefulness of quantitative techniques in this particular area. Clearly, in one chapter, we cannot achieve the scope and depth of studies such as [150], and the reader seeking more details on the industrial side is advised to consult McArthur and Scott as a general, basic source, and to look at the chapters on energy (Chapter 4), industry (5), and transport and telecommunications (6) in [94] for an expanded version of the Plan account in these particular sectors.

[2]   The network is discussed in [113], p. 21, and in [151], p. 39.

[3]   See again [113], pp. 27—31.

[4]   The Plan itself acknowledges this rigidity: '... the relative specialisation of certain financial channels could produce over the next year a surplus of their resources over their traditional uses ...; some investment projects might have to be sacrificed or suffer from inadequate resources; others would be privileged, perhaps to excess'. It also speaks of 'redundant

specialised agencies', but actually recommends that 'maximum possible use should be made of their collecting capacity' (!) thus emphasising the great shortage of investment finance. Special legislation is proposed in order to by-pass the qualifying conditions of these redundant agencies. [112], p. 37.

5   This is Stoleru's definition, [152], p. 10.

6   [152], p. 10.

7   This special booklet is [148].

8   Co-ordinating the national interest and the firm's interest is the theme of Goux's paper [153], where the firm in Goux's context is a large multinational enterprise, thus raising a whole new set of problems which we do not consider in this chapter.

9   Apparently the concept also causes confusion among French economists: the material in this section is taken from an internal CGP paper [154], from which one gets the impression that there was perhaps some doubt amongst the members of the multi-departmental team who first calculated the rate of actualisation associated with the Sixth Plan. I have asked a number of English-speaking French economists for an acceptable translation of 'taux d'actualisation', and the commonest answer has been 'discount rate' but with so many qualifications that it seems simplest to give and use the literal translation. This is the translation that Alain Bernard of the CGP used throughout his lectures on the subject to National Economic Planning postgraduates in Birmingham in March 1971.

There is also a Part I to reference [154], but it is not listed separately here because it has since been published as [152]. To my knowledge, Part II has not been published.

10   The literature on social discount rates is huge: all the texts on cost-benefit analysis and project appraisal have to grapple with the problem of choosing an appropriate value for the rate. 'In a perfect world, the rate of interest would be equal to both the marginal social rate of time preference and the marginal rate of return on investment net of risk; there would be no problem about choosing a discount rate. In practice, however, one is forced to choose'. [149], p. 110.

11   This is known as the E_0 model, and is described in Appendix II of [95].

12   Described in [155].

13   See [96], [97], and [98].

14   The edge effect is a complaint that all finite horizon, macro-economic linear programming models, that have investment as a decision variable suffer from. Investment in periods towards the end of the time horizon is clearly not in the interests of optimality, since no opportunity will

228

exist to reap the benefits of such investment *within* the period covered by the model. Various devices exist to force some investment to take place in the later periods; see, among others, Manne [156].

[15] I do not have a precise reference for this study, but Desport describes a linear programming model in [157], which CERMAP (now CEPREMAP) developed for the French Ministry of Agriculture, and in which SEDES (Société d'Études pour le Developpement Économique et Social) participated.

[16] The material in this section comes from [158]. Alain Bernard was also involved in a much more ambitious study prior to this, designed 'to explore different Sixth Plan development strategies, and to compare their long-term consequences'. The model involved in this earlier study is known as the ANTOINE model [159]. Rather strangely, there is no reference to it at all in [158]; one can only put this down to the fact that the results were rather poor, mainly because of extremely bad estimates of the production function parameters. A rate of actualisation was calculated, but not presented with any confidence.

There are additional notes and references to this and other chapters at the end of Chapter 10.

References

[148] Commissariat Général du Plan, *L'Entreprise face à la décision d'investir* (The firm faced with the decision to invest), published in the series 'Travaux pour le Plan' (Analyses in support of the Plan) by La Documentation Française, November 1968, 128 pp.

[149] K.B. Griffin and J.L. Enos, *Planning Development*, Addison-Wesley, London 1970, 262 pp.

[150] J.A. McArthur and B.R. Scott, *Industrial Planning in France*, published by Division of Research, Harvard Business School, Boston, Mass., 1969, 592 pp.

[151] J. Ardagh, *The New France*, Penguin Books, 1973, 700 pp.

[152] L. Stoleru, 'Taux d'interest et taux d'actualisation' (The rate of interest and the rate of actualisation), *Économie et Statistique* no. 5, October 1969, pp. 3–11.

[153] C. Goux, 'The relations between the economy and the plans of companies' *Metra* vol. VIII no. 4, 1969, pp. 483–92.

[154] Commissariat Général du Plan (Quantitative Economic Analysis Department), 'Taux d'actualisation et rationalité économique. Deuxième

Partie: L'évaluation numérique du taux d'actualisation associée au VIe Plan' (The rate of actualisation and economic rationality. Part II: The numerical calculation of the rate of actualisation associated with the Sixth Plan), Working Paper, October 1968, 48 pp.

[155] P. Massé, *Cahiers du Seminaire d'Économetrie* no. 11, 1969.

[156] A.S. Manne, 'Key sectors of the Mexican economy, 1962–1972', Chapter 10 of I. Adelman and E. Thorbecke (eds), *Theory and Design of Economic Development*, Johns Hopkins Press, 1966.

[157] L. Desport, 'Forecasting the supply response of French agriculture with a linear programming model' *European Economic Review* vol. 1, no. 2, 1969, pp. 212–56.

[158] A. Bernard, 'Une nouvelle évaluation du taux d'actualisation pour l'économie française' (A new evaluation of the rate of actualisation for the French economy), *Revue Économique* vol. XXIII, no. 3, May 1972, pp. 506–33.

[159] A. Bernard and J. Mairesse, 'Un modèle de croissance à long terme linéarise pour l'économie française' (A linearised, long-term growth model for the French economy), *Cahiers du Seminaire d'Économetrie* no. 12, 1970.

8 The Regions and the Plan: the PRDE Exercise

The regionalisation of the Sixth Plan is only the beginning; an event of major importance will next be built on this foundation: the introduction of the new regional reform. The bringing together of the technical base supplied by the regionalisation of the Plan and the political change supplied by the regional reform makes it possible to hope for new development on all sides, technical, social and political.

Michel Rousselot, [160], p. 53.

We have so far avoided speaking of the 'regionalisation of the Plan', a term that has frequently been used to refer to the Fifth Plan's regional analyses. This expression is indicative of a state of mind of a methodology that should really be set aside.

Jacques Antoine, [161], p. 41.

It would be a reasonably straightforward matter to describe the 'regionalisation' of the Sixth Plan from a purely technical viewpoint; this side of the Plan is so underdeveloped in fact that we should find it difficult to justify a full chapter on the subject. To proceed in such a way, however, would be to ignore one of the most interesting and fascinating features of French economic, social and political life: the great debate on regional development. Countless authors have talked of the 'French desert'[1] (which was said to start on the outskirts of Paris), the 'two economies of France',[2] the 'mirage of balanced regional development',[3] and the 'regional obsession'.[4] 'Aménagement du territoire' (which means 'regional development' in its widest sense, but is also used to mean simply 'town and country planning') has become something of a cult among French economists, urban planners, administrators, sociologists, futurologists, and geographers, and it is extremely confusing to try and find some kind of order and structure in the masses of articles, periodicals, books and conferences that have appeared or been held within the last five to ten years. It is beyond the scope of this book to attempt to define this structure, but in describing the regional aspects of the Plan we are obliged to acknowledge the influence of all these other activities.

Although there are explicit regional objectives in the Sixth Plan (see Table 6.4), many of these are still couched in rather abstract terms; those that are explicit nearly all relate to the same 'industrialisation' priority as dominates the technical tools we have discussed in previous chapters. The two other major priorities of the Plan (improved living conditions, and 'solidarity') convey very little meaning when described at the national level. It is only when the debate is conducted at local and regional levels that the quality of life objective takes on any real substance: housing, schools, rural areas, leisure facilities, etc. In this sense, it is seen to be essential to prepare the Plan at a local and regional level, as well as at the national level, if the new social awareness that is apparent in French society is to find any expression at all. The national level is fine for analysing macro-economic equilibrium, and it may even be desirable (as we have argued in previous chapters) to introduce an international level to this sort of analysis. But real social problems are felt at the sub-national levels, and it is important to create channels of communication between these levels and the levels at which the national planners operate.

This at least is how the theory goes. But is it true in practice? Is there real regional planning in France? We shall show in this chapter that there is a long way to go yet before the regions have any proper authority over their own development, although, as the quotation from Rousselot at the head of the chapter shows, there is hope that the regional reforms of 1972 will accelerate this process. We begin in section 8.1 by trying to unravel the mystifying world of ZEATs, OREAMs, ZPIUs and other creations of the French economic administration. This is followed by a description of the Sixth Plan's regionalisation machinery (Antoine (quoted above) and others feel that the term 'regionalisation' should not be used because it implies a process in which all the national objectives are determined first, leaving very little room for any regional initiatives, all their decisions and freedom being constrained by fixed national constraints. We sympathise with this view, but, as will become clear later, regionalisation is an unfortunately accurate description of the regional procedure involved in the Sixth Plan). In section 8.3, we examine the way in which the regional population and employment forecasts were produced. Although the need for regional economic accounts had been acknowledged in the Fifth Plan, delays in compiling suitable regional statistics meant that changes in population and employment were the only available quantitative indicators of regional economic development that could be used. Section 8.4 follows the step-by-step construction of the regional development and equipment programmes (PRDEs), impressively titled but essentially reducing to a regional breakdown of the social overhead capital figures described in

Table 6.5. Finally, we briefly discuss the other aspects of regional policy related to the Plan and the role of DATAR (Délégation à l'Aménagement du Territoire et à l'Action Régionale), the self-styled troubleshooters of French regional planning.

8.1 On forms of region and sub-region

What is a region? This apparently simple question does not have a simple answer, or at least it did not until the 1972 reform legalised the concept

Fig. 8.1   Map of the 95 departments and 22 programme regions
Source: [163], p. 292

233

of a region as a French institution. Before that, all sorts of different geographical bases were being used by ministries and the planners. The two basic administrative units are of course the department and the commune, both dating back to Napoleon. There are now 95 departments (see Fig. 8.1), many of which still have the same boundaries as when they were first created (however, six new departments were created in the Paris region in 1964). There are too many departments to carry out a proper regional analysis at this level, and the CGP suggested in the late fifties that a bigger unit should be used for the purposes of checking implementation of the Plan. Thus, in 1959–60, 21 'circonscriptions d'action régionale' (regional action districts, more commonly referred to as programme regions) were set up, and these have since been used in both preparation and implementation of the Plan. The number of programme regions was increased to 22 in 1970 when Corsica was separated (in a planning sense) from Provence–Côte d'Azur; all 22 regions are shown in Figure 8.1 and it can be seen that each region contains from one to eight departments. It is these 22 regions that the 1972 reform has turned into administrative institutions.

But as the regional aspects of Plan preparation became more technical, it was found that, whereas the post-Plan regionalisation procedure (regional programming of social overhead capital expenditures) could be carried out in terms of 21 or 22 programme regions, the pre-Plan preparation stages could not, mainly because the statistical resources would not stretch to 21 or 22 sets of regional accounts. The preparatory work on the Fifth Plan was therefore undertaken in terms of three large regions: the Paris region, France East, and France West (see Fig. 8.2). This was a suitable breakdown in so far as it allowed the problems of the regions in western France to be shown to be different from those of the regions in eastern and northern France. But there were a number of regions, especially in the centre, for which this partition was not very satisfactory. There was an alternative, more disaggregated breakdown available in the EEC's regional pattern: the EEC's Statistical Office (OSCE) used nine large regions to cover France (see Fig. 8.3), and the INSEE published some of its regional statistics in this framework. The EEC pattern was rather subjectively drawn, however; as we have pointed out, regional statistics were not very plentiful in the early sixties, and it was not possible to ensure the homogeneity of the areas constituting each region. The INSEE performed such an analysis (as far as the statistics would allow) in 1967, and this led to the creation of eight 'zones d'études et d'aménagement du territoire' (regional development and analysis areas, or ZEATs for short). The eight ZEATs formed the basis of the Sixth Plan's preparatory regional

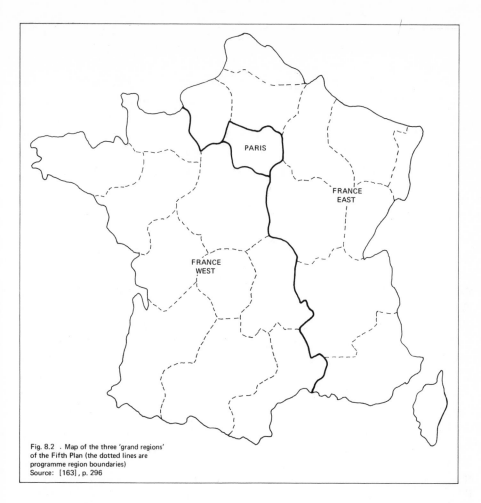

Fig. 8.2 . Map of the three 'grand regions'
of the Fifth Plan (the dotted lines are
programme region boundaries)
Source: [163], p. 296

analyses; Figure 8.4 shows their relationship to the 22 programme regions.
The constraints behind their definition are discussed in [162].

The answer to the question, 'What is a region?' is thus clear, at least in
an administrative and a planning sense. But in a socio-political sense, the
picture is complicated by the existence of another hierarchy based on the
commune. Just as 95 departments are too many 'regions' for effective
regional analysis, so 37,708[5] communes are too many 'local areas' for
effective local or sub-regional analysis. Between the department and the
commune there are two other subdivisions: the canton and the arrondissement, but the local level of life in almost every sense is based on the
commune. The central government has offered numerous incentives to
small communes to encourage them to merge, and although many cling to
their traditional identity there is now a bewildering range of agglomera-

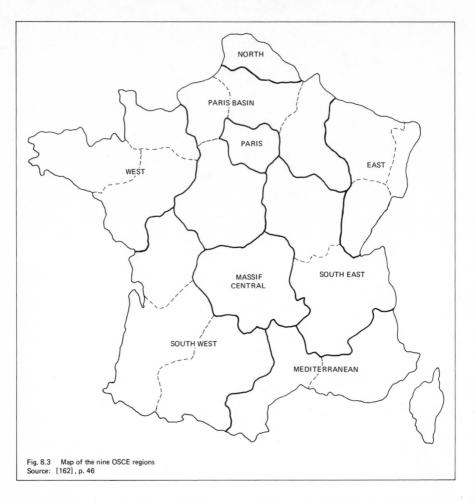

Fig. 8.3   Map of the nine OSCE regions
Source: [162], p. 46

tions, urban communities, districts, syndicates, isolated towns, and ZPIUs (the interested reader will find more details on these forms of local organisation in Appendix VII). These will not worry us too much in this chapter, but they are important for the work going into the construction of the REGINA model, in which an attempt is to be made to allow for analysis of the urbanisation phenomenon; more on this in Chapter 10.

8.2   The preparation of the Sixth Plan at the regional level

The regional phases of the preparation of the Sixth Plan began in February 1968 and extended well into 1972, although the events of May–June 1968 and their consequent effects lengthened this period in much the

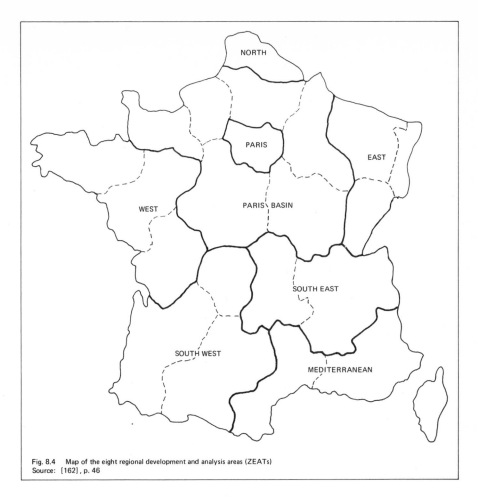

Fig. 8.4 Map of the eight regional development and analysis areas (ZEATs)
Source: [162], p. 46

same way as that of the national preparation procedure (i.e. about one year's delay occurred). Our purpose in this section is to describe the various national–regional consultations that took place, fit them into the overall Plan preparation context (described in Chapter 1), and draw one or two conclusions on the effect that the regional work had on the national 'concertation'. It should be pointed out at the outset that we are not in this section talking of a 'regional planning process' in the proper sense of the term; the following two sections on the methodology of the regionalisation procedures will gradually reveal the national dominance in such matters as employment policy, social overhead capital expenditures, and so on. Although starting out with very few constraints placed upon them, the regions were slowly but surely manoeuvered into a final situation where they had very little control over regional development policy. Regional planning gradually became, therefore, regional programming within fixed national constraints. Thus, it is apparent that the early stages offered the greatest opportunity to the regions to express their own ideas on development. Were they able to do this?

This question has to be answered against the background of two key factors: first, the experience of previous Plans, and secondly the much broader concept of a socio-political regional identity. Experience of regional planning in previous Plans was not extensive. It is possible to trace the origins of regional planning back to the fifties, to the programmes of regional action suggested by the CGP in 1955. But the following quotation within a quotation immediately dispels any idea that this was anything more than a tentative step forward:

> The programmes were scarcely satisfactory. They were intended to be co-ordinated with the national plan but the legislation did not specify how they should be drawn up and how the regional interests should participate. M. Bauchet is particularly critical. 'The preparation of the reports ... was first done by Parisian civil servants who, in order to avoid collusion, were required not to visit the regions. But without power and without sufficient means of information in Paris, they gradually abandoned their task'.[6]

The next step was taken in 1958 with the formation of the Committee of Regional Plans in the CGP. This body called for the preparation of separate economic and social development plans for each region. By 1966, all these plans had been published, but

> unfortunately, these regional plans have tended to be plans in name only, since for the most part they constitute inventories of what existed in a given region at a given time. Moreover, their appearance at different times over a period of ten years means that even this aspect of the various plans is not really comparable. As to future projections, orders of priority generally are not specified and modes of finance are at best only vaguely hinted.[7]

In 1962, the CGP introduced 'regional sections' (or 'tranches opératoires', meaning literally operational slices) into the Fourth Plan, but this was 'regionalisation' in the sense of the word used by Jacques Antoine above: the rest of the Plan had already been approved.

These observations appear rather disparaging, but we feel it to be essential in a brief summary such as this to reduce the French regional experience to the bare facts of its essential results rather than the optimistic hopes expressed for it at the time these various measures were introduced.

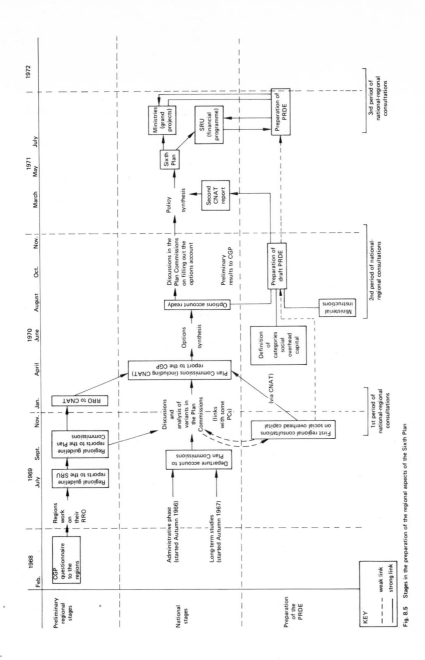

Fig. 8.5   Stages in the preparation of the regional aspects of the Sixth Plan

239

This early experience, although unfortunate in many respects, did have the value of bringing out the obstacles to the creation of a 'regional face' to the Plan. Reduced to their basic common denominator, these obstacles were mainly institutional. The reforms of 1963 and 1964 (see Appendix VII) attempted to deal with this side of the picture, and the procedure for the Fifth Plan was altogether different. The regions were consulted, via the Regional Prefects and the CODERs, *before* the Plan became too rigid, and although there were delays in completing the consultations, understandable with new institutions, the important channels of communication between the national and regional levels were strengthened and allowed more time to function.

The procedure in the Sixth Plan is very similar in fact to the Fifth Plan procedure: Figure 8.5 summarises the main stages involved in the Sixth Plan, and a similar diagram can be found in [175] relating to the Fifth Plan.[8] We examine this procedure in more detail now, still focusing on the extent to which the regions were able to make their presence felt at the national level. A useful framework for this analysis is formed by the three different reports produced by each region during the four-year preparation period: the regional guideline reports ('rapports régionaux d'orientation', or RRO for short), the draft regional development and equipment programmes (referred to as 'esquisses régionales' in the French literature), and the definitive regional development and equipment programmes (PRDE); it can be seen in Figure 8.5 that these reports are at the heart of the three national–regional consultation periods.

The RRO, compiled according to the CGP instructions of February and December 1968 by the regional missions, contain (or are supposed to contain):

(a)   the major desirable directions of regional development linked to the long-term options for the planning of the region;
(b)   forecasts of medium-term growth in the different sectors of activity.

The regions attempted to prepare reports along these lines in the context of population and employment forecasts, which we discuss in section 8.3. In general, the reports reflect national preoccupations: industrialisation in the west, conversion in the north and east, and the major urban developments already formulated in the structure plans for Paris, the Seine Basin, and the balancing metropolises in the north and Lorraine. The reports are also significant in their desire to see a satisfactory equilibrium between industrial and urban development on the one hand, and agricultural and rural activities on the other. Fears are expressed about the profit motive leading to a concentration of capital in rapidly developing areas, with the

240

consequent neglect of others. These and other anxieties come across clearly, but policies to deal with them do not. As we shall see in the details of the next two sections,

> the regions, faced with proposed objectives, define their means hardly at all and then only in terms of public investments. But could it be otherwise when the main regional planning policies are directed from Paris, and the regions know very little of the means and techniques behind their own development, when they have at their disposal only a weak consultative power which deconcentration restricts to public investment procedures (and even then excludes the most 'attractive' infrastructure facilities) and aids to small industries, and finally, above all, when the size of certain regions makes it difficult to put forward specific policies? [9]

This lack of ideas on the policy side was not too serious a problem in the RRO because, as Chapter 1 and Figure 8.5 reveal, the corresponding national phase in the preparation of the Plan was mainly dealing with bringing out problems and analysing variants. The main channel for feeding the RRO into the national level is the CNAT which, unlike the other Plan Commissions, is a permanent body. The RRO were also made available to the other Plan Commissions, but there is little evidence that they had any real influence, other than in such areas as towns, rural affairs, and employment; in the other commissions, regional data were considered as secondary. All expressions of regional interests were thus relying on the CNAT report to sway the options synthesis their way. With 24 other Plan Commissions pursuing other interests, it is hardly surprising that there was little enthusiasm on the part of the regions to be very specific with regard to anything but public investment.

The draft PRDE phase held out more hope for the regions, because the constraints were now more clearly defined, and it was a question of putting forward concrete proposals for the allocation of social overhead capital programmes, still with the possibility of affecting the overall financial constraint. Rousselot regards these second national—regional consultations as more significant than the first: '... at this moment, the national plan was not yet determined, and the regional analyses based on correctly calculated financial constraints contributed new and valuable information to the (national) deliberations'. [10] The regional analyses were particularly influential in urban development and transport expenditures, as is shown in section 8.4. This section also brings out the gradual process of 'nationalisation' that was applied to certain categories of social overhead capital. Within each category, however, the regions were free to suggest how the overall financial allocation should be spent, working with a low and a high hypothesis. These choices were then submitted to a comparison with the national-level analyses. There was a number of important differences, which were then resolved by the central authorities, the regions gaining one or two 'concessions', as stated above. Generally, this second round of consultations made both levels aware of each other's problems, the regions reluctantly accepting tighter financial constraints, and the national level accepting a slightly different order of priorities with regard to social overhead capital expenditures.

The definitive PRDE were established after the Plan had been voted, and so it was not possible to modify the overall financial constraints any further; this phase is very similar to the 'regional sections' phase of previous Plans. More sectors were taken outside the regional financial envelopes, and the regions were told they had to respect the national and ministry decisions on category I and 'grand project' expenditures (these categories are explained in section 8.4). There was some reluctance on the part of the regions to do this, and even more so to accept the recommendations from above for categories II and III. The ensuing national—regional consultations were clarified when

> the Prime Minister, faced with the desire for regional autonomy and recognising the centralist tendencies of the administration, spelled out the principles of regional planning: the regional bodies must respect the national priorities defined by the Sixth Plan, and especially subordinate their own forecasts for category I to ministerial decisions, but in return they would be able freely to propose their category II and category III programmes, provided they kept within the global financial constraints. The rules of the game implied that the 'Government would not feel bound by the detail of the proposed programmes but it would act, during the deliberations on the Budget, to facilitate their maximum effective realisation'.[11]

It was left to the CGP, and the SRU in particular, to persuade the regions and the ministries to abide by this ruling; but differences still existed when the PRDE finally came to be published, amounting in some cases to 10–15 per cent (and in one exceptional case to over 27 per cent) within individual expenditure categories. This may seem significant, but in fact the regions were responsible in the end for only 28 per cent of all social overhead capital programmes (see section 8.4). The differences have been allowed to persist, in the expectation that any changes made to the Plan in mid-term or during an annual Budget will take them into account.

On balance, the Sixth Plan regional experience, considered against the background of previous Plans, was probably beneficial for the regions, if only because the obstacles placed in their way (some of which were of their own making) so frustrated some of them that a new regional spirit began to appear. A lot of faith is now being placed in the 1972 regional participation in future Plans. It is interesting, in closing this section, to recall the statements made in another English text on French planning six years ago, just after similar optimistic hopes had been placed in the 'new' Fifth Plan regional procedures and the 'new' reformed institutes (CNAT, DATAR, and the Regional Prefect):

> It is, however, important to note that despite the proliferation of new bodies at the regional level, regional policy in France is still essentially determined by the national authorities.... The centralist nature of French administration has been little altered by the emergence of regionalism.... Regional development in France has a long way to go. [12]

Whilst the emergence of a regional identity and effective institutions is doubted by many, what is not in doubt is that the methodology on the regional side of future Plans will be much improved (due to the REGINA model, considered in Chapter 10, and the ancillary work on regional economic accounts that it is encouraging) compared with the Sixth Plan techniques, which we consider in the next two sections.

8.3 The regional employment patterns

We have previously referred to the shortage of regional economic data. In this section, it will become clear just how great this shortage was during the preparation of the Sixth Plan. Although the need for regional statistics had been foreseen during the Fifth Plan, and the INSEE has started to compile experimental regional accounts soon after, it was necessary to ask the regions to base their medium-term growth and long-term development options on population and employment projections. The intention was to compile a long-term picture of the regions, followed by a medium-term analysis in the context of this long-term view. The first long-term projections were contained in regional pattern 1 ('fresque régionale no. 1'), which was a very crude picture of 1985 based on the eight-ZEAT regional breakdown. This was communicated to the regions, but since it did not incorporate the results of the 1968 population census, it did not play a significant role in the following stages. It became submerged in the aftermath of the May–June 1968 events, which allowed more time for processing the census returns.

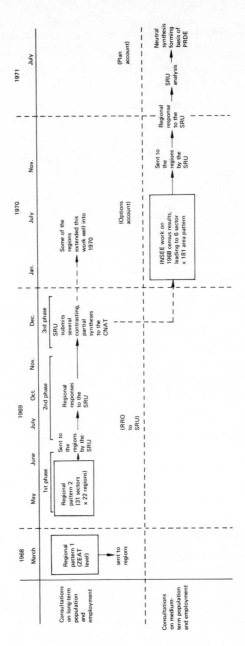

Fig. 8.6   The regional consultations on population and employment

244

The second regional pattern ('fresque régionale no. 2') was based on the 1968 census results. It contained a trend extrapolation of population and employment on a 31 sector by 21 region basis. It was sent to the regional missions in May 1969, and was supposed to serve as the point of departure for their discussions on long-term regional development. [13] The regions were expected to 'correct' the forecasts for their area by taking account of known or expected changes in employment (e.g. major projects such as the Fos industrial complex, which would cause employment in Provence–Côte d'Azur to grow faster than the trend) and migration. Comparing Figures 8.5 and 8.6, it is clear that the technical consultations were already out of phase with the RRO, which is perhaps unfortunate but not critical because the planners aimed to complete the long-term synthesis by the time the options were complete at the national level, and to complete the medium-term synthesis by July 1971 in order to form a basis for the allocation of social overhead capital in the PRDE (an allocation mainly achieved on the criterion of regional population, as is illustrated in the next section). The fact that the consultations were out of phase did cause a certain amount of confusion, however, and undoubtedly reduced the impact of the regional analyses at the national level. The regional responses on the long-term exercise were in fact only partially synthesised by the SRU and the CNAT: no definitive synthesis has been published. Some of the results from the partial synthesis are shown in Table 8.1. There is very good agreement between the overall employment figures (the new national figure of 23·6 million is roughly halfway between the two regional figures) and the figures for agriculture. The regions have clearly overestimated their attractiveness and competitiveness with regard to industrial jobs, however; the planners regarded the productivity increases underlying the regional projections as too high.

The medium-term projections were based on a much more detailed analysis of the 1968 census returns (a quarter sample instead of a twentieth, which was used for the long-term projections) and consequently allowed a finer regional breakdown. All ZPIU (industrial or urban populated areas) with more than 60,000 inhabitants in 1968 were distinguished, and the other communes were aggregated into three sets: those ZPIU with populations between 20,000 and 60,000, the ZPIU with populations of less than 20,000, and communes outside a ZPIU, giving 181 areas in all. An example of the INSEE projection is given in [179]. This was useful not only in employment analysis, but housing and social overhead capital studies too, enabling all the main urban areas to be treated individually. INSEE's employment trend extrapolations were not sent to the regions

Table 8.1

Results from the first partial syntheses
of the national–regional, long-term employment consultations

Sectors (results in millions)	Census years			Projections for 1985			
	1954	1962	1968	RP2	New national*	Low regional	High regional
Agriculture (01)†	5·0	3·7	3·0	1·8	1·6	1·6	1·7
Industry, building and public works (02 to 24)	6·7	7·3	7·7	9·0	8·9	9·4	9·9
Tertiary (24 to 37)	7·1	8·0	9·2	12·3	13·1	12·2	12·8
Employed working population	18·8	19·1	19·9	23·1	23·6	23·2	24·4

Sectors	Changes between 1968 and 1985					
	New national*		Low regional		High regional	
	(millions)	(%)	(millions)	(%)	(millions)	(%)
Industry, building and public works	1·2	23·5	1·7	38	2·2	36
Tertiary	3·9	76·5	3·0	62	3·6	64
All non-agricultural sectors	5·1	100	4·7	100	5·8	100

* Calculated after the RP2 was sent to the regions
† National accounts branch numbers

Source: [178], pp. 63–4

because they were not regarded as sufficiently meaningful, but an aggregated version of them was used by the SRU in its synthesis exercise in the first half of 1971. The main feature of the regional responses was that many of them tended to exaggerate their total population figures, mainly because it was known that the most important criterion for allocating social overhead capital expenditures in the PRDE would be total population in each region. The SRU had to adjust these regional figures, and seek a reasonable fit with the national figures;[14] a comparison between Tables 8.2 and 6.9 reveals a slight discrepancy, which is explained by the small time difference between the two dates to which the forecasts refer.[15]

To summarise, the population and employment consultations, although based on a similar approach in the Fifth Plan, suffered from a number of shortcomings. There was no proper link between the long-term projections and the medium-term projections, because the medium-term work had to be started before the completion of the long-term syntheses, which consequently were not concluded. The national—regional technical linkages were also very weak, the two sets of projections being compiled separately and then adjusted by the SRU in a discretionary manner. The SRU, in fact, were responsible for nearly all the communication that did take place between the two levels. The final difficulty has already been alluded to in

Table 8.2

The July 1971 population and employment forecasts for January 1976, on which the PRDE were based
(figures in thousands)

| Region | Total population 1 January 1976 | Total population working in | | | | Total employed working population |
		Agriculture	Industry	BPW*	Tertiary	
Paris region	10,354	42	1,400	383	2,971	4,796
Champagne	1,382	69	170	47	268	554
Picardie	1,723	72	254	54	315	695
Upper Normandy	1,679	53	233	61	347	693
Centre	2,165	116	249	100	408	873
Lower Normandy	1,334	134	125	49	249	557
Burgundy	1,583	84	182	55	302	623
North	4,038	87	579	112	664	1,442
Lorraine	2,439	54	360	85	421	920
Alsace	1,570	42	283	54	308	627
Franche-Comté	1,074	44	188	33	166	431
Loire Country	2,735	220	292	109	480	1,101
Brittany	2,583	220	182	106	503	1,011
Poitou-Charentes	1,532	125	124	61	283	593
Aquitaine	2,575	176	240	104	515	1,035
Midi—Pyrenées	2,258	157	185	97	414	853
Limousin	747	72	70	29	133	304
Rhône—Alpes	4,929	146	712	200	968	2,026
Auvergne	1,365	100	156	57	236	549
Languedoc—Roussillon	1,802	97	101	75	335	609
Provence—Côte d'Azur	3,712	85	270	175	821	1,351
Corsica	232	10	5	13	42	70
All France	53,811	2,205	6,300	2,059	11,143	21,713

* Building and public works

Source: [182], tables 16 and 33

the statement about the incomplete long-term syntheses. The subsequent further delays affected the preparation of the PRDE, which had to begin before the population figures were available, and the information submitted to the CNAT was apparently not specific and decisive enough to allow a quantitative expression of regional development policy in the Plan, as is confirmed by the following: on the long-term syntheses,

> ... it was impossible to present a single synthesis of the regional responses. That is why several variants were submitted to the CNAT, who considered the total industrial employment given by the national model as a constraint. They were expressed in six large regions, obtained by aggregating some of the ZEAT, and according to an aggregated sector classification [16]

on the medium-term synthesis,

> Taking into account their variability, the results have only been published in an aggregated form (employment by ZEAT and major sector, total population by region) [17]

and on the techniques used to analyse regional development policy,

> There was, therefore, no fundamental methodological innovation and this explains why the Sixth Plan's regional policy (which is defined in simple terms in six major regions) is very qualitative. [18]

8.4   The PRDE exercise

We have already outlined the essentials of the preparation of the PRDE in section 8.2 and Figure 8.5; in this section we fill out these essentials by presenting some of the relevant results, and attempt to read between the lines of the global presentation of social overhead capital in Chapter 6 (Tables 6.5 and 6.6). As is apparent from Figure 8.5, it is convenient to fit this discussion into yet another three-phase sequence: the expression of regional needs regarding social overhead capital (in November 1969; the regional contribution to the options preparations in the public equipment side); the preparation of the draft PRDE, starting in June 1970 (the regional contribution to the specification of the Plan itself); and the elaboration of the definitive PRDE, beginning in July 1971.

As we have stated several times above, the technical side of the PRDE exercise was based on the corresponding phase in the Fifth Plan, so much so in fact that the regions were initially asked to indicate their preferences in terms of the Fifth Plan equipment categories and the actual Fifth Plan

248

credits (i.e. they had to assume that only the same financial provisions would be made). They were also asked to put forward similar indications based on more optimistic credit programmes: the Fifth Plan figure plus 30 per cent, and finally a completely unconstrained financial allocation. The regions in fact refused to accept that no increase at all would be granted, and subsequently submitted their priorities in terms of the latter two assumptions. This stage was thus extremely useful in that the regions were allowed a great deal of freedom to amplify their requirements. On the economic side, the order of priorities was: telecommunications, transport equipment (especially roads), and research facilities; on the social equipment side, the preferences were for urban development facilities. These regional opinions were channelled into the options preparation at the national level, and as we have seen, there was a favourable response to the urban development and transport priorities.

At the same time as this phase was being completed, new definitions of regional development sectors and equipment categories were being compiled by the central administration. There were nine sectors, showing modifications in comparison with the Fifth Plan in order to be consistent with new budgetary and national accounting classifications. The first three cover the main collective functions: education, health, and social and cultural affairs; the second three are more inclined to the regional interest: protection of the natural environment, urban development, and communications; and the final three are not public equipment sectors, but they are areas in which the central government makes substantial financial contributions: economic development (e.g. regional industrial incentives), housing, and research. The social overhead capital categories were also changed: the A—B—C (national—regional—departmental) classification was replaced by a I—II—III—IV (national—regional—departmental—local) system, which will become clearer when the programming phases are illustrated numerically below. It is important to point out here that this system did not apply to all nine sectors, in some cases for obvious reasons. A feature of the whole exercise is the regularity with which certain facilities were 'de-regionalised', so that eventually the regions were left with only a small say in spending the money allocated to their area; this is one of the conclusions to which the tables given in this section lead.

These technical definitions were not formalised officially until December 1970, [19] but they were recognised during the draft PRDE phase, which began in June 1970. The first withdrawals from the regional financial envelopes were made at this point: telecommunications, housing, and research were termed 'non-localisable'; a new concept of 'grand projects' was introduced to refer to such major developments as the Languedoc—

Table 8.3

The regional financial envelopes in the draft PRDE and the definitive PRDE
(millions of 1970 francs)

| | Draft PRDE | | | | PRDE | |
| | Low hypothesis | | High hypothesis | | Low hypothesis | High hypothesis |
	PA*	GFCF†	PA	GFCF	PA	PA
Paris region‡	13,910	48,440	16,380	54,270	13,970	15,050
Champagne	1,000	3,400	1,180	3,730	1,020	1,110
Picardie	1,300	3,870	1,540	4,460	1,370	1,480
Upper Normandy	1,340	4,830	1,600	5,260	1,440	1,560
Centre	1,700	6,160	2,000	6,700	1,730	1,875
Lower Normandy	1,110	3,290	1,310	4,350	1,160	1,260
Burgundy	1,200	4,230	1,420	4,550	1,240	1,340
North	3,230	9,540	3,940	11,130	3,310	3,660
Lorraine	1,990	5,880	2,430	6,850	2,020	2,275
Alsace	1,860	3,580	1,520	4,250	1,380	1,520
Franche-Comté	830	2,710	980	2,990	825	920
Loire Country	2,500	7,980	3,010	8,850	2,455	2,700
Brittany	2,270	7,010	2,710	7,780	2,170	2,380
Poitou–Charentes	1,290	4,110	1,540	4,780	1,370	1,485
Aquitaine	2,130	6,620	2,600	7,480	2,170	2,380
Midi–Pyrénées	2,000	6,470	2,410	7,480	2,000	2,180
Limousin	730	2,440	860	2,720	685	745
Rhône–Alpes	4,690	15,780	5,550	17,650	4,380	4,760
Auvergne	1,250	4,080	1,480	4,440	1,155	1,260
Languedoc–Roussillon	1,320	4,310	1,560	4,730	1,410	1,525
Provence–Côte d'Azur	2,940	10,160	3,570	11,740	3,275	3,540
Corsica	200	620	250	690	255	275
All France	50,190	166,120	59,840	186,880	50,790	55,290

* Programme appropriations
† Gross fixed capital formation (see footnotes to Table 6.5)
‡ Including grand projects

Source: Tables III and VII, [176], p. 38 and p. 46

Roussillon tourism programme, new towns, the port complexes at Fos, Dunkirk, etc., [20] and the ministries were given responsibility for their financial programming (making complete rigour at the regional level impossible); category I facilities, although left in the regional financial envelopes, were also decided at the national and ministry level, as were those category II and III expenditures associated with grand projects. This meant that the SRU was dealing with an overall financial envelope of approximately 60×10^9 francs (1970), based on two hypotheses (8·5 per cent and 10·0 per cent) concerning the average annual rate of growth of total social overhead capital expenditures. An approximate appreciation of the size of the non-regionalised categories can be gained by noting that the eventual (i.e. July 1971) figure for the financial envelope (see Table 6.5) was 129×10^9 1970 francs, (i.e. over half the envelope had been taken away from the regions already); this global figure reappears below in Table 8.6 relating to the definitive PRDE. The criteria used to break down this global financial envelope into 22 regional financial envelopes mainly depend on the medium-term population forecasts. 80 per cent of the available finance is allocated to regions on the basis of their forecast population on 1 January 1976, their special needs as expressed in the previous phase, and the urban concentration present in their area. Therefore, reduced to its simplest terms, this means that the biggest regions receive the most finance (Table 8.3 confirms this), but the balance is redressed a little by using the remaining 20 per cent according to specific criteria: there is a share to encourage industrialisation, another to assist conversion from declining industries, a third for regions containing a balancing metropolis or a special town in the Paris Basin ring (see Fig. VII.3 in Appendix VII), and a final share for regions in which there are rural renovation areas (see Fig. VII.2). These activities are very much within the domain of the DATAR and the regional development incentives (i.e. they come under sector 7, defined above), but they form only a part of the overall programme: some of the central government aid that is allocated to the economic development of the regions is clearly not capable of 'regionalisation' at this stage of the Plan period; a certain proportion of the aid has to be held back for eventualities that may occur towards the end of the Plan. Prud'homme and Allouche give more details on the regional allocation criteria. [21]

The regions had to respect their own financial allocation, but within this constraint they were free to choose between the different equipment categories. Their choices were compared with the national choices (made by the Plan Commissions) in March 1971 (i.e. before the Plan had been approved); Table 8.4 contains a summary of the results of this comparison. The regional preferences for urban development, transport, and health are readily apparent, and as we know from earlier sections, these were accepted and written into the Plan, except for the health sector preference. Generally, with proposals coming from three sources (the regions, the Plan Commissions, and the ministries), the regional figures were

Table 8.4

Comparison between the regional and national draft PRDE
social overhead capital choices (March 1971)

	Low hypothesis		High hypothesis	
	Regional	National	Regional	National
	(millions of 1970 francs)			
Education and training	19,184	20,500	21,211	22,500
Social action	1,579	1,600	1,851	2,000
Cultural affairs	1,755	1,800	1,971	2,000
Sport and socio-educational activities	2,325	2,400	2,692	2,650
Health	3,660	3,400	4,311	3,900
Urban development	15,952	15,300	19,700	18,100
Water	561	9,300	702	11,100
Rural development	8,694		10,258	
Transport facilities	14,188	13,700	16,473	15,700
Total	67,898	68,000	79,169	77,950
	(percentages)			
Education and training	28·25	30·15	26·79	28·86
Social action	2·33	2·35	2·34	2·57
Cultural affairs	2·59	2·65	2·49	2·57
Sport and socio-educational activities	3·42	3·53	3·40	3·40
Health	5·39	5·00	5·44	5·00
Urban development	23·49	22·50	24·88	23·22
Water	0·83	13·67	0·89	14·24
Rural development	12·80		12·96	
Transport facilities	20·90	20·15	20·81	20·14
Total	100	100	100	100

Source: Table IV, [176], p. 41

not likely to cause major changes in the programme, but in certain sectors
they were more concrete, showed more social awareness, and were more
rigorous (because of the explicit financial constraint within which they
had been elaborated) than the national figures.

The constraints became much tighter of course after the Plan had been approved. The elaboration of the PRDE was subject not only to regional financial constraints but sector constraints too: Table 6.5 contains the sector figures. Further sections of the regional financial envelope were excluded from the regional programming procedure, including rural renovation, certain administrative facilities, and social overhead capital that still had to be finally located. The overall situation, compared with the draft PRDE stage, was characterised by a reduction in the total programme appropriation, although the low hypothesis figure increased slightly (see Table 8.3, bottom row). There were changes in the allocation criteria too: more emphasis was to be given to the Paris-decentralisation policy, which meant a bigger share for regions having a balancing metropolis or a special town in the Paris Basin ring; and improved population forecasts were available (see Fig. 8.6) at this time, thus introducing a number of additional changes in the regional allocations. Comparing columns 1 and 5 in Table 8.3, it can be seen that Alsace, Franche-Comté, Brittany, Midi–Pyrenées, Limousin, Rhône–Alpes, and Auvergne all have smaller allocations, due mainly to the removal of rural renovation from the regional envelopes (Fig. VII.2 in Appendix VII confirms that all these regions contain rural renovation areas); conversely, all the Paris Basin regions (Champagne, Picardie, Upper Normandy, Centre, Lower Normandy, Burgundy, and the North) have increased allocations, reflecting the bigger attention given to decentralisation from Paris.

The regions were thus asked to make final allocations, respecting regional financial quotas and national sector quotas, and making allowances for the grand projects and other non-regionalised facilities expected to be located in their area. As we pointed out at the end of section 8.2, there was a certain reluctance (or inability) on the part of some regions to 'conform' in this way, and differences emerged in the PRDE between national and regional programmes; Table 8.5 brings out the major areas of disagreement, and indicates perhaps the regions' lack of interest in the special manpower training programmes which are such a feature of the Sixth Plan. Rousselot feels that allowing differences to persist between the two levels of programming is not necessarily a bad thing:

> Such differences are not only acceptable, they are desirable. These differences have now been made explicit. The Government is obliged to take them into account every year in the regionalisation of the Budget. ... The Government is also obliged to retain these differences as one of the important factors to be examined when the Plan comes up for review in 1973. [22]

The differences remain then, and we can now put a rough numerical

Table 8.5

Comparison of the regional and CGP PRDE forecasts*

Ministries	Normal hypothesis (Plan)				Low hypothesis			
	CGP (N)	Regional (R)	R−N	$\frac{R-N}{N}$ %	CGP (N)	Regional (R)	R−N	$\frac{R-N}{N}$ %
	(millions 1970 francs)				(millions 1970 francs)			
Cultural Affairs	2,000	1,837	−163	−8·2	1,669	1,627	−42	−2·5
Agriculture	9,835	9,770	−65	−0·7	9,128	8,925	−203	−2·2
National Education	17,000	16,787	−213	−1·3	16,717	15,995	−722	−4·3
Equipment	25,760	25,891	+131	+0·5	24,040	25,190	+1,150	+4·8
Interior	5,085	5,834	+749	+14·7	4,655	4,558	−97	−2·1
Justice	550	499	−51	−9·3	492	420	−72	−14·6
Health	4,850	5,089	+239	+4·9	4,139	4,415	+276	+6·7
Manpower training, Prime Minister's Office, and Ministry of Labour	1,700	1,238	−462	−27·2	1,373	1,062	−311	−22·7
Prime Minister's Office, Youth and Sport	2,500	2,337	−163	−6·5	2,209	2,154	−55	−2·5
Transport	3,900	3,898	−2	0	3,510	3,586	+76	+2·2
Total	73,180†	73,180	0	0	67,932	67,932	0	0

* Excluding research, rural renovation, and overseas departments and territories

† This figure is total regionalised credits, and should agree with the sum of the first eight items of column 1 in Table 6.5, and again with the figure for total regionalised credits in Table 8.6; the small discrepancy is unexplained, but is insignificant

Source: Table VIII, [176], p. 50

Table 8.6

Sixth Plan social overhead capital five-year expenditures
broken down by category and degree of regionalisation

	Programme appropriations (millions 1970 francs)
A Non-regionalised credits:	
Research	21,400
Telecommunications	5,995
Posts	1,777
	29,172
B Credits regionalised according to a special procedure:	
Telecommunications	1,023
Posts	22,405
	23,428
C Credits regionalised within the PRDE procedure:	
(a) outside the regional envelope:	
grand projects (category I)	17,113
new towns (II and III)	747
(b) inside the regional envelope:	
centralised (I)	20,818
decentralised (II, III and IV)	34,472
Total regionalised credits	73,150*
Total credits	125,750†

* See second note to Table 8.5
† This figure excludes allocations to overseas departments and territories, which amount to 3,820; the total then agrees with the total in Table 6.5

Source: Table IX, [176], p. 51

figure to the limit of regional responsibility over Government expenditures in their area. Table 8.6 shows how the 129,570 million francs (1970) are distributed between categories and different responsibilities. The key figure from the regions' point of view is 34,472 million francs, representing approximately 28 per cent of all public equipment programmes. Regional development in France indeed has a long way to go, for as Antoine

255

puts it 'qui paie, commande' (who pays, commands): 'the only true instrument of decentralisation would be a profound change in taxation, radically increasing the share of local finances in comparison with the central government budget'[23].

8.5   Regional development policy

Allocating social overhead capital expenditures to the regions is only one aspect of the Sixth Plan's regional development policy. As is shown in Table 6.4, there are other objectives concerned with job creation in declining and under-industrialised regions: tourism, protection of the environment, and improving the quality of life. Social overhead capital, of course, goes some way towards meeting these objectives, but in most cases additional measures have to be found. The traditional approach is a system of regional investment incentives and tax exemptions, systems that most European countries operate. We shall focus on the French system in this section, but we should also say a little about the other components of regional policy, in which the DATAR plays an important 'implementing' role. These components relate to the urban environment, the rural areas, and tourism.

The dominant theme in the latest national statement of regional policy [171] is 'quality as well as quantity'; in other words, emphasis is to be placed on the quality of life objective, which is one of the Sixth Plan's three priority objectives (the other two are industrialisation and more equality), as well as on the sharing out of the fruits of growth in a quantitative sense. Thus, there is a quality element in the traditional decentralisation policy: in addition to maximising the number of jobs created in the regions through encouraging firms to expand or create new factories there, an effort is to be made to locate a higher proportion of 'top jobs' in the regions. The incentives depend not only on where the new jobs are to be located but also on what types of jobs are involved. Research, upper services (banks, etc.), computer and scientific jobs all increase the grants that are paid to decentralising firms, and there are additional incentives if the firm's head office moves too. This last point is a conscious effort to try and increase the decision-making power located in the regions, and thus add in some way to the authority and character of the regions.

The 'quality' objective is also present in the urban and rural components of the policy. The urban policy has been based on the balancing metropolises for some years now, and indeed they are to continue to be

256

the focal points for development in their region. But it is recognised that large cities can create more problems than they solve once a certain critical size is reached. The planners argue that French cities in general have not yet reached this limit, [24] and that there is still time to redirect the urbanisation phenomenon to other areas. Accordingly, the middle towns policy has been introduced, [25] placing the emphasis on towns with populations between 50 and 200 thousand inhabitants. The intention, according to an announcement by the Minister of Regional Development on 7 February 1973, is to negotiate contracts between individual towns and the Government, under which finance will be made available to improve the quality of developments in the towns. 15 towns had submitted proposals by October 1973, and the first agreed programme (for Rodez) set in motion. Rural policy is to focus on 'vulnerable areas' ('espaces fragiles'), meaning the mountains and the coast, to protect them from exploitation, undesirable competition, and degradation. The mountain policy has been included in special measures aimed at rural renovation areas (ZRR) for several years (since 1967), and further brief details are given in Appendix VII. The interest in the coast is relatively new, however, and is still at the discussion stage, [26] but there is little doubt that it will receive increasing attention in the future.

There are changes on the traditional policy side too. France has had a regional industrial incentive programme since 1954. This was revised in 1960 and again in 1966, and reformed in 1972. The bases of the systems are incentives and controls: incentives to firms to locate in the priority regions, and controls to prohibit excessive development in Paris, but a new development is likely to put a different complexion on the system in the future. Development contracts have been introduced to enable a more flexible relationship to be formed between the Government and private industry than is possible under fixed incentives and controls. The policy is aimed at large firms (projects involving investments amounting to less than 5 million francs are negotiable at the regional level), and, in addition to the usual financial provisions, allows benefits which are specific to each individual case to be written in. The contracts can also run beyond the normal three years applying to other incentives. Seven such contracts were signed in 1973, and the policy is clearly seen as the administration's attempt to put a new face on industrial decentralisation. This of course is the big drawback to incentive systems: once all the firms that can obviously benefit from the scheme have done so, the system becomes redundant, runs down, and new ideas have to be introduced. Another move in this direction is the open encouragement being given to foreign firms to locate branches in the regions of France. The DATAR has responded to

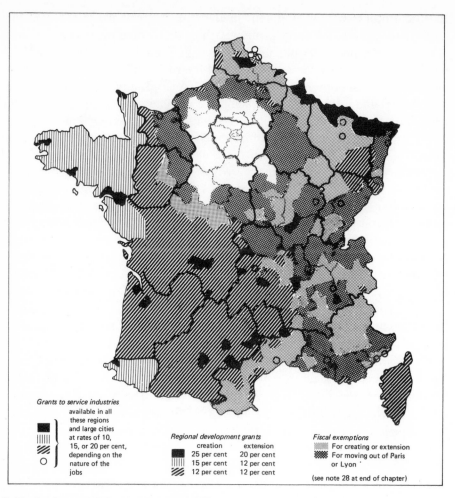

Grants to service industries
available in all
these regions
and large cities
at rates of 10,
15, or 20 per cent,
depending on the
nature of the
jobs

Regional development grants		
---	creation	extension
■	25 per cent	20 per cent
|||||	15 per cent	12 per cent
/////	12 per cent	12 per cent

Fiscal exemptions
For creating or extension
For moving out of Paris
or Lyon

(see note 28 at end of chapter)

Fig. 8.7   Map of grants available for regional development in 1972
Source: [170], p. 22

the Sixth Plan's competition policy by opening offices in New York
(1969), Frankfurt (1970), Tokyo (1970), Great Britain (1972), Switzerland (1972), Sweden (1972), and Spain (1973), to compete for foreign
firms' investment and persuade them to locate it in France. [27]

The changes made in 1972 to the regional incentive system are shown
in Figure 8.7, and the system it replaced is shown in Figure 8.8. It can be
seen that the aided areas are still very much the same ones as were eligible
for assistance in 1964, but the rules have changed. The new top investment grant is 25 per cent for new sites, and the lower rates are also raised
in certain cases. The decentralisation of service industries is encouraged by

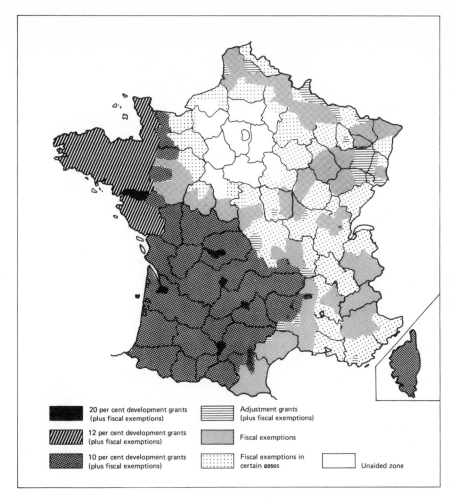

Fig. 8.8   Map of aid for regional industrial expansion in 1966
Source: [169] , p. 18 (see note 29 at the end of this chapter)

Legend:

- 20 per cent development grants (plus fiscal exemptions)
- 12 per cent development grants (plus fiscal exemptions)
- 10 per cent development grants (plus fiscal exemptions)
- Adjustment grants (plus fiscal exemptions)
- Fiscal exemptions
- Fiscal exemptions in certain cases
- Unaided zone

a new system introduced at the same time as the new industrial system. The old services system was little short of totally ineffective: whereas 2,100 applications for industrial grants were received in the four years 1968–1971, only 28 applications were received for service industry grants. Any area that now qualifies for a regional development grant (this is the new name replacing industrial development and industrial adjustment grants) also qualifies for a service activity grant, and the fact that service activities tend to locate in cities is recognised by extending the assisted areas to a number of cities that are not included in the regional development areas but are in special need of additional employment opportunities; these cities are marked on Figure 8.7. This system depends on the type and number of jobs created, as well as on the area in which they are located. The rates quoted below the map in Figure 8.7 for service activity grants depend on the nature of the jobs: quality jobs (as defined earlier in this section) qualify for higher grants, and the lower limit rates (at least 100 jobs are needed for an application to qualify) are also waived (schemes involving 50 jobs qualify if they are in certain priority activities such as research or computers). Further changes were made to the system in the 1974 Finance Act. The maximum regional development rate can now apply to areas exposed to strong international competition in assisted areas, irrespective of the number of jobs created. Further concessions have also been made for developments in middle towns, thus giving more teeth to this policy. They now qualify for higher rates of grant than would normally apply in the area where they are located. A special system for research and computer activities is mentioned in the Act, indicating that the services activity system is still not having the desired effect in these particular sectors; it is stated that the new system will be introduced during the period covered by the Act.

Finally, Table 8.7 gives an indication of the effect of the measures in 1971 and 1972. The new incentive system does not appear to have had a marked effect, although it has only been in operation for a year and the figures shown are not altogether accurate (see the first footnote to Table 8.7), so that the final figures could tell a different story. It does seem, however, that the number of major industrial decentralisations has passed its peak: the total number of new jobs created or expected to be created during the five years 1968–1972 are: 1968, 36,000; 1969, 44,000; 1970, 65,000; 1971, 45,837 (or 39,700, depending on which Finance Act is accurate); 1972, 38,428. [28] There is a remarkable symmetry about these figures, clearly pointing to a continued decline in the number of industrial jobs. This is also confirmed by more detailed figures for the industrial redeployment policy in the north, and the industrial development policy in the west and south-west (policies that no longer exist as separate policies: they now come under the 'regional development' policy): Table 8.8, which is perhaps not as clear as it might be, due to the way in which the data are presented in the 1972, 1973, and 1974 Finance Acts, illustrates the same symmetrical pattern with a peak around 1970, and a steady decline since then, a decline more marked in the industrial conversion regions than in the newly industrialising regions. Table 8.7 also shows that although the number of grants is increasing, the average size of each grant is falling, as is the number of jobs expected to be created by each grant. The encouragement being given to foreign investors and the increased

Table 8.7

Industrial jobs expected to be created due to grants
allocated under the regional development systems of 1971 and 1972

	1972*			1971*		
	Number of grants	Finance involved (m. francs)	Jobs anticipated	Number of grants	Finance involved (m. francs)	Jobs anticipated
Alsace	12	6·5	895	10	5·0	1,235
Aquitaine	31	82·3	7,000	33	15·9	5,041
Auvergne	21	6·1	743	12	7·6	893
Burgundy	10	4·9	907	7	2·5	915
Brittany	94	23·9	4,005	67	29·0	5,828
Centre	2	0·2	110	4	1·5	272
Champagne	10	8·5	875	5	1·9	324
Languedoc	14	3·2	532	7	9·0	1,019
Limousin	37	5·5	919	23	8·4	1,291
Lorraine	42	21·2	3,029	20	20·0	2,829
Midi–Pyrenées	63	22·8	4,032	47	22·0	3,870
North	10	29·3	3,627	14	62·8	5,866
Upper Normandy	9	5·9	924	0	0	0
Lower Normandy	17	5·9	1,136	13	4·1	492
Franche-Comté	1	0·5	200	2	0·4	115
Loire Country	63	21·6	3,845	36	39·0	5,629
Picardie	4	1·2	532	2	1·2	208
Poitou–Charentes	36	18·2	3,132	30	50·5	5,258
Rhône–Alpes	32	9·2	1,688	22	30·0	3,712
Provence–Côte d'Azur	5	1·3	258	2	7·1	1,040
Corsica	3	0·3	39	0	0	0
Total	516	278·5	38,428	356	317·9	45,837[†]

* The 1971 figures relate to a period when the 21 May 1964 system of incentives was in force, whereas the 1972 figures refer to a period when the 11 April 1972 system (applicable from 1 January 1972) was in force

† This is the figure given in the 1973 Finance Act, but reference is made to only 39,700 expected jobs stemming from 349 grants made in 1971 in the 1974 Finance Act. This may be an attempt to put the 1972 figures in a better light, or it could just mean that columns 3 and 6 in particular, and all the columns in general, are subject to revision in subsequent years

Source: columns 1, 2, 3: [171], p. 39; columns 4, 5, 6: [170], p. 25

Table 8.8

The results of the industrial policies in the north, west, and south-west, 1967–1972

North and Lorraine	Number of jobs created or expected to be created				
	1967–1969	1969–1970	1970–1971 II	1971	1972
North	45,000	29,700	15,000	5,866	3,627
Lorraine	12,000	13,800	8,000	2,829	3,029
Total	57,000	43,500	23,000	8,695	6,656
West and south-west	1967–1968	1969	1970	1971	1972
Brittany	6,400	11,000		5,828	4,005
Loire Country	3,500	10,300		5,629	3,845
Aquitaine	2,200	10,000		5,041	7,000
Midi–Pyrenées	1,500	7,000		3,870	4,032
Poitou–Charentes	2,200	5,700		5,258	3,132
Lower Normandy	0	2,200		492	1,136
Limousin	1,500	1,800		1,291	919
Total	19,000	15,500	34,500	27,409	24,069

Note: All figures are inclusive of all years in the stated period, 1971 II meaning up to the end of the first half of 1971[29]

Sources: North and Lorraine: columns 1 and 2, [186], pp. 4–5; column 3, [185], p. 10; columns 4 and 5, see Table 8.7
West and south-west: column 1, [186], p. 6 (the total is probably more reliable than the individual figures, which do not agree with the total); columns 2 and 3, [186], p. 6 and [185], p. 9 (again the totals are more reliable than the individual figures); columns 4 and 5, see Table 8.7

attention to service industry incentives are clearly important for the continued development of the regions.

Notes

[1] The 'French desert' was first referred to in the title of Jean-François Gravier's book *Paris et le désert français*, published in 1947. Gravier was attached to the CGP at the time, and his book is generally regarded as the original spark from which much of later official policy flowed.
[2] 'In France there are two economies that uneasily co-exist: a modern

262

one, most of it implanted since the war by the technocrats and a few big State and private firms; and below it, an old creaking infrastructure, based on artisanship, low turnover with high profits, and the ideal of the small family business.' [151], p. 22. There is constant friction between the two societies that run these two economies, and one of the obvious outlets for it is in the regional–national administrative machinery.

³   A term used by Parodi in [111].

⁴   Ardagh again, in [151], p. 175.

⁵   This is the 1968 census figure, as listed in [163], p. 288.

⁶   The whole quotation is from [60], p. 316, and Bauchet's quotation is from [173], p. 106.

⁷   [174], p. 78.

⁸   The Fifth Plan diagram of Viot is also given in [174], p. 98. We have omitted the sub-regional branch from Figure 8.5, for reasons of space and brevity in dealing with the regional side of the Plan in only one chapter. The sub-regional branch deals with the urban PME (modernisation and equipment programmes) for the Sixth Plan. These are discussed in [87], [94], pp. 314–15, and [112] pp. 250–4.

⁹   [176], p. 29.

¹⁰   [160], p. 35.

¹¹   [176], p. 48. The quotation from the Prime Minister, M. Chaban Delmas, is taken from a speech he made to the Poitou–Charentes CODER on 4 November 1971.

¹²   An example of the type of population and employment table that was sent to the regions is given in [179].

¹³   The national employment model, integrated with the FIFI model, is discussed in [180].

¹⁴   A more recent article by Salais [181] updates the figures, and sets them in a 1985 context, which should have been done during the Plan preparation phases.

¹⁵   [94], p. 309.

¹⁶   Ibid. This confirms that [182] was not widely distributed.

¹⁷   [183], p. 13.

¹⁸   Order No. 70-1222 of 23 December 1970, part of which is described in Appendix 3 to Rousselot's paper [160].

¹⁹   Progress reports on the grand projects are included in the regional section of the annual budget. For example, there are detailed maps on the Languedoc–Roussillon project in [170], pp. 80–3.

²⁰   See [184]. There is also a diagram in [160], p. 25, showing how the criteria are used to break down the global financial envelope (the diagram is taken from [184]).

21 [160], pp. 40–1.

22 [161], p. 74.

23 France has remarkably few large cities: only Paris, Lille, Bordeaux, Lyons and Marseilles have over a half million inhabitants; whereas Britain has nine and West Germany has 11 (these figures relate to 1970 or earlier, and are taken from [163], p. 173). Not surprisingly, in view of this, France has one of the lowest population densities in Europe: 94 inhabitants per sq. km, compared with 245 in West Germany, 318 in Belgium, 114 in Denmark, 182 in Italy, 131 in Luxembourg, 358 in Holland, 105 in Portugal, 228 in the UK, and 152 in Switzerland (figures, from [163], p. 16, relate to 1970 or 1971).

24 Very few details on this policy are available, because it is so new. There is a short section devoted to it in [171], pp. 75–8.

25 The whole of no. 6 of *Revue 2000* (the official publication of the DATAR) is devoted to 'Conflict sur le littoral' (Conflict on the coast), and includes a statement from the Regional Development Minister, Oliver Guichard.

26 Their success is shown on a map of new foreign investments in France in [171], p. 34.

27 The figures for 1968, 1969 and 1970 are taken from [185], p. 31.

28 Fiscal exemptions include reduced conveyance duties, exemption from the local authority business tax (the 'patente'), and exceptional depreciation terms. They also apply in the regional development grant areas, and play an increasingly important role in the regional policy, as the figures below for the 1970–1972 period show:

	1970	1971	1972
Reductions in conveyance duties	293	322	314
'Patente' exemptions	771	917	1,006
Exceptional depreciation terms	246	262	292
Total fiscal exemptions	1,310	1,501	1,612

The source of these figures is [171], p. 42 (the 917 is given as 325 in [170], p. 26, but that is probably a misprint).

29 References [169] and [186] are obtainable from the Press and Information Department, French Embassy, 58 Knightsbridge, London SW1. This series of papers covers nearly all aspects of French life, and is regularly updated.

There are additional notes and references to this and other chapters at the end of Chapter 10.

References

[160] M. Rousselot, 'La regionalisation du VIème Plan' (The regionalisation of the Sixth Plan), *Aménagement du Territoire et Développement Régional* vol. 6, Institut d'Études Politiques de Grenoble January 1973, pp. 40–96.

[161] J. Antoine, 'La préparation du VIe Plan dans sa dimension régionale' (The regional aspect of the preparation of the Sixth Plan), *Aménagement du Territoire et Développement Régional* vol. 2, IEP Grenoble March 1969, pp. 39–78.

[162] INSEE, 'Les huit zones d'études et d'aménagement du territoire' (The eight regional development and analysis areas), *Économie et Statistique* no. 5, October 1969, pp. 45–7.

[163] INSEE, 'Statistiques et indicateurs des régions françaises. Édition 1973' (1973 edition of French regional statistics and indicators), *Les Collections de l'INSEE*, série R, no. 14, December 1973, 314 pp.

[164] M-C. Gérard, 'Les unités urbaines et les zones de peuplement industriel ou urbain' (Urban units and industrial or urban populated areas), *Économie et Statistique* no. 20, February 1971, pp. 54–6.

[165] J. Labasse, 'Les orientations de la recherche en matière d'urbanisation au sein de la Délégation Générale à la Recherche Scientifique et Technique' (Directions of research into urbanisation within the General Delegation of Scientific and Technical Research), *Aménagement du Territoire et Développement Régional*, IEP Grenobel.

[166] DGRST/DAFU, 'Rapport du comité d'orientation de la recherche urbaine' (Report of the urban research steering committee), Paris, March 1971, 24 pp. (This is reprinted in *Aménagement du Territoire et Développement Régional* vol. 5, IEP Grenoble January 1972.)

[167] J. Bodiguel, 'Les communautés urbaines' (The urban communities), *Aménagement du Territoire et Développement Régional* vol. 2, IEP Grenoble March 1969, pp. 347–99.

[168] R. Moss, 'France: a divided nation. A survey' *The Economist*, 23 February 1974, 42 pp.

[169] French Embassy, *Regional Planning in France*, Document B/42/2/8, Press and Information Department, London, February 1968, 31 pp.

[170] DATAR, *La Politique d'aménagement du territoire en 1973* (Regional development policy in 1973), November 1972, 123 pp.

[171] DATAR, *La Politique d'aménagement du territoire en 1974* (Regional development policy in 1974), November 1973, 93 pp.

[172] L. Marce, 'Les zones de rénovation rurale' (The rural renovation areas), *Aménagement du Territoire et Développement Régional* vol. 2, IEP Grenoble March 1969, pp. 487–518.

[173] P. Bauchet, *Economic Planning, the French Experience*, Heinemann, 1964.

[174] N.M. Hansen, *French Regional Planning*, University Press, Edinburgh, 1968.

[175] P. Viot, 'Les institutions de l'aménagement du territoire' (The regional development institutions), *Revue de l'Action Populaire* no. 189, June 1965.

[176] M. Astorg, 'La régionalisation du VIᵉ Plan' (The regionalisation of the Sixth Plan), *Bulletin de Liaison et d'Information de l'Administration Centrale l'Économie et des Finances* no. 60, July–September 1972, pp. 22–55.

[177] INSEE, 'Une consultation sur l'emploi régional en 1985' (Consultation on regional employment in 1985), *Économie et Statistique* no. 4, September 1969, pp. 69–71.

[178] P-A. Muet, 'Fresque régionale no. 2: premières synthèses' (First syntheses of (responses to) regional pattern 2), *Économie et Statistique* no. 10, March 1970, pp. 62–4.

[179] F. Cazin, 'Un instrument de planification régionale: les perspectives démographiques de 181 unités géographiques' (An instrument of regional planning: the demographic projections of 181 geographical units), *Économie et Statistique* no. 10, March 1970, pp. 65–7.

[180] B. Grais, 'Le système français de prévision de l'emploi' (The French employment forecasting system), *Économie et Statistique* no. 34, May 1972, pp. 51–8.

[181] R. Salais, '25 millions d'actifs en 1985' (25 million workers (assets) in 1985), *Économie et Statistique* no. 35, June 1972, pp. 3–13.

[182] SRU (CGP), 'Evaluation de la population et de l'emploi par région pour le VIème Plan' (Calculation of regional population and employment for the Sixth Plan), Working Paper, 10 March 1972, 44 pp.

[183] R. Courbis and J-C. Prager, 'Analyse régionale et planification nationale: le project de modèle "Regina" d'analyse interdépendante'. (Regional interdependent analysis), *Les collections de l'INSEE*, série R, no. 12, May 1973, pp. 5–32.

[184] R. Prud'homme and C. Allouche, 'La répartition entre les régions des autorisations de programmes pour les équipments publics' (The distribution of the public equipment programme appropriations between the regions), *Chroniques d'actualité de la SEDEIS* vol. VI, no. 4, April 1972.

[185] DATAR, *La Politique d'aménagement du territoire en 1972* (Regional development policy in 1972), November 1971, 142 pp.

[186] French Embassy, *French Regional Development Results 1969–1970*, Document B/62/4/71, Press and Information Department, London, April 1971, 27 pp.

9 Monitoring the Plan. Indicators, Economic Budgets and Annual Reviews

The current situation usually changes pretty violently every year or so and a plan that looked reasonable at the beginning of the year may well look near-impossible at the end. Should one then still try to steer towards the original objectives and leave the long-term programme untouched? Or should one alter course at once and try to effect some fresh reconciliation between short-term and long-term objectives? Reason may suggest the latter; but planning is not in practice the rational process that it may be in principle and few countries, if any, make a practice of engaging in continuous modification of development plans except in minor respects

Sir Alec Cairncross, [187], p. 171.

This chapter is concerned with yet another area in which balance is vitally important: to what extent is the annual budget an instrument of medium-term planning? What other methods are used in France to check the implementation of the Plan, and what feedback is there between these monitoring devices and short-term policy decisions? There are obvious dangers in putting into practice the extreme answers to these questions and the ones raised by Cairncross, and equally serious obstacles to steering some form of middle course between the two extremes. The answers depend not only on economic considerations, but also on administrative and cultural traditions, and any discussion on this subject is bound to come uncomfortably close to the thorny problem (briefly raised in earlier chapters) of who runs the French economy: the Ministry of Finance or the CGP? It is possible to construct plausible arguments in favour of both sides. There is plenty of evidence to support some commentators' claims that the Plan is no longer important (and it is, therefore, pointless to monitor it), and that the Minister of Finance makes all the key economic decisions. For example,

... since the late 1960s the plan has increasingly been questioned and ignored.... It has been steadily downgraded into a government policy document and a battlefield on which rival ministries fight for bigger shares of the budget. M. Giscard (the Finance Minister) has shown unconcealed hostility towards the commissariat. Whenever the time comes to reach for the axe, governments have chopped first at the plan's cherished targets for the published sector.[1]

And yet the same article from which this quotation is taken is entitled 'A planner as President of France? ', revealing the great uncertainty that exists in the present situation. On the other side, many features of short-term policy are clearly (although not always explicitly stated to be) framed within the medium-term growth, employment and industrial objectives of the Plan. The CGP's work, as well as being concerned with formulating problems and influencing decisions at the preparatory stage, is also very much involved with the co-ordination and supervision of decisions to be implemented by others. This role is not always apparent, but it is strongly defended. A number of articles and books by prominent members of the economic administration in support of the Plan have appeared recently. A collective work [2] by 13 such writers speaks of the 'political crisis of planning', and seeks to answer some of the many criticisms that the Plan has come under. Its final chapter is a good, short summary of the case for planning in France. And if further arguments are needed in support of the Plan, then Claude Gruson's book [3] is highly recommended. Henri Guitton describes it as follows:

> One would imagine that the Plan had ceased to exist, because [according to the title of Gruson's book] it is now re-born. In truth, it was never dead. All who participated in the preparation of the Sixth Plan know this better than anyone. But it has to be recognised that in spite of all its merits, so often proclaimed, French indicative planning is criticised, and its future is questioned. It is necessary, therefore, to read this book to regain confidence in it.[4]

Our purpose in this chapter is not to arrive at a definite conclusion about which 'side' is right or stronger at the present time.[5] We are more concerned with the machinery that exists to monitor the Plan, and the information it has supplied in the first three years of the Plan. A lot of this information remains unpublished, and it is therefore impossible to know how much influence it has played in policy decisions taken within the three-year period. It is also certain that continuous analysis is taking place on the effect of short-term demand management policy on the medium-term picture of the economy, but this analysis too remains unavailable to us. Consequently, the material that we have gathered together in this chapter is drawn from different sources (including both 'sides'), and

270

the observations made are necessarily tentative. Hopefully, the reader will be provided with sufficient evidence to help him make up his own mind about the respective roles of the Plan and the Budget in the formulation of short and medium-term economic policy.[6]

We have included the 1974 forecasts of the economic budget prepared in September 1973 in one of the tables, mainly to gauge how far the original 1971–1975 Plan targets have been changed. But recent events in the Middle East have made it certain that the 1974 forecasts and the Plan itself will have to be revised. A special programme for 1974–1976 has been prepared by the CGP, but it is presently awaiting the outcome of the Presidential election. It contains various possible programmes based on different assumptions about the future price of oil, but its results have not been published. One source [7] puts the revised growth rate at 4·0 per cent but gives no other revised targets. Recent press statements by M. Giscard d'Estaing have admitted that the balance of payments will not be back in balance until 1976 at the earliest. Clearly then, the targets we shall be referring to in this chapter are now outdated, and it will be interesting to see for how long the original Plan targets continue to be published in *Les Indicateurs Associés Au 6e Plan.*[8]

In the first section below, we examine how the indicators have changed since the fifth Plan, when indicators were used for the first time. Following this, we look at the precise formulation of each indicator, and discover the constraints imposed on the system by national accounting and statistical conventions. The quarterly performance of 13 of the indicators is reviewed before, in the last section, we compare changes in the main economic aggregates during 1971–1973 with the original annual average Plan figures, and look at the interim position of the collective function programme.

9.1 From flashing lights to passive indicators

Pierre Massè, head of the CGP between 1959 and 1965, used to speak of the self-implementing characteristic of the Plan. For him, the great stress that was placed on internal consistency between the various targets and forecasts during the preparation stages was sufficient to persuade the different economic agencies to conform to the Plan. Emphasis was thus placed on endogenous methods of implementation, and this gave rise to the term 'the internal force of the Plan'. This conception of the Plan still has many adherents today. They regard the Plan itself as an instrument that serves to implement the Government's economic and social policy, and the mere fact that it is there is, provided it is well-prepared, sufficient to ensure movement towards the Government's medium-term objectives. 'Economic and social policy is not the instrument of the Plan. It is the Plan that is an instrument (among others) of economic and social policy'.[9] This view is acceptable only if the Plan as an instrument of policy is distinguished from the Plan as a statement of objectives. The confusion that frequently surrounds the use of the words 'Plan' and 'planning' in a French context is responsible for many misinterpretations in the literature. In this chapter, we mean by 'the Plan' a statement of Government objectives, intentions and forecasts relating to the medium-term. [10] This is what the various devices described below were set up to monitor and review. The Plan as an instrument of policy can be properly discussed only in conjunction with other instruments and their respective performance; this is not our purpose here.

With entry to the Common Market and subsequent increased exposure to international competition, various external forces began to be recognised as possible dangers to the Plan, and it was felt that an early-warning system should be set up to detect automatically undesirable influences on certain key targets of the Fifth Plan. At the same time, it was hoped (perhaps rather optimistically) that the same system would give reminders to the short-term policy-makers to stay on or close to the Plan's growth path. A third intention was to educate the public into accepting changes in strategy and policy whenever the economy entered a critical zone (the Third and Fourth Plans both had to be rescued by short-term stabilisation programmes towards the end of their period of currency: the Third by the Interim Plan of 1960–61, and the Fourth by the Stabilisation Plan of 1963, both events that did nothing to enhance the Plan's public image).

A series of monthly indicators was accordingly set up to monitor the Fifth Plan, each indicator having a fixed threshold beyond which a warning signal flashed to trigger off automatically a revision of economic policy or re-examination of the Plan. The important variables that had an indicator associated to them were:

(a) the price level: this indicator flashed if, for three consecutive months, the annual rate of increase in consumer prices was more than 1 per cent higher than in France's main trading partners;
(b) balance of payments: flashed if the coverage of imports (c.i.f.) by exports (f.o.b.) was less than 90 per cent for three consecutive months (it was estimated that equilibrium corresponded to a coverage of 92 per cent);
(c) gross domestic product and industrial output: flashed if the annual

rate of increase in either fell below 2 per cent (annual indicator);

(d) productive investment: this indicator flashed if the annual rate of growth fell below 2·5 per cent (annual indicator);

(e) employment: flashed if the number of people looking for jobs exceeded 2·5 per cent of the working population for three consecutive months.

Time and progress schedules ('tableaux de bord') were also submitted to the spring and autumn meetings of the National Accounts and Economic Budgets Commission to help them follow the execution of the Plan and recommend any necessary changes in the annual economic budgets (the economic budget procedure is discussed in more detail in Appendix VI). But the monthly indicators occupied a privileged place and had a spectacular appeal to public opinion, at least in the early period of the Plan. This publicity turned sour, however, when the expected 'automatic' policy changes did not take place. The problem was that some of the indicators were too sensitive and were flashing all the time (the prices indicator was active continuously between January 1968 and February 1970), while others reacted too slowly to situations that clearly called for more immediate action by the authorities. The assumption had been too well-planted in people's minds that as soon as an indicator crossed its threshold for the stated three consecutive months, either a change in policy would be undertaken to redirect the offending aggregate back onto the Plan's growth path, or one or more of the Plan's objectives would be changed. It had been overlooked that the Plan implicitly assumed *regular* growth paths towards its targets five years hence, and that the thresholds were therefore too close to the targets. It was recognised, belatedly, that there were many feasible paths between 1966 and 1970, all of which would meet the original targets but many of which would diverge from the regular growth path built into the indicators.

This account is perhaps a little oversimplified because there were clearly also actual situations where flashing indicators did call for appropriate action to be taken, but for one reason or another it was not forthcoming. There was also an element of confusion, still persisting with the Sixth Plan indicators, between a system designed to safeguard medium-term objectives, and the usual battery of statistical surveys and indices that all industrialised economies operate to follow short-term trends.

In an attempt to remove some of this confusion, the Sixth Plan monitoring system has some new features. To begin with, there is a distinction between indicators designed to follow the achievement of various key *objectives* (i.e. similar to the Fifth Plan indicators), and indicators intended to follow the *assumptions* built into the Plan account on changes in the international environment. A third set of indicators monitors the important necessary *conditions* for realising certain Plan objectives. The objective indicators are shown with reference to a 1975 value derived from the associated Plan targets, so that implementation can be closely followed, but there are no reference values in the graphs and tables of the international environment and French industrial performance (the third category) indicators, emphasising the fact that these latter two categories refer to forecasts and not targets.

Secondly, no thresholds are associated with any of the indicators, and there is therefore no flashing light mechanism as in the Fifth Plan. This is to emphasise that there is to be no automatic policy or target revision if the indicators fail to achieve their reference values for any period. Instead of revision at dates determined by the state of the indicators, regular periodic revision and review dates are explicitly mentioned in the Plan itself (i.e. there is in the Sixth Plan no direct link between operation of the indicators and review of the Plan).

Thirdly, the indicators are calculated once every quarter instead of monthly as in the Fifth Plan. This is an attempt to avoid the sensitivity displayed by some of the previous indicators (some of which have been retained in the Sixth Plan system) to short-term fluctuations that do not constitute a significant threat to medium-term development. To emphasise further the association of the indicators to the medium-term picture of the economy, the performance of each indicator is presented in a long-term perspective as well as the more immediate context of the Sixth Plan (i.e. values of the indicators have been calculated for the previous 20 years or so to try to bring out the structural changes in the long-term trends that the Plan is supposed to achieve). While the placing of the movement towards medium-term objectives within a longer-term framework is undoubtedly a useful move, it is in many respects unfortunate that the annual statement of short-term policy (i.e. the economic budget) is not explicitly placed within the medium-term framework formed by the Plan. As Hayward puts it, the economic budget 'should provide the vital link between short and medium-term economic forecasting and the economic policy pursued, without which the objectives of economic planning are unlikely to be achieved'.[11] Although data from the past three or four years are always given in economic budgets, I can find no similar tables in which the economic budget forecasts for the coming year are compared with the Plan account figures (other than in 'Plan' years like 1971). Still, to expect to find such explicit recognition of the Plan by the Ministry of Finance is perhaps to ignore the traditional administrative factors to which we referred above.

274

But it is regrettable in some respects that the operation of the indicators is now divorced from the automatic revision of policy that existed under the Fifth Plan system; admittedly, the automatic revision did not always happen, but the existence of the procedure focused attention on one of the most important shortcomings of the French planning system: the short-term, medium-term linkage problem. On the positive side, however, this attention did encourage some interesting technical work on the linkage problem. [12]

The indicators focus almost entirely on 'the central condition of the achievement of the Plan', namely industrial competitiveness, [13] although to some extent the choice of indicators reflects the availability of quarterly and other short-term economic indices. There are six main objective indicators:

(1) a comparative price indicator (similar to (a) above), the aim of which is to follow the competitiveness of French products;
(2) a general foreign trade indicator, similar to (b);
(3) a more specific foreign trade indicator focusing on the trade balance in industrial goods;
(4) a growth indicator based on the index of industrial production;
(5) the first of a series of indicators of the labour market situation, this one following the creation of new industrial jobs;
(6) other indicators of the general labour market situation, none of which is too accurate, but perhaps the most useful is the number of unsatisfied demands for jobs (the variable DENS, used in the wage–price–unemployment relationship in the FIFI model; see Chapter 5) corrected for statistical drift (explained in the following section).

The international environment indicators correspond to two of the key assumptions underlying the Plan account (see Table 6.1):

(7) an indicator of growth in important foreign economies;
(8) an indicator of foreign price movements, also involved in (1).

The indicators monitoring the key conditions for realising the Plan objectives all relate to the performance of French industry:

(9) a series of indicators to measure the share of foreign markets taken by French products compared with those of France's main competitors;
(10) two indicators to measure the penetration of foreign products on the French domestic market;
(11) an indicator of apparent industrial labour productivity;
(12) an indicator of unit wage costs in industry.

275

These indicators cover much more ground than the Fifth Plan indicators, but it is disappointing to see that all of them are aimed at monitoring the industrialisation priority. Although the solidarity and living standards priorities come much more under the direct control of the Government, and in that sense do not need monitoring (because the Government presumably knows how well it is doing), it would considerably help the public image of the Plan if the social overhead capital, housing, social assistance benefits, and regional development figures were published along with the economic indicators.

9.2 The calculation and performance of the indicators

Not all the indicators are calculated with the same degree of accuracy, because the reliability and efficiency of the statistical machinery varies from field to field. Increasing demands are being made on the data base maintained by the INSEE and other parts of the administration, and as responses are made to these demands so particular fields become richer and better established. As we have stated above, the quarterly Plan indicators have only been in operation since the beginning of 1972, and it is to be expected, therefore, that some of the calculations involved and the data used are still crude and experimental. The quarterly indicators are intended to give a more rapid service than the national accounts (updated versions of which appear twice a year; see Appendix VI), and so it is important to maintain regular contact with firms and commerce in order to keep the data base up to date. This is done by means of direct personal contact and the use of sample surveys and enquiries; literally hundreds of surveys and specialised enquiries are carried out every year.[14] There is a distinction between economic enquiries and statistical questionnaires: the former seek mainly qualitative answers from firms on how they see the current economic situation, and how they intend to behave in the short-term future: [15] such indications are important for the assumptions built into economic budgets. Statistical questionnaires seek hard data to feed in to the national accounts and the growing system of economic indicators (this system is not the same as the Plan indicator system, but it provides the basis for several of the Plan indicators, as is shown below). The basic structure of the industrial statistics system is shown in Figure 9.1.

The main economic indicators, published separately from the Plan indicators, [16] are:

(a) the rapid (monthly) index of industrial production (see [195] and

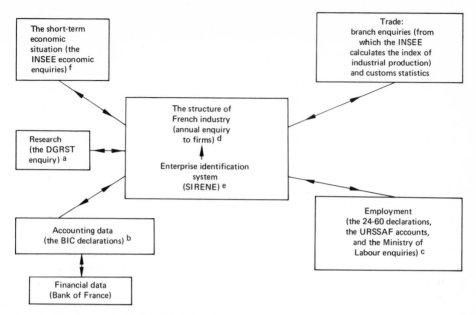

Fig. 9.1   The administration's industrial statistics systems

a   The DGRST ('Délégation Générale à la Recherche Scientifique et Technique', the General Delegation for Scientific and Technical Research, attached directly to the Prime Minister's office) carries out an enquiry on industrial research several times a year

b   BIC ('bénéfices industriels et commerciaux', industrial and commercial profits) declarations are made by firms to the Finance Ministry's Tax Directorate

c   The 24–60 declarations are annual returns made by employers on wages (see [189]).

The URSSAF accounts are held by the Social Security administration, and contain regularly updated (monthly and quarterly) information on social security payments and family allowances.

See [190] for full details on all employment statistics

d   The annual statistical survey of industry covered all French industry for the first time in 1970 (see [191] and [192]). The results are published by the SCSII ('Service Centrale de Statistiques et d'Information Industrielle', the Central Statistical and Industrial Information Department of the Ministry of Industry)

e   The SIRENE ('Système Informatique pour la Répertoire des Entreprises et Établissements') is a computerised list of over 2·5 million firms and establishments held by the INSEE (see [193] and [194])

f   See note 15 at the end of this chapter

Source: Based on a diagram in [192], p. 62

[196]), available approximately 40 days after the month to which it refers, and calculated by the INSEE from data held by the SCSII (see note below Fig. 9.1) and collected in many cases by professional bodies;

(b) the monthly consumer price index, relating to urban households, and recently revised (see [197]) (the old index was called the '159-article' index);

(c) the general hourly wage rate index;

(d) other less accurate indicators on unemployment and foreign trade.

These act as an intermediary between the short-term forecasts and hard, national accounts, which clearly cannot be made available quickly enough to check the execution of the Plan. However, the recent introduction of quarterly national accounts does go some way towards making 'instant' national accounts a reality. The first three quarterly national accounts were published in January 1973 [198], and the intention is to publish between four and seven quarterly accounts in simplified overall economic table form every quarter (the four for the previous year plus the 0, 1, 2, or 3 of the current year, with updating every quarter). The idea behind them is simple: if a reasonably stable correlation can be found over a long enough period between the annual average values of the economic indicators and the related annual values of the national accounting aggregates, then the quarterly values of the economic indicators can be regarded as approximate values of the quarterly national accounting aggregates. Of course, there are difficulties in doing this, such as trying to find a suitable economic indicator for all the aggregates in the non-financial section of the overall economic table, and making corrections for seasonal effects. But these difficulties are outweighed by the advantages of having available very quickly a tool to check and update economic budgets.

All the Plan indicators draw their numerical expression from this statistical system, although there are a number of gaps between what the indicators are designed to monitor and what the statistics actually measure. One of these gaps is evident in the first objective indicator, which monitors French and foreign prices. Ideally, a measure of industrial goods' prices, exclusive of taxes, at home and abroad is required to assess the competitiveness of French industrial goods. But the nearest available statistic is the consumer price index, which includes agricultural goods and services that are not internationally competitive. There are also problems in combining different countries' indices, and so the OECD indices are used. The indicator is calculated as follows:

$$P_q = \frac{FP_{nq}}{FP_{n-1,q}} - \frac{CP_{nq}}{CP_{n-1,q}} \qquad (9.1)$$

278

where FP_{nq} = the value of the French consumer price index (the 295-article index) in quarter q of year n;

CP_{nq} = the value of the consolidated consumer price index in quarter q of year n.

The consolidated index covers France's six main trading partners, assigning weights of 31 to West Germany, 28 to the USA, 13 to the UK, 11 to Belgium and Luxemburg, 10 to Italy, and 7 to the Netherlands. These weights reflect the importance of these countries in industrial trade, according to 1967–1969 data. There is no indication in *Les Indicateurs* that the weights have been updated since their original calculation. The Sixth Plan target is $P_q \leqslant 0$, and the actual performance of the indicator (see Table 9.1) shows that after a satisfactory beginning, French prices grew more quickly than foreign prices. The anti-inflation package of December 1972,[17] designed to take effect from 1 January 1973, had a marked effect for the first half of 1973, but it appears to be losing its impact in the third quarter. It should be emphasised again that care has to be taken in interpreting movements in P_q and some of the other indicators. A significant element in the rapid increase in the French consumer price index in 1972 was the very fast rise in food prices. A rise in P_q in 1972 does not necessarily mean, therefore, that French industrial products were losing their competitive edge. Other indicators have to be looked at in conjunction with P_q to assess this possibility.

The foreign trade indicator, corrected for seasonal variations, is

$$FT_q = \frac{\text{exports}_q \ (\text{f.o.b.})}{\text{imports}_q \ (\text{f.o.b.})} \tag{9.2}$$

calculated one quarter back, and one year back. Initially, it was felt that more weight should be given to the most recent quarters in the one-year coverage indicator, but this has since been changed to give equal weights to all four quarters. The Sixth Plan target, which most observers regard as ambitious, is for $FT_q \geqslant 106$ per cent. The performance of the annual coverage indicator confirms that perhaps the target is a little high, although it was almost achieved in 1973. The figures shown in Table 9.1 are, therefore, reasonably satisfactory, although there is other evidence (some of which is apparent from the data in Table 9.2) which shows that insufficient capacity prevented French exporters from achieving their potential, and hence, possibly, meeting the Plan target. In addition to this global indicator of foreign trade, there is a separate indicator to monitor industrial trade:

$$IT_q = \frac{\text{exports}_q \ (\text{f.o.b.})}{\text{imports}_q \ (\text{c.i.f.})} \tag{9.3}$$

279

Table 9.1

Changes in the main quarterly Plan indicators during 1971–1973

Indicators*	year	1970		1971		
	quarter	III	IV	I	II	III
Objective indicators						
1　Comparative prices (French price ratio– foreign price ratio)		0·8	0·3	−0·3	−0·3	−0·3
2　Foreign trade (per cent coverage)		100	101	102	102	103
3　Industrial foreign trade (per cent coverage)		104	106	107	108	108
4　Growth (index number, 1962 = 100)		159	161	165	164	170
				(163)	(166)	(168)
5　New industrial jobs (number employed in industry at beginning of each quarter, in thousands)		5,713	5,724	5,732	5,750	5,764
					(5,747)	(5,762)
6　Labour market situation: DENS (with correction for drift) (quarterly average in thousands)		234	249	264	286	291
PDRE (linearly interpolated, in thousands)		227	241	251	262	266
International environment indicators						
7　Foreign growth (index number, 1962=100)		150	151	152	152	152
				(153)	(155)	(156)
8　Foreign prices (index number, 1970=100)		100	102	103	105	106
				(103)	(104)	(104)
Industrial performance indicators						
9　Penetration of foreign markets (percentage ratio)		9·1	9·0	9·2	9·6	9·8
10　Domestic market share taken by imports (percentage ratio)		34·5	36·2	35·4	36·1	36·5
11　French export effort (percentage ratio)		37·4	38·0	39·0	39·3	38·4
12　Apparent labour productivity (index number, 1962=100)		155	157	162	159	167
13　Wage cost per unit produced (index number, 1962=100)		121	122	122	127	125

* See text for definition of indicators

1971	1972				1973			Sixth Plan target or assumption
IV	I	II	III	IV	I	II	III	
0·2	0·4	0·6	0·9	0·9	−0·1	−0·5	−0·1	≤0 all the time
104	103	104	104	104	105	105	105	≥106 all the time
108	106	106	107	106	107	105	104	≥111 all the time
173	177	179	182	188	196	195	199	215 by 1975
(171)	(174)	(176)	(179)	(182)	(184)	(187)	(190)	
5,779	5,796	5,805	5,821	5,836	5,864	5,904	5,924	6,004 by 1975
(5,777)	(5,792)	(5,807)	(5,822)	(5,837)	(5,852)	(5,867)	(5,882)	
306	313	321	304	283	267	287	291	≤1·5 per cent of working population
275	279	285	277	261	253	268	278	
152	154	158	158	165	168	170	170	194 in 1975
(158)	(160)	(162)	(164)	(165)	(167)	(169)	(171)	
107	109	110	112	114	116	119	120	121 in 1975
(105)	(106)	(107)	(108)	(109)	(110)	(110)	(111)	
9·8	9·7	9·8						Increases (unquantified) generally expected
35·9	38·1	40·1	38·6	41·2	41·5	43·3		
38·4	38·4	44·0	42·0	43·3	42·8	43·6		
169	173	172	177	181	187	185		
126	127	131	131	131	131	138		

Source: *Les Indicateurs Associés Au 6e Plan* no. 4, 1973. The figures in brackets are rounded approximations (not given in source) to a regular growth path towards the Plan targets or assumptions.

It is not possible to make the conversion from c.i.f. to f.o.b. figures for industrial imports, because of statistical limitations. Further allowances have to be made for the fact that the customs data supporting exports in (9.3) does not include exports of armaments, whereas exports in (9.2) does. The target for industrial trade coverage (see Table 6.4) corresponds to $IT_q \geqslant 111$ per cent. When it is recognised that the global foreign trade target written in f.o.b./c.i.f. terms is $FT_q \geqslant 99$ per cent (note that equilibrium in the Fifth Plan foreign trade target corresponded to a coverage of 92 per cent), this industrial trade target is indeed formidable. Table 9.1 shows that it has not once been met in the 11 quarters recorded in 1971–1973. This again reflects the rapid rise (especially in 1973) in imports, which have entered France to satisfy domestic demand that industrial capacity has not been able to meet. As with FT_q, IT_q is calculated every quarter, both one year back and one quarter back; the one-year coverage indicator is recorded in Table 9.1.

The fourth objective indicator monitors economic growth, or more precisely industrial output. There are two such indices available, a monthly (rapid) index and a quarterly index, the first of which clearly has the advantage of being available more quickly, and the second of which compensates by covering a wider field. Both are used in the indicator: the monthly index is adjusted and plotted on the same graph as the quarterly index. There are problems in converting the Sixth Plan target (which is expressed in national accounting terms) into industrial index terms, but it has been estimated that an average annual growth rate of 7·3 per cent for industrial value added (the Plan target) corresponds to a 6·2 per cent p.a. growth rate for the index of industrial output. The regular growth path targets are shown in brackets below the actual recorded values in Table 9.1, and it is clear that apart from one early slip, this target has been comfortably met.

The labour market indicators suffer from the traditional problems surrounding French employment and unemployment statistics. We have already referred to this problem in Chapters 3 and 5 when discussing the FIFI model's wage–price–unemployment relationship. The main problem is that unemployment is measured only in official census years, and so some alternative measure has to be found for non-census years. From the many that have been suggested, we have recorded two in Table 9.1: the number of unsatisfied demands for jobs (the DENS variable, which occurs in the FIFI model) recorded at the end of every month, and the working population looking for a job ('population disponible a la recherche d'un emploi', or PDRE for short) which is measured by the responses to certain questions in the regular employment enquiries. As with the other suggest-

282

ed measures, there are difficulties in interpreting DENS and PDRE; the DENS time-series has been considerably distorted in recent years by the activities of the National Employment Agency, set up in 1968 to provide guidance to job-seekers, channel the long-term unemployed into retraining schemes, and help place young and female workers in work. The NEA now has 84 departmental offices (there are 95 departments in France), 270 local agencies and 226 temporary offices, [18] the net effect of which is to encourage more people to register as unemployed than would otherwise be the case. The number of additional registrations is referred to as the drift ('derive'), and there are ways of estimating it. The data shown in Table 9.1 are DENS corrected for the drift. We also show PDRE, which, even in census years, does not always agree with unemployment; it was found in 1968 that the PDRE was approximately 70,000 less than unemployment as measured by the 1968 official census. [19] With so many statistical uncertainties, neither DENS nor PDRE can satisfactorily monitor the Plan objective of full employment (i.e. unemployment $\leqslant$ 1·5 per cent of total working population), but they are useful for keeping an eye on the trend.

The other employment indicator listed in Table 9.1 is much more directly linked to a Plan objective: the number of new industrial jobs created. This can be monitored by means of the INSEE series, which records the number of wage-earning industrial employees. The Sixth Plan target (see Table 6.4) is 250,000 new industrial jobs by 1975, and this, taking account of the expected reduction in non-wage-earning industrial jobs, corresponds to a target of 300,000 new wage-earning industrial jobs by 1975. Apart from three very marginal shortfalls in 1972, this indicator points to a very satisfactory performance, although there are doubts about the quality of the new jobs being created. We come back to this point below when discussing the productivity indicator.

The two international environment indicators rely on OECD statistics. The index of industrial production, as measured and standardised by the OECD, is taken as the growth indicator, and weights are applied to the indices of six countries according to the share of these countries in French industrial exports. The weights differ from those used in the price indicator decribed above because EFTA (European Free Trade Area) trade is included in the UK total, and all non-EEC, non-EFTA trade is included in the USA total. The weights are: West Germany 28, the UK 20, the USA 15, Belgium and Luxemburg 15, Italy 15, and Holland 7. Converting the Sixth Plan foreign growth assumptions (see Table 6.1) into an index number reveals that this indicator should attain the level of 194 in 1975. We have inserted the values corresponding to regular progress towards this

1975 assumed level in brackets in Table 9.1, where it can be seen that, although the 1972 performance made up for the stagnation in 1971, the world economy shows signs of slowing down again, with consequent effects on French exports. The foreign price indicator (which is merely the second component of (9.1)) should have followed the path shown by the values in brackets in line nine of Table 9.1 if the assumption made in the Plan account (an average annual growth rate of 3·2 per cent) had been accurate. Foreign prices have in fact grown much faster than this, and in the process have removed one of the key instruments of the competition policy. As foreseen by the Plan, exposed sector enterprises were freed from any administrative constraint in determining their prices with effect from 1 June 1972, [20] but they were brought back under the scheme of supervised price fixing in November 1973, [21] reflecting the fact that competition from abroad was not sufficient to keep domestic prices from growing too fast.

The importance attached to the market share model in the FIFI model (see Chapter 3) is confirmed by the fact that three of the five industrial performance indicators monitor various aspects of it. The first indicator is a global measure of the market penetration of French industrial products compared with France's main competitors:

$$IC_q = \frac{\text{imp}_{fq}}{\text{imp}_q} \tag{9.4}$$

where imp_{fq} = French industrial imports into EEC, EFTA, and North American countries in quarter q;

imp_q = total industrial imports into the same countries in the same quarter from all EEC, EFTA, and North American countries.

The indicator is corrected for seasonal variations, and its values during the first one and a half years of the Plan are shown in Table 9.1. France appears to be holding on to the gains made in 1971, but the picture is not the same in all markets. Specific indicators, calculated in the same way as (9.4) but relating to individual foreign markets, show a maintenance of the 1971 position in the USA, West Germany and Italy, a deterioration in the UK and Belgium, and an improved situation in only one of the six cases: the Netherlands.

The penetration of foreign products on the French market is measured by PFI_q, where

$$PFI_q = \frac{\text{imports of manufactured products}}{\text{total domestic consumption of manufactured products}} \tag{9.5}$$

and total domestic consumption covers production plus imports minus exports. This indicator is established from the new quarterly national accounts, and is complemented by

$$EE_q = \frac{\text{exports of manufactured products}}{\text{total domestic consumption of manufactured products}} \quad (9.6)$$

which measures the French industrial export effort. Recent values of these two indicators shown in Table 9.1 show a rise in PFI_q at a time when world trade generally was slowing down. This supports the earlier contention that French industrial capacity was not capable of meeting the strong domestic demand, and more imports were thus allowed to enter.

The last two indicators are supposed to monitor industrial costs and productivity, but the statistical measurement problems are such that both are to be interpreted with caution. The growth of productivity is another important assumption underlying the Plan account, and the FIFI model has demonstrated the favourable effects that this growth should produce. Accordingly, a quarterly measure of productivity has been devised, but it is rather approximate:

$$ALP_q = \frac{\text{quarterly index of industrial production}}{\text{INSEE activity index}} \quad (9.7)$$

where ALP_q is the quarterly index of apparent labour productivity and the INSEE activity index measures the change in the number of hours worked in a week, comparing the first week of each successive quarter. [22] The 7·0 per cent p.a. assumption shown in Table 6.2 cannot really be compared with the values of this indicator shown in Table 9.1, first because the index of industrial production covers a different field to the industry sector in the FIFI model, and secondly because only wage-earning employees are included in the INSEE activity index. A more accurate impression of changes in productivity can be obtained from a report prepared for the annual meeting of the Industry Plan Commission, which we briefly discuss in the next section.

The unit industrial wage cost indicator is more uncertain still, because it includes all the uncertainties surrounding the productivity indicator (by using it as the denominator) and introduces more because of having to leave out a number of elements that affect the wage cost but cannot be measured:

$$WC_q = \frac{\text{hourly remuneration index}}{ALP_q} \quad (9.8)$$

The hourly remuneration index is a derivative of the hourly wage-rate index which is published in *Tendances de la Conjoncture*. Although it is not possible to attach any real meaning to the individual values of the indicators shown in the last two rows of Table 9.1, the series taken as a whole does indicate the rapid rise in wages, that successive annual economic budgets have confirmed, and the recent slowdown in productivity, which is taking some of the gloss off the apparent success in achieving the new industrial jobs target.

9.3 Annual reviews, revisions, and economic budgets

Unlike the situation in the Fifth Plan, the Sixth Plan indicators have no direct link with automatic policy or target revisions. Their use is mainly psychological; they provide publicity for the Plan, and keep its key objectives and assumptions in the minds of the policy-makers. The annual reviews of Plan implementation by the Plan Commissions are of far more importance for possible policy changes or target revisions. The Plan itself spells out the annual review procedure and also mentions the particular significance associated with the mid-term (i.e. 1973) review. At the beginning of each year, the CEGF assesses how the Plan is working on the basis of two principal elements of information: the Plan indicators presented in graphical and tabular form, and time and progress schedules ('tableaux de bord') drawn up by the CGP. These schedules, which exist in two forms, show the degree to which the Plan's targets have been reached. [23] A simplified schedule is established on the basis of the forecast national accounts for the current year and assumptions for the following year, as published at the time of the debate on the Finance Act in October. More detailed and retrospective schedules are then drawn up in May or June on the basis of the annual Report on the National Accounts prepared by the INSEE with the assistance of several other Government departments.

Any modifications that are thought to be necessary as a result of examining these schedules are submitted by the CGP to Parliament in the Report on the Execution of the Plan, which is presented in October with other economic and financial documents accompanying the Finance Act. The outcome of these debates and discussions is the Economic and Financial Report for the current year and the economic budget [24] for the following year. Both these documents are valuable sources of data, forecasts and policy statements, and they form the basis for Table 9.2 below, which compares economic performance during 1971–1973 with Sixth Plan and economic budget forecasts. This sort of 'before' and 'after' comparison is useful for assessing where the main weaknesses in the original forecasts

Table 9.2

Changes in the main macro-economic aggregates 1971–1973 compared with Sixth Plan and economic budget forecasts (average annual growth rates, volume terms)

	Departure account 1970/1975	Plan account 1970/1975	Forecast 1971	Actual 1971*	Forecast 1972	Actual 1972†	Forecast 1973	Actual 1973‡	Forecast 1974
Resources									
Gross domestic production (PIB)	5·4	5·9	5·7	5·6	5·2	5·6	5·8	6·6	5·5
Imports	9·8	9·3	8·7	7·3	7·2	12·8	11·2	16·9	12·5
Uses									
Total consumption	5·2	5·3	5·1	6·1	5·2	5·6	5·7	5·6	5·5
of which: households	(5·3)	(5·4)	(5·1)	(6·1)	(5·4)	(5·6)	(5·6)	(5·8)	(5·6)
administrations	(4·0)	(3·3)	(3·7)	(4·7)	(1·6)	(4·8)	(5·7)	(3·5)	(2·4)
financial institutions	(6·8)	(6·0)	(9·7)	(7·2)	(4·8)	(7·6)	(7·0)	(2·7)	(3·7)
Gross fixed capital formation	5·5	6·4	6·6	6·1	5·6	6·8	6·0	8·2	6·3
of which: productive	(5·4)	(6·8)	(7·4)	(6·3)	(5·8)	(6·5)	(6·2)	(8·0)	(7·0)
housing	(4·8)	(4·6)	(3·5)	(7·3)	(4·6)	(8·2)	(4·6)	(8·0)	(4·5)
administrations	(7·0)	(7·6)	(7·0)	(2·8)	(5·8)	(6·1)	(6·7)	(9·9)	(5·7)
financial institutions	(3·6)	(6·5)	(5·1)	(16·5)	(3·8)	(9·9)	(8·6)	(8·2)	(7·8)
Exports and net services	8·2	10·0	9·3	10·9	8·0	11·6	11·1	13·0	11·7

* The definitive national accounts for 1971 are not finalised until the end of 1974, and are then published in May 1975. The values in column 4 are, therefore, subject to change
† Ditto, but read 1972, 1975, 1976 for 1971, 1974, 1975
‡ Ditto, but read 1973, 1976, 1977 for 1972, 1975, 1976

Sources: columns 1 and 2, Table 6.8; column 3, [205], p. 33; columns 4 and 6, [206], p. 12; column 5, [207], p. 23; column 7, [208], p. 59; column 8, [209], p. 69; column 9, [209], p. 84

appear to be, but there are pitfalls in drawing definite conclusions about the success or otherwise of the Plan. Many analyses have been carried out in the past, seeking to determine whether or not the French plans have been successfully implemented. For instance, Vera Lutz in [147] uses a realisation index defined by

$$A = \frac{R_a}{P_a} \times 100$$

where R_a = realised quantity in the terminal year;
P_a = predicted quantity in the terminal year.

Thus, perfect realisation is represented by $A = 100$. But it is important to recognise that this and other measures like it are forecast-realisation indices and not Plan-implementation indices: just because a forecast has been perfectly realised does not necessarily mean that the Plan has been consciously perfectly implemented. This point is better appreciated by referring to the Third and Fourth Plans,[25] both of which were replaced by other programmes before the end of their term. To compile a table of original Third or Fourth Plan targets and corresponding terminal year realisations is a meaningless exercise if aimed at checking the successful implementation of these Plans, when both have clearly been abandoned. [26] Such analysis is widely questioned in the literature. McArthur and Scott point out some obvious difficulties, in [150] :

1   Is the Plan precise enough to be implementable?
2   Do the growth and development objectives of the Plan provide a sound guide that companies might reasonably follow in setting their own development objectives?
3   When Government agencies intervene, as they frequently do, is it the objectives of the Plan they are seeking to implement, or other, perhaps quite different, objectives?

They go on to agree that it is possible to find 'before' and 'after' figures that are remarkably similar, even for sectors and sub-sectors; '... this has lent support to the wide belief that national planning in France has been effective'. McArthur and Scott conclude:

> The usual before-and-after comparisons are not the most appropriate way to test the implementation of the Plan or to measure the impact of the planning process. What is needed is a case-by-case approach, with a focus on actual decision-making. 'Who did what and why?' Are the interventions of the State to implement the Plan, or for some other reason?

Table 9.2 is, therefore, only a starting point. It helps to point out where the forecasts seem to be wide of the mark. This should encourage deeper structural analysis into the reasons: what economic, social or political mechanisms were missed or misread? And even where perfect realisation appears to have been achieved, further analysis is still required to discover whether this was by design or happy accident. All this may appear discuraging to the student of economic planning, but there really is no alternative to a project-by-project and firm-by-firm approach to the problem of measuring Plan implementation. It is an area in which much research remains to be done.

For our part, we can merely hope to point the student in the right direction and provide him with some of the basic data, sources, and ideas. We have indicated at the beginning of this chapter that the Sixth Plan is likely to be amended or replaced by the as yet unpublished 1974—1976 programme, and in this light Table 9.2 is probably as far (in time) as any Sixth Plan before-and-after comparisons could be taken. Bearing in mind the further imprecisions introduced by the fact that the 'actual' values are not firm national accounts' values, the broad impressions one gains are as follows. First, imports have grown incredibly fast, making up the shortfall in domestic capacity, which has been unable to satisfy a demand growing at a faster than forecast pace. Exports, taken by themselves, have shown a better than forecast performance, but the foreign trade target has not been met because of capacity limitations. The growth and industrial output situations are, on the figures shown in Table 9.2, generally satisfactory, but further analysis reveals some causes for concern. A report prepared for the Industry Plan Commission [210] concludes that although the employment, investment, and capital objectives included in the Plan account have so far been met, the productivity of labour has not increased as rapidly as expected and the length of the working week has decreased more quickly than anticipated. As the earlier chapters show, these two factors are critical to the Plan account, and the fact that the original assumptions concerning them have so far proved to be not quite so accurate is largely responsible for the observed differences in the before-and-after comparisons on the volume side. This has led to further work on productivity analysis, [27] following the procedural chain of events (i.e. before and after comparisons generating deeper structural analyses) we have outlined above.

The major problems have been on the value side, however, with wages and prices far outstripping the Plan account forecasts. [28] This has tended to focus attention on inflation and demand management policies in the recent annual economic budgets and OECD economic surveys, with the

Table 9.3

The state of implementation of the Sixth Plan's social overhead capital programmes

Functions	Sixth Plan		Actual[f] (millions of 1970 francs)				Implementation percentage	
	9 per cent assumption	Low assumption	1971	1972	1973	Total 1971–1973	9 per cent assumption (6/1)	Low assumption (6/2)
	1	2	3	4	5	6	7	8
Education and training	19,150	18,800	3,354·3	3,578·6	3,697·7	10,630·6	55·5	56·5
of which: manpower training	(2,000)	(1,700)	(166·5)	(252·0)	(314·6)	(733·1)	(36·7)	(43·1)
Social action	1,800	1,600	204·9	203·6	266·4	674·9	37·5	42·2
of which: Ministry of Health and Social Security	(1,250)	(1,100)	(139·5)	(164·5)	(196·1)	(500·1)	(40·0)	(45·5)
Ministry of Justice	(550)	(500)	(65·4)	(39·1)	(70·3)	(174·8)	(31·8)	(35·0)
Health	3,600	3,100	428·0	528·9	806·6	1,763·5	49·0	56·9
Sporting and socio-educative activities	2,500	2,250	328·7	387·6	399·9	1,116·2	44·6	49·6
Cultural affairs	2,000	1,700	219·8	283·1	371·7	874·6	43·7	51·4
Urban development	19,050	17,850	2,869·3	3,074·4	3,457·0	9,400·7	49·3	52·7
Rural development	9,800	9,300	1,699·6	1,799·4	1,818·2	5,317·2	54·3	57·2
Transport[a]	15,250	14,300	1,988·6	2,469·0	3,098·2	7,558·8	49·5	52·8
Research	21,400	19,500	3,255·3	3,575·3	3,896·2	10,726·8	50·1	55·0
Overseas departments	2,900	2,700	340·5	424·2	442·6	1,207·3	41·6	44·7
Overseas territories[b]	920	850	106·0	137·9	156·2	400·1	43·5	47·1
Telecommunications[b]	28,400	27,300	3,630·0	4,640·0	5,561·3	13,831·3	48·7	50·7
Posts[c]	2,800	2,500	299·0	419·3	483·2	1,201·5	45·5	51·3
Total disaggregated programme appropriations	129,570	121,750	18,724·0	21,521·3	24,455·2	64,700·5	49·9	53·1

Non-disaggregated programme appropriations:[d]							
environment		24·2					
FIAT and rural renovation funds[e]			62·2	87·4			173·8
			249·8	267·4			517·2
global equipment subsidy paid to local authorities			178·3	178·3			178·3
General total	129,570	121,750	18,748·2	21,833·3	24,988·3	65,569·8	50·6	53·9

[a] This refers only to budgetary programme appropriations. About 480 million francs should be added for complementary programmes agreed in 1972 and financed by borrowing. The implementation rates for 'programme appropriations + complementary financing' are as follows: 9 per cent, 52·7 per cent; low 56·2 per cent

[b] As above, with the added figure being 1,400 million francs. This makes the implementation rates 53·8 per cent on the 9 per cent assumption, and 55·9 per cent on the low assumption

[c] The realisation percentages have been calculated using financial envelopes reduced by 160 million francs. This is because certain items have been substituted by apparatus that is not financed by programme appropriations

[d] As in previous years, part of the Ministry of the Environment's programme credits have been attributed to 'cultural affairs' (2·8 million) and 'rural development' (34·6 million)

[e] The FIAT figures for 1971 have been attributed to the various benefiting categories. This distribution is no longer possible for the following years; neither is it possible for the rural renovation fund

[f] Including FAC ('Fonds d'Action Conjoncturalle'), which the Government holds in reserve to meet particular short-term contingencies

Source: Table VI, [218], pp. 40–1. Columns 1 and 2 are also given in Table 6.5 above, and subsumed in various tables in Chapter 8 (particularly Table 8.5)

Plan mentioned very rarely, if at all. It is regarded only as a framework for investment programmes for the period 1971–1975, and as a guide for economic expansion and social progress. [29] Following the work on value programming that went into the Fifth Plan, and the endogenisation of prices in the FIFI model used in the Sixth Plan's preparation, the planners had reason to hope for better results than this. But there are features of any plan that are wildly optimistic, stubbornly conservative, or politically naive. They are the points at which logic and rationality give way to emotion, and where the analysis has failed to come up with an acceptable answer; a value is inserted to maintain consistency with the others, but it has no deep, structural support (i.e. it goes against acknowledged or expressed economic and social mechanisms). Wages and incomes are in this category in the Sixth Plan. We have described the criticisms of the wage–price–unemployment relationship in earlier chapters, and the Plan itself openly admits defeat on an incomes policy:

> In the absence of a minimum of co-operation from the parties involved, the Government has given up the idea of including the principles of a concerted incomes policy in the Sixth Plan, thus continuing the multiyear programming in value terms initiated under the Fifth Plan. The fact remains that the French people have in mind orders of magnitude for the increase in nominal income that are incompatible with the maintenance of balance. It is essential to the success of the Plan that a more reasonable rate be accepted. [30]

Nearly three years later, the same sentiments were being expressed in the 1974 economic budget.

> It seems that the attitudes adopted by the social partners in France are, in the present circumstances, more opposed to central, imperative regulation of their incomes than in some other countries....The root of the problem is, in effect, the growing mismatch of the desires of individuals, groups and enterprises and the physical possibilities of the economy. As long as behaviour built on illusions persists the problem of inflation will not be fully solved. [31]

It is clear that any analysis of the Sixth Plan at the macro-economic aggregate level is bound to reveal poor results on the wages and prices front. It is equally clear that any analysis of the short-term policy situation is certain to focus on the major immediate problem, which is inflation, so that extreme impressions of the role and success of the Plan are encouraged. We emphasise again that this is not a satisfactory way of assessing the success of the Plan; it omits altogether the social and regional aspects that we have spent so much time discussing in previous chapters. In addition to a simplified overall economic table, an overall social table should be compiled to help guide the analysis of the performance of the Plan in this direction. Tables 9.3 and 9.4 are certainly simplified, and they do focus on some of the social aspects of the Plan. They record the progress made in the first three years of the Plan in implementing the five-year social overhead capital and goal-oriented programmes. Tables 6.5 6.6 and 6.7 show the original intentions with respect to these program- mes. Generally, the figures in Table 9.3 are quite good, although not one of the 13 overall programmes is on the regular growth path (i.e. 60 per cent implemented after three years). The priority programmes appear to be rural development, health, education and research, with sport, overseas departments and territories and social action at the other end of the spectrum. It is remarkable that the 1973 figure is, in every case, the highest figure, indicating either a gradual build-up in all programmes which, if continued (18·7 million francs in 1971, 21·5 in 1972, 24·5 in 1973, 27·5 in 1974, 30·5 in 1975), will achieve the low target, or, more likely, indicating that the 1973 figures, which are estimates (the source of the figures is dated November 1973), are optimistic. The apparent time-lag between the formulation of the programmes and their implementation can also be explained by the traditional lack of synchronisation between pub- lic investment programmes and budget expenditures. Hayward[32] quotes a court of public accounts report that found that between one-quarter and one-third of the funds allocated to ministries every year were not spent until up to four years later.

An interesting development designed to help put this situation right are 'plan contracts', which considerably extend the field of application of previous contractual arrangements (the Fourth Plan used quasi-con- tracts as a means of Plan implementation), and specifically bring in public enterprises and local authorities. 'The Fifth Plan did not achieve its social overhead capital objectives, because local authorities were not able to ensure their share of the financing',[33] and this fact has led directly to the legislation of December 1970 introducing plan contracts. Pimont gives a good description of their intended mode of operation, but it is too soon to assess their effectiveness with respect to the implementation of the Sixth Plan. They provide a good opportunity for us to add the contract- by-contract method of checking Plan implementation to the previously mentioned firm-by-firm and project-by-project approaches, and reinforce our contention that much research remains to be done on the extent to which French plans are actively implemented, and the roles played by the various instruments we have discussed in this chapter.

Table 9.4

The state of implementation of the Sixth Plan's goal-oriented programmes

Title of programme and contributions by ministries [a]	Sixth Plan total (millions of 1970 francs)	Actual (millions of 1970 francs)				Implementation percentage (5/1)
		1971	1972	1973	Total 1971–1973	
	1	2	3	4	5	6
1 New towns						
Total	3,340					
Central government	2,410	232·2	426	413	1,071·2	44
of which: Housing		116·9	138·0	147·0		
Interior		35·6	63·0	45·7		
National Education		34·7	94·9	121·0		
Youth and Sport		9·9	19·8	26·2		
Social Affairs		1·6	41·1	16·3		
Aid to new towns		40·6	64·2	85·0		
Other grants			36·2	20·0		
2 Road safety						
Total	2,349					
Central government	1,450	171·2	199·7	228·0	598·9	41·3
of which: Housing		131·1	157·0	182		
Interior		27·85	29·3	37·3		
Health		20·3	14·25	19·3		
Other ministries		7·67	14·82	18·6		
3 Mother and child care						
Total	2,588					
Central government	74	10·3	10·0	12·7	33·0	44·6
of which: Health		10·34	10·2	13·4		

294

	Total					
4 *Labour market*						
Central government (Min. Lab.) Total	805[c]	145.1	177.3	223.2	545.6	70
of which: Handicapped adults	45	2.1	6.0	[d]		
5 *Old people*						
Total	1,128		21.4	23.5	[e]	
Central government (Min. Health)	265					
6 *Mediterranean forests*						
Total	492	42	62	75.4	179.4	45
Central government	395					
of which: Agriculture		31.3	46.44	57.6		

[a] Central government and Plan figures are in constant 1970 francs, but ministry figures are in current francs

[b] Figure not given in source

[c] Figure expressed in 1971 francs

[d] Figure not given in source

[e] Figure not given in source, because of difficulty in distinguishing this aid from other benefits granted to old people

Source: Table VIII, [218], pp. 44–7, which also gives details on the goal programme objectives and sub-programmes. Note that the tentative Plan figure (2,850) quoted in Table 6.6 is very much an underestimate

Notes

[1] From *The Economist*, 13 April 1974, p. 107.

[2] This work [246], was compiled just after the preparation of the Sixth Plan had begun. The 'today' in its title refers to early 1970. It provides a good picture of how the state of the Plan looked, from the inside, at that time. The 13 contributors are: Michel Aglietta, Jacques Bertherat, Jean Jacques Bonnaud, Raymond Courbis, Paul Dubois, Catherine Girardeau, Bernard Grais, Jean-Pierre Pagé, Christian Sautter, Claude Seibel, Lionel Stoleru, Bernard Ullmo, and Yves Ullmo. These names will be recognised by the reader as the source of a lot of material covered elsewhere in this book.

[3] See [247]. Claude Gruson has been called the father of French national accounting. He was a member of the committee of experts on national accounting set up in March 1950, and then appointed head of the SEEF (at that time attached to the Treasury) in the same year. This department was very much involved in creating the national accounting system. He was Director of the INSEE from 1961–1966.

[4] Quoted from a review of [247] by Henri Guitton, a professor at the University of Paris and the editor of *Revue d'Économie Politique*, in vol. 82, no. 3 (May–June 1972), p. 563, of this journal.

[5] To do so would be difficult at the best of times, but in the present (April 1974) pre-presidential election period, it is impossible to judge which way the balance of economic power will move.

[6] Cairncross' paper, written in 1966, is a good general introduction to the problem of finding the right balance between medium-term planning for structural change and short-term demand management policy. French articles on the subject are surprisingly few and far between, and there is little alternative to reading between the lines in the Economic and Financial Report, submitted to Parliament every autumn during the discussions on the annual Finance Act. The Report is usually published, along with the forecast national accounts for the same year and the economic budget for the following year, in the October issue of *Statistiques et Études Financières*, Série Rouge, published by the Ministry of Finance (and hence the need to read between the lines to find references to the Plan!). Summary articles on the Report are also frequently carried by the November or December issues of *Économie et Statistique*.

[7] An article by Alain Vernholes in *Le Monde*, 20 March 1974, states that the CGP submitted its report to M. Messmer, the Prime Minister, 'last week' . It also states that the work 'will probably not by made public', so

the 4·0 per cent growth rate is either an educated guess or a piece of inside information. It is unlikely that the report is very detailed because M. Messmer only asked the CGP to prepare it at the end of January 1974.

[8] *Les Indicateurs Associés au 6e Plan* (Indicators associated with the Sixth Plan) is published every quarter, by the CGP and the INSEE. It carried graphs and tables of the indicators described in this chapter. The first issue contains 'information available on 15 February 1972', and the last issue of 1973 'information available on 15 December 1973'. There is no apparent change in the original targets between those two issues. Both carry the same brief description of the indicators, a description that is also given, word for word, in [188]. This last source also carries a complete graphical record of the performance of the Fifth Plan indicators.

[9] [146], p. 38, in a chapter written by Paul Dubois.

[10] Perhaps we should qualify the use of the word 'Government' in relation to these objectives, intentions, and forecasts. As we have seen, other social groups are involved in their preparation, but many would argue (including some of the social groups themselves, notably the unions) that it is too idealistic to refer to the final outcome (i.e. the Plan) as reflecting society's preferences. This is yet another interesting debate that we have to sidestep here. It occurs again in Chapter 5, with reference to the critical balance between the open 'concertation' phases and the closed administrative phases of Plan preparation, in Chapter 7 where we discuss the social time preference discount rate, and in Chapter 8 where the true meaning of the word 'regionalisation' is highlighted.

[11] [250], p. 179.

[12] This is the OPTIMIX study, which used a version of the DECA model to analyse the problem of defining strategies aimed at counteracting uncontrolled factors that might occur during the lifetime of a Plan. It also specially constructed a preference function for the Sixth Plan. As is confirmed by Table 5.1 the study was probably before its time. A summary of all the work done in the OPTIMIX study is given in [248], which is a paper written by three CEPREMAP researchers and translated into English by Liggins. The derivation of the Sixth Plan objective function is given in [249].

[13] The quotation is from [112], p. 163.

[14] It would be impossible to give even a brief summary of the hundreds of economic surveys and statistical series carried out by the INSEE and other Government data-gathering services. I have compiled a list of references (in [101]) which may prove useful to readers wishing to find out more about French economic statistics.

[15] The results of these economic enquiries are published in *Information Rapides*, an INSEE publication, which appears approximately 140 times per year.

[16] The main weekly, monthly, and quarterly statistical series and economic indicators are published in the *Bulletin Mensuel de Statistique* (monthly) and *Tendances de la Conjoncture* (appearing 11 times a year), two more INSEE publications.

[17] For details see [199], p. 74.

[18] According to a footnote on p. 20 of [200].

[19] More discussion on PDRE and DENS can be found in [201], which discusses some of the results of the March 1973 employment enquiry. Further results of the same enquiry are given in [202].

[20] See [199], p. 75.

[21] See [203], p. 60. Annual price programmes in France run from 1 April to 31 March in the following year. Price norms are written into contracts drawn up between firms and the administration, and must be respected. The norm can be exceeded on some products only if prices of other products are reduced by a corresponding amount below the norm. Not all firms have to sign contracts, but those choosing not to do so still remain bound by other regulations requiring them to submit price lists for their products to the Price Directorate in the Ministry of Finance. The Ministry employs a large number of price inspectors to police the scheme. Details of successive annual programmes are usually given in the OECD surveys on France, such as [199] and [203].

[22] The article by Ponsot and Sautter [204] discusses the difficulties in establishing the productivity and wage cost indicators, and gives detailed step-by-step description of how both are calculated.

[23] There is an example of a Fifth Plan time and progress schedule in [246], pp. 70–1, (also given in Appendix IV later in this book).

[24] The various types of economic budget and national account and the procedures according to which they are compiled are described in Appendix VI, along with the DECA model, which is used to prepare exploratory economic budgets.

[25] In fact, we could refer to all six Plans to make this point. We have already mentioned that the Sixth will probably be replaced by the 1974–1976 proposals (or some other interim measure introduced by the new President), and Hayward very neatly deals with the other five: 'The First Plan's targets were achieved a year late; the Second Plan, thanks to Edgar Faure's '18 month plan' of 1953–1954, exceeded its targets; the Third Plan was scaled down by an Interim Plan covering 1960–1, only for the results to be nearer the original targets; the Fourth Plan was modified

by the 1963 'stabilisation plan'; while the Fifth Plan was going badly until it was unexpectedly rectified by the May—June 1968 crisis and devaluation in 1969' (from [250], p. 185).

[26] Stephen Cohen supports this view: 'Any attempt to compare actual patterns of economic activity in 1961 with the targets of the Third Plan promises to be especially futile and misleading' (from [251]).

[27] Notably by Malinvaud, [211].

[28] The reader is referred to [199], [200], and [203] for the numerical details.

[29] Quoted from [212], p. 59, which in turn is based on the Bill describing the Plan in the *Journal Officiel* of 16 July 1971.

[30] [112], p. 22.

[31] [200], p. 29. Footnote to the passage from which this quotation is taken is as follows: 'Other European countries have also experienced rapid increases in wages: between 11 and 13 per cent per annum with a high point of 18·9 per cent in 1970. Taking labour productivity into account (gross value-added per wage-earning employee), the wage cost per unit produced has increased by 6·6 per cent in 1972 in France, compared with 5·9 per cent in Great Britain, 7·5 per cent in Italy, 4·5 per cent in West Germany, 7·5 per cent in Belgium, and only 1·5 per cent in the USA. It should increase by 7·8 per cent in France in 1973 according to the forecast national accounts'.

[32] [250], pp. 185—186.

[33] [252], p. 703.

There are additional notes and references to this and other chapters at the end of Chapter 10.

References

[187] A. Cairncross, 'Economic planning: the short term and the long', pp. 159—83 in A. Cairncross, *Essays in Economic Management*, George Allen and Unwin , London 1971, 219 pp.

[188] INSEE, 'Les indicateurs associés au VIe Plan' (The indicators associated with the Sixth Plan), *Économie et Statistique* no. 26, September 1971, pp. 3—26.

[189] M. Perrot, 'Où retrouver les statistiques de salaires' (Where to find wages statistics), *Économie et Statistique* no. 5, October 1969, pp. 61—71.

[190] INSEE, 'Les principales statistiques sur l'emploi disponibles en

France' (The main available statistics on employment in France), *Économie et Statistique* no. 18, December 1970, pp. 58–69.

[191] INSEE, 'L'enquête annuelle d'entreprise a couvert toute l'industrie en 1970' (The annual industrial enquiry covered the whole of industry in 1970), *Économie et Statistique* no. 43, March 1973, pp. 59–63.

[192] G. Ader, 'Le système francaise de statistiques industrielles' (The French system of industrial statistics), *Économie et Statistique* no. 12, May 1970, pp. 51–66.

[193] P. Letoquart and J-M. Reffet, 'Le projet SIRENE vise à unifier la procédure d'immatriculation des entreprises' (The SIRENE project aims to unify the enterprise registration procedure), *Économie et Statistique* no. 6, November 1969, pp. 67–8.

[194] J. Peskine, 'La classification par activités économiques dans la fichier des enterprises SIRENE' (Classification by economic activity in the SIRENE enterprise index), *Économie et Statistique* no. 50, November 1973, pp. 56–60.

[195] P. Koepp, 'La nouvelle base de l'indice de la production industrielle 1962 = 100' (The new base year of the industrial output index is 1962), *Économie et Statistique* no. 3, July–August 1969, pp. 23–31.

[196] INSEE, 'Les indices de la production industrielle, base 100 en 1962' (Industrial output indices, base 100 in 1962), *Les Collections de l'INSEE*, séries E, no. 9, April 1971.

[197] J-M. Rempp, H. Picard, Ph. Sigogne and F. Fabre, 'Les nouveaux indices de prix à la consommation (1970 = 100)' (The new consumer price indices, base year 1970), *Économie et Statistique* no. 21, March 1971, pp. 3–13.

[198] Ph. Nasse, 'Premières publications des comptes économiques trimestriels' (First publication of the quarterly economic accounts), *Économie et Statistique* no. 43, March 1973, pp. 56–58.

[199] OECD, *Economic Survey of France*, Paris, February 1973, 99 pp.

[200] Ministry of Finance, 'Le rapport économique et financier' (The economic and financial report), *Statistique et Études Financières*, Série Rouge, no. 298, October 1973, pp. 3–58.

[201] F. Eymard-Duvernay, 'Selon l'enquête-emploi le chomage avait sensiblement diminué entre mars 1972 et mars 1973' (Unemployment fell significantly between March 1972 and March 1973 according to the employment enquiry), *Économie et Statistique* no. 50, November 1973, pp. 49–53.

[202] R. Poal, P. Laulhé and F. Eymard-Duvernay, 'La population active

en 1972' (The working population in 1972), *Économie et Statistique* no. 44, April 1973, pp. 35–51.

[203] OECD, *Economic Survey of France*, Paris, February 1974, 85 pp.

[204] J-F. Ponsot and Ch. Sautter, 'La croissance de la productivité du travail dans l'industrie s'est accélérée dès 1967' (The growth of industrial labour productivity has accelerated since 1967). *Économie et Statistique* no. 13, June 1970, pp. 13–28.

[205] INSEE, 'Principales hypothèses économiques pour 1971' (Main economic assumptions concerning 1971), *Économie et Statistique* no. 17, November 1970, pp. 27–39.

[206] INSEE, 'Rapport sur les comptes de la nation de l'année 1972' (Report on the national accounts for 1972), vol. 1, *Les Collections de l'INSEE*, série C, no. 23, June 1973, 108 pp. (also published in *Statistiques et Études Financières*, Série Rouge, no. 294, June 1973). 1973).

[207] INSEE 'Principales hypothèses économiques pour 1972' (Main economic assumptions concerning 1972), *Économie et Statistique* no. 28, November 1971, pp. 21–30.

[208] INSEE, 'Le budget prévisionnel pour 1973' (The forecast budget for 1973), *Économie et Statistique* no. 40, December 1972, pp. 58–62.

[209] INSEE, 'Comptes prévisionnels de la nation pour 1973 et principales hypothèses économiques pour 1974' (Forecast national accounts for 1973 and main economic assumption concerning 1974), *Statistiques et Études Financières,* Série Rouge, no. 298, October 1973, pp. 59–89

[210] J-P. Devichi, 'La situation de l'industrie francaise en 1972' (The situation of French industry in 1972), *Économie et Statistique* no. 48, September 1973, pp. 17–31.

[211] E. Malinvaud, 'Une explication de l'évolution de la productivité horaire du travail' (An explanation of the change in the hourly labour productivity), *Économie et Statistique* no. 48, September 1973, pp. 46–50.

[212] OECD, *Economic Survey of France,* Paris, February 1972, 85 pp.

[213] Containay, Girardeau, Sirel, Bonnans, Bréguet, Dupart, de Laparent, and Tuchman, 'Le contenu des fonctions collectives' (The meaning and content of the collective functions), *Notes et Études Documentaires* no. 4037–4038, 6 November 1973, 47 pp.

[214] Ph. Herzog and G. Olive, 'L'élaboration des budgets economiques' (The construction of economic budgets), *Études et Conjoncture* no. 8, 1968, pp. 3–30.

301

[215] D. Liggins, Translation of [214] into English, *NEP Research Papers* no. 61, University of Birmingham, February 1972, 37 pp.

[216] J. Billy, 'Méthodes et travaux de la Direction de la Prévision' (The Forecasting Directorate's methods and work), *Le Bulletin de Liaison et d'Information de l'Administration Centrale de l'Économie et des Finances* no. 63, April–September 1973, pp. 56–89.

[217] J-M. Callies, 'Révision annuelle des comptes nationaux' (Annual revision of the national accounts), *Économie et Statistique* no. 40, December 1972, pp. 63–64.

[218] B. Billaudot, 'Le modèle DECA model' (The DECA model), *Statistiques et Études Financières*, Série Orange, no. 1, 1971, 46 pp.

[219] D. Liggins, Translation of [218] into English, *NEP Research Papers* no. 65, University of Birmingham, May 1972, pp. 23–61.

[220] P. Malgrange, 'Étude analytique du modèle DECA' (Analytical study of the DECA model), CEPREMAP Working Paper, Paris, November 1972, 75 pp.

10　On FIFITOF and REGINA

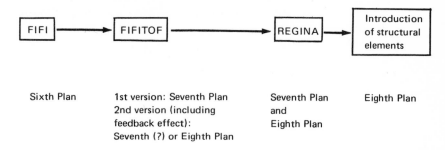

FIFI	FIFITOF	REGINA	Introduction of structural elements

| Sixth Plan | 1st version: Seventh Plan
2nd version (including
feedback effect):
Seventh (?) or Eighth Plan | Seventh Plan
and
Eighth Plan | Eighth Plan |

Raymond Courbis, [120], p. 338.

In this final chapter, we report progress on the models that are to be used in the preparation of the Seventh Plan. The above diagram, produced by Courbis in May 1973, just after the start of the administrative phase in the preparation of the Seventh Plan, is suitably uncertain about whether the models will be ready on time, and the reader is referred to section 5.4 above to remind himself of some of the doubts and criticisms voiced by planners, administrators, participants and others on the use of 'bigger and better models'. We do not need to repeat those views here, but they should be borne in mind when reading this chapter, and weighed against the analytical descriptions we give (drawn from mainly technical sources that tend to ignore the social feelings and priorities expressed in Chapter 5). The arguments for including financial operations and regional problems in the 'model' have also been referred to many times (in Chapters 1, 3, and 5 particularly), and so no further justification for including FIFITOF and REGINA in this chapter is given here.

10.1　The FIFITOF project

This project takes its name from the FIFI model and the financial operations table (TOF being the initials of the French term 'tableau d'opérations financières'), which are both to be integrated in one single model, along with a number of 'financial mechanisms'. Work to this end has been going on for a number of years now, dating back to the preparation of the Fifth Plan. The first projection of the TOF,[1] and the first detailed projection of enterprise accounts by sector,[2] including their financial account,

303

marks the real beginning of the proper analysis of financial problems in the Plan preparation process. It is clear, however, that

> these financial forecasts were carried out as the last link in the chain, after the analysis of the real resources equilibrium and the income and expenditure equilibrium. It follows therefore that the development of financial circuits was dependent on a large body of assumptions introduced at earlier stages, a fact that placed limits on the confidence in the final results that were reached. A complete reiteration of all the earlier stages of the model-building process was not considered possible within the context of the preparation of the Fifth Plan.[3]

The Sixth Plan took this work further by basing the TOF projection on a better economic projection (produced by the FIFI model), and experimenting with 'manual' feedback (i.e. some of the FIFI's parameters were changed by hand as a result of examining the projected TOF). Several financial variants were produced in this way.[4] An important innovation in the Sixth Plan financial studies was the long-term financing table (TFLT), compiled by the DP. This was designed to analyse the total supply of long-term (meaning medium-term too, in a planning context) capital and its allocation. We have referred before to the fragmentation of the French capital market, and the way in which some sources can be left holding a surplus because no potential borrowers can meet their lending conditions, while others suffer a shortage; the TFLT highlights these surpluses and shortages and points the way to possible changes in policy (its use is apparent in the statement taken from the Plan given in note 4 to Chapter 7). The TFLT associated with the Sixth Plan account is given in [94], p. 302.

We mentioned in Chapter 6 the TOF associated with the reference account of January 1970. Further TOFs were calculated in association with the options account (August 1970) and the Plan account (July–August 1971),[5] but each one had to be constructed according to a procedure that was distinct from the computerised calculations involved in the associated economic account. There was very little possibility of any feedback from the economic equilibrium described by the associated central account, and the financial side of the post-options phase was very much the same as in the Fifth Plan. One of the aims of the FIFITOF project is to include the TOF and TFLT projection in the same package as FIFI, so that every time an economic account is produced, an associated financial account is also constructed. This stage was reached in 1972, so that the FIFI model now has a TOF block[6] which

(a)   takes the economic projection produced by FIFI's other blocks and calculates the use of finance by economic agencies, using separate sub-models for housing and administrations;[7]

(b)   a disaggregation is then made by category of financial operation and type of financial institution, bringing out the structure of use made by the various financial institutions;

(c)   the TFLT can then be constructed directly.

But there is still no feedback from the TOF projection to the economic projection, mainly because of doubts as to which financial mechanism to use to carry this interaction. Courbis' ideas, originally put forward in 1969,[8] focus on enterprises' self-financing behaviour and the way in which France's traditional shortage of long-term capital affects this behaviour. As we have seen in section 3.1, a global consideration of this behaviour is one of the key features of the FIFI model. The purpose of Courbis' theoretical model, and the later work on FIFITOF, is to disaggregate the structure of long-term finance external to the enterprises, and explain the mechanisms involved. The rate of interest does not have a prominent role in this theoretical model, for reasons that are explained in Chapter 7. This

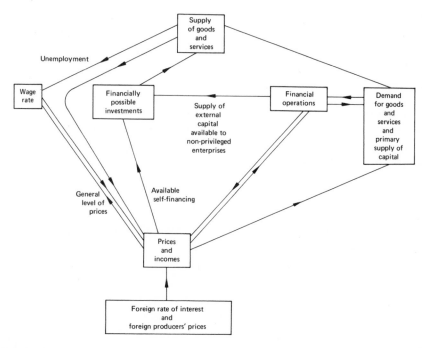

Fig. 10.1   Structure of the FIFITOF model
Source: see note 9

305

makes it more difficult to incorporate monetary policy into the model, but Courbis defends the assumption of passive behaviour on the part of the monetary authorities by emphasising that the model aims to analyse the medium-term impact of an insufficient supply of long-term external finance, and not primarily to aid the definition of monetary policy.

There are also practical problems, mainly of a statistical nature, involved in a proper integration of financial mechanisms in FIFI. It is no longer satisfactory to consider just one large category of enterprises, nor to work only with 'financial institutions' as the usual overall economic table and national accounts do. Public, private, and individual enterprises behave differently in seeking finance (some public firms have privileged access to particular sources), and the various types of financial institution compete in a different way to satisfy this demand. But the standard statistics are incapable of reflecting these distinctions, a situation that has necessitated a great deal of work (particularly by the Financial Operations Statistical Research Department (SESOF) of the Bank of France) on compiling retrospective disaggregated series. Figures relating to the sources of finance used by public and private enterprises broken down according to FIFI's seven sectors and going back to 1962 are now available.

The model proposed in 1969 has thus been generalised and put forward as a practical proposition; its basic structure is shown in Figure 10.1. Comparison with the diagrams in Chapter 3 makes it clear that FIFITOF is by no means a new model; what is involved here is the addition of more equations to the existing FIFI model. The five-stage sequence of operations in the financial block is as follows:

(i) disaggregation of the capital accounts of households (distinguishing farmers, other entrepreneurs (self-employed), wage earners, and pensioners) to improve the calculation of savings rates, and enterprises (distinguishing 11 categories, the seven included in FIFI with further breakdowns of sectors 3, 4, 5 and 6);

(ii) detailed projection of the TOF, analysing the behaviour of nine large finance networks in detail and that of the Treasury; [10]

(iii) having thus calculated the supply of long-term capital available to each agency, modification of:

    (a) investment (for agricultural enterprises),

    (b) level of self-financing (for enterprises in exposed sectors), investment (for enterprises in non-competitive sectors), distribution of profits etc.,

    (c) average level of saving and investment in housing (for households),

(d)   investment and share of internal financing (for local authorities);

(iv) calculation of transfer between different finance networks (where
possible);

(v) repetition, with new values of parameters and variables changed in
steps (i)–(iv).

This framework was suggested in 1971,[11] but at about the same time
the CGP established a money–growth discussion group to discuss how
best to integrate financial operations. The observations of this group have
tended to slow down progress towards a fully integrated model, at least as
far as Courbis' original expectations are concerned. His 1971 proposals
anticipated using an integrated model in the preparation of the Seventh
Plan, but, as we have pointed out, this will not now happen (unless attempts are made to use such a model in the later Plan preparation stages,
which is unlikely). The difficulties raised by the group concern the reduced role given to the rate of interest (plans to create a larger, more
homogeneous capital market will assign a bigger role to the rate of interest, it is argued), the passive behaviour of the monetary authorities, and
the lack of explicit allowance for the interaction between the money supply
and inflation. The proposed model also ignores the time dimension (as do
the other first generation models), wealth, and international financial
operations, all factors that are clearly significant, but which cannot be
handled in the present state of knowledge and modelling competence. A
three-sector experimental version of the model, known as MINIFIFITOF,
is currently being tested,[12] but it remains to be seen how quickly the
fully integrated model can be made operational.

10.2   The REGINA project

1971 was also a critical year for the work being done on integrating
regional aspects with the national model. Up to that time, it had seemed
likely that a very ambitious project involving a disaggregated interregional
model, known as MURAT, would make significant contributions to regional analysis in the Seventh Plan. In the event, a high-level policy decision cut off the flow of funds to the MURAT project, and official backing
was given instead to the REGINA project, now being run by Raymond
Courbis with financial support from the CGP. It is interesting, however,
briefly to examine the MURAT project, in order to see what might have
been, and why it was not allowed to proceed.

MURAT was part of the SESAME which, as we have seen in Chapter 2, was also behind the 2000 study and other, mainly long-term, analytical developments. The SESAME is basically a DATAR undertaking, and several of its personnel were members of the MURAT team, along with members of OTAM (also involved in the 2000 study) and CERAU ('Centre d'Études et de Recherches d'Aménagement Urbain', Centre for Research and Analysis in Urban Development). CEPREMAP, involved in a lot of modelling work on the planning side, was also contributing researchers to the team, and it is significant that the leader of the group, Michel Horps, was at that time a member of the CGP, thus indicating that MURAT was originally very much in the planners' minds. Like the objectives of the SESAME itself, the MURAT project appears to have been too ambitious. Although focusing primarily on regional employment problems, it also encompassed regional production and investment, and at a very micro level compared with previous studies. Its main level of analysis was to be at the department level, operating below regional levels. Considering that there are 95 departments and 22 regions, and that French regional statistics were not exactly abundant, this was the major obstacle to gaining the approval of the people in the DATAR and the CGP who were expected to use the model.

It is extremely difficult to summarise the model because it was so large, but basically it consisted of four sub-systems:

(i) a production and investment sub-system, functioning mainly at the regional level, and setting up fundamental (i.e. industrial) employment and facilities in the different sub-regions (i.e. departments);

(ii) an employment supply sub-system, determining for each sub-region the number, nature and qualifications of the jobs offered by firms:

(iii) an employment demand sub-system, defining the number and qualifications of the jobs by households in each sub-region;

(iv) a local labour-market sub-system, attempting to balance the job supply and demand situation in each sub-region.

The overall system operated in a simulation manner, rather like the FIFI model, with the main regional development policy instruments being industrial investment incentives, subsidies to social housing, and central government financing of social overhead capital. These are numbered from 100 upwards in Figure 10.2, which gives an impression of the structure of the model. Other important parameters are the various 'keys' which are used to disaggregate national and regional aggregate figures into regional and local quantities. We have already come across such a 'key' in Chapter 8 in the Sixth Plan regional programming procedure: 80 per cent of central government social overhead capital credits were allocated to regions on the basis of their population and urban concentration, and the remainder according to other criteria. The MURAT team suggested that population should continue to be used as the main key, but it is possible to introduce alternatives which derive from special policies.

There are several other features of the model that are similar to keys in that they can reflect deliberate changes of behaviour, which in turn could be induced by policy changes. In the absence of such policy changes, they would be calculated from past statistical series:

(a) fidelity coefficient: reflecting the tendency of local producers to invest in their own region;
(b) dynamism: reflecting the extent to which local authorities use their own finance to provide social overhead capital;
(c) propensities: the usual consumer propensities to save and spend;
(d) stone coefficient: denoting the proportion of their savings invested in housing by households;
(e) attractiveness and fecundity indices: indicating the attractiveness of local areas to potential employers, and clearly depending on the area's existing job structure, available manpower, and the stock of productive facilities;
(f) attraction and repulsion indices: similar to (e), but reflecting the features of an area from the potential migrating employee's viewpoint. Important considerations here are housing, other social amenities, population structure, etc.

Figure 10.2 gives an idea of the role played by these coefficients and indices. They provide a good example of the way in which economic and social indicators can be used in a model of this type. Even though MU-RAT has now been scrapped, these particular features are likely to be useful in themselves in other regional analyses.

Although the problems of providing data for these coefficients on the scale demanded by MURAT were formidable, and strongly supported the mounting pressures for discontinuing the project, they would probably have been tolerated and gradually overcome if it had not been for another serious difficulty: there was no suitable national model to fasten into the system. The approach of the team had been to start from the bottom and build upwards, concentrating on the local and regional adjustment mechanisms. When they reached the top (horizontal dotted line in Figure 10.2), however, and looked around for a model that would complement the features they had already built in to the interregional model, all the obvious candidates were found to be lacking in one or several ways.[13] CEPREMAP Research Report of February 1971 carries a paragraph on the

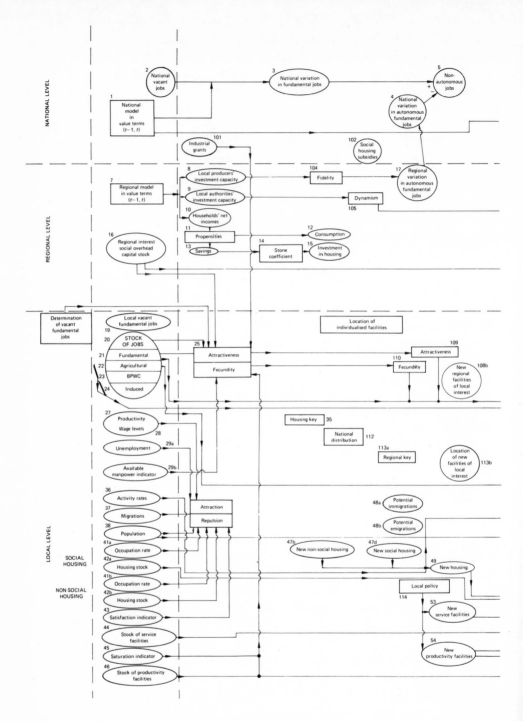

Fig. 10.2   The dynamic linkages and iterative processes of the MURAT model
Source: [235]

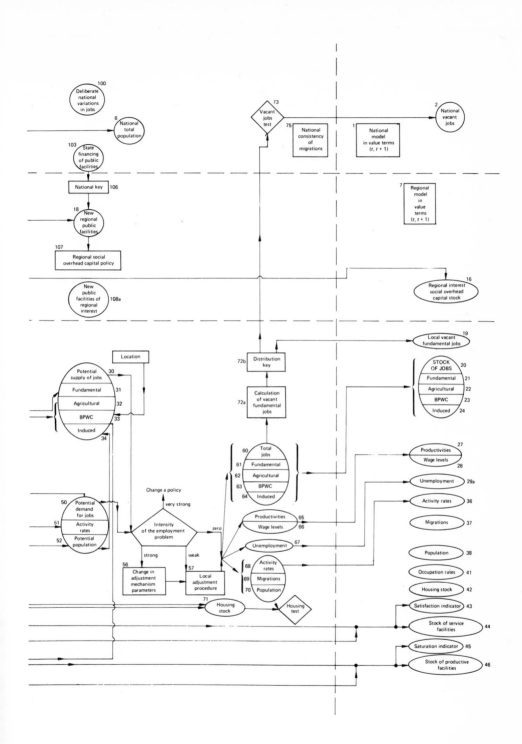

311

312

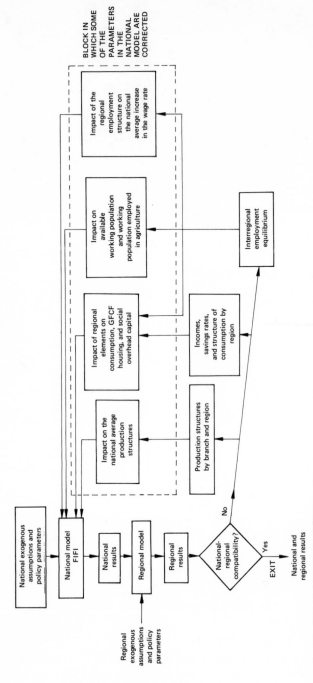

BLOCK IN
WHICH SOME
OF THE
PARAMETERS
IN THE
NATIONAL
MODEL ARE
CORRECTED

Impact of the
regional
employment
structure on
the national
average increase
in the wage rate

Impact on
available
working population
and working
population employed
in agriculture

Impact of regional
elements on
consumption, GFCF
housing, and social
overhead capital

Impact on the
national average
production
structures

Incomes,
savings rates,
and structure of
consumption by
region

Interregional
employment
equilibrium

Production structures
by branch and region

National exogenous
assumptions and
policy parameters

National model
FIFI

National
results

Regional model

Regional
results

National-
regional
compatibility?

Regional
exogenous
assumptions
and policy
parameters

No

Yes

EXIT

National and
regional results

Fig. 10.3   The original structure of the REGINA model
Source: [243], p. 29 and [244], p. 21

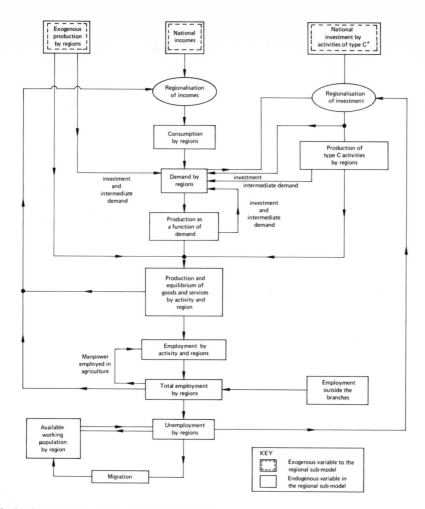

Fig. 10.4   The structure of the regional sub-model in the original REGINA project

*   Activities of type C are those for which location does not primarily
    depend either on demand or geographical factors

Source: [243], p. 23 and [244], p. 16

'regionalisation' research (numbered B6 in CEPREMAP's overall research programme), financed by the CGP, and aimed at the search for a national model. The project was still live in September 1971, [14] and in October of the same year, Michel Horps gave a paper on MURAT to the First Franco-Soviet Colloquium on the use of models in planning, a gathering that brought together only the top French and Soviet planners and at which only the 'meaningful' models were discussed. But a CEPREMAP Research Report dated April 1973, and containing a summary of the 1971 research programme, makes no mention at all of the 'regionalisation' project: B6

313

Table 10.1

Level of analysis of the different variables in REGINA

Level	Variables

Sub-regional	Employment and demographic
	    Employment by activity (branches and non-branch)[a]
	    Foreign immigration
	    Inter-area migrations, and distribution of net regional
	        migration
	    Border workers
	    Available working population and unemployment
	    Population and number of households
	    Two-way Paris—suburbs migrations
	
	Incomes and demand
	    Wage bill by activity (branches and non-branch)
	    Rent expenditures

Regional	Demographic
	    Inter-regional migrations (workers, non-workers under
	        60 years old, retired people)
	
	Goods and services
	    Regional input—output tables (TEIR), interregional
	    flows of goods and services, and flows abroad
	    Production and investments by branch[b]
	    Household consumption
	    Housing investments
	
	Agents' accounts
	    Household accounts
	    Local authority accounts
	    Agricultural accounts
	
	Wage-rates and prices
	    Regional wage-rates
	    Certain prices[c]

National	Enterprise accounts by sector, and prices Rest of the overall economic table (TEE) (non-local administrations, financial institutions, abroad) Financial operations table (TOF)[d]

^a Employment is determined by region first of all, and then disaggregated into sub-regions

^b For activities that are not constrained to a particular location, investment is initially directly determined at the national level (as a function of demand in the case of a 'sheltered' sector, and as a function of financing possibilities for an 'exposed' sector), and then calculated by region depending on location behaviours

^c The trend of prices is determined at the national level, but some prices can be regionalised

^d Some elements of which can be regionalised, or even determined directly by region

Source: [244], p. 20

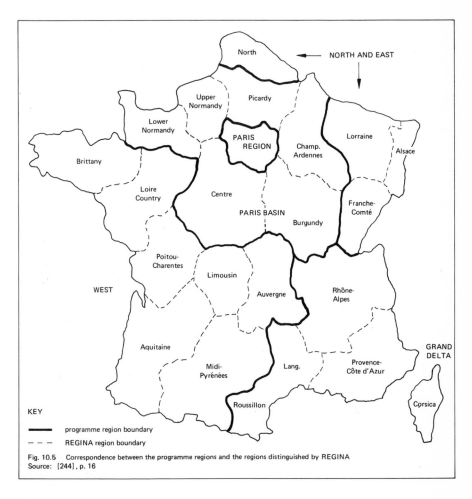

Fig. 10.5   Correspondence between the programme regions and the regions distinguished by REGINA
Source: [244], p. 16

does not appear. The search for a national model had not yielded any positive results by the time CGP came to review its research budget at the end of the year, and the contract with CEPREMAP was not renewed.

Michel Horps moved to the DATAR, and continued to work on MURAT, but on a much-reduced scale. A simplified version of the model, known as MURAT-O, was used to analyse the working of the local labour markets in two departments, Loire and Isère. [15] But the main spotlight, as far as the planners were concerned, was pointed elsewhere, on the REGINA project. Significantly, a paper [16] on REGINA was also presented at the Franco-Soviet Colloquium, a fact that obviously allowed both projects to be compared and their relative merits assessed. The major factor acting in favour of REGINA was that it was to be built around FIFI (i.e. from the top down, as against the opposite approach of the MURAT project), which already existed and worked well. The originally proposed structure is shown in Figure 10.3, and the regional sub-model in Figure 10.4. The points to note here are, first, that MURAT could conceivably have been designed to fit a framework similar to the one shown in Figure 10.3 (i.e. accepting FIFI as the national model from the outset, and designing the rest of the system to be compatible with it); and secondly, the focus in the regional model is again on employment but the other activities are far

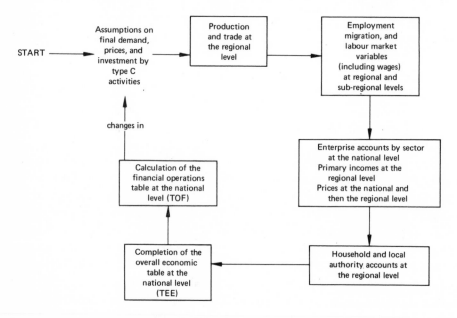

Fig. 10.6   The algorithmic structure of the REGINA model
Source: compiled from Chapter VIII in [245]

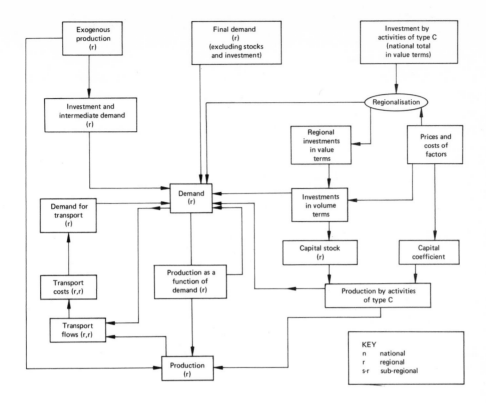

Fig. 10.7   The production block in the REGINA model
Source: Diagram 3, [245], p. 207

more traditional (in a national accounting or economic sense) than the corresponding ones in MURAT. This last point reflects the fact that RE-GINA is constructed at a much more aggregated level than MURAT was.

An experimental version of the regional sub-model, known as MOTREX ('modèle trirégional expérimental', experimental three-region model) was constructed and programmed in 1971 to test the responses of the mechanisms to different assumptions, particularly concerning the location of investments. [17] Just as the self-financing behaviour of firms plays an important role in the FIFI model, it appears likely that the investment location behaviour of firms will be a key element in REGINA. Three types of activity are distinguished: those whose location depends on natural resources and geographical factors (e.g. agriculture and extractive industries), activities whose location is determined by demand (because of heavy transport costs or the nature of the product), and other activities, not locationally constrained but looking for the right sort of opportunities. There is no explicit mention in the REGINA papers of attractive-

317

ness indices (as used in MURAT), but some similar concept is clearly of obvious use in analysing location behaviour, especially that of the 'free' category of enterprises.

The first half of 1972 saw a great deal of thought on which project to back financially. It was reasonably certain during the whole of this period that REGINA would win the official support, but it was not until the autumn of 1972 that Courbis and his GAMA group ('Groupe d'Analyse Macroéconomique Appliquée', Applied Macro-economic Research Group) at the University of Paris were confident enough to be able to embark on phase two of their project. And the months of reflection led to a number of changes in the structure of the model shown in Figure 10.3. A third, sub-regional level was introduced (and again, one cannot avoid drawing a

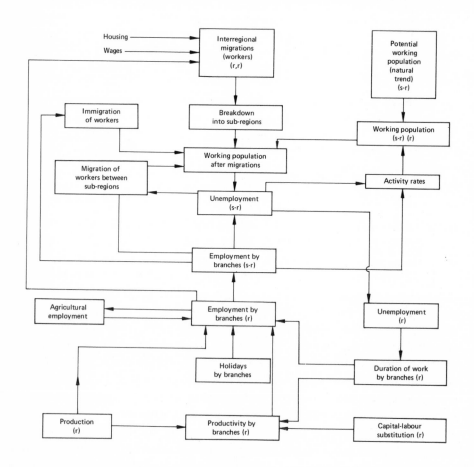

Fig. 10.8   The employment block in the REGINA model (Key as in Fig 10.7)
Source: Diagram 4, [245], p. 208

direct line between this move and the same structure in MURAT) in order to obtain a clearer picture of activity rates, the needs and demands for housing, social overhead capital, and the structure of household consumption, all of which depend on whether or not they are being considered in an urban, rural, or 'Parisienne' setting. The three sub-regions now included within each region are:

(i) rural areas (consisting of all rural communes not belonging to a ZPIU ('urban or industrial populated zone'; see Appendix VII));

(ii) moderately urbanised areas (defined as all ZPIU in the region having fewer than 60,000 inhabitants);

(iii) heavily urbanised areas (meaning the set of all ZPIU with more than 60,000 inhabitants).

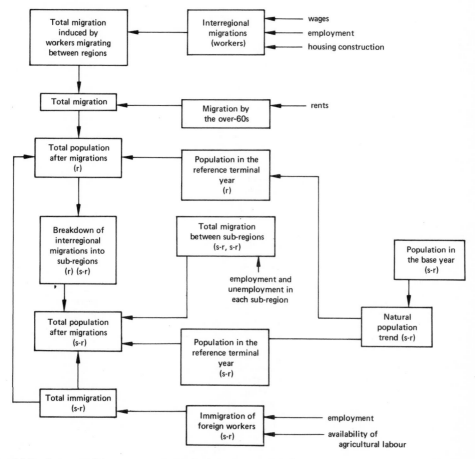

Fig. 10.9   The migration block in the REGINA model (Key as in Fig. 10.7)
Source: Diagram 5, [245], p. 209

319

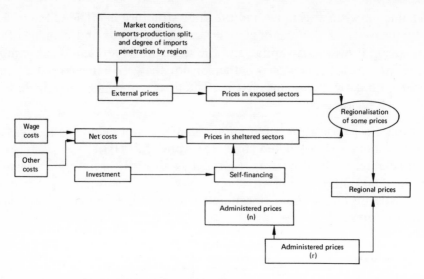

Fig. 10.10   The prices block in the REGINA model (Key as in Fig. 10.7)
Source: Diagram 6, [245], p. 210

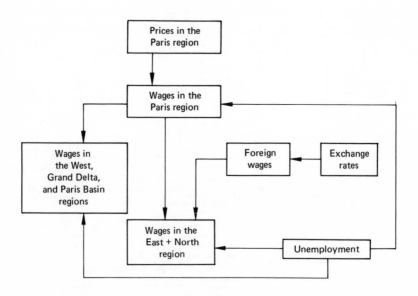

Fig. 10.11   The wages block in the REGINA model (Key as in Fig. 10.7)
Source: Diagram 7, [245], p. 210

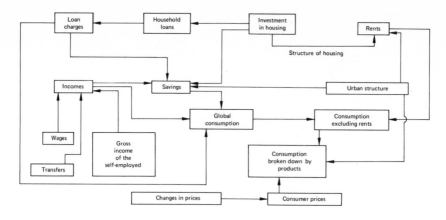

Fig. 10.12 Household consumption in the REGINA model
Source: Diagram 8, [245], p. 211

For the Paris region, there is a special sub-regional breakdown: Paris city, Paris suburbs, and the rest of the region.

The Paris region is one of five regions considered in the model; Figure 10.5 shows how REGINA's five regions correspond to the 22 programme regions. There are thus 15 spatial units in the model, and nine branches (FIFI's seventh branch is disaggregated into (7) building and public works; (8) services; (9) commerce. It can of course be just as simply reconstituted, so that consistency with FIFI is not difficult to achieve), recognising that the mechanisms operating at the regional level in building must clearly be distinguished in order to allow a meaningful analysis of housing and social overhead capital problems. Other economic agencies are handled in the same way as in FIFI. Table 10.1 lists the variables contained in REGINA, and the level at which each one is calculated (note that variables not listed at the regional and national levels are obtained by aggregating corresponding variables at the level below).

At the moment, the model is still being put together, so it is not possible to give a precise formulation of it, nor, obviously, any results produced by it. [18] Figure 10.6 summarises the intended algorithmic structure of the model, showing the sequence in which various blocks in the model will be calculated. Unlike MURAT and the first version of RE-GINA, there is no dichotomy between regional and national levels of analysis: the analysis is carried out at whichever level is the most appropriate from a decision-making point of view. Thus, the sequence mixes the national, regional, and sub-regional, aggregating and disaggregating where necessary. Figures 10.7–10.13, which are given according to the sequence depicted in Figure 10.6, show the economic structure of each successive

321

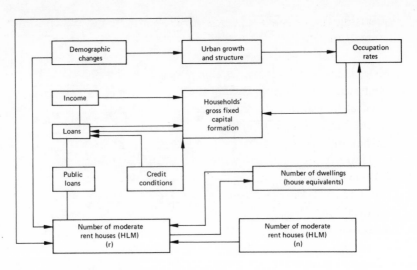

Fig. 10.13   The housing block in the REGINA model (Key as in Fig. 10.7)
Source: Diagram 9, [245], p. 212

block; the arrows in them do not convey the algorithmic structure, which remains to be finally specified.

Notes

[1] The way in which the TOF was projected in the Fifth Plan is described in detail in [77], Appendix III, Chapter 3, pp. 157—68, and in [221], which includes the projected TOF for 1970.

[2] See [76].

[3] Quoted from [222], p. 64.

[4] The results are reported in [97] and [98].

[5] Very little has been published on the early Sixth Plan TOFs and TFLTs. The only sources I have been able to find are internal DP working papers: the financial flows consistent with the departure account are given in [223], the TOF associated with the reference account in [224], and the TOF constructed on the basis of the options account in [225]. The TFLT associated with the reference account is more widely available, in [226], pp. 18—19. We give the TOF associated with the Plan account in Appendix II.

[6] The TOF sub-model was formalised by A. Coutière and M. Mousel of the DP, and built into the FIFI model by Ph. Rossignol and D. Fouquet of the INSEE. Again, details are available only in working papers, [227], [229], and [230].

[7] The housing finance sub-model is given in [145], and the administrations' financial sub-models, CONFI 1 and CONFI 2 are shown in Figure 3.6.

[8] Courbis' ideas derive from the time he first worked on firms' self-financing behaviour and prices during the Fifth Plan. His theoretical model is discussed at length in [61], and more briefly in [63].

[9] This same diagram is in [59], [74], [82] and [226]

[10] The other nine financial intermediaries are the Bank of France; other banks; the Deposit and Consignments Office ('Caisse des dépôts et consignations'); savings banks and lenders to local authorities; the National Agricultural Credit Bank ('Crédit Agricole'); the 'Crédit National' and other industrial-loan banks; 'Crédit Hotêlier' and miscellaneous loan banks; instalments and hire-purchase credit institutions; insurance companies and variable capital investment companies (SIGAV).

[11] In [226] and [231].

[12] As usual, no firm details are available other than in working papers that are not very easy to obtain, [232], [233], and [234].

[13] A series of CEPREMAP papers describe the features that the team were looking for in a national model (see for example [236] and [237]), and a later series outline the reasons why existing national models (FIFI, DECA (used in the preparation of economic budgets; see Appendix VI)), and ANTOINE (an experimental long-term programming model that in a practical planning context was never used; see note 16 to Chapter 7)) were not suitable (see [238], [239] and [240]).

[14] A short presentation on the 'regionalisation' project was given by CEPREMAP to a group of students that I led in Paris in September 1971.

[15] Horps was still working on MURAT-O when I visited the DATAR in March 1972. The local labour market studies are reported in [241] and [242].

[16] This paper is [243]. It has been reproduced for wider circulation in [183], published 18 months later.

[17] Appendix III in [243] and [183] briefly discusses the MOTREX model.

[18] The latest paper on REGINA is [244], which was written in May 1973. This paper will also appear in Volume VII of *Aménagement du Territoire Développement Regional* in 1974, and in *Economics of Planning* (I have prepared an English translation of the paper on behalf of Courbis). The massive report prepared by Courbis and his team [245] brings together in great detail the work so far completed on the various components, and outlines the next stages. It appears to contain no major advances since [244].

References

[221] S. Barthelemy, 'La méthode de projection a moyen terme des circuits financiers utilisée dans la préparation du Ve Plan français' (The financial circuit medium-term projection method used in the preparation of the Fifth French Plan), *Review of Income and Wealth*, series 15, no. 1, March 1969, pp. 77–100.

[222] A. Kidel, 'Techniques and methodology of the French fifth plan' *Long Range Planning* vol. 1, no. 3, March 1969, pp. 60–7.

[223] P. Vajda, 'Note technique relative à une première projection tendancielle des flux financières en 1975' (Technical note on a first trend-oriented projection of financial flows in 1975), Working Paper, Financial Operations Division, Forecasting Directorate, Ministry of Finance, November 1969.

[224] P. Vajda, 'Nouvelles perspectives financières pour 1975. Présentation d'un TOF associé au compte de référence' (New financial prospects for 1975. Presentation of a TOF associated with the reference account), Working Paper, FOD, DP, MEF, February 1970.

[225] P. Vajda, 'Présentation d'un tableau des opérations financières associé au compte d'option' (Presentation of a financial operations table associated with the options account), FOD, DP, MEF, October 1970.

[226] R. Courbis and P. Vajda, 'Financement et planification' (Financing and planning), *Économie et Statistique* no. 24, June 1971, pp. 13–29.

[227] D. Fouquet, 'Les équations du bloc financier de FIFITOF' (The equations of FIFITOF's financial block), INSEE and DP Working Paper no. 320/1378, September 1972.

[228] M. Rochefort, C. Bidault and M. Petit, 'Aménager du Territoire' (Regional Planning) Editions du Seuil, Paris 1970, pp. 144.

[229] A. Coutière, 'Le tableau des financements à moyen et long terme dans FIFI-TOF' (The medium and long-term financing table in FIFITOF), Working Paper, FOD, DP, MEF, August 1971.

[230] A. Coutière and P. Roux-Vaillard, 'Fiches techniques sur le traitement dans FIFI-TOF des intermédiaires financiers et du marché financier' (Technical papers on the way in which financial intermediaries and the finance market are handled in FIFITOF), INSEE and DP Working Paper, December 1971.

[231] R. Courbis, 'L'intégration des opérations financières dans le modèle à moyen terme FIFI utilisé pour la préparation du Plan français' (Integration of financial operations in the FIFI medium-term model

used in the preparation of the French Plan), Paper presented at the Fifth International Conference on Input–Output Techniques, Geneva, January 1971.

[232] P. Roux-Vaillard, 'Presentation du mini-modéle FIFI-TOF à 3 secteurs' (Presentation of the FIFITOF mini-model in three sectors), INSEE Working Paper no. 320/1308, March 1972.

[233] Ph. Rossignol and P. Roux-Vaillard, 'Résultat du modèle MINIFIFITOF avec rétroaction des variables financières sur l'équilibre économique' (Results of the MINIFIFITOF model including feedback of the financial variables on the economic equilibrium), INSEE Working Paper, December 1972.

[234] Ph. Rossignol and P. Roux-Vaillard, 'Modèle MINI-FIFI-TOF. Quelques résultats concernant la FBCF des ménages (sous-modèle logement)' (The MINIFIFITOF model. Some results on households' gross fixed capital formation (housing sub-model)), INSEE Working Paper, December 1972.

[235] R. Prudhomme, 'Un cadre pour l'analyse du développement interrégional. Proposition d'architecture du modèle MURAT' (A framework for interregional development analysis. Structural proposals concerning the MURAT model), OTAM/CERAU Paper, March 1971, 26 pp.

[236] CEPREMAP, 'Problèmes posés par les relations entre le modèle interrégional et un modèle global' (Problems surrounding the linkages between the interregional model and a global model), Internal Paper, June 1970.

[237] CEPREMAP, 'Problèmes relatifs au modèle national: entrées-sorties' (Problems relating to the national model: entering it and leaving it), Internal Paper, December 1970, 10 pp.

[238] CEPREMAP, 'Le modèle FIFI at le modèle interrégional' (FIFI and the interregional model), Internal Paper, February 1971, 21 pp.

[239] CEPREMAP, 'Le modèle FIFI et le modèle interrégional. Comment tenir compte des renseignements que nous donnera MURAT sur l'évolution de la population active occupés? (FIFI and the interregional model. How should the information generated by MURAT on changes in working population be taken into account?), Internal Paper, April 1971.

[240] CEPREMAP, 'Reflexions sur quelques modèles nationaux' (Thoughts on some national models), Internal Paper, June 1971, 25 pp.

[241] H. Coing, 'Le marché de l'emploi dans le département de l'Isère de 1962 à 1968' (The labour market in the Isère department from

1962 to 1968), DATAR-CERAU Paper, July 1971, 38 pp.

[242] G. Dupuy and H. Coing, 'Marché de l'emploi de la Loire et de l'Isère. Conclusions méthodologiques' (The Loire and Isère labour markets. Methodological conclusions), DATAR-CERAU Paper, February 1972, 24 pp.

[243] R. Courbis and J-C. Prager, *Analyse régionale et planification nationale. Une tentative d'analyse interdépendante. Le project REGINA* (Regional analysis and national planning. A proposal for a simultaneous approach. The REGINA project), Paper presented at the First Franco-Soviet Colloquium on the Use of Models in Planning, Paris, October 1971, 53 pp.

[244] R. Courbis, *Le Modèle REGINA d'analyse interdépendante des problèms régionaux et nationaux* (The REGINA model for simultaneous analysis of national and regional problems), Paper presented at the Montpellier meeting on econometric, regional development models, June 1973, 31 pp.

[245] R. Courbis, J. Bourdon, D. Bonnet, C. Pommier, D. Vallet, G. Cornilleau, and F. de Massougnes, *Le Modèle REGINA: analyse économique du modèle. Rapport de synthèse de la 1ère phase d'élaboration du modèle* (The REGINA model: economic analysis of the model. Report on the first phase of constructing the model), GAMA Paper no. 43, October 1973, 214 pp.

[246] Atreize, *La Planification française en pratique* (French planning in practice), Editions Ouvrières, Paris 1971, 382 pp.

[247] C. Gruson, *Renaissance du Plan* (Rebirth of the Plan), Editions du Seuil, Paris 1971, 149 pp.

[248] M. Deleau, R. Guesnerie, and P. Malgrange, 'Planning, uncertainty, and economic policy. The OPTIMIX study' in *Economics of Planning* (forthcoming).

[249] R. Guesnerie and P. Malgrange, 'Formalisation des objectifs à moyen terme. Application au VIème Plan' (Formalising the medium-term objectives of the Sixth Plan), *Revue Économique* vol. 23, no. 3, 1972, pp. 442–91.

[250] J. Hayward, *The One and Indivisible French Republic*, Weidenfeld and Nicolson, London, 1973, 306 pp.

[251] S. S. Cohen, *Modern Capitalist Planning. The French Model*, Weidenfeld and Nicolson, London, 1969.

[252] Y. Pimont, 'Les contrats de Plan' (Plan contracts), *Revue de Science Financière* vol. LXIII, no. 4 (October–December 1971), pp. 697–750.

[253] G. Lord, *The French Budgetary Process*, University of California Press, Berkeley, 1973.

[254] D. Pickles, *The Government and Politics of France*, 2 vols, Methuen, London 1973.

[255] G. Dupuis et al., *Organigrammes des institutions françaises* (Organisation charts of French institutions), Armand Colin, 1971.

[256] INSEE, '25ᵉ anniversaire de l'INSEE' (25th anniversary of the INSEE), *Économie et Statistique*, Supplement to no. 24, June 1971 xx pp.

[257] A. Kuyvenhoven, *The French and the Standardized System of National Accounts*, Discussion Paper No. 10, Centre for Development Planning, Netherlands School of Economics, Rotterdam, January 1971, 26 pp.

[258] S. and J-L. Fauré, *Comment s'élaborent les comptes de la nation* (How the national accounts are drawn up), published by the National Information Centre for Economic Progress (CNIPE), Paris 1973.

[259] INSEE, same title as [258], *Économie et Statistique* no. 51, December 1973, pp. 57–9.

[260] J-E. Chapron, 'Le nouveau système européen de comptabilité économique (The new European system of economic accounting), *Économie et Statistique* no. 31, February 1972, pp. 23–38.

[261] INSEE, 'L'introduction du nouveau système de comptabilité nationale' (The introduction of the new national accounting system), *Économie et Statistique* no. 25, July–August 1971, pp. 57–8.

[262] B. Brunhes, 'Présentation de la comptabilité nationale française' (Presentation of the French national accounts), *Les Collections de l'INSEE*, série C, no. 1, 1971 (third edition), 86 pp.

[263] J. Hackett and A-M. Hackett, *Economic Planning in France*, Allen and Unwin, London 1963.

[264] C. P. Kindleberger, 'French planning' in M. F. Millikan (ed.), *National Economic Planning*, Columbia University Press, New York 1967, pp. 279–303.

[265] M. Anderson, *Government in France. An Introduction to the Executive Power*, Pergamon Press, Oxford, 1970, 217 pp.

Additional notes to Chapters one to ten

The information given here was received too late to be included in the notes following the relevant chapter. It is not linked to precise locations in the text by numbers, as other notes are, but the reader should be able to relate the note to the appropriate section. To avoid any possible confusion with the original note numbers, these additional notes are numbered differently.

Chapter 1

(i)   'Concertation' is taken from the French and means converting of efforts, close co-operation between participants. It is a favourite description of the French planning process. See (276).

(ii)   Strictly speaking, the French Plan does not have the force of law, but it does go before Parliament to be voted. Hayward discusses the finer details of this point; see (250) p. 185. For a wider discussion of the role of Parliament in planning, with particular reference to the first five plans, see Corbel (274).

(iii)   An interesting insight into the intense power structure of the Plan-Finance groups is given by the following quotation: '... the Ministry of Finance plays a dominant role in the French Government; its tasks and traditional problems do not exceed the short-term, and its connections with the Director of the CGP are at the same time strict and nonexistent. As far as the Ministry of Finance is concerned, planning involves risks because of its medium-term budget orientations, and so it is not concerned with appraising the real situation, it is not compelled to limit its range of action, and consequently it loses its privileged position in the administration ... On the other hand, the Economic Authority [CGP?] is a small administration with only its persuasive power and the technical quality of its work; the relation between these two institutions is of most unequal character', Ullmo (124) pp. 10–11.

(iv)   A fascinating account of what it is like to sit on a Plan Commission is given in (277).

Chapter 3

The models used to discuss the competitioned economy theory in this chapter are earlier than the ones used to criticise the theory in Chapter 5.

Chapter 5

Hayward emphasises the inbalance between open and closed 'concertation' in the preparation of the Sixth Plan: '... neither the Plan Commissions nor Parliament share in this (first phase), the longest and most crucial preparatory phase', (250), p. 183.

Chapter 6

More details on the preparation of social overhead capital programmes, and on the distinction between collective functions and earlier concepts can be found in (271), (269), (213), (246) p. 183 and (275).

Chapter 7

The very early publication of (272), intended to assist in the preparation of the Seventh Plan, tends to suggest that the rate of actualisation is an essential guide to early thinking on public investment projects.

Chapter 8

(i) For the essential facts on French regional economic policy in the sixties, (228) is recommended.
(ii) The question 'What is a region?' is very well answered in (270).
(iii) For more details on the role of DATAR and its changing place in the administration, see (250), Chapter 2 and pp. 170–3.
(iv) The regionalisation procedure is amplified in (213) and (269).
(v) Hayward (see (250)) does not share Rousselot's optimistic expectations about the regional reforms. He describes them as 'retrograde', and 'managerial delegation, not democratic participation'. He points out that the new regions are not territorial authorities (like communes and departments) but mere public establishments with specific functions primarily concerned with national planning. There is no directly elected assembly, and the regional prefect remains in managerial command. He states that the basic choice is essentially between more centralisation (leading to greater rationalisation, but more local irresponsibility) and more decentralisation (meaning less rationality but more effective local contributions to regional development in the long term). Thus, another area in which the right balance is vital is brought out.

Chapter 9

Another recent reference on the unemployment measurement problems is given in (273).

Additional References to Chapters one to ten

[266] DATAR 'Investment incentives in France' Paris, August 1973 p. 31.

[267] P. de Castelbajac, 'Ces aides à l'expansion industrielle régionale dans les pays du Marché commun' (Assistance to regional industrial expansion in the Common Market countries), *Notes et Études Documentaires*, No. 3917, 11 September 1972, p. 39.

[268] European Community Press And Information, 'Working the regional policy', *European Community*, November 1973, pp. 10–12.

[269] Contenay, Girardeau, Sirel, Bonnans, Bréquet, Dupart & Fournier, Functions collectives et planification, *NED*, 3991–3992, June 1973, 71 pp.

[270] M. Boucher, 'La région', *Cahier Français*, No. 158–159, 1973

[271] B. Lion, 'Les programmes finalisés dans le VIe Plan' (Goal programmes in the Sixth Plan), *Notes et Études Documentaires*, Nos. 3959–3960, 5 February 1973, 57 pp.

[272] Commissariat Général Du Plan, 'Calcul économique et planification', (Economic computation and planning), Volume 1 of the collection 'Économie et Planification', La Documentation Française, 1973, 110 pp.

[273] R. Salais, Ça mesure du chômage dans l'enquête emploi', (Measuring unemployment in the employment enquiry), *Économie et Statistique*, No. 54, March 1974, pp. 3–17.

[274] P. Corbel, 'Le parlement français et la planification', (The French parliament and planning), Cahier de l'institut d'Études Politiques de l'Université de Grenoble, Editions Cujas, Paris 398pp.

[275] 'Les programmes finalisés du VIe Plan' (The goal programmes of the Sixth Plan), *Rationalisation des Choix Budgétaires*, no. 6, December 1971

[276] G. Mignot, 'La concertation dans la preparation des plans', ('Concertation' in plan preparation), *Droit Social*, Special issue, no. 4–5, April–May 1972, pp. 10–20.

[277] C. Grandjeat, 'Simples réflexions' (Some thoughts (on plan preparation)), *Droit Social*, Special issue, no. 4–5, April–May 1972, pp. 68–75.

Appendix I: The Central Economic Administration

These notes are by no means comprehensive, but they should answer some of the more obvious questions that might occur to the non-specialist reader. For more details, not only on the economic administration but French government and political administration in general, four very good English texts are Avril [10] (translated from the French), Hayward [250], Anderson [265], and Pickles [254].

I.1 The Planning Commission (CGP)

The CGP (or, to give it its full title, the General Planning Commissariat for Equipment and Productivity) came into being in 1946. It is attached to the Prime Minister's office, and is not a ministry in the usual sense of the word, but, in addition to the Planning Commissioner (the head of the CGP), there is now a Deputy Minister for the Plan attached to the Prime Minister. This politicisation of the Plan is comparatively recent and in marked contrast to the original status of the CGP as a politically neutral organisation, carefully avoiding controversial issues and thereby remaining in existence. It is the essential instrument of planning in France and is responsible for preparing the Plan and submitting it for Government approval. Subsequently, it is responsible for implementing the Plan and reporting on its results. CGP is therefore a formulator, preparer, co-ordinator and supervisor of work that others do and decisions that others implement. This has to be so because the CGP has so few permanent staff: there are approximately 50 senior 'planners', organised in social, urban and regional (this department, the SRU, is discussed in Appendix VII), financial, long-term, quantitative, industrial, agricultural, and transport groups, ranging in size from one (Bernard Cazes is the long-term studies co-ordinator and has to call on outsiders or other group members to undertake the CGP's futures research and long-term analysis) to a dozen or more. These staff rarely stay for more than four or five years, moving to other parts of the administration or to industry via 'the network' (see note 2 to Chapter 7).

Since 1946, there have been only five men in charge of the CGP, all of them extremely skilful at steering the CGP around the obstacles that many thought would have destroyed it. The first was Jean Monnet, the father of Europe, and the first of many prominent planners to move on into key positions in European bodies. He headed the CGP from 1946 to 1952, and was followed by Étienne Hirsch. He held the post for seven years, and left to go into Euratom. Pierre Massé was the next Plan Commissioner, and was responsible for guiding the plan through the difficult transition from being a set of investment programmes to becoming an overall economic and social development programme. His theory of indicative planning and his 'new look' which followed are important milestones in the story of French planning. Francois Ortoli succeeded Massé in 1966, but this was only a brief interlude in a career which has seen him occupy many high-ranking positions (he has been Minister of Finance, Education, Industrial and Scientific Development, and Public Works and Housing, and is now Head of the EEC Commission). René Montjoie took over as Plan Commisioner in 1967.

The obstacles referred to in the last paragraph were largely built by other political and administrative bodies, and it is only through the considerable personal qualities of the five Commissioners, and their access to the highest level in the French power structure, that the CGP has managed to survive. At best, relations between the CGP and various divisions in the Finance Ministry can be described as 'competitive'; the rest of the time, the two senior economic organisations coexist somewhat uneasily.

I.2   The Ministry of the Economy and Finance (MEF)

On paper, there should really be 'no contest', with the 130,000 officials of the MEF facing the 50 or so officials of the CGP. But to draw conclusions from this simple numerical comparison is to ignore the personalities of the five men mentioned above, the 'protection' the CGP is able to derive from its position in the Prime Minister's office, and the important fact that the MEF is not one huge ministry but rather a federation of directorates and departments. Figure I.1 gives some idea of the structure of the MEF, and conveys a little of the economic expertise that the Ministry is able to call on. The key areas as far as medium-term planning is concerned are the Forecasting Directorate (DP) and the National Institute of Statistics and Economic Research (INSEE), but the real centres of power in the MEF are the Budget Directorate (DB) and the Treasury, the former controlling central government expenditure, and the latter (along with the Bank of France)

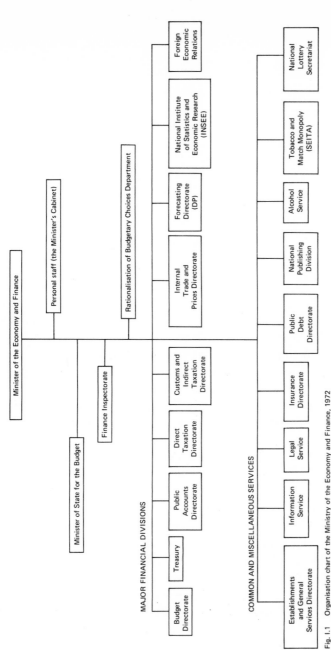

Fig. I.1 Organisation chart of the Ministry of the Economy and Finance, 1972

Note: Other departments, which Hayward omits from this diagram, but whose activities are regularly reported in *Le Bulletin de Liaison et d'Information de l'Administration Centrale de l'Économie et des Finances*, include the General Inspectorate of the National Economy, the Central Markets Commission, the Control of Agreed Expenditures Service, the Pensions Service, the Money and Medals Administration

Source: [250], p. 161

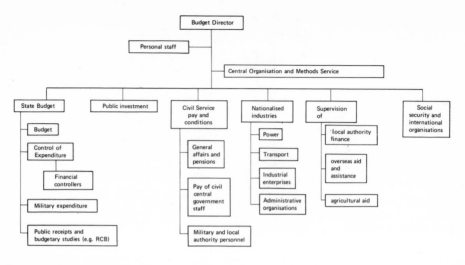

Fig. I.2   The structure of the Budget Directorate, 1970

being responsible for monetary policy. The structure of the DB is shown
in Figure I.2. The critical division here is the one dealing with the State
Budget, and within that division, the Control of Expenditure department
carries the most weight. It consists of a small number of financial control-
lers, each attached to different ministries of the administration to check
and advise on the implementation of the Budget. They are one of the
means by which the MEF is able to maintain its superiority over other
ministries.

The structure of the Treasury is shown in Figure I.3. There are here two
potentially powerful instruments for implementing the Plan's investment
proposals: the Deposit and Consignment Office ('Caisse des Dépôts et
Consignations', or Caisse for short) and the Economic and Social Development Fund (FDES). Both are important agencies in the selective financing
of public and private investment. Hayward describes the Caisse as 'the
Plan's investment bank'. Certainly all its loans have to be within the
framework of the Plan, but significantly the Minister of Finance retains
the right of veto. The membership of the management council of the
FDES reads like an economic 'Who's who': it is chaired by the Minister of
Finance, and consists of all the top ministers, the Planning Commissioner,
the Governor of the Bank of France, the Regional Planning Delegate (head
of the DATAR), the directors of the Budget, Treasury, Forecasting, and
Price Directorates in the MEF, and the Director General of the Caisse.
Thus, although the Council is formally only advisory, in practice it wields
a great deal of decision-making power. The fact that the Finance Minister

334

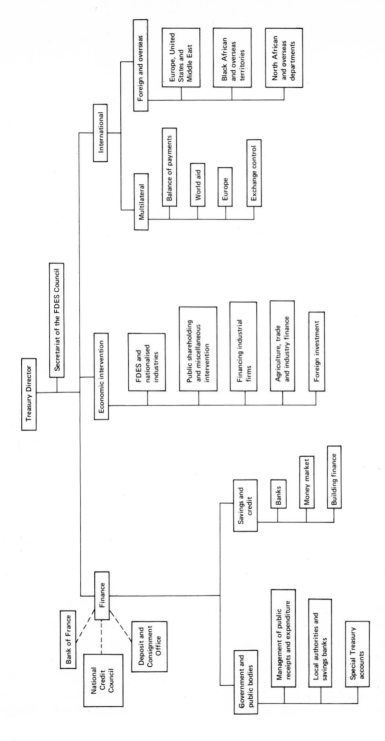

Fig. I.3 The structure of the Treasury, 1970
Source: [250], p. 163, which in turn is from [255], p. 208

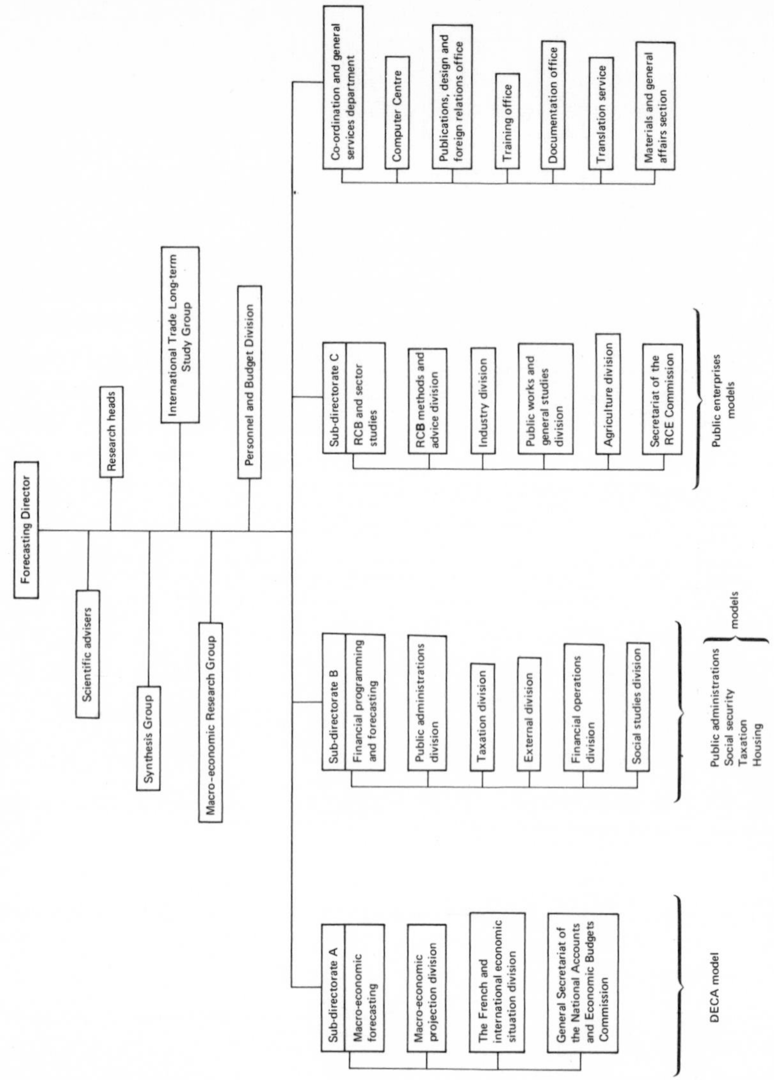
Forecasting Director
Scientific advisers
Research heads
Synthesis Group
International Trade Long-term Study Group
Macro-economic Research Group
Personnel and Budget Division
Sub-directorate A
Macro-economic forecasting
Macro-economic projection division
The French and international economic situation division
General Secretariat of the National Accounts and Economic Budgets Commission
DECA model
Sub-directorate B
Financial programming and forecasting
Public administrations division
Taxation division
External division
Financial operations division
Social studies division
Public administrations
Social security
Taxation
Housing
models
Sub-directorate C
RCB and sector studies
RCB methods and advice division
Industry division
Public works and general studies division
Agriculture division
Secretariat of the RCE Commission
Public enterprises models
Co-ordination and general services department
Computer Centre
Publications, design and foreign relations office
Training office
Documentation office
Translation service
Materials and general affairs section

Fig. I.4 Organisation chart of the Forecasting Directorate
Source: [216], p. 56

is in the chair again brings out the superior position of the MEF over another important area of economic policy.

The rivalry between the MEF and the CGP also extends to the forecasting and programming field, where the DP operates. Its structure is shown in Figure I.4, which also shows examples of the models (mainly short-term) constructed by the three sub-directorates. The DP makes significant contributions to the FIFI model, and will probably take on a bigger role with respect to the FIFITOF model. Another area in which the

DP's influence is likely to increase in the near future is that of RCB studies, although a number of ministries are still resisting the pressure from the MEF to quantify their decision-making procedures. Billy's paper [216] is a very good up-to-day survey of the work being done by the DP in this and other methods.

The co-operation of the INSEE is also vital to the smooth operation of models such as FIFI for which the CGP is responsible (in a formal way, effective day-to-day running of the model remaining in INSEE hands). Rivalries here are not so intense, however, because the INSEE mainly fulfils the role of a central statistical office and plays a comparatively minor role in policy-making. It does contain within its various divisions (see Figure I.5) a great deal of economic and econometric expertise, however, and although it formally serves the data requirements of the MEF and the CGP, its role and influence go far beyond those of mere number-crunchers. None of the other economic research groups in the MEF, the CGP, or any other ministry is large enough or has sufficient technical know-how to undertake planning and policy analyses without (usually major) contribution from the INSEE. The reader who has reached this stage after going through most of the earlier material in the book will not need reminding of how and where the INSEE operates. Its history is recorded in [256].

I.3   The Centre for Mathematical Economic, Long-term Research Applied to Planning (CEPREMAP)

Strictly speaking, CEPREMAP is not part of the economic administration, but it provides an economic planning research service for the CGP and other Government departments. In the sixties, when the centre was known as CERMAP and was lead by Professor Nataf, a great deal of macro-economic modelling work was done here. We have referred earlier in the book to the working hours model (see note 20 to Chapter 3), and other linear programming models were also built at the CEPREMAP (including the linearised long-term growth model known as ANTOINE (see note 16 to Chapter 7)). But, as the ministries set up their own programming and economic research units, CEPREMAP was called upon to do less and less 'mathematical economic modelling applied to planning', and the advent of the FIFI model in the late sixties, operated by the INSEE, brought down the final curtain on CEPREMAP's macro-model contributions.

Bessière, himself a man of considerable modelling experience from his

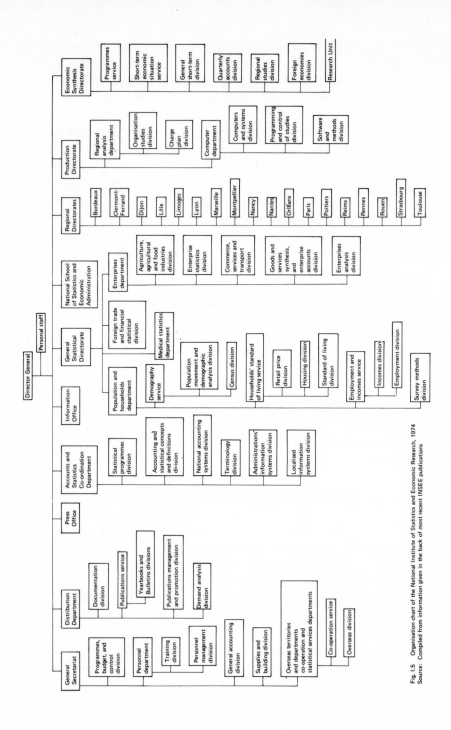

Fig. I.5 Organisation chart of the National Institute of Statistics and Economic Research, 1974.

Source: Compiled from information given in the back of most recent INSEE publications

338

days at Electricité de France, became director and in his report proposing research to be undertaken in 1971 outlined the new directions CEPRE-MAP would be following. The emphasis is now on general and normative economics (i.e. theoretical and conceptual), and monographic and descriptive economics (i.e. practical and empirical), covering a very wide range of subjects. Under the first category, research was undertaken on:

(i)   economic equilibrium and the theory of games;
(ii) economic organisation and the theory of teams;
(iii) the dynamic linkage problem (completion of the OPTIMIX study);
(iv) monetary economics; and
(v)   environment policy.

The research programmes listed in the second major category were:

(i)   statistical analysis of education;
(ii) analysis of French public expenditure;
(iii) foreign trade;
(iv) French housing policy; and
(v)   a production function for the cement industry.

(These topics are taken from a report issued by CEPREMAP in April 1973, and, apart from the regionalisation study involving MURAT (see Chapter 10), confirm that the change of emphasis proposed by Bessière has taken place.) The current director is G. Delange.

Appendix II: Definition of the TEE, TOF and PIB

This appendix is designed to clarify doubts that the reader might still have on the difference between the French system of national accounts and the United Nations system of national accounts (usually known as the standardised system of national accounts, or SNA for short). It concentrates mainly on the overall economic table (TEE), the financial operations table (TOF), and the main accounting aggregates (PIB, etc.). Other sources that are very useful to the reader who requires more detailed information are Kuyvenhoven [257], S. and J-L. Faure [258], (with a 'review' in [259]), Brunhes [262], Chapron [260], and [261] which outlines the stages involved in converting the French national accounts procedures to the European system of Integrated Economic Accounts, ESA (the EEC version of the SNA). The Seventh Plan will be prepared according to data based on both the French system and the ESA, and after that (from 1976, it is estimated), the only official system in France will conform to ESA conventions. The following comparisons are derived from Appendix I in [94].

II.1 Classification of agents under the two systems

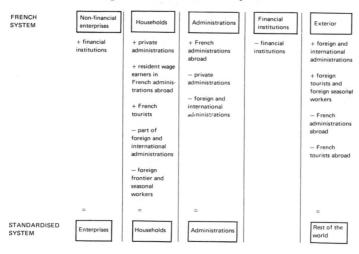

341

II.2 From PIB to GDP and GNP

Taking the 1975 Plan account as an example, the accounting relationships are as follows:

	Millions of 1975 francs
Gross domestic production (PIB)	1,119,816
Part of the value added of financial institutions	18,214
Value added by wage earners employed by households and private administrations	14,348
Value added by wage earners employed by public administrations	112,562
Other items	−1,080
Gross domestic product	1,263,860
Balance of the factor incomes received from the exterior less incomes paid (wages and interest)	215
Gross national product	1,264,075

There is no apparent easy way of distinguishing gross domestic production and gross domestic product in French: both have the same initials (PIB). But as usual, the French have a way out of this difficulty: gross domestic production is feminine ('*la* production intérieure brute'), and gross domestic product is masculine ('*le* produit intérieur brut').

II.3 The calculation of gross national expenditure

FRENCH
SYSTEM

Household consumption	Administrations consumption	Gross fixed capital formation

+ remuneration of wage earners employed by households

− consumption by private administrations

+ consumption of private administrations and remuneration of their wage-earning employees

− consumption by foreign and international administrations

<table>
<tr><td></td><td>+ consumption of services supplied by financial institutions</td><td>+ consumption by French administrations abroad</td><td></td></tr>
</table>

| | + consumption of services supplied by financial institutions

– consumption in France by non-resident house-holders (tourists, military, diplomats, and foreign frontier workers)

+ consumption by corresponding categories of French residents abroad

– some other payments to households by public administrations | + consumption by French administrations abroad

+ remuneration of French public administrations' wage-earning employees | |

STANDARDISED SYSTEM = private consumption + public consumption + gross capital formation = gross national expenditure

The gap between the two systems can be quite wide in some of these concepts. Taking the Plan account figures again:

	Milliards of 1975 francs
Household consumption	721·6
Private consumption	756·8
Administrations' consumption	32·4
Public consumption	152·0

II.4   The external account

There is a great deal of difference between the two systems here, but only in the intermediate balances, the final balances corresponding almost exactly (the difference in this final balance is due to the financing capacity of foreign and international administrations, which is very small: it is assumed to be zero in the Plan account). Table II.1 summarises the numerical details.

Table II.1

The external balance in 1975
according to the two national accounting systems
(millions of current francs)

French system		*Standardised system*	
1 Goods balance (exports (f.o.b.) — imports (c.i.f.))	484	1 Goods balance (exports (f.o.b.) — imports (f.o.b.))	9809
2 Net services balance	12958	2 Services balance	−2006
3 Balance of operations on goods and services (= 1 + 2)	13442	3 Goods and services balance (= 1 + 2)	7802
4 Balance of distributive operations	−14373	4 External income payments	215
		5 Trade balance (= 3 + 4)	8017
		6 Balance of current transfers	−8808
		7 Current account balance (= 5 + 6)	−791
		8 Balance of capital transfers	−140
5 France's financing need (−) or capacity (+) (= 3 + 4)	−931	9 France's financing need (−) or capacity (+) (= 7 + 8)	−931

Source: [94], p. 349

II.5 The standardised resource—use accounts

These are shown in Tables II.2 and II.3, the 1975 figures corresponding to the Plan account (compare Table 6.8 and others in Chapter 6).

II.6 The financial operations table

The TOF is established after the TEE, but since the TEE in its proper

344

Table II.2

The SNA Sixth Plan resource—use equilibrium (volume terms)

	Milliards of 1965 francs		Average annual growth rates
	1970	1975	1970—1975
Resources			
Gross national product	608·7	801·6	5·7
Uses			
Private consumption	364·2	479·5	5·7
Public administrations' consumption	69·0	83·0	3·8
Gross capital formation	172·3	232·9	6·2
Gross national expenditure	605·5	795·4	5·6
External balance (goods, services and factor incomes)	+3·2	+6·2	

Source: [94], p. 350

form is usually presented with some financial operations in it, we give the TOF first here. The object of the TOF is to discover how equilibrium can be established between lenders and borrowers at the levels laid down in the TEE. The TOF associated with the Sixth Plan account is shown in Table II.4. The notation used there is as follows.

Operations: 90 cash
91 other deposits
92 short-term securities
93 debentures
94 shares
95 short-term credits
96 medium-term credits
97 long-term loans
98 gold and foreign exchange
99 bills of deposit and advances between financial intermediaries
8f balance of credits and debts

	8c'	financing requirements
	8c	financing capacity
	0	adjustments
Agents:	A	enterprises
	B	households
	C	administrations other than central government

              C1   local authorities and semi-public organisations (OSPAEs)

              C2   social security and other authorities

          D   abroad

          E   overseas countries in the franc area

          F   banking system

              F1   Bank of France

              F2   other banks

          G   other financial institutions

              G1   deposit offices and savings banks

              G2   other financial bodies

          H   treasury

The projection method used in the Sixth Plan is described in Chapter 15 of [94], and the one used in the Fifth Plan in Chapter 3 of Appendix III in [77].

II.7 The overall economic table

The TEE brings together for a given year all the various agents' accounts distinguished in the French national accounts. In its full form, it is the most complete summary of the economy that can be given in one table. The rows distinguish operations, and the columns agents' accounts, every one balancing. Table II.5 shows an example of a TEE (for 1966) in full form; numerous simplified versions are used in other parts of this book.

Table II.3

The SNA Sixth Plan resource—use equilibrium (nominal value)

	Milliards of current francs		Average annual growth rates
	1970	1975	1970–1975
Resources			
Remuneration of wage earners	389·5	611·4	9·4
Income from property and enterprise	241·4	358·5	8·2
National income	630·9	969·9	9·0
Indirect taxation	119·7	185·9	9·2
Operating subsidies	−15·6	−21·0	6·1
Net national product at market prices	735·0	1134·8	9·1
Depreciation	84·6	129·3	8·8
Gross national product at market prices	819·6	1264·1	9·0
Imports and payment of incomes abroad	135·9	203·2	8·4
Total	955·5	1467·3	9·0
Uses			
Private consumption	482·2	756·8	9·4
Public administrations' consumption	99·3	152·0	8·9
Gross capital formation	235·0	347·3	8·1
Gross national expenditure	816·5	1256·1	9·0
Exports and payment of incomes from abroad	139·0	211·2	8·7
Total	955·5	1467·3	9·0

Source: [94], p. 350

Table II.4   The financial operations table associated with the Plan account (figures in milliards of francs)

Nature of operations	Changes in assets		Administrations other than the state		Overseas	Franc area	Banking system		Other financial institutions		Treasury	Total
	Enterprises	Households										
	A	B	C1	C2	D	E	F1	F2	G1	G2	H	
90	2·5	15·8						1·5		1·0		20·8
91	4·1	43·4	0·2	1·4						1·0		50·1
92	0·6	7·1					0·6					8·3
93	3·2			0·1	0·5				2·4	7·5		13·4
94		7·3		0·1	2·5			0·5	0·5	7·0	5·3	23·5
95	0·3		0·2	0·4			21·1		3·0	3·0		28·0
96							8·4			0·9		9·3
97	9·7		2·0	0·3	1·6		10·5		19·8	36·4	5·0	85·3
98						0·3						0·3
99								1·0				1·0
Total	20·4	73·6	2·4	2·3	4·6	0·3	43·6		25·7	56·8	10·3	240·0
Debt recovered												
93												
97												
Total					3·3	4·4						7·7
Net changes												
8f	63·1				3·0							76·4
8c'		43·7	9·8	1·8				3·5	3·5	17·5	6·5	75·9
8c												
0						4·4						7·7
Total	63·1	43·7	9·8	1·8	6·3	4·4		3·5	3·5	17·5	6·5	160·0

Nature of operations	Changes in liabilities											
	Enterprises	Households	Administrations other than the state		Overseas	Franc area	Banking system		Other financial institutions		Treasury	Total
	A	B	C1	C2	D	E	F1	F2	G1	G2	H	
90							5·5	9·6	20·2	3·4	2·3	20·8
91								24·5	2·0	5·2	0·2	50·1
92	3·0									4·8	1·5	8·3
93	12·3		2·3		0·4			0·2		8·5	−1·0	13·4
94	23·6				3·0			0·2		8·0		23·5
95	7·9	3·3		0·3	0·8							28·0
96		1·4										9·3
97	33·4	25·2	9·9	0·2	6·4	0·8		0·1		9·5	−0·2	85·3
98					0·3							0·3
99											1·0	1·0
Total	80·2	29·9	12·2	0·5	10·9	0·8		40·1	22·2	39·4	3·8	240·0
Debt repaid												
93												
97												
Total												
Net changes												
8f	59·8		9·8		6·3	0·5						76·4
8c'		39·3		1·8		3·9		3·5	3·5	17·4	6·5	75·9
8c	3·3	4·4										7·7
0												
Total	63·1	43·7	9·8	1·8	6·3	4·4		3·5	3·5	17·4	6·5	160·0

Source: Table 188, [94], pp. 300–1

Table II.5

The overall economic table for 1966
(figures in millions of francs)

a. Uses	Non-financial enterprises			Households			Administrations		Financial institutions		Abroad	Franc area	Total
	Profit	Appropriation	Capital and financial	Profit	Appropriation	Capital and financial	Appropriation	Capital and financial	Appropriation	Capital and financial			
Operations on goods and services													
6a Gross domestic production													—
6b Consumption					311,051		18,973		2,035				332,059
6c Gross fixed capital formation			85,984			26,482		18,529		1,044			132,039
6d Changes in stock and other operations			11,463			-818		818					11,463
6e Exports											48,041	7,634	55,675
6f Net Services and uses											3,685	1,597	5,282
6g Imports													—
Total			97,447		311,051	25,664	18,973	19,347	2,035	1,044	51,726	9,231	536,518
Distributive operations													
70 Wages and social security contributions	187,216			169	7,929		37,977		6,321				239,612
71 Social security benefits	2,720						76,492		194				79,406
72 Interest, dividends and rents	16,135	9,312		2,386	616		5,463		8,300		2,280	407	44,899
73 Taxes	83,521	8,652		2,206	22,421		1,634		3,819				122,253
74 Transfers	2,205						47,872				424		50,501
75 Insurance	8,664			425	4,488	1,346	239		6,478		63		21,703
76 External receipts and expenditure					5,669		3,763		27		6,040	654	16,153
77 Miscellaneous distributive operations	4,123	115			6,972		1,152		669		1,532	260	14,823
78 Gross income of self-employed		106,156											106,156
79 Financing of capital formation by the self-employed						15,245							15,245
Total	304,584	124,235		5,186	48,095	16,591	174,592		25,808		10,339	1,321	710,751
Financial operations													
9a Cash			1,882			10,867		701		1,819	643	201	16,113
9b Other securities, bonds and shares			3,512			19,982		5,758		5,675	1,399	399	36,725
9c Short-term credits			2,674			177		1,805		18,864	-195		23,325
9d Other loans and borrowing			1,377					4,466		22,321	296	-93	28,367
9e Gold and foreign exchange						348		379		4,310	2,703	-1,247	6,493
9f Bills of deposit and advances between financial intermediaries								-75		-2,422			-2,497
Total			9,445			31,374		13,034		50,567	4,846	-740	108,526
Accounting balances													
8e Gross profits	166,268			17,424									183,692
8a Gross savings		53,092			57,508		19,648		6,583				136,831
8c Financing capacity						15,365		301		6,885	1,034	3,284	26,869
8c' Financing requirement			26,869										26,869
0 Adjustment			1,291							1,265	2,636	4,020	9,212
General total	470,852	177,327	135,052	22,610	416,654	88,994	213,213	32,682	34,426	59,761	70,581	17,116	1,739,268

b. Resources	Non-financial enterprises			Households			Administrations		Financial institutions		Abroad	Franc area	Total
	Profit	Appro-priation	Capital and financial	Profit	Appro-priation	Capital and financial	Appro-priation	Capital and financial	Appro-priation	Capital and financial			
Operations on goods and services													
6a Gross domestic production	454,950			22,610									477,560
6b Consumption													—
6c Gross fixed capital formation													—
6d Changes in stock and other operations													—
6e Exports													—
6f Net Services and uses													—
6g Imports											51,082	7,876	58,958
Total	454,950			22,610							51,082	7,876	536,518
Distributive operations													
70 Wages and social security contributions					174,328		65,284						239,612
71 Social security benefits					78,682						256	468	79,406
72 Interest, dividends and rents		3,937			15,566		3,214		20,430		1,693	59	44,899
73 Taxes	776						121,477						122,253
74 Transfers	13,507	6,634			12,541		15,488				878	1,453	50,501
75 Insurance	307		2,241		3,634	112	41		13,914	1,346	108		21,703
76 External receipts and expenditure					5,827		803		64		6,624	2,835	16,153
77 Miscellaneous distributive operations	1,312	488			2,496		6,906		18		2,458	1,145	14,823
78 Gross income of self-employed					106,156								106,156
79 Financing of capital formation by the self-employed			15,245										15,245
Total	15,902	11,059	17,486		399,230	112	213,213		34,426	1,346	12,017	5,960	710,751
Financial operations													
9a Cash								2,631		13,482			16,113
9b Other securities, bonds and shares			8,494					1,266		26,220	779	−34	36,725
9c Short-term credits			16,526			1,353		4,188			1,283	−25	23,325
9d Other loans and borrowing			12,585			8,773		3,741		2,617	596	55	28,367
9e Gold and foreign exchange										2,703	3,790		6,493
9f Bills of deposit and advances between financial intermediaries								−2,422		−75			−2,497
Total			37,605			10,126		9,404		44,947	6,448	−4	108,526
Accounting balances													
8e Gross profits		166,268			17,424								183,692
8a Gross savings			53,092			57,508		19,648		6,583			136,831
8c Financing capacity						15,365		301		6,885	1,034	3,284	26,869
8c' Financing requirement			26,869										26,869
0 Adjustment						5,883		3,329					9,212
General total	470,852	177,327	135,052	22,610	416,654	88,994	213,213	32,682	34,426	59,761	70,581	17,116	1,739,268

Source: Table 19, [262], pp. 58–9

Appendix III: The First Four Plans

These notes are usually given to my own students when I start my course on French planning. They are not by any means comprehensive, but they set the scene and add perspective. Their incompleteness also encourages students to consult the original sources. A number of good English texts are available, including Lutz [147], Cohen [251], Denton, Forsyth and Maclennan [60], and Hackett and Hackett [263]. All four of these sources are books, and thus contain many additional references and details of French sources. Of the many shorter articles, Kindleberger's [264] is hard to beat, and the comments by Wellisz which follow his paper are especially good on measuring the effectiveness of planning.

III.1   The First Plan (1947 to 1952–53)

(1)   Focused on investment in a number of key sectors: coal, electricity, oil, steel, cement, railways, tractors, and fertilisers. No overall growth target was set.

(2)   The original targets were over-optimistic, and were effectively revised downwards when the Marshall aid administration, which was responsible for over one third of the planned investment, requested 1952 as the terminal year for the European recovery programme. The original Plan terminal year, 1950, was changed to harmonise with this, but no new investment was introduced to cover the additional years.

(3)   The Plan was prepared from very little data and no reliable set of national accounts. There had been no agricultural census since 1929 and no industrial census since 1931.

(4)   It was also prepared at a time of runaway inflation:

	wholesale price index (1938 = 100)	hourly wage index (1946 = 100)
January 1946	479	100
April 1946	559	104
July 1946	571	111
September 1946	727	138

January 1947	874	143
April 1947		147
September 1947	1,096	179
December 1947	1,217	
February 1948	1,537	239
April 1948	1,555	246
July 1948	1,698	249
January 1949	1,946	287

This complicated the target choice: short-term stabilisation or long-term growth?

(5) The Plan chose growth and investment, and made no attempt to influence short-term policy. This brought the CGP into conflict with the Treasury and the numerous governments of the period who tried to tackle inflation. Who then kept the Plan going? Who supported it? The Treasury certainly did not: they were looking for *cuts* in expenditure. There was some support from the basic sectors benefited by the Plan, but most of all from the administrators of Marshall aid (it is difficult to find documentary evidence of this, but Cohen's personal interviews (reported in [251] support it).

(6) Another important factor was the extraordinary personal qualities of Jean Monnet, the first head of the CGP. He recognised the constraints and the possible pitfalls of getting involved in controversial issues. He accepted the supremacy of the Ministry of Finance, and kept well away from any attempt to rationalise agriculture.

(7) A feature of this and later Plans was the very ambitious housing target (2 million dwellings to be repaired by 1950 plus half a million new dwellings by the same date), which was not reached (by 1950 only 174,000 new dwellings and 789,715 repaired dwellings had been completed) because the money was never granted. Housing was completely omitted from the 1948 revisions to the Plan: Cohen calls it 'the Cheshire cat smile of the Monnet Plan'.

(8) Finally, and significantly, the ease of Plan preparation and implementation in the basic sectors owed a great deal to the fact that several of these industries were nationalised monopolies (coal, electricity, railways), which came to the CGP with their investment plans already drafted (in many instances in a (technically speaking) very sophisticated and skilful fashion).

III.2 The Second Plan (1954–1957)

This Plan was prepared against a vastly different set of external and internal circumstances:

(a) Marshall aid was over (at least, for non-military purposes);

(b) The entire productive apparatus now needed the modernising that had taken place in the basic sectors in the First Plan.

(c) Monnet had gone. Étienne Hirsch took over in 1952.

(d) The Governments's attitude to the Plan was not friendly; two Finance Ministrers ignored the Plan and substituted their own personal economic programmes:

    (i) Antoine Pinay's personal anti-inflation programme of March–December 1952;

    (ii) Edgar Faure's personal 18-month plan for economic expansion between the autumn of 1953 and the spring of 1955.

CGP was detached from the Prime Minister's office in 1954 and located in the Finance Ministry.

In spite of this de-emphasis, the Plan did expand, and the first of the three harmonising Plans (a term later due to Massé) was prepared, consisting of two principal components: the concerted economy, investment part, and a general resource allocation part intended to cover the whole economy.

1   The basic sector targets were achieved almost exactly: coal, electricity, steel, gas, railways, aluminium, even housing, all coming within 10 per cent of their planned increase in output.

2   The intermediate sector targets were a long way out, in both directions: automobiles 380 per cent; paper 208 per cent; chemicals 280 per cent; farm machinery 200 per cent; miscellaneous manufacturing 200 per cent; wood 246 per cent; machine tools 50 per cent; electrical equipment 233 per cent; textiles 213 per cent; all manufacturing 196 per cent of planned increase in output.

3   This last point brings out the cautious attitude of the planners, who were new at the general resource allocation aspect of the Plan.

4   The level of detail attempted in the projections, encouraged by a much richer data base, was much too fine.

5   To attempt such comprehensiveness without at the same time constructing a framework for co-ordinating short-term policy, constituted the basic political failure of the Plan.

III.3 The Third Plan (1958–1961)

The Third Plan came too early to reflect the changes that the planners already recognised were needed to avoid the failures of the previous Plan. It was simply a more sophisticated version of the Second Plan, based on better data and a bigger sector breakdown; but this technical elegance was not matched on the political side. The Plan did not appear until February 1959, and was officially laid aside in 1960, being replaced by the Interim Plan. The numerical aspects and the outcome of both Plans, are summarised (a great deal!) below:

| | Four-year growth rates | | |
| | Planned | | Actual (1961) |
	Third Plan	Interim Plan	
Gross domestic product	27	23·3	24·9
Gross fixed investment	28	26·5	28
Private consumption	24	17·6	20
Administrations' consumption	12	17·2	11
Imports	10	18·2	26
Exports	35	60	60

Source: [147]

III.4 The Fourth Plan (1962–1965)

The Fourth Plan was the last of the harmonising Plans, still mainly focusing on structural objectives and generally ignoring financial imbalances. It too was replaced, by Giscard d'Estaing's Stabilisation Plan in September 1963. The Fourth Plan was similar to the Second and Third in that

(a) it was effective only within the concerted economy part;
(b) it provided a very detailed picture (made up of physical output targets) of the Plan year (1965);
(c) incomes policy was treated as an awkward residual;
(d) short-term policy was still 'external' to the Plan.

But new features are discernible, many deriving from 'the continual adaptation of the theory of the Plan to the practice' under Pierre Massé's influence. The distribution of the benefits of growth, achieved in the previous Plans and once again written into the Fourth, was given much more prominence: social investment and regional policy objectives appeared for the first time. In addition, the beginnings of an integrated prices and incomes policy are apparent, and the degree of detail and technical sophistication contained in the physical projection reached proportions never previously attained. This last point (taken alongside France's impressive growth record) was probably responsible for the considerable interest shown in French planning by other European countries, notably Britain, at this time.

The record of the Plan is well documented in the sources cited above. Our purpose here is to bring out the fact that this Plan marked the end of the second phase (consisting of the Second, Third and Fourth Plans) of French planning. With entry to the EEC, the increased foreign competition, and the added emphasis this placed on price stability, it became essential to transfer resources away from more detail and sophistication on the physical side to first attempts at comprehensive value planning.

This appendix perhaps appears to be too critical, but there are many sources that the reader can turn to to see 'how successful the early Plans were'. We have also omitted all details of how the Plans were prepared, how many commissions there were, etc., because information on these aspects is also reasonably plentiful. All we need here is sufficient to make the following points about French planning:

(a) it has never been fully comprehensive;
(b) it has never adequately tackled the short-term, medium-term linkage problem;
(c) it has always worked better on the basic sector, concerted economy side than on the general resource allocation side;
(d) the inclusion of value planning (prices) is comparatively recent;
(e) when one speaks of social and regional planning, it is an illusion to imagine that France has 'six Plans' experience' in these fields;
(f) the technical and administrative aspects of French planning are extremely well-organised and amongst the most sophisticated in the world. This is where most of the benefits of France's 'six Plans' experience' are to be found.

Appendix IV: The Fifth Plan

This Plan is better documented than any of the previous Plans because it marks the beginning of a new phase in French planning, and most of the sources cited in Appendix III were written during the Fifth Plan period, thus focusing on that particular Plan. The technical details are interesting in that they represent the first iteration of the process described in this book. Figures IV.1 and IV.2 below provide a very useful background to similar diagrams and discussions in Chapters 1, 3, 5, and 8. The following brief notes are intended to explain some of the jargon and notation used in the figures; more explanation is given in [77], and a much shorter presentation of the same material in English is given in [222].

IV.1 The technical Plan preparation phases

Phase 1 (September 1962 to March 1964). Technical preparation of the major guidelines.

E_0, E_1 : roughing out stage.

E_2 : reference projection, established by synthesising detailed analyses.

E_3 : drawing up of the Plan Commissions' work programme for 1964.

Phase 2 (April to November 1964). The options phase.

E_4 : determination of the Fifth Plan options by political bodies.

Phase 3 (December 1964 to November 1965). Plan specification phase.

E_5 : despatch of directives to the consultative bodies (the Plan Commissions' work programme for 1965) following the vote by Parliament on the main options.

E_6 : synthesis of the Commissions' detailed analyses and final choices by the Government.

Phase 4 (December 1965 to mid-1966). Regionalisation of the Plan.

The E_i refer to the successive projections used throughout the preparation

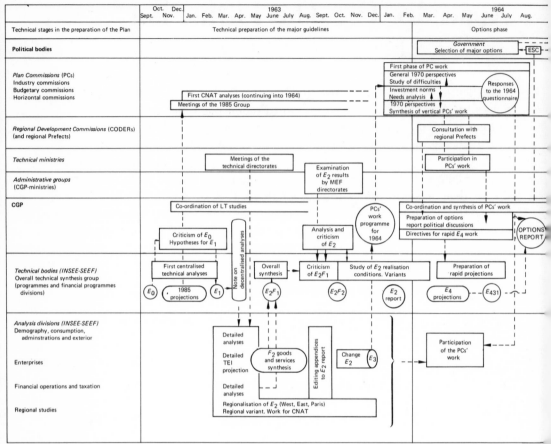

Fig. IV.2   Stages involved in the preparation of the Fifth Plan
Source: Table X, [77], facing p. 121

of the Plan; a numerical version of the actual model is given in Appendix VIII. A single subscript denotes a synthesised, central projection, a second subscript the same projection modified at a later intermediary phase, and a third subscript a variant of the central projection.

The important projections are E_2 (the reference projection), E_{431} (associated with the options report), and E_{62} (associated with the Plan itself), corresponding to the departure account, the options account, and the Plan account in the Sixth Plan. The way in which these projections changed during the preparation of the Plan is shown in Table IV.1. The

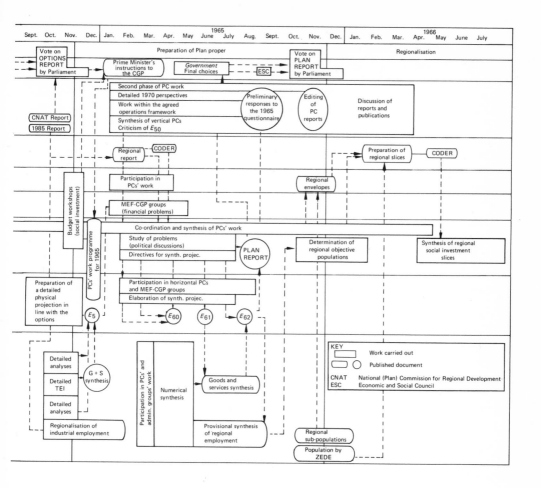

way in which the exogenous and endogenous variables are indicated there also conveys the technical limitations of the model, at least compared with the FIFI model in the Sixth Plan. As is well-known, the Fifth Plan was modified following the May–June events; the revised targets and projections are shown in the last column of Table IV.2. This is a time and progress schedule used for checking the execution of the Plan (see Chapter 9). There is a lot of tantalising material here that should incite the reader to seek explanations and answers; much research remains to be done on the Fifth Plan now that material such as this is available.

361

Fig IV.1 The characteristics and time scales of the Fifth Plan projections

Plan preparation phases	E0 (1962)	E1 (1963)	E2 (1963)	E3 (Dec 1963)	E4 (1964, options phase)	E5 / E50 (critical analysis)	E6 / E60, E61, E62 (preparation of the plan proper)
Successive projections	E_0	E_1	E_2	E_3	E_{40} E_{41} E_{42} E_{43} / E_{421} E_{431} Variants	E_{50}	E_{60} E_{61} E_{62}
General nature of the projection	Semi-global, Partially formalised TEI, Formalised TEE		Detailed TEI, TEE, and TOF	Variant of E_2 (44½ hour working week)	Semi-global projections based on the detailed E_2 analyses	Detailed TEI, Global TEE and TOF	E_{60}: semi-global TEI, detailed TEE and TOF; E_{61}: detailed TEI; E_{62}: detailed TEI, TEE and TOF
Basis of the projection	1960 on old 1956 base year. Interpolation of IVth Plan 1965	Global account on new 1959 base year	Definitive 1960 account on new 1959 base year. 1962 population census. First 1965 forecast account established at the end of 1963	Same as E_2	Definitive 1960 account on new 1959 base year. 1965: E_{40}: P1B 65/63 assumed = 9 per cent 1965 forecast. E_{41}, E_{42}, E_{43}: May 1964 forecast	December 1963 version of the 1962 account. The September 1964 (Finance Act) version of 1965 account	Definitive 1962 account. May 1965 version of 1965 account
Units used: Volume terms	1959 francs	Projection 1959 francs, Global 1960 francs	1960 francs	1960 Francs	1960 francs	1962 francs	1962 francs
Value terms	Real value 1960 francs 1970 relative prices	Real value 1960 francs 1970 relative prices	Real value 1960 francs at 1970 relative prices	Same as E_2	E_{40} and E_{41}: real value 1960 francs at 1970 relative prices; E_{42} and E_{421}: nominal value 1970 francs at 1970 prices; E_{43} and E_{431}: real value 1963 francs at 1970 relative prices	Real value 1962 francs at 1970 relative prices	Real value 1962 francs at 1970 relative price
Degree of detail in the 1970 projection: Goods and services table	4 branches	4 branches, 5 sectors (trial)	67 branches (a)	same as E_2	8 branches. Continuation of E_{431} results (15 sectors in E_{432})	67 branches	E_{60}: 8 branches; E_{61}: 67 branches; E_{62}: 67 branches
Enterprise accounts by sector TEE	No	No	12 sectors and 40 public enterprise accounts. Yes with detailed external and administration accounts		Yes (marginal revision of E_{431})	29 sectors and 40 public enterprise accounts. Yes (marginal revision of E_{431})	E_{60}: Yes (b); E_{61}: No; E_{62}: Yes
TOF	No Global	No Global	Yes		Yes for E_{431}	Yes, with variants	E_{60}: Global; E_{61}: No; E_{62}: Yes
Demographic projections	Global	Global	Detailed (1954 and 1962 censuses)		Global (marginally revised versions of E_2)	Employment in 28 branches	Global — Employment 28 branches
Regional projections	No	No	Population, employment, migration for West, East, and Paris.		Employment in three regions	Regional breakdown of industrial employment	Provisional synthesis of employment by branch and region

Plan preparation phases (time scale):
- 1962 – 1963: Technical preparation of the major guidelines (E_0 to E_3). E_2 reference projection. E_2 realisation conditions, variants, updating.
- 1964: The options phase (E_4).
- 1965: Preparation of the plan proper (E_5, E_6). Critical analysis of E_{50}.

Main variants around the central projection

From E_0:
V1: more social investment and housing
V2: shorter working week
V3: more productive investment
V4, V5, V6: changes in production functions: lower productivity
V7: faster agricultural exodus
V8: external forces

E_2 variants:
V1: higher female population
V2: shorter working week
V3: more productive investment
V4: greater agricultural migration
V5: faster rate of growth
V6: more social investment and housing
V7: less migration from the west
V8: higher indirect incomes

E_4: Complementary analyses to those of E_2 (marginal revisions), plus
V9: slower rate of growth
V10: more private consumption

(a) Parametric projection of household consumption in 300 products, and a very detailed analysis of other final demand items (foreign trade, administrations' consumption, gross capital formation)
(b) Synthesis of the administrative groups' detailed analyses and those of the CEEGF
(c) Synthesis of the industry commissions' analyses
(d) The Fifth Plan projection, the physical equilibrium being a revision of E_{61}, and the TEE and the TOF revisions of E_{60}

Source: Table IX, [77], facing p. 120

Table IV.1

Changes in the key aggregates from the reference projection to the Plan projection (Fifth Plan)

(a)   Physical equilibrium

Characteristic variables in 1970	E_2	E_{431}	E_{62}	Observations
Working population minus armed forces and overseas forces	21,015	20,830	21,050	In thousands
Easing of the labour market	−50	−200	−260	In thousands. Defined as 'changes in the job supply' or the 'rate of activity'
Total employment	20,715	19,980	20,140	In thousands, assuming a 44½ hour working week and 4 weeks' paid holiday in 1970
Hourly productivity (recall that yearly rate between 1954 and 1962 was 4·5 per cent)	4·2%	4·0%	4·0%	Representing the average annual growth rate in industry and services between 1962 and 1970
Gross domestic production (PIB)	5·5%	5·0%	5·0%	Average annual growth rate between 1965 and 1970
External balance (volume terms)	0·06m. (1960 fr.)	0·5m. (1960 fr.)	1·90m. (1962 fr.)	
Household consumption	5·1%	4·5%	4·5%	Average annual growth rate between 1965 and 1970
Productive gross fixed capital formation	6·3%	5·7%	5·8%	Ditto
Administrations' gross fixed capital formation	11·3%	9·1%	8·2%	Ditto
Housing gross fixed capital formation	450	470	480	Thousands of houses built in 1970. Increase in quality between 1960 and 1970

KEY

Exogenous variables:
⬚ via a technical hypothesis

⬚ via a detailed analysis

⬚ via a received instruction

Endogenous variables: no frame

(b) Overall economic equilibrium

Characteristic variables in 1970	E_2F_2	E_{431}	E_{62}	Observations
Households' savings rate	11·5%	12%	12·4%	Ratio of savings to consumption
Non-financial enterprises' rate of self-financing	65·5%	70%	69·5%	Ratio of companies' undistributed incomes plus the proportion of non-agricultural self-employed's savings channelled to the financing of their investments to gross capital formation
Administrations' financing requirement	5·15m. (1960 fr.)	6·6m. (1960 fr.)	1·3m. (1962 fr.)	
Annual growth rate of per capita wages		3·3%*	3·5%*†	* Real per capita growth rate from 1965 to 1970
Annual growth rate of per capita gross income of the non-agricultural self-employed	4·0% (1960–1970)	3·3%	3·3%	† Increase consistent with 3·3 per cent p.a. in each branch
Annual growth rate of per capita agricultural incomes		5·4%	4·8%	
Relative price of agricultural output 1970/1960	98·9	106	102	1965–1970 index for E_{62}
Social security benefits index	136	138·6	138	Index of 1965–1970 programmes
Elasticity of $\dfrac{\text{social contributions}}{\text{wages}}$	1·1	1·06	1·12	
Direct taxation on households	7·24%	8·0%	8·7%	Percentage of consumption
Indirect taxation on enterprises	18·55%	19·3%	20·0%	Percentage of output
Subsidies to enterprises	21·3m. (1960 fr.)	21·0m. (1960 fr.)	14·0m. (1962 fr.)	Gradual return to economic prices within the Common Agricultural Policy

Source: Table II, [77], p. 76 (also in [222], p. 66)

Table IV.2

The revision and execution of the Fifth Plan main aggregates

	Economic budgets and forecast accounts (annual growth rates)					Average over the period (annual growth rates)				Fifth Plan
	1965–66	1966–67	1967–68	1968–69	1969–70	1965–67	1967–69	1969–70	1965–70	1965–70
Growth and its uses (volume terms)										
PIB	5·9	4·7	4·6	8·0	6·2	5·3	6·3	6·2	5·9	5·7
Household consumption	4·8	4·7	5·0	7·1	4·1	4·7	6·0	4·1	5·1	5·3
Productive investment	10·3	6·3	7·8	11·4	7·5	8·3	9·6	7·5	8·7	6·0
Administrations' investment	8·2	13·0	2·8	3·4	6·6	10·6	3·1	6·6	6·8	10·4
Investment in housing	6·5	4·7	8·3	6·2	6·7	5·6	7·2	6·7	6·5	3·8
Exports	5·6	6·0	11·8	16·0	20·8	5·8	13·9	20·8	11·9	7·5
Imports	12·4	5·6	12·7	21·4	9·2	8·7	16·8	9·2	12·2	8·4
Prices and incomes										
General price level	2·8	2·7	4·2	7·0	5·1	2·7	5·6	5·1	4·4	1·5
Hourly wage rate	3·1	3·1	6·7	4·0	4·7	3·1	5·3	4·7	4·4	3·3
Gross income of non-agricultural self-employed	6·4	4·7	5·5	7·2	3·1	5·6	6·3	3·1	3·7	3·8
Gross income of agricultural workers	4·9	6·8	1·7	2·0		5·9	1·9			4·8
Social security benefits	7·3	7·2	5·8	8·5	7·1	7·2	7·1	7·1	7·1	7·3
Average net wage per head	3·2	3·2	7·0	5·0	4·2	3·1	6·0	4·2	4·5	3·8

Source: Table 2, [246], pp. 70–1

365

Appendix V: An Algebraic Presentation of the FIFI Model

The full version of FIFI has not yet been published (other than in [90], which is not easy to obtain), although a second volume to [82] is promised for later in 1974. In the meantime, enthusiasts have to make do with 'simplified' versions which frustratingly conceal all the interesting features. The presentation we give here is the one given in an appendix to Courbis' contribution in [82] (pp. 71–4). It corresponds to the 1967–68 version of FIFI, as distinct from the 1972 version discussed in Chapter 10.

V.1 Notation

V.1.1 General conventions

(a)   A sector or a group of products is indicated by the subscript i or j (the sector i generally corresponds to the product group i); where a double subscript occurs, the first corresponds to the sector and the second to the product group (e.g. K_{ij} is sector i investment demand for product j). The number of sectors and product groups is n (in FIFI $n = 7$).

(b)   For goods and services, X represents measurement in 'volume' terms (value in constant prices) and $\hat{X}$ the same magnitude in 'value' terms (at current prices); $\hat{X}/X$ is the relative price index for the magnitude being considered.

(c)   Variables written with a bar on top (e.g. $\overline{X}$) are exogenous.

V.1.2 Symbols used

Goods and services

$$
\begin{aligned}
Q_i &= \text{production of good or service } i \\
I_i &= \text{imports of product } i \\
H_{ij} &= \text{intermediate consumption of product } j \text{ in sector } i
\end{aligned}
$$

C_i = household consumption of product i
K_{Mi} = use of product i in household investment
G_i = administrations' demand (consumption + investment) for product i
K_{ij} = sector i investment demand for product j
E_i = exports of product i
D_{ETi} = foreign demand for product i
$\hat{K}_i$ = sector i total investment in value terms
$\hat{C}$ = total household consumption in value terms
$\hat{G}$ = total administrations' demand in value terms
$\hat{K}_M$ = total household investment in value terms

Employment

N_i = labour employed in sector i
N_A = labour employed by administrations
N = total employed labour
N_a = available working population
N_T = total population
U = unemployment
u = rate of unemployment

Wages and prices

p_i = production price of good i
p_{Ii} = import price of good i
p_{Ei} = export price of good i
p_{ui} = internal utilisation price of good i
p_{ETi} = foreign market price of good i
p_g = general price level
w = reference wage rate
w_A = administrations' average wage rate

Distributive operations and accounting items

W_i = wages paid by sector i enterprises
W_A = wages paid by administrations
RE_i = non-wage incomes paid to households by sector i enterprises
F_i = taxes and obligatory payments paid by sector i enterprises
F = total fiscal receipts and obligatory payments over all enterprises

J	= taxes paid by households
T	= social transfers
R	= households' gross income
R_d	= households' disposable income
A_i	= self-financing available to sector i enterprises
S	= households' savings
B_i	= financing requirement of sector i enterprises
B_A	= adminstrations' financing requirement
CF_M	= households' financing capacity
Z	= external financing requirement (current balance of payments

Other symbols

n_i	= labour needed to produce a unit of good i
h_{ij}	= sector i technical coefficient relating to intermediate consumption of product j
k_{ij}	= sector i productive investment rate (at constant prices) for product j
ξ	= parameter that measures the variation of the available working population as a function of the labour market situation (level of unemployment)
ϵ_i	= structural difference (for 'exposed' sectors) between the product price and the import price of good i
λ_i	= weight given to ith price in calculating the general price level
a_i	= sector i's self-financing rate
C_{zi}	= households' minimum consumption (in volume terms) of product i
γ_i	= share of households' disposable income (excluding disposable income spent on minimal consumption) spent on product i
g_i	= ratio between sector i average wage and the reference wage rate w (wage 'drift')
g_A	= ratio between the average wage rate paid by administrations and the reference wage rate w

V.2   System of equations

Equilibrium of goods and services in volume terms:

(1) $\quad Q_i + I_i = \sum_{j=1}^{n} H_{ji} + C_i + \bar{G}_i + \sum_{j=1}^{n} K_{ji} + \bar{K}_{Mi} + E_i, \ i = 1,2,...,n$

Production functions:

intermediate consumption –

(2) $\quad H_{ij} = h_{ij}\, Q_i, \ i, j = 1,2,...,n$

employment –

(3) $\quad N_i = n_i\, Q_i, \ i = 1,2,...,n$ (except for agriculture where N is exogenous)

investment –

(4) $\quad K_{ij} = k_{ij}\,(Q_i)\, Q_i, \ i = 1,2,...,n$

Employment and unemployment:

(5) $\quad N = \sum_{i=1}^{n} N_i + \bar{N}_A$

(6) $\quad N_d = \bar{N}_d^* - \xi\, U$

(7) $\quad U = N_d - N$

(8) $\quad u = \dfrac{U}{N_d}$

Foreign trade (in volume terms):

(9) $\quad E_i = E_i\,(\bar{D}_{ETi}, \bar{p}_{ETi}, Q_i, p_{Ei}, ...)$ or $\bar{E}_i, \ i = 1,2,...,n$

(10) $\quad I_i = I_i\,(Q_i, p_{Ii}, p_i, ...)$ or $\bar{I}_i$ (sheltered and publicly controlled sectors)

$\qquad$ or $\qquad\qquad\qquad\qquad$ (exposed sector)

$\qquad p_i = p_{Ii} + \bar{\epsilon}_i \qquad\qquad\qquad i = 1,2,...,n$

Wages and prices:

(11) $\quad p_g = \sum_{i=1}^{n} \lambda_i\, p_i$

(12) $\quad w = w(u, p_g),$ $\qquad$ (Phillips–Lipsey relation)

(13) $\quad p_{Ii} = \begin{cases} \bar{p}_{Ii} & \text{, 'complementary' imports} \\ p_{Ii}\,(I_i), & \text{'substitutable' imports (exposed sector)} \end{cases}; i = 1, 2, ..., n$

(14) $\quad p_{Ei} = \bar{p}_{Ei}$ or $p_{Ei}(p_{ETi}, p_i, ...)$, $\quad i = 1,2,...,n$

(15) $\quad p_{ui} = \dfrac{p_i\, Q_i + p_{Ii} - p_{Ei}\, E_i}{\sum\limits_j H_{ji} + C_i + \bar{G}_i + \sum\limits_j K_{ji} + \bar{K}_{M\,i}}$, $i = 1,2,...,n$

Enterprise accounts and incomes arising from production:

(16) $\quad W_i = N_i\, g_i\, w$ $\qquad\qquad\qquad\qquad$, $i = 1,2,...,n$

(17) $\quad RE_i = RE_i\,(Q_i, p_i, ...)$ $\qquad\qquad$, $i = 1,2,...,n$

(18) $\quad F_i = F_i\,(Q_i, p_i, W_i, ...)$ $\qquad\qquad$, $i = 1,2,...,n$

(19) $\quad A_i = p_i\, Q_i - \sum\limits_{j=1}^{n} H_{ij}\, p_{uj} - w_i - RE_i - p_i,$ $\quad i = 1,2,...,n$

(20) $\quad \hat{K}_i = \sum\limits_{j=1}^{n} K_{ij}\, p_{uj},$ $\qquad i = 1,2,...,n$

Enterprise behaviour:

(21) $\quad A_i - a_i\, \hat{K}_i = 0,$ $\qquad i = 1,2,...,n$

$\qquad$ meaning that either $\begin{cases} A_i = a_i\, \hat{K}_i & \text{, non-competitioned sector} \\ K_i = \dfrac{1}{a_i}\, A_i, & \text{competitioned sector} \end{cases}$

$\qquad\qquad$ or $\quad p_i = p_i \qquad$ for publicly controlled sectors

(22) $\quad n_i = n_i - \mu_i\,(I_i\,/\,Q_i)$

(23) $\quad g_i = g_i\,(a_i - a_i^*) = g_i\,(I_i\,/\,Q_i)$

(24) $\quad a_i = a_i^* - v_i\,(I_i\,/\,Q_i)$

$\left.\begin{array}{l}\text{for exposed sectors, } \mu_i \text{ and } v_i \text{ are} \\ \text{increasing functions of } I_i/Q_i, \text{ and} \\ g_i \text{ is a decreasing function of } I_i/Q_i, \\ \text{for other sectors, } n_i, g_i \text{ and } a_i \text{ are} \\ \text{exogenous.}\end{array}\right.$

Nevertheless n_i depends on weekly hours of work (a function of the labour market situation (i.e. of u)) for non-agricultural sectors, and is fully determined for agriculture because employment is exogenous there.

Households' account:

(25) $\quad R = \sum\limits_{i=1}^{n} W_i + W_A + \sum\limits_{i=1}^{n} RE_i + T$

(26) $\quad J = J(R, ...)$

(27) $\quad R_d = R - J$

(28) $\quad \hat{K}_M = \sum\limits_{i=1}^{n} p_{ui}\, \bar{K}_{Mi}$

(29) $\quad CF_M = S - \hat{K}_M$

Households' behaviour:

(30) $\quad S = S(R_d, p_g, \hat{K}_M, ...)$

(31) $\quad \hat{C} = R_d - S$

(32) $\quad p_{ui} C_i = p_{ui} \bar{C}_{zi} + \gamma_i \left[\hat{C} - \sum_{j=1}^{n} p_{uj} \bar{C}_{zj} \right] , i = 1, 2, .., n$

Administrations' account:

(33) $\quad \hat{G} = \sum_{i=1}^{n} p_{ui} \bar{G}_i$

(34) $\quad W_A = \bar{N}_A \, g_A \, w \text{ or } \bar{N}_A \, \bar{w}_A$

(35) $\quad F = \sum_{i=1}^{n} F_i$

(36) $\quad T = T(\bar{N}_T, w, p_g, ...)$

(37) $\quad B_A = \hat{G} + W_A + T - F - J$

Balance of payments (reduced here to the trade balance, for simplification):

(38) $\quad Z = \sum_{i=1}^{n} p_{Ei} E_i - \sum_{i=1}^{n} p_{Ii} I_i$

Appendix VI: Economic Budgets and the DECA Model

This appendix provides brief details on the short-term forecasting and economic budgeting exercises that impinge on the medium-term planning process at the technical level and Plan monitoring stages. The material here is taken from [101] where further references are given. Details of the financial budgeting process can be found in [253].

VI.1 The economic budget procedure

Economic budgets have been the central instrument with which the DP (Forecasting Directorate, Ministry of Finance) have carried out their short-term forecasting and policy evaluation tasks for a number of years. The procedure according to which economic budgets are prepared is well laid down ([214], [215], [216]) and very much tied in with the Finance Act ('Loi de Finances'), which is debated by Parliament every year in October and November, and which contains a statement of Government intentions and expectations for the coming year. There are two types of economic budgets: exploratory budgets and forecast budgets. The former look at the problems likely to occur during the next 18 months to two years, and assess whether the foreseeable trends over this period are satisfactory with respect to the general objectives of equilibrium and growth set by the Government in the Plan. It is in the preparation of this type of budget that the DECA model is used, together with other decentralised models (some of which also serve in the medium-term model system described in Figure 3.6), and it is common for the DP to put forward several variants, depending on the different types of external economic forces that might intervene and the different economic policy assumptions associated with them. Forecast budgets concern the coming year, and are consistent with the economic policy measures written into the Finance Act; if the Government changes its policy after the presentation of the Act, then the forecast budget is revised. The DECA model is not the main

373

instrument used in preparing forecast budgets: the procedure is much too complex, as is shown in Figure VI.1.

The whole process revolves around the production of economic budgets for the two meetings of the CCBE ('Commission des Comptes et Budgets Économiques', the National Accounts and Economic Budgets Commission), usually held in May and October. The CCBE includes members of the administration, the Economic and Social Council, the Plan Commission (CGP), and various people with 'economic competence'. It is chaired by the Finance Minister, and the DP provides the secretariat.

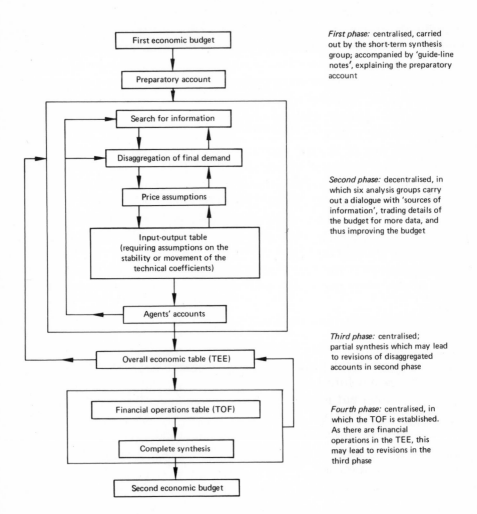

First phase: centralised, carried out by the short-term synthesis group; accompanied by 'guide-line notes', explaining the preparatory account

Second phase: decentralised, in which six analysis groups carry out a dialogue with 'sources of information', trading details of the budget for more data, and thus improving the budget

Third phase: centralised; partial synthesis which may lead to revisions of disaggregated accounts in second phase

Fourth phase: centralised, in which the TOF is established. As there are financial operations in the TEE, this may lead to revisions in the third phase

First economic budget

Preparatory account

Search for information

Disaggregation of final demand

Price assumptions

Input-output table (requiring assumptions on the stability or movement of the technical coefficients)

Agents' accounts

Overall economic table (TEE)

Financial operations table (TOF)

Complete synthesis

Second economic budget

Fig. VI.1   Main stages in the construction of a forecast economic budget
Source: based on a diagram in [214]

374

Taking year n as the year for which short-term forecasts and economic budgets are to be produced, the timeable of events is as follows:

Late in year $n-2$: work starts on the first economic budget (FEB) for year n. This is an exploratory budget and the DECA model is used to construct it.

May in year $n-1$: the FEB for year n is presented to the CCBE. It includes variants on the rate of growth, fiscal receipts, execution of the Plan, etc., and tries to set year n in a two- to three-year context.

May to September in year $n-1$: work proceeds on the second economic budget (SEB) for year n. This is a forecast budget.

October in year $n-1$: the SEB for year n is presented to the CCBE. It is a projection based on the Finance Act, and is published (in the Economic and Financial Report). The SEB is generally a precise form of one of the variants contained in the FEB.

May in year n: the third economic budget (TEB) for year n is drawn up, using first quarter data to make any necessary amendments to the forecasts and policy.

October in year n: the last projection for year n is established, but it now takes on the nature of a *forecast national account* rather than an economic budget. Its essential purpose is to act as a basis for the year $n+1$ economic budgets. It is published (for example, see [209]).

Early in year $n+1$: the provisional national accounts for year n are constructed, and clearly serve to aid the preparation of the FEB for year $n+2$ and the TEB for year $n+1$.

Late in year $n+1$: the first semi-definitive national accounts are available.

Late in year $n+2$: the second semi-definitive national accounts are drawn up.

Late in year $n+3$: the definitive national accounts for year n are finally compiled.

The whole process depends on, and eventually turns itself into, the preparation of various forms of the national accounts, an exercise that involves many personnel but is essential for the economic planning and budgeting procedures (see [217]).

To summarise, the various national accounts and economic budgets that are available at the two key meetings of the CCBE, again taking year n as the year in question, are:

	National accounts	Economic budgets
May *n* :	*National accounts*	*Economic budgets*
	Definitive *n*−4	FEB *n*+1
	Second semi-definitive *n*−3	TEB *n*
	First semi-definitive *n*−3	
	Provisional *n*−1	
October *n*:	Forecast *n*	SEB *n*+1

VI.2 The DECA model

The DECA ('Demande et Comportement d'Autofinancement', Demand and self-financing behaviour) model was constructed by the DP in 1968 to produce an annual projection of the overall economic table (TEE). It succeeds the ZOGOL I, II, and III models (ZOGOL I appeared in 1966), which were the first attempts to formalise completely the forecasting techniques introduced by the SEEF ('Service des Études Économiques et Financières', Department of Economic and Financial Research, created in 1950, modified in 1961 (part of the SEEF going to the INSEE), and becoming the DP on 9 July 1965) and then the DP, with participation from the INSEE. DECA is a global, Keynesian demand model, which currently excludes financial operations, and is distinguished from ZOGOL by the introduction of the dynamic, self-financing behaviour of firms. There are problems surrounding the self-financing concept (see [218], [219], for details).

To appreciate the structure of DECA, it is necessary to understand that it was originally expected to contribute to the following four needs expressed by the policy-makers in the DP:

(i)   to provide a framework of consistency for successive forecast economic budgets;

(ii)   to serve as a one- to two-year forecasting model for exploratory economic budgets;

(iii)   to analyse the effects of economic policy variants and unforeseen external 'shocks';

(iv)   to act as a time-path ('cheminement') model, describing the intermediate years between the base year and the terminal year of the Plan.

Perhaps it was naive to expect that a single model could satisfy all these needs; in any event, the choice of a single model did mean that economic policy variants were compatible with the projections, that there was continuity between the various economic budgets, and that computational flexibility was gained by having the whole model computer-programmed once, needing only to vary the control cards to switch from one mode of operation to another.

The efficiency with which DECA can fulfil needs (i)–(iv) is of course rather variable, and there are particular shortcomings with regard to (iv). It cannot really be said to be a time-path model because allowance is not made in its equations for all the structural changes that the economy will go through in a three- to five-year period, especially behavioural changes. But there is a device in the model such that *given* time-paths can be compared via their effects on the results of the model: this is the device of using deviation variables ('variables d'écart'). Work has been going on for a number of years on a separate time-path model, called STAR, which is being constructed by the Macro-economic Research Group in the DP.

Every equation in the DECA model contains a deviation variable. It is a parameter that effectively enables the coefficients in a relationship to be changed at will. For example, it may be known (via another analysis) that the behaviour of a particular economic agency, which is faced with an exceptional situation of *short* duration, will change (i.e. it will diverge from the recent trend). To accommodate this, a value can be given to the deviation variable in the relevant equation, and the appropriate dependent variable modified accordingly.

Yet another way in which the deviation variables are useful is in the model's inverted operating mode. An economic budget may be calculated in some way that does not essentially involve DECA. All the items of the base year and the projected year are thus known. These can be fed into the model, and the values of the deviation variables necessary to produce them as results of the model automatically calculated. The list of deviation variables generated in this way signifies that the economic budget being considered verifies the equations of the model with the exception of these deviations: they indicate that the projected year has some peculiarity with respect to past trends. Every annual forecast can in the end be characterised by a list of the deviation variables and exogenous data that have enabled DECA to produce it. Thus, two variants can be compared immediately, simply by looking at the two lists of deviation variables and making judgement on them.

The model itself is used to generate two sorts of projections. Its main use is in projecting one year ahead, when all effects from preceding years are naturally exogenous, and all that are needed to start off the iterations are some items from the agricultural account and a starting value for the PIB growth rate. There is a simple representation of the reduced form of the one-year equilibrium model in an appendix to Billaudot's paper ([218], [219]). The main simplifying assumptions in this use of the model are:

(a)   there is no disagreement between supply and demand, because of the role assigned to changes in stocks;

(b)   there is sufficient capacity to satisfy all demand levels;

(c)   the growth of prices does not depend directly on the growth of costs.

The solution is obtained by calculating the volume of output such that household consumption in value terms (the balancing item in the goods and services equilibrium) is equal to the result of applying the household consumption function to their disposable income. The rate of growth of output is then compared with the starting value, and, if significantly different, further iterations are carried out.

The second use of the model is in producing annual forecasts two to three years ahead. Some of the items which act as exogenous input to the model in its one-year mode of operation now form dynamic linkages between separate years. Each dynamic linkage is constructed around two particular components: a driving relationship of a structural type (i.e. representing underlying structural forces that determine the evolution of particular economic variables in the short and medium term), and self-regulating mechanisms attempting to bring together the actual evolution of the variable and the underlying trend (or structural force). Many such dynamic linkages clearly exist, but not all of them have yet been sufficiently understood to be included in DECA. The ones that are described in the model involve imports and four variables dependent on the self-financing behaviour of the private sector: prices, wages, exports, and investment.

The following version of DECA is taken from Malgrange [220] where it is called the MO model. The MO model is itself derived from another version of DECA used in the OPTIMIX study (see note 12 to Chapter 10). Malgrange shows how to convert the OPTIMIX version of DECA into MO in an appendix to [220]. It is just about possible to convert MO back into the OPTIMIX version of DECA (and thus obtain a better feel for the actual DECA model), but we do not have the space to do that here.

The symbolic conventions adopted in MO are as follows.

(a)   Underlined symbols are exogenous, although not necessarily constant over time, nor close to zero. Confusion can arise from the same notation being used in equations for an endogenous variable and an exogenous quantity (e.g. X_2 and $\underline{X}_2$ in (3): the $\underline{X}_2$ is *not* an exogenous value of the variable X_2; it is an exogenous quantity involved in the enumeration of X_2;

(b)   Time-lags (in years) are indicated by negative superscripts.

(c)   The variables x_i and X_i represent the various goods and services

378

equilibrium aggregates in volume and value terms, respectively (each value of i corresponds to a different aggregate, as defined after the model);

(d)   a tilde (wavy line) over a symbol indicates a growth index (e.g. $\tilde{x}_i = \dfrac{x_i}{X_i^{-1}}$);

(e)   a hat over a symbol indicates a growth rate (e.g. $\hat{x}_i = \tilde{x}_i - 1$);

(f)   an asterisked symbol indicates the value the symbol takes on a reference path (i.e. on an average trajectory).

The equations of MO are as follows:

$$(1) \quad x_1 + x_2 = \sum_{i=3}^{9} x_i$$

$$(2) \quad X_1 + X_2 = \sum_{i=3}^{9} X_i$$

$$(3) \quad X_2 = [\mu_2' \, (p_1 - p_2 + p_1^{-1} - p_2^{-1}) + v_2'] \sum_{i=3}^{9} X_i \, (m_i + m_i' t + n_i \tilde{x}_i)$$
$$\qquad + \underline{X}_2$$

$$(4) \quad X_3 = a_3 S_1 + b_3 S_2 + c_3 X_1 + d_3 X_3^{-1} p_3 + e_3 \, (S_1^{-1} + S_2^{-1} + S_a^{-1})$$
$$\qquad + \underline{\underline{X}}_3$$

$$(5) \quad x_4 = (a_5 \hat{x}_1 + APF + b_4 APF^{-1} + c_4) \, (X_4^{-1} - p_4^{-1} \, \underline{x}_4^{-1}) + \underline{x}_4$$

$$(6) \quad X_5 = a_5 \, (X_1 - X_1^{-1}) + \underline{X}_5$$

$$(7) \quad x_i = \underline{x}_i \qquad i = 6 \; 7 \; 8$$

$$(8) \quad x_9 = [a_9 \, (TF^{-1} + TF^{-2} - TF^{-3} - TF^{-4}) + b_9] \, [X_9^{-1} - p_9^{-1} \, \underline{x}_9^{-1}]$$
$$\qquad + \underline{x}_9$$

$$(9) \quad p_1 = \mu_1 \tilde{x}_1 + v_1 \, [TF^{-1} - TF^{-3} + v_0' \, (TF^{-1})] + \underline{p}_1$$

$$(10) \quad p_2 = v_2 + \underline{p}_2$$

$$(11) \quad p_i = \mu_i p_1 + v_i + \xi_i \underline{p}_2 \, \dfrac{X_2^{-1}}{X_1^{-1} + X_2^{-1}} \qquad i = 4 \; 6 \; 7 \; 8$$

$$(12) \quad p_5 = \mu_5' p_1 + \mu_5' p_1^{-1} + \xi_5 p_2 \, \dfrac{X_2^{-1}}{X_1^{-1} + X_2^{-1}}$$

$$(13) \quad p_9 = \mu_9 \left(TF^{-1} + TF^{-2} + TF^{-3} + TF^{-4} \right) + v_9$$

$$(14) \quad S_1 = \left(1 + \sigma_1 p_1 + \sigma_2 \frac{x_1}{x_1^*} + \sigma_3 \hat{x}_1 + \sigma_4 APF + \underline{\hat{s}}_1 \right) S_1^{-1}$$

$$(15) \quad S_2 = \left(1 + \sigma_1 p_1 + \sigma_2 \frac{x_1}{x_1^*} + \underline{\hat{s}}_2 \right) S_2^{-1}$$

$$(16) \quad APF = \sum_{i=1}^{5} \theta_i' \left(TF^{-i} - TFT^{-i} \right)$$

$$(17) \quad TFT = TFT^{-1} + \theta_2 + \theta_3 \left(X_4^{-1} + X_4^{-2} - X_4^{-6} - X_4^{-7} \right)$$

$$(18) \quad TF = \frac{1}{X_4} \left[\theta_4 X_1 + \theta_5 \left(X_3 + X_6 + X_7 \right) + \theta_6 X_5 + \theta_7 S_1 + \theta_8 S_2 \right. $$
$$\left. + \underline{\underline{E}}_0 \right]$$

where
$$\underline{\underline{X}}_3 = \underline{X}_3 + f_3 \underline{S}_a + c_3 \underline{RBE} + g_3 \underline{RNS}$$

$$\underline{\hat{s}}_1 = \hat{s}_1 - \sigma_5 \frac{Pd_1}{Pd_2} + (1 - \sigma_6) \underline{\hat{DT}} - \sigma_6 \hat{\pi} + \hat{TS}$$

$$\underline{\hat{s}}_2 = \hat{s}_2 - \sigma_5 \frac{Pd_1}{Pd_2} + \hat{TS}$$

$$\underline{\underline{E}}_p = \underline{E}_p + \theta_1 \underline{RBE}$$

and $p_i = \dfrac{X_i}{x_i} =$ the price of aggregate i;

$S_1 =$ gross wages paid by non-agricultural enterprises;

$S_2 =$ gross wages paid by administrations, financial institutions and agricultural enterprises;

$S_a =$ gross wages paid by households (for domestic help, etc.) plus a contingency allowance for wages paid by administrations;

[Note: DECA distinguishes five separate categories of wage earners, and these have been aggregated in MO].

$\underline{Pd}_1$	= non-agricultural working population
$\underline{Pd}_2$	= total working population;
TF	= actual rate of self-financing;
TFT	= trend rate of self-financing;
APF	= state of financing possibilities;
$\underline{RNS}$	= exogenous part of households' non-wage income (through

380

	which a variation in IRPP would appear);
$\hat{\underline{DT}}$	= exogenous part of rate of growth of the length of the working week;
$\hat{TS}$	= exogenous part of rate of growth in the hourly wage rate;
$\hat{\pi}$	= exogenous part of rate of growth in hourly productivity
$\underline{E}_p$	= exogenous part of financial year savings of private companies;
$\underline{RBE}$	= exogenous part of gross profits of private companies (through which a change in VAT would appear);
t	= time index, equal to zero in 1971;
i	= index corresponding to the different aggregates in the TEE:

$i = 1$ corresponds to PIB,

$i = 2$ corresponds to imports.

$i = 3$ corresponds to household consumption,

$i = 4$ corresponds to enterprises' productive GFCF,

$i = 5$ corresponds to stock variations,

$i = 6$ corresponds to enterprises' GFCF in housing,

$i = 7$ corresponds to administrations' and financial institutions' expenditure,

$i = 8$ corresponds to households' GFCF,

$i = 9$ corresponds to exports;

$IRPP$	= income tax ('tax on the income of physical persons').

There are many additional equations involved in the aggregation from OPTIMIX-DECA to MO; see the appendix to [220] for the details. There are no deviation variables in MO because the model relies exclusively on the mechanisms it contains when used to generate time-paths (which is the main purpose of Malgrange's study).

To aid interpretation of equations (1)–(17), the following brief comments might be useful:

(1) and (2) merely express accounting equilibrium;

(3) determines imports in value terms from the import contents of the different final demand items;

(4) is the consumption function;

(5) states that the growth of productive investment in volume terms is a linear increasing function of PIB, and depends also on financing possibilities;

(6) gives variations in stocks as proportional to the change in PIB;

(8) shows that exports are mainly exogenous, and vary according to previous rates of self-financing;

(9) the general level of prices p_1 depends on the growth in activity and early self-financing;

(11) and (12) p_1 is the main determining factor in these demand item prices;

(14) and (15) summarise the links between the wage rate, productivity, employment, prices and enterprises' financial condition: they are based on a Phillips curve;

(16) gives *APF* as a function of self-financing;

(18) defines the actual rate of self-financing.

The special treatment that DECA gives to the building sector is omitted from MO, and [220] contains the reason why. But apart from this and one or two minor modifications, MO contains the essential DECA mechanisms. As a final guide to understanding MO (and hence DECA), the numerical values of the coefficients are given in the table opposite.

	1	2	3	4	5	6	7	8	9
a_i			0·64	1·32	0·29				0·27
b_i			1·15	-0·8					
c_i			0·10	1·005					
d_i			0·25						
e_i			-0·05						
f_i			0·77						
g_i			0·4						
μ_i	0·15			1	7	1	0·92	1	-0·18
μ_i'		0·25			-6				1·01
v_i	-0·095	1·01		-0·006		-0·003	-0·068	0	
v_i'	0·25	0·985			0				
ξ_i				1·15	1·1	0·85	0·85	0·85	
m_i			-0·06	-0·19	0·16	0·05	-0·14	-0·21	-0·12
m_i'			0·002	0·005	0·006	-0·0012	0·0025	-0·0015	-0·002
n_i			0·16	0·35	0	0	0·24	0·22	0·24
σ_i	0·7	0·23	0·64	0·05	0·81	1·19			
θ_i		-0·1	-0·1	0·6	-0·08	-0·14	-0·78	-0·73	
θ_i'	0·9	0·8	0·6	0·3	0·1				

383

Appendix VII: Forms of Urban and Regional Organisation

These brief notes are intended to provide general background to the discussion in Chapter 8.

VII.1　The regional political administration

The basic administrative unit is the department (see Fig. 8.1) each of which has a Prefect and a General Council. The Prefect is the representative of the central government in the department, and is appointed by the Ministry of the Interior. He is a very high ranking civil servant whose job it is to supervise the communes and the General Council, and to co-ordinate the various Government activities within his department. Whereas previously ministries maintained their own local agencies in the regions, the reforms of 1964 placed all their services under the authority of the Prefect.

To assist him in this complex task, the Prefect has a staff of sub-prefects and 'bright young men', usually graduates from the top civil service school, the ENA (École Nationale d'Administration). These staff form the departmental mission, and are very much the driving force behind the preparation of the regional and departmental aspects of the Plan. The Regional Prefect was created along with the new programme regions in 1960, and he is the Prefect of the department in which the regional capital is located. He guides and supervises the other Prefects in his region, and is responsible for the preparation and implementation of the regional development and equipment programmes (PRDE).

Advisory bodies known as CODERs (Commission de Développement Économique Régional', Regional Economic Development Commissions) form the link between the above central government organs and local opinion. They were set up in 1964 'to give opinions on the implementation of economic, social and territorial development policies in the region', and were constituted of local mayors, members of the General

Table VII.1 Relations between ZEATs, regions, and departments

Regional development and analysis area (ZEAT)	Regions		Constituent departments			
	Code*	Name	Code†	Name	Area (sq. km)	Average 1972 population (thousands)
Paris region	1.1	Paris region	75	Paris	105	2,460·7
			77	Seine-et-Marne	5,917	675·8
			78	Yvelines	2,271	970·2
			91	Essonne	1,811	835·5
			92	Hauts-de-Seine	175	1,513·8
			93	Seine-Saint-Denis	236	1,357·0
			94	Val-de-Marne	244	1,233·2
			95	Val-d'Oise	1,249	791·5
Paris Basin	2.1	Champagne—Ardenne	08	Ardennes	5,219	313·9
			10	Aube	6,002	281·7
			51	Marne	8,163	523·0
			52	Haute-Marne	6,216	217·5
	2.2	Picardie	02	Aisne	7,378	532·7
			60	Oise	5,857	583·4
			80	Somme	6,175	527·6
	2.3	Upper Normandy	27	Eure	6,004	401·5
			76	Seine-Maritime	6,254	1,170·1
	2.4	Centre	18	Cher	7,228	311·1
			28	Eure-et-Loir	5,876	321·6
			36	Indre	6,778	242·1
			37	Indre-et-Loir	6,124	469·6
			41	Loir-et-Cher	6,314	280·0
			45	Loiret	6,742	462·5
	2.5	Lower Normandy	14	Calvados	5,536	548·7
			50	Manche	5,947	453·2
			61	Orne	6,100	295·0
	2.6	Burgundy	21	Côte-d'Or	8,765	444·8
			58	Nièvre	6,837	248·5
			71	Saône-et-Loire	8,565	561·6
			89	Yonne	7,425	292·7

North	3.1	North	59	North	5,738	2,490·8
			62	Pas-de-Calais	6,639	1,416·2
East	4.1	Lorraine	54	Meurthe-et-Moselle	5,235	726·1
			55	Meuse	6,220	205·1
			57	Moselle	6,214	1,016·9
			88	Vosges	5,871	399·3
	4.2	Alsace	67	Bas-Rhin	4,787	865·5
			68	Haut-Rhin	3,523	609·5
	4.3	Franche-Comté	25	Doubs	5,228	460·3
			39	Jura	5,008	238·0
			70	Haute-Saône	5,343	217·7
			90	Territoire de Belfort	610	124·7
West	5.2	Loire Country	44	Loire-Atlantique	6,893	900·1
			49	Maine-et-Loire	7,131	605·2
			53	Mayenne	5,171	255·4
			72	Sarthe	6,210	475·2
			85	Vendée	6,721	427·9
	5.3	Brittany	22	Côtes-du-Nord	6,878	508·7
			29	Finistère	6,785	782·9
			35	Ille-et-Vilaine	6,758	682·0
			56	Morbihan	6,763	546·8
	5.4	Poitou-Charentes	16	Charente	5,953	332·5
			17	Charente-Maritime	6,848	492·3
			79	Deux-Sèvres	6,004	330·5
			86	Vienne	6,985	345·8

Table VII.1 *continued*

Regional development and analysis area (ZEAT)	Regions		Constituent departments		Area (sq. km)	Average 1972 population (thousands)
	Code	Name	Code	Name		
South-West	7.2	Aquitaine	24	Dordogne	9,184	367·2
			33	Gironde	10,000	1,040·4
			40	Landes	9,237	283·4
			47	Lot-et-Garonne	5,358	292·9
			64	Pyrénées-Atlantiques	7,629	526·2
	7.3	Midi–Pyrénées	09	Ariège	4,890	136·0
			12	Aveyron	8,735	271·4
			31	Haute-Garonne	6,301	733·3
			32	Gers	6,254	177·8
			46	Lot	5,228	150·5
			65	Hautes-Pyrénées	4,507	229·7
			81	Tarn	5,751	334·6
			82	Tarn-et-Garonne	3,716	182·9
	7.4	Limousin	19	Corrèze	5,860	237·8
			23	Creuse	5,559	152·0
			87	Haute-Vienne	5,512	350·1
Centre–East	8.2	Rhône-Alpes	01	Ain	5,756	357·0
			07	Ardeche	5,523	261·0
			26	Drôme	6,525	366·6
			38	Isère	7,474	823·8
			42	Loire	4,774	737·2
			69	Rhône	3,215	1,420·8
			73	Savoie	6,036	303·2
			74	Haute-Savoie	4,391	415·1
	8.3	Auvergne	03	Allier	7,327	388·6
			15	Cantal	5,741	166·4
			43	Haute-Loire	4,965	204·7
			63	Puy-de-Dôme	7,955	577·9

Mediterranean	9.1	Languedoc–Roussillon	11	Aude	6,232	275·5
			30	Gard	5,848	494·4
			34	Herault	6,113	621·1
			48	Lozère	5,168	71·4
			66	Pyrenées-Orientales	4,086	286·9
	9.3	Provence–Côte d'Azur	04	Alpes-de-Haute-Provence	6,944	106·2
			05	Hautes-Alpes	5,520	90·3
			06	Alpes-Maritimes	4,294	760·6
			13	Bouches-du-Rhône	5,112	1,553·4
			83	Var	5,999	586·4
			84	Vaucluse	3,566	373·7
	9.4	Corsica	20	Corsica	8,681	218·7
Totals					543,998	51,703·0

* This is the INSEE's code and determines the order in which they present their regional statistics. The first number is the ZEAT number

† Departments were originally numbered in alphabetical order, but the creation of new departments in the Paris region upset the sequence. Most departments are named after rivers, and their remarkably similar size is due to the fact that the Prefect had to be able to reach anywhere in his department on horseback in a day

Source: [163], pp. 293–4

Councils (the departmental elected assembly) and delegates from trade unions and chambers of commerce. According to Ardagh, 'The CODERs were a facade: they met only twice a year, they had no proper funds or secretariats, they were not properly elected, and there was little evidence that the state ever took much notice of their advice' ([151], p. 253).

The past tense is used in this context because the CODERs have been affected by the regional reforms of 1972. The CODER is now replaced by two new assemblies in each of the 22 regions. The first is a CODER under another name, but the second is regarded as a further step towards full regional democracy. It is a Regional Assembly made up of deputies and senators representing the region in Paris, plus members of the General Councils and local officials. It has its own budget (small), and is to be consulted on the regional aspects of the preparation of the Seventh Plan, The size and population of each of the ZEATs, regions and departments is given in Table VII.1.

VII.2   The local political and economic administration

This is based on the commune, ranging in size from a population of less than ten people to over 100,000 people. Above this is the canton, which is the electoral constituency for the departmental General Council. The next stage is the arrondissement, headed by a sub-prefect, and these together form the department. Table VII.2 contains the relevant statistics on this four-tier, ancient structure. As stated in Chapter 8, considerable efforts have been expended to encourage communes to merge to form larger units, pooling their resources and thus being able to undertake bigger capital expenditure programmes. There are many cultural and traditional obstacles to such change, and the central government is also more than a little wary about possible undesirable political consequences: opposition control of large urban units is an important factor to be borne in mind.

Nevertheless, communes have been persuaded to merge, albeit slowly. Where a number of adjacent communes form a continuous urban area, an 'agglomeration' can be formed, either voluntarily or under one or more of the several laws which have been set up for the purpose. If the resulting total population of the agglomeration exceeds 50,000, then an urban community can be created: the benefits of such an authority are described in Law 66–1069 of 31 December 1966. Four such authorities were set up by the Government immediately this law came into force: at Bordeaux, Lille, Lyon, and Strasbourg, and the municipal councils of various other communes have since agreed to merge to form four more: at Dunkerque,

390

Table VII.2

Relations between regions, departments, arrondissements, cantons and communes (situation at 1 January 1973)

Region	Number of			
	Departments	Arrondissements	Cantons	Communes
Paris region	8	22	242	1,283
Champagne–Ardenne	4	15	118	1,955
Picardie	3	13	113	2,303
Upper Normandy	2	6	92	1,431
Centre	6	19	157	1,845
Lower Normandy	3	11	124	1,819
Burgundy	4	15	150	2,035
North	2	13	121	1,553
Lorraine	4	19	128	2,339
Alsace	2	14	69	919
Franche-Comté	4	9	102	1,804
Loire Country	5	17	175	1,522
Brittany	4	15	172	1,280
Poitou–Charentes	4	14	131	1,464
Aquitaine	5	18	202	2,288
Midi–Pyrenées	8	22	247	3,028
Limousin	3	8	84	749
Rhône–Alpes	8	25	271	2,918
Auvergne	4	14	131	1,311
Languedoc–Roussillon	5	14	149	1,546
Provence–Côte d'Azur	6	16	175	1,000
Corsica	1	5	62	361
Totals	95	324	3,215	36,753

Source: [163], p. 11

Le Creusot and Montceau-les-Mines, Cherbourg, and Le Mans [167]. Other forms of association are possible where it is apparent that local services cannot be handled by single communes. Law 59–30 of 5 January 1959 enabled communes to form 'urban districts', and this was modified in 1970 to allow 'rural districts' too, the distinction being discontinued henceforth and the associations referred to as just 'districts'. Another form of association is rather similar, and is known as a 'syndicate'. At the end of 1972, there were 111 districts (involving 966 communes), and 1,437 syndicates (including 14,164 communes); the eight urban communities covered 243 communes. As already stated, the advantage of such unions is a bigger budget and hence more flexibility in terms of capital expenditures. If the communes actually agree to merge fully, then there are also numerous tax advantages and loans made available. Over the last ten years, approximately 10,000 communes have linked together in some form of association, but less than 1,000 have agreed to full mergers. This emphasises the gap that exists between the (mainly Paris-based) town and country planning and regional development élite, who publish the masses of articles and attend all the conferences referred to in the introduction to Chapter 8, and the man in the commune street, who remains largely untouched (or possibly confused) by the bureaucratic gymnastics taking place in the other stages of the urban and regional hierarchy, and who consequently feels no identity at all with his region (except of course in such places as Brittany, the Basque country, and the Catalan country, the last two of which unfortunately do not coincide with programme regions).

The INSEE uses various other definitions to refer to local units in its population and demographic statistics. Any agglomeration with a population exceeding 2,000 is known as an 'urban unit', and if this urban unit contains only one commune, then it is known as an 'isolated town'. The 1968 population census revealed 1,519 urban units (793 isolated towns plus 726 agglomerations) involving 4,306 communes. In this 11 per cent of all the communes lived almost 70 per cent of the total population of France, a statistic that vividly conveys the rural nature of local French life. The next level of aggregation in the INSEE system is the ZPIU ('zone de peuplement industriel ou urbain', industrial or urban populated area), denoting a set of communes with a low agricultural population, an industrial site within it or close to it, and a considerable flow of people between homes and jobs. A ZPIU can thus contain rural communes, if such communes house people who work in a neighbouring urban or industrial commune; all communes not belonging to a ZPIU are clearly rural. Almost 80 per cent of the population live in a ZPIU according to the 1968 census [164]

VII.3 SRU, DATAR, and regional policy instruments

The SRU ('Service Regional et Urbain' Urban and Regional Department) is part of the CGP, and acts as the go-between for the regional and national work involved in the preparation of the Plan. It supervises the work of several Plan Commissions, notably the Towns Commission and the National Commission for Régional Development (CNAT), and regards itself as the mouthpiece of regional opinion at the national level. It has only a very small staff (10 to 12 at the most), and so everyone has to look after two or three regions. SRU also promotes research on urban and regional planning, although its influence in this area has been considerably affected by the CORU ('Comité d'Orientation de la Recherche Urbaine', Urban Research Steering Committee), set up under the joint auspices of the DAFU ('Direction de l'Aménagement et de l'Urbanisme', the Land-Use Planning and Urban Department of the Ministry of Equipment and Housing) and the DGRST ('Délégation Générale à la Recherche Scientifique et Technique', the General Delegation for Scientific and Technical Research, attached directly to the Prime Minister's office). The CORU apparently is to continue the research programme originally supervised by the DGRST's Urbanisation Committee [165], and is to promote and allocate research contracts on topics that fit into its overall view of urban research. Its programme can be found in [166]. The view has been expressed to me by many members of the planning administration that the CORU, and other bodies like it, 'over-organise' social research, and this is one of the main reasons for the dearth of operational social research results. Although the SRU is free to place its own research contracts, there is pressure to place them through the CORU.

The DATAR ('Délégation a l'Aménagement du Territoire et à l'Action Régionale', Delegation for Town and Country Planning and Regional Action (this is but one of the many English translations of DATAR's name!)) is the other main central body involved in regional economic affairs. It does not play as prominent a role in the preparation of the Plan as the SRU, but it sits on the CNAT and is generally 'involved'. It was set up in 1963, again attached directly to the Prime Minister's office. In the words of Robert Moss,

> DATAR is an élite strike-force of fewer than 100 young technocrats, commanded by M. Jérôme Monod. They are the practitioners, in the words of *Le Figaro*, of 'a sort of economic terrorism'. The way that DATAR operates is certainly a fascinating example of how the talents of a highly trained, largely Parisian élite, formed in the best traditions of one of the most highly centralised administrations in the world, has been able to put itself at the service of decentralisation and the encouragement of local initiative. ... DATAR is there to push, to jostle, to coax reluctant businessmen on with cash grants and tax incentives. It has easy access to those in power, ... but it does not have budgetary powers ([168], p. 34).

This way of operating does not please the SRU very much, because the DATAR is not constrained by normal bureaucratic procedures or the

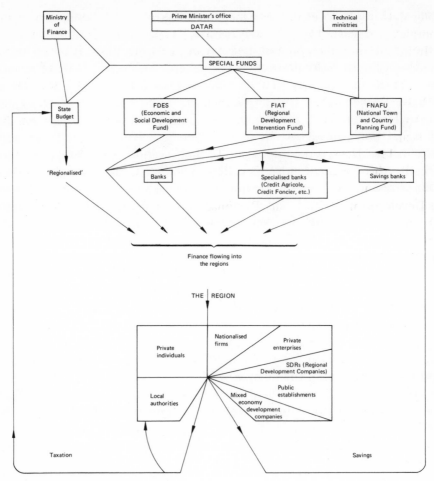

Fig. VII.1   Financial circuits affecting the region

Note: arrows denote financial flows; other lines indicate direct influence

Source: [169], p. 6

planning machinery. It works to its own priorities, and spends the money from the FIAT ('Fonds d'Intervention pour l'Aménagement du Territoire', Regional Development Intervention Fund) in an 'unplanned' way (although the FIAT is only 1 or 2 per cent of the national social overhead capital budget). DATAR is able to cut corners, and start urgent operations which then have to be taken over by the Government department concerned. It can also amend the priorities and choices of a ministry in order to overcome a particular problem, and it can provide extra money for complex operations that require various forms of financing. A member of the SRU told me that 'the DATAR operates cheque-by-cheque, and we feel obliged to react to everything they do'. Figure VII.1 shows part of the complex regional aid system, with the DATAR in a privileged position.

In addition to the special funds shown in Figure VII.1, there are many other specialised bodies involved in regional policy, particularly in agriculture. These include the SAFER ('Sociétés d'Aménagement Foncier et d'Établissement Rural', Land Development and Rural Settlement Companies) whose purpose is to improve agricultural structures, increase the size of farms, and generally to rationalise small-scale agriculture. They date back to 1960, and, according to [163], there are now 29 of them, covering virtually the whole of France but based on regions that do *not* coincide with the boundaries of the programme regions. Since the SDRs ('Sociétés de Developpement Régional', Regional Development Companies, of which

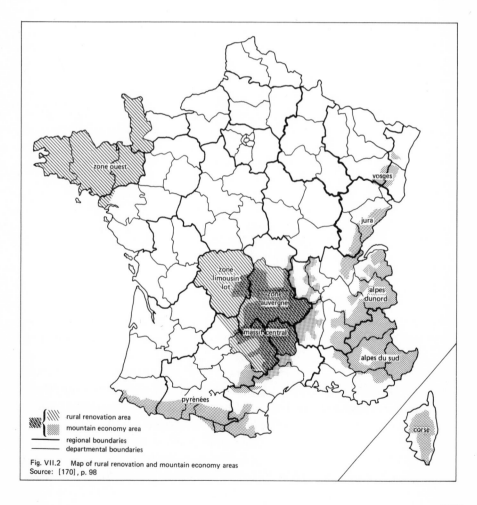

Fig. VII.2   Map of rural renovation and mountain economy areas
Source: [170], p. 98

395

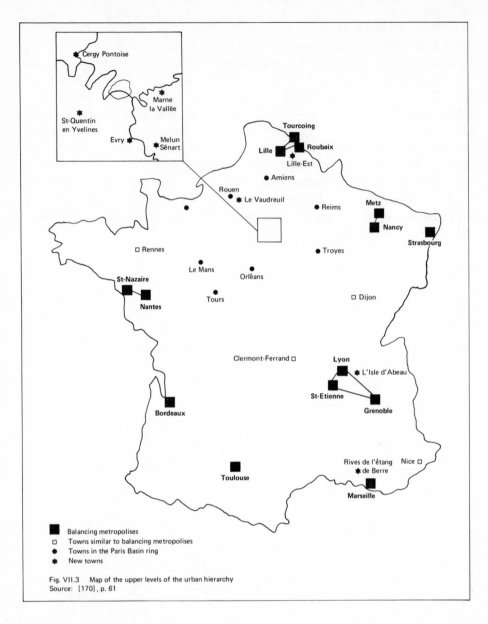

Cergy Pontoise

Marne
la Vallée

St-Quentin
en Yvelines

Evry

Melun
Sénart

Tourcoing

Roubaix

Lille

Lille-Est

Amiens

Rouen
Le Vaudreuil

Reims

Metz

Nancy

Strasbourg

Rennes

Troyes

Le Mans

Orléans

St-Nazaire

Tours

Dijon

Nantes

Clermont-Ferrand

Lyon

L'Isle d'Abeau

St-Etienne

Grenoble

Bordeaux

Rives de l'étang
de Berre

Nice

Toulouse

Marseille

■ Balancing metropolises
□ Towns similar to balancing metropolises
● Towns in the Paris Basin ring
✱ New towns

Fig. VII.3   Map of the upper levels of the urban hierarchy
Source: [170], p. 61

[163] lists 15 in 1972) also have their own definition of a region, yet another complicating factor is introduced into the regional planning framework.

Finally, we should mention ZEM, ZRR, and OREAM. The ZEM ('zones
d'economie montagnarde', mountain economy areas) are shown in Figure VII.2. They qualify for special benefits under the regional aid policy
administered by the DATAR, and are included in the PRDE of several

396

regions. The 'mountain policy' dates back to 1967 (see [170], pp. 96–8; [171], pp. 61–2; and [172]), as do the ZRR ('zones de rénovation rurale', rural renovation areas), also shown in Figure VII.2. These areas should be compared with those shown as aided in the maps in Chapter 8 in order to obtain a more complete picture of how French regional aid is distributed. The OREAM ('Organisms d'Études d'Aménagement des Aires Métropolitaines', Study Organisations for the Development of Metropolitan Areas) are at the other end of the urban–rural scale. They are associated with eight balancing metropolises ('métropoles d'équilibre'), cities chosen to act as counter-magnets to Paris and to be the driving forces behind regional development; they are shown in Figure VII.3. It is the OREAM's job to prepare a structure plan ('schéma directeur') for its associated metropolis; very good brief details (maps, etc.) on the plans that have already been prepared can be found in [170] and [171]. There was a fundamental revision in the balancing metropolis policy in March 1972: on the surface, it appears that the OREAMs have been given more authority, with the extension of their area of competence to include the whole of the region in which a metropolis associated with them is located. But in reality, they are to work with the new Regional Assemblies. This step, taken alongside the new middle towns policy, is a sign that the eight balancing metropolises are not to be allowed to grow too big and thus create urban problems on a Parisian scale.

VII.4   Important dates in urban and regional development

30 June 1955: FDES and SDRs created.

5 January 1959: syndicates and urban districts instituted.

2 June 1960: programme regions officially set up.

5 August 1960: SAFERs introduced.

4 August 1962: Budget to be 'regionalised' henceforth.

14 February 1963: DATAR, FIAT, CNAT, and FNAFU created.

14 March 1964: the title of Regional Prefect introduced. CODERs set up in each programme region.

October 1964 (Finance Act for 1965): all towns with more than 50,000 inhabitants obliged to prepare a modernisation and equipment programme (PME).

24 February 1966: OREAMs established for a number of balancing metropolises.

31 December 1966: urban communities introduced.

24 October 1967: ZRRs and ZEMs created.

31 December 1970: Districts (urban and rural) instituted, updating 1959 law.

5 July 1972: Programme regions given the name 'region' for administrative as well as programming purposes. Regional Assemblies introduced.

Appendix VIII: Algebraic Presentation of the E_O Model

This model was used in compiling long-term projections in both the Fifth and Sixth Plans (see especially section 2.1 in Chapter 2), and takes its name from the E_0 projection in the Fifth Plan (see Appendix IV). We take this version of the model from [94], Appendix II, which also contains a projection for 1980 based on the Sixth Plan account and constructed with the model. An earlier version of the model is given in [77], Appendix II, where it is referred to as the semi-global physical projection model.

The model distinguishes seven products and eight branches (branch 8 has no product):

branch	name
1	agriculture
2	agricultural and foodstuffs industries
3	energy
4	industry
5	transport and telecommunications
6	housing
7	building, public works, and services
8	commerce

This breakdown is chosen in this particular instance ([94]) in order to harmonise with the FIFI model which was involved in the elaboration of the Sixth Plan account; earlier versions used a different branch breakdown.

The exogenous variables and parameters are as follows:

$\bar{c}_i$ and $\bar{\bar{c}}_i$: parameters in households' product consumption functions ($i = 1, 2, \ldots 7$);

F and F_i: administrations' and financial institutions' (i.e. outside the branches) total consumption and consumption of product i ($i = 1, 2, \ldots 7$);

399

t_4 and t_7: the rates of productive investment with respect to value added at domestic prices for products 4 and 7;

J_2: gross fixed capital formation in housing, demand for which concerns only product 7;

J_a, J_{a4} and J_{a7}: gross fixed capital formation by administrations and financial institutions, in total and by product;

S, S_2, S_3, and S_4: changes in stocks, in total and by product;

$Ex, Ex_1, Ex_2, Ex_3, Ex_4, Ex_5$, and Ex_7: total exports and exports of products;

$\theta, \theta_2, \theta_3$, and θ_4: the difference between domestic and f.o.b. prices, in total and by product;

I, I_1, I_2, I_3, and I_4: total imports and imports of products;

DTI, DTI_1, DTI_2, DTI_3, and DTI_4: import duties and taxes, in total and by product;

a_{ij}: input–output coefficients $(i = 1, 2, ..., 7; j = 1, 2, ..., 8)$;

μ_1, μ_2, μ_3, and μ_4: trading margin rates on household consumption in products 1 to 4;

L: total employment;

L_1, L_6, and L_{hb}: employment in branches 1 and 6, and outside the branches;

D_j: the length of the working week in branch j;

CA: annual holiday index;

π_j: index of hourly productivity in branch j $(j = 2, 3, 4, 5, 7$ and $8)$.

The 47 endogenous variables are:

$5 + x$: average annual rate of growth of total household consumption between 1965 and 1980 (in per cent);

C and C_i: total consumption and consumption by product $(i = 1, 2, ..., 7)$ of households;

J_p, J_{p4}, and J_{p7}: total productive investment and productive investment in branches 4 and 7;

V and V_j: value added at domestic prices, in total and in branch j $(j = 1, 2, ..., 8)$;

V_j^1: value added at real prices in branch j $(j = 1, 2, ..., 8)$;

P_j: production at domestic prices in branch j $(j = 1, 2, ..., 7)$;

M: production at domestic prices in branch 8;

M_j: trading margin on product j $(j = 1, ..., 4)$;

L_j: employment in branch j $(j = 2, 3, 4, 5, 7 + 8)$;

PIB: gross domestic production.

The 47 equations are as follows.

Consumption behaviour:

(1) – (7) $C_i = \bar{c}_i + \bar{\bar{c}}_i x$, $(i = 1, 2, ..., 7)$

Total consumption:

(8) $C = \sum\limits_{i=1}^{7} C_i$

Productive investment:

(9) $J_{p4} = t_4 V$

(10) $J_{p7} = t_7 V$

(11)   total $= J_p = J_{p4} + J_{p7}$

Equilibrium of resources and uses:

(12) $P_1 + M_1 + I_1 + DTI_1 = \sum\limits_{j=1}^{7} a_{1j} P_j + C_1 + F_1 + Ex_1$

(13) $P_2 + M_2 + I_2 + DTI_2 = \sum\limits_{j=1}^{7} a_{2j} P_j + a_{28} M + C_2 + F_2 + S_2 + Ex_2$

(14) $P_3 + M_3 + I_3 + DTI_3 = \sum\limits_{j=1}^{7} a_{3j} P_j + a_{38} M + C_3 + F_3 + S_3 + Ex_3$

(15) $P_4 + M_4 + I_4 + DTI_4 = \sum\limits_{j=1}^{7} a_{4j} P_j + a_{48} M + C_4 + F_4 + J_{p4} +$

$J_{a4} + S_4 + Ex_4$

(16) $P_5 = \sum\limits_{j=1}^{7} a_{5j} P_j + a_{58} M + C_5 + F_5 + Ex_5$

(17) $P_6 = C_6 + F_6$

(18) $P_7 = \sum\limits_{j=1}^{7} a_{7j} P_j + a_{78} M + C_7 + F_7 + J_{p7} + J_2 + J_{a7} + S_7 + Ex_7$

(19) – (22) $M_i = \mu_i C_i$, $(i = 1, 2, 3, 4)$

(23) $M = \sum\limits_{i=1}^{4} M_i$

401

$$(24) - (30) \quad V_j = (1 - \sum_{i=1}^{7} a_{ij}) P_j, \quad (j = 1, 2, ..., 7)$$

$$(31) \quad V_8 = (1 - \sum_{i=1}^{7} a_{i8}) M$$

$$(32) \quad V = \sum_{j=1}^{8} V_j$$

$$(33) - (40) \quad V_j^1 = V_j - \theta_j, \quad (j = 1, 2, ..., 8)$$

$$(41) \quad PIB = V - \theta + DTI$$

Production functions:

$$(42) - (45) \quad L_j = \frac{V_j}{D_j \times CA \times \pi_j}, \quad (j = 2, 3, 4, 5)$$

$$(46) \quad L_{7+8} = \frac{V_7 + V_8}{D_{7+8} \times CA \times \pi_{7+8}}$$

Total employment:

$$(47) \quad L = \sum_{j=1}^{6} L_j + L_{7+8} + L_{hb}$$

Appendix IX: French and European Incentives

The details given here are intended to complement the discussion of the French regional investment incentive system in Chapter 8, and to broaden the picture a little by giving some European comparisons. The two main sources are a booklet issued in English by the DATAR [266], designed for and aimed at British and American industry, and Castelbajac [267].

IX.1 The French system in detail

As is apparent from Figure 8.7, there are four main investment areas in which differing scales of assistance apply. These are referred to as A, B, C, and D in [266], A denoting the area in which maximum benefits are vailable, B and C reduced benefits, and D none at all (or negative benefits (i.e. controls)). The eight types of assistance are available as follows:

Type of assistance	A	B	C	D
1 Regional development grants (at various rates)	Yes	No	No	No
2 Decentralisation indemnity	Yes	Yes	Yes (for transfers out of Paris and Lyons)	No
3 'Patente' exemptions	Yes	Yes	Yes (ditto)	No
4 Conveyance duty reductions	Yes	Yes	Yes (ditto)	No
5 Exceptional depreciation terms	Yes (in west)	No	No	No
6 Capital gains tax reductions (on sale of land)	Yes	Yes	Yes	No

7 Personnel training subsidies and removal expenses	Yes	Yes	Yes	No
8 Service industry grants	Yes	Yes (in certain metropolitan areas)		

The conditions relating to each of these types of assistance are given in full in [266]; the following lists are only summaries of these conditions.

1 Regional development grants

Available to industry (not agriculture and foodstuffs) and research and development firms for the creation of new activities or the extension of existing ones, subject to

(a)   creation: the proposed investment being of at least half a million francs (excluding taxes), resulting in the creation of at least 30 permanent jobs, and being completed within three years;
(b)   extension: the same requirements as in (a), and in addition an increase in the labour force of at least 30 per cent, or at least 100 persons (for transfers out of Paris, first expansions, or certain labour retraining schemes).

A new site within 30 km of a firm's existing activities is regarded as an extension. For rural and mountain economy areas (see Appendix VII), the limits in (a) are 300,000 francs and 15 jobs (or less in special cases), and in (b) 300,000 francs, 15 jobs, and 20 per cent (if the project creates 15–50 jobs) or 10 per cent (50–100 jobs). The grant may apply outside A if the project helps to solve particular socio-economic problems, involves at least 20 million francs, and creates at least 400 jobs.

The grant is available in varying rates (see Fig. 8.7), and new areas are regularly added (permanently or for a limited period) to A, B, C, and D ([266] gives a very detailed list of areas that qualify, almost on a commune-by-commune basis). It may not exceed

(a)   15,000 francs per job created for the creation of new activities;
(b)   12,000 francs per job for extensions.
However, this job ceiling can be, and frequently is, waived.

2 Decentralisation indemnity

Industrial firms located in the Paris region are eligible for partial reimbur-

404

sement of expenses involved in moving all or part of their production facilities elsewhere. The conditions are, that

(a)   at least 500 sq.m must be vacated;
(b)   relocation must be made outside the Paris Basin (the definitions of Paris, the Paris region, and the Paris Basin are all different);

and the rate is 60 per cent of disassembly, transportation, and reassembly costs, or less if the indemnity exceeds half a million francs.

3, 4, 5, and 6   Fiscal exemptions

The benefits available under all four schemes may be cumulated, but relief is not automatically given in every case.

(a)   'Patente' exemptions vary according to the rates charged by different local authorities, but they can be 100 per cent for a maximum period of five years. Each case is determined by the local authority concerned.
(b)   Conveyance duty reductions can be from 17·2 per cent to 2 per cent (for purchase of a business) and from 13·8 per cent to 2 per cent (for purchase of plant that is more than five years old). This tax does not apply in all cases, so that benefits may not be possible.
(c)   Exceptional depreciation (25 per cent of construction cost immediately on completion) may be granted.
(d)   Capital gains tax reductions (half the tax) may be given on land sales if the proceeds are reinvested in specified activities (i.e. conforming with regional development objectives).

7   Subsidies for job training and personnel removal

Training benefits are granted by the National Employment Fund (designed to aid transfers out of Paris) and appropriations provided by a 1971 law relating to the training of personnel (the latter fund is constituted by a tax on all enterprises with more than ten employees).

Removal and relocation expenses are granted to employees who follow an enterprise when it moves under one of the above schemes.

8   Service industry grants

A grant of up to 20 per cent is available to non-industrial facilities locating in the areas in Figure 8.7. It cannot be cumulated with the regional development grant and must result in the creation of

(a) at least 100 jobs; or

(b) at least 50 jobs (in the case of research and development facilities or the relocation of a firm's head office).

The figures in (a) and (b) rise to 200 and 100 respectively if the project involves several facilities. Like the regional development grant, the service industry grant is applicable to three-year projects, but the limit may be extended to five years if 300 jobs are created. Job ceilings again apply: the grant may not exceed 15,000 francs per job created, and investments in real estate may not exceed 50,000 francs per job created.

IX.2 European comparisons

The French regional investment incentive system is generally regarded as comparable with most of the schemes operated by other EEC countries (on a comparison of *maximum* grants available), but when the qualifying conditions of the French system are taken into account, the comparison is less favourable (thus, the *average* grant made under the French system is low in comparison). This, and other facts, come out of Castelbajac's study [267], from which the following details are taken. Most of the figures relate to pre-1972, and this means that the French system, which was amended in April 1972, is evaluated on the basis of old legislation, as possibly the systems of other countries are; it also means that references to the EEC are to the EEC of the six original member countries. There are other difficulties in making comparisons: not all grants are explicit enough to allow comparison; some schemes operate grants and others preferential loans; there are differences between schemes in the delay between the realisation of the investment and the giving of assistance; and taxation conditions vary from country to country. Where possible, allowances are made for these factors in Castelbajac's work, but the results nevertheless must be interpreted with caution.

In addition to the complexities of individual countries' incentive systems, the rules pertaining to the EEC regional policy further complicate the picture. It is sufficient here to acknowledge that the EEC is divided into two main areas for EEC policy purposes: central areas of the EEC in which the maximum rate of assistance can be 20 per cent of the investment involved in a project, and other areas where this limit does not apply. Within these other areas, known as peripheral EEC areas, member countries are generally free to operate their own systems above the 20 per cent limit. Allowing for taxation on the benefits, the differing time-scales of grant payments, and rounding the figures to the nearest five per cent, Castelbajac's study reveals the following list of *maximum* regional investment grants which may be available to firms:

Italy	50 per cent + exemption from taxation of benefits for ten years + employment premium
Britain	30 per cent + employment premium
Norway	25 per cent + partial exemption of benefits
Ireland	25 per cent + (other industry and sector grants)
Germany	25 per cent
France	25 per cent
Denmark	20 per cent
Holland	20 per cent (EEC central area limit)
Belgium	20 per cent (EEC central area)

The comment made after the Irish figure highlights the fact that this comparison refers only to *regional* incentives. Some countries also operate general industrial and sectoral incentive schemes. If these schemes were included in the comparison, then the rates shown would be different, particularly for Ireland. The following figures on the *average* grants made to firms under regional investment schemes show the Irish situation in a truer setting since both regional aid and general aid are considered; for the other countries, the figures relate only to regional aid:

Ireland (1970)	50 per cent
Britain (March 1969–March 1970)	24 per cent
Denmark (several years average)	15 per cent
Germany (1972)	15 per cent
Italy (1970)	14 per cent
Holland (1970	14 per cent
France (1970)	11 per cent

At the time of writing, the final amount to be voted to the EEC's regional development fund had not been agreed. Proposals on the use of the fund once established are briefly discussed in [268], which also lists in detail the regions, districts and, in some cases, towns that would benefit.

Subject Index

Indexer's note: References to any organisation, model, etc., that is normally referred to by an abbreviation or acronym will be found in the list of abbreviations and acronyms. Authors are also indexed separately.

Accounts, departure, of Sixth Plan (1969) 106-13
Actualisation, rate of, *see* Industry *under* Sixth Plan
Administration, central economic 331-9
Annual growth rate (AGR) 108
Annual reviews, *see* Sixth Plan *under* Monitoring
Average annual growth rate (AAGR) 43

Budgets, *see* Sixth Plan *under* Monitoring

Capital market and industry 208-12
Central Economic Administration 331-9; The Planning Commission 331-2; Ministry of the Economy and Finance 332-7; Centre for Mathematical Economic, Long-term Planning 337-9
Chronology of events, Sixth Plan 2-4
Cobb-Douglas production functions 31, 33, 150, 215-16
Criticisms of FIFI, *see under* FIFI Model

Departments, map of French 233
Disaggregation 191-203

Economic administration 331-9
Economic Budgets and DECA Model 373-83
Economic Budgets, *see* Sixth Plan *under* Monitoring
Economy, theory of competitioned, *see* FIFI Model, development of
E_O Model, algebraic presentation of 399-402

FIFI Model, development of: main theoretical assumptions 76-8; sector equilibrium, determination of 78-83; macro-economic equilibrium, determination of 83-8; from theory to

model 88-9; households, public administrations and the exterior 89-93; overall structure 93-6; criticisms of, in planning process, theoretical structural foundations 138-46, model's effect on policy choices 146-9, improvements to model 149-51, techniques of seventh and later plans 151-5; algebraic presentation of 367-72; *see also* Sixth Plan
FIFITOF and REGINA 303-22: FIFITOF project 303-7; REGINA project 307-22
Fifth Plan 359-65
First Plan 353-4
Fourth Plan 356-7

Giscard d'Estaing 271, 356

Hirsch, Étienne 332, 355

Incentives, French and European 403-7: French system, regional development grants 404, decentralisation indemnity 404-5, fiscal exemptions 405, subsidies for job training and personnel removal 405, service industry grants 405-6; in Europe 406-7
Indicators, *see* Sixth Plan *under* Monitoring
Industry and Sixth Plan, *see* Sixth Plan
Investment in industry 208-12
Improvements to FIFI model 149-51

Keynes, theory of 75-89

Languedoc 249-50
Lipsey 143, 146, 150, 370

Monnet, Jean 332, 354-5
Moss, Robert 393; *see also* Author Index

409

Ortoli, François 332

Phillips 77, 85, 141, 143, 146, 150, 370
Pinay 355
Plan account, *see* Sixth Plan *under* Projections of 1975
Plans one to five: No. 1 (1947–53) 353-4; No. 2 (1954–57) 355; No. 3 (1958–61) 356; No. 4 (1962–65) 356-7; No. 5 (1962–66) 359-65
Policy choices, effect of model on 146-9
PRDE Exercise 231-61; *see also* Sixth Plan, regions and the

REGINA and FIFITOF, *see* FIFITOF and REGINA
Regional and Urban Organisation, forms of 385-98
Regions and the plan, *see* Sixth Plan *under* Regions
Regions, maps of departments by 233, 235
Reviews, annual, *see* Sixth Plan *under* Monitoring
Roussillon 250

Second plan 355
SESAME Project 28, 54-9, 71, 308
Sixth Plan, preparation of: chronology of events 2-4; innovations, institutional 4-9, technical 9-16; role of central model 16-21; main studies carried out, table of 12-13; long-term studies in preparation: preliminary projections 28-33, study groups 33-40, macroeconomic projections 40-50, social

indicators 50-4, SESAME project 54-68; accounts and variants of, departure account (1969) 106-13, sensitivity variants 113-21, uncertainty variants 121-8, policy analysis variants 128-9, policy synthesising variants 129-33; variants: sensitivity 113-21, uncertainty 121-8, policy analysis 128-9, policy synthesis 129-33; projections of 1975 on contents of plan account, main assumptions of 166-78, main results of 178-87, from departure account 187-91, disaggregation of 191-203; summary of objectives and policies 171-5; industry and rate of actualisation: investment, savings and capital market 208-12, relation of rate of actualisation to other concepts 212-14, rate of actualisation 214-22, new rate of actualisation 222-7; regions and the, forms of region and sub-region 233-6, preparation at regional level 236-43, employment patterns 243-8, PRDE Exercise 248-56, development policy 256-62; monitoring, flashing lights to passive indicators 271-6, indicators, calculation and performance of 276-86, annual reviews, revisions and economic budgets 286-95; *see also* FIFI Model

Third Plan 356

Urban and regional organisation, forms of 385-98

List of Abbreviations
and Acronyms

AEC	Atomic Energy Commission	109, 170
ANTOINE	A CGP long-term growth model	229, 323, 337
APIE	A public administrations model	92, 100
BD	Budget directorate	332
BIC	Industrial and commercial profits	277
CCBE	National Accounts and Economic Budgets Commission	374
CEGF	General Economic and Financing Commission	6, 17, 18, 21, 126, 130, 132, 135, 140, 154-6, 159, 164, 286
CEGFTG	Technical Group of the General Economic and Financing Commission	6
CEPREMAP	Centre for Mathematical Economic Long-term Research	99, 155, 158, 229, 297, 302, 308-9, 313, 316, 323, 325, 337-9
CERAU	Centre for Research and Analysis in Urban Development	308, 325-6
CERMAP	Previous name of CEPREMAP	99, 216, 229
CFCFIE	Contribution to the Financing of Capital Formation by Individual Entrepreneurs	118-19, 188
CFDT	French Democratic Labour Confederation (trade union)	18, 159, 204
CGP	Planning Commission	3-4, 7-9, 12-13, 18, 28-9, 37, 52, 56, 70, 133, 155, 159, 165, 198, 203, 211, 215-16, 218-19, 220-4, 234, 238-40, 242, 254, 262, 266, 269-71, 286, 297, 307, 328, 331-2, 336-7, 354-5, 374, 392
CGT	General Confederation of Labour (trade union)	18, 156
CIE	Economic Information Planning Commission	6
CML	Short-medium-long linkage model	152
CNAT	National Commission for Regional Development	6, 239-45, 248, 392-3, 397
CNIPE	National Information Centre for Economic Progress	327

411

Author Index

417